J. J. Keller®

Tractor-Trailer Driver Training Manual

3rd Edition

Based on the FHWA Model Curriculum
Follows PTDI's curriculum standards

J. J. Keller
& Associates, Inc.®
Since 1953

Copyright 2016

J. J. Keller & Associates, Inc.
3003 Breezewood Lane
P.O. Box 368
Neenah, Wisconsin 54957-0368
Phone: (800) 327-6868
Fax: (800) 727-7516
JJKeller.com

Library of Congress Catalog Card Number: 2015933041

ISBN: 978-1-68008-047-6

Canadian Goods and Services Tax (GST) Number: R123-317687

Third edition, May 2016

Printed in the U.S.A.

TRACTOR-TRAILER DRIVER TRAINING MANUAL

Published & Printed by

J. J. Keller & Associates, Inc.
3003 Breezewood Lane, P.O. Box 368
Neenah, Wisconsin 54957-0368
Phone: (800) 327-6868
Fax: (800) 727-7516
JJKeller.com

EDITORIAL

director – editorial resources	**PAUL V. ARNOLD**
project editor	**JILL M. SCHULTZ**
sr. editorial manager – transportation	**BETTY J. B. WEILAND**
sr. editor – transportation management	**THOMAS E. BRAY**
sr. editor – transportation safety	**DAREN B. HANSEN**
sr. editor – hazardous materials transportation	**THOMAS J. ZIEBELL**
editor – transportation safety	**KATHY L. CLOSE**
editor – transportation management	**RICHARD J. MALCHOW**
editor – transportation operations	**HEATHER L. NESS**
editor – transportation management	**ROBERT J. ROSE**
associate editor	**RANDALL J. SKOOG**
sr. metator/xml analyst	**MARY K. FLANAGAN**
technical review	**ROB BEHNKE***
technical asssistance	**SAM EUSTICE***

PUBLISHING GROUP

chairman	**ROBERT L. KELLER**
vice chairman & treasurer	**JAMES J. KELLER**
president & ceo	**MARNE L. KELLER-KRIKAVA**
evp & chief operating officer	**RUSTIN R. KELLER**
chief financial officer	**DANA S. GILMAN**
sr. director of product development	**CAROL A. O'HERN**
sr. product development manager	**JENNIFER M. JUNG**
product development specialist	**SUZANNE IHRIG**
product development specialist	**ASHLEY C. PUCKER**
director of manufacturing	**TODD J. LUEKE**
sr. electronic publishing & prepress manager	**GERALD L. SABATKE**

The Editorial Staff is available to provide information generally associated with this publication to a normal and reasonable extent, and at the option of, and as a courtesy of, the Publisher.

*The Editor would like to thank Rob Behnke and Sam Eustice of Fox Valley Technical College, Appleton, Wisconsin, for their expertise and assistance with this publication.

▌ Chapter 1

Orientation 1

- ◆ Welcome to the trucking industry
- ◆ A regulated industry
- ◆ Obtaining your commercial driver's license (CDL)
- ◆ Driver qualifications
- ◆ Driver disqualification
- ◆ Alcohol and drug testing
- ◆ The commercial motor vehicle — an overview
- ◆ Summary
- ◆ Orientation Quiz
- ◆ General knowledge CDL pre-test

▌ Chapter 2

Control systems 19

- ◆ Engine controls
- ◆ Primary vehicle controls
- ◆ Secondary vehicle controls
- ◆ Vehicle instruments
- ◆ Summary
- ◆ Control systems Quiz
- ◆ General knowledge CDL pre-test

▌ Chapter 3

Vehicle systems 33

- ◆ Frame
- ◆ Suspension system
- ◆ Axles

- ◆ Engine
- ◆ Fuel system
- ◆ Air intake and exhaust system
- ◆ Lubrication system
- ◆ Cooling system
- ◆ Electrical system
- ◆ Drive train
- ◆ Brake system
- ◆ Wheels and tires
- ◆ Steering system
- ◆ Coupling system
- ◆ Summary
- ◆ Vehicle systems Quiz
- ◆ General knowledge CDL pre-test

▊ Chapter 4

Vehicle inspection 57

- ◆ The importance of inspections
- ◆ Types of inspections
- ◆ Conducting an inspection
- ◆ Pre-trip inspection
- ◆ En-route inspection
- ◆ Post-trip inspection
- ◆ Special rigs
- ◆ Summary
- ◆ Vehicle inspection Quiz

▊ Chapter 5

Basic control 75

- ◆ Starting, warming up, and shutting down
- ◆ Putting the vehicle in motion and stopping
- ◆ Straight line backing
- ◆ Turning
- ◆ Summary
- ◆ Basic control Quiz
- ◆ General knowledge CDL pre-test

▌ Chapter 6

Shifting 87

- ◆ Key elements of shifting
- ◆ Shifting gears
- ◆ Shifting patterns
- ◆ Summary
- ◆ Shifting Quiz
- ◆ General knowledge CDL pre-test

▌ Chapter 7

Backing 99

- ◆ Backing principles and rules
- ◆ Sight side and blind side backing
- ◆ Basic backing maneuvers
- ◆ Summary
- ◆ Backing Quiz
- ◆ General knowledge CDL pre-test

▌ Chapter 8

Coupling and uncoupling 109

- ◆ Coupling tractor-trailers
- ◆ Uncoupling tractor-trailers
- ◆ Coupling twin trailers
- ◆ Uncoupling twin trailers
- ◆ Other combinations
- ◆ Summary
- ◆ Coupling and uncoupling Quiz
- ◆ General knowledge CDL pre-test

▌ Chapter 9

Visual search 123

- ◆ Seeing ahead and to the sides
- ◆ Use of mirrors
- ◆ Adjusting mirrors
- ◆ Seeing to the rear
- ◆ Summary

- ◆ Visual search Quiz
- ◆ General knowledge CDL pre-test

▌ Chapter 10

Communication 133

- ◆ Communicating intent
- ◆ Communicating presence
- ◆ Communication from others
- ◆ Summary
- ◆ Communication Quiz
- ◆ Combination vehicle CDL pre-test

▌ Chapter 11

Speed management 143

- ◆ Stopping distance
- ◆ Road conditions
- ◆ Road shape
- ◆ Speed and visibility
- ◆ Speed and traffic flow
- ◆ Use of cruise control
- ◆ Obeying the speed limit
- ◆ Summary
- ◆ Speed management Quiz
- ◆ Combination vehicle CDL pre-test

▌ Chapter 12

Space management 153

- ◆ Managing space
- ◆ Turning space
- ◆ Space when crossing and entering traffic
- ◆ Summary
- ◆ Space management Quiz
- ◆ Combination vehicle CDL pre-test

Chapter 13

Night driving.. 161

- ◆ Night driving factors
- ◆ Night driving procedures
- ◆ Summary
- ◆ Night driving Quiz
- ◆ Combination vehicle CDL pre-test

Chapter 14

Extreme driving conditions 171

- ◆ Vehicle preparation
- ◆ Emergency equipment
- ◆ Tire chain installation
- ◆ Cold weather starting
- ◆ Driving hazards
- ◆ Skidding and jackknifing
- ◆ Slippery surfaces
- ◆ Wet brakes
- ◆ Freeing a stuck vehicle
- ◆ Breakdowns
- ◆ Mountain driving
- ◆ Summary
- ◆ Extreme driving conditions Quiz
- ◆ General knowledge CDL pre-test

Chapter 15

Hazard perception... 189

- ◆ Hazard recognition
- ◆ Road hazards
- ◆ User hazards
- ◆ Plan ahead
- ◆ Summary
- ◆ Hazard perception Quiz
- ◆ General knowledge CDL pre-test

▌ Chapter 16

Railroad crossings 199

- ◆ The regulations
- ◆ Types of warning devices
- ◆ Signs and signals
- ◆ Safety tips
- ◆ Summary
- ◆ Railroad crossings Quiz
- ◆ General knowledge CDL pre-test

▌ Chapter 17

Emergency maneuvers 211

- ◆ The role of emergency maneuvers
- ◆ Evasive steering
- ◆ Emergency stopping
- ◆ Off-road recovery
- ◆ Brake failure
- ◆ Blowouts
- ◆ Summary
- ◆ Emergency maneuvers Quiz
- ◆ General knowledge CDL pre-test

▌ Chapter 18

Skid control and recovery 223

- ◆ Skid dynamics
- ◆ Causes of skids
- ◆ Tractor-trailer skids
- ◆ Skid recovery
- ◆ Summary
- ◆ Skid control and recovery Quiz
- ◆ General knowledge CDL pre-test

▌ Chapter 19

Special rigs 233

- ◆ Multiple articulation vehicles
- ◆ Oversize vehicles

- High center-of-gravity vehicles
- Special cargo vehicles
- Summary
- Special rigs Quiz
- General knowledge CDL pre-test

▌ Chapter 20

Preventive maintenance 245

- Types of maintenance
- Your responsibility
- Regulatory requirements
- Pitfalls of poor vehicle maintenance
- Summary
- Preventive maintenance Quiz
- General knowledge CDL pre-test

▌ Chapter 21

Diagnosing and reporting malfunctions 257

- Diagnosing and reporting malfunctions
- Troubleshooting
- DVIR requirements
- Summary
- Diagnosing and reporting malfunctions Quiz
- General knowledge CDL pre-test

▌ Chapter 22

Handling cargo 265

- The importance of proper cargo handling
- Principles and methods of cargo securement
- Principles of weight distribution
- Safe loading responsibilities
- Loading/unloading tools
- Summary
- Handling cargo Quiz
- General knowledge CDL pre-test

▌ Chapter 23

Cargo documentation 277

- ◆ Basic definitions
- ◆ Basic documents
- ◆ Pickup and delivery procedures
- ◆ Summary
- ◆ Cargo documentation Quiz
- ◆ CDL air brake pre-test

▌ Chapter 24

Hazardous materials 289

- ◆ What is a hazardous material?
- ◆ The CDL and hazmat endorsement
- ◆ Hazard classes and divisions
- ◆ Shipping papers
- ◆ Shipping paper accessibility
- ◆ Loading and unloading
- ◆ On the road
- ◆ Summary
- ◆ Hazardous materials Quiz
- ◆ CDL air brake pre-test

▌ Chapter 25

Hours of service 299

- ◆ Who is regulated?
- ◆ 11 hours driving rule
- ◆ 14 consecutive hours duty rule
- ◆ Mandatory break provision
- ◆ On-duty time
- ◆ 60-hour/7-day and 70-hour/8-day limits
- ◆ Record of duty status/electronic logging device
- ◆ Exceptions
- ◆ Summary
- ◆ Hours of service Quiz
- ◆ CDL air brake pre-test

Chapter 26

International driving 315

- Operating in Canada
- Crossing the Canadian border
- Border crossing programs
- Returning to the United States from Canada
- Motor carrier safety and licensing
- Vehicle sizes and weights
- Metric measurements and conversions
- Summary
- International driving Quiz
- CDL air brake pre-test

Chapter 27

Trip planning 327

- The five basic steps of trip planning
- Paperwork
- Route selection
- Vehicle and cargo restrictions
- Estimating time
- Estimating fuel usage
- Estimating trip expenses
- Summary
- Trip planning Quiz
- CDL air brake pre-test

Chapter 28

Accident procedures 341

- Definitions
- Accident register
- Securing the scene
- At the scene
- Hazardous materials
- Vehicle fires
- Summary
- Accident procedures Quiz
- CDL air brake pre-test

▌ Chapter 29

Security of cargo, truck, and driver 355

- ◆ Cargo theft
- ◆ Personal security
- ◆ In-transit security tips
- ◆ Summary
- ◆ Security of cargo, truck, and driver Quiz
- ◆ General knowledge CDL pre-test

▌ Chapter 30

Personal health and safety 365

- ◆ Personal health and driving
- ◆ Weight, diet, and exercise
- ◆ Stress
- ◆ Fatigue
- ◆ Alcohol use and drug abuse
- ◆ Safety equipment and practices
- ◆ Summary
- ◆ Personal health and safety Quiz
- ◆ General knowledge CDL pre-test

▌ Chapter 31

Public and employer relations 379

- ◆ Trucking industry image
- ◆ Contact with the public
- ◆ Customer relations
- ◆ What do employers look for?
- ◆ Company policy
- ◆ Whistleblower protection
- ◆ Coercion
- ◆ Opportunities for advancement
- ◆ Applying for a job
- ◆ Summary
- ◆ Public and employer relations Quiz
- ◆ General knowledge CDL pre-test

▍Chapter 32

Basic business practices 393

- ◆ Cost determination and control
- ◆ Fuel management
- ◆ Growing revenue
- ◆ Summary
- ◆ Basic business practices Quiz
- ◆ General knowledge CDL pre-test

▍Chapter 33

CSA 401

- ◆ What is CSA?
- ◆ Data collection
- ◆ Safety measurement system (SMS)
- ◆ Behavior Analysis and Safety Improvement Categories (BASICs)
- ◆ Assigning value
- ◆ Safety evaluation
- ◆ Interventions
- ◆ Your role in CSA
- ◆ CSA-related data
- ◆ Summary
- ◆ CSA Quiz
- ◆ General knowledge CDL pre-test

Troubleshooting guide 413

Glossary 417

Index 447

Orientation

OBJECTIVES

Upon completion of this chapter, you should have a basic understanding of:

- The importance of the trucking industry
- The importance of compliance with applicable regulations
- The procedure for obtaining a commercial driver's license (CDL)
- The qualifications you are subject to in this industry
- Basic vehicle definitions

1 Orientation

- WELCOME TO THE TRUCKING INDUSTRY
- A REGULATED INDUSTRY
- OBTAINING YOUR COMMERCIAL DRIVER'S LICENSE (CDL)
- DRIVER QUALIFICATIONS
- DRIVER DISQUALIFICATION
- ALCOHOL AND DRUG TESTING
- THE COMMERCIAL MOTOR VEHICLE — AN OVERVIEW
- SUMMARY

INTRODUCTION

This chapter will introduce you to some of the basics when it comes to the trucking industry — how it is regulated, the qualifications you must meet, and some of the terms you need to understand.

■ Welcome to the trucking industry

The trucking industry is essential to our nation's economy. Trucks deliver everything from raw materials to manufacturers, to completed products to warehouses, stores, and homes. Trucks deliver seed and fertilizer to the farm and food to our nation's grocers. Virtually everything, at one time or another, is moved by a truck.

According to the American Trucking Associations (ATA), 9.96 billion tons of freight (primary shipments only) was transported by trucks in 2014. This represents over two-thirds (68.8 percent) of total domestic tonnage shipped. In 2013, just over seven million people were employed throughout the economy in jobs related to trucking activity (excluding the self-employed). In 2014, there were 3.4 million people employed as truck drivers.*

Source: ATA: "American Trucking Trends 2015"

Interstate vs. intrastate

A motor carrier may operate in interstate commerce, intrastate commerce, or both. When discussing compliance with the regulations it is important to understand the following terms.

Interstate commerce: You are involved in interstate commerce if you drive a commercial motor vehicle (CMV) that hauls cargo from state-to-state, from overseas, or across U.S. borders. Hauling interstate cargo within a state is also considered interstate commerce.

Intrastate commerce: You are involved in intrastate commerce if you drive a CMV that hauls cargo within a state and never crosses a state line. The cargo's trip must begin and end in the same state, the cargo can not cross state lines by any form of transportation such as rail, air, ship, or truck.

Most states adopt at least some of the FMCSRs for intrastate operations. Requirements do vary from state to state. If operating in intrastate commerce, make sure you understand the state regulations before hitting the road.

■ A regulated industry

The trucking industry is subject to government regulation, intended in part to ensure safety for those in the industry as well as the general motoring public. Part of being a professional driver is knowing and complying with the regulations that affect you and your industry.

Federal Motor Carrier Safety Administration (FMCSA)

The Federal Motor Carrier Safety Administration (FMCSA), an agency of the U.S. Department of Transportation (USDOT), issues and enforces the bulk of the regulations that interstate motor carriers and drivers must follow. These regulations are commonly referred to as the Federal Motor Carrier Safety Regulations (FMCSRs).

The FMCSRs establish basic safety rules and standards for motor carriers, drivers, other employees of motor carriers, and commercial motor vehicles. Topics covered in the FMCSRs include driver qualification and disqualification, hours of service, commercial driver's license (CDL) standards, drug and alcohol testing, and vehicle condition and inspection.

Pipeline and Hazardous Materials Safety Administration (PHMSA)

The Pipeline and Hazardous Materials Safety Administration (PHMSA), an agency of the USDOT issues and enforces the hazardous materials regulations (located in 49 CFR Parts 105 to 180). The hazardous materials regulations apply to individuals who offer for transport hazardous materials including individuals responsible for their preparation and transport, and those transporting these materials.

The regulations, as a whole, apply when hazardous materials are offered in commerce for transport to, and transported by:

- Rail, air, motor vehicle, and vessel carriers;
- Interstate, intrastate, and foreign carriers.

The hazardous materials regulations address several issues including:

- Classification;
- Emergency response;
- Incident notification and reporting;
- Labeling;
- Marking;
- Placarding;
- Shipping papers; and
- Training.

Other regulations

Drivers and their carriers are also responsible for complying with other regulations that apply to their industry, including workplace safety, environmental, and tax laws.

Obtaining your commercial driver's license (CDL)

In order to become a professional driver you must possess a CDL. The first step in this journey is to obtain a commercial learner's permit (CLP).

Commercial learner's permit (CLP)

A CLP must be issued before a CDL is issued by a state.

A CLP is considered a valid CDL for the purposes of behind-the-wheel training on public roads and highways.

In order to obtain a CLP, you must pass a general knowledge test for the class of vehicle you expect to operate. You will also have to pass a combination vehicle test and an air brake test if the vehicle you will be driving has air brakes.

You may also have to take and pass other written tests if you plan on adding an endorsement (such as tank) to your CLP.

There are additional requirements, including certifying that you are not subject to disqualification, providing proof of citizenship, and completing the CDL/med card merger process, that must be met as part of the process of obtaining a CLP. Complete details are listed in your state's CDL manual, issued by your state's licensing agency.

When operating a CMV, the CLP holder must, at all times, be with the holder of a valid CDL who has the proper class and endorsement(s) necessary to operate the CMV.

The CDL holder must directly supervise the CLP holder by being in the front seat of the vehicle, next to the CLP holder.

A CLP holder is not eligible to take the CDL skills test in the first 14 days after the issuance of the CLP.

A CLP is valid for 180 days, but may be renewed for an additional 180 days.

Commercial driver's license

In order to obtain your CDL, you will need to pass a driving or skills test in a motor vehicle representative of the type you want to operate. In other words, if you want to operate tractor-trailers that require a Class A CDL, you will need to take your skills test in a tractor-trailer.

You will also have to provide documentation and paperwork similar to when you applied for your CLP. Consult your state's CDL manual, issued by your state's licensing agency, for complete details.

CDL classes

The federal regulations describe three vehicle groups for the purpose of the CDL. The groupings, commonly referred to as Classes, are covered in Sec. 383.91 of the FMCSRs. The Groups/Classes are as follows:

Combination Vehicle (Group A) — Any combination of vehicles with a gross combination weight rating (GCWR) of 26,001 pounds (11,794 kilograms) or more provided the gross vehicle weight rating (GVWR) of the vehicle(s) being towed is in excess of 10,000 pounds (4,536 kilograms);

Heavy Straight Vehicle (Group B) — Any single vehicle with a GVWR of 26,001 pounds (11,794 kilograms) or more, or any such vehicle towing a vehicle not in excess of 10,000 pounds (4,536 kilograms) GVWR;

Small Vehicle (Group C) — Any single vehicle, or combination of vehicles that meets neither the definition of Group A nor that of Group B, but is designed to transport 16 or more passengers (including the driver) or is used in the transportation of hazardous materials.

Endorsements

If you plan on driving a CMV that requires an endorsement on your CDL, you must take and pass a specialized test for each endorsement.

You must get an endorsement on your CDL to operate the following specialized vehicles:

- Double/triple trailers (T);
- Passenger (P);
- Tank vehicle (N);
- Hazardous materials (H);
- A combination of tank vehicle and hazardous materials (X); and
- School bus (S).

To obtain a hazardous materials endorsement, you must comply with Transportation Security Administration (TSA) requirements. This includes providing proof of citizenship or lawful permanent residency and submitting to criminal history and intelligence-based background checks.

You are required to take a written test to get an endorsement for doubles/triples, tankers, and hazardous materials. You are required to take both a written and road/skills test to get a passenger or school bus endorsement.

Restrictions

Restrictions may also be placed on your CDL for various reasons. Air brake, intrastate-only, vision (glasses/contacts), and manual transmission are common restrictions that may be placed on a driver's CDL.

States may have additional codes for endorsements and restrictions. Codes and restrictions are explained on the license.

▌ Driver qualifications

As you will find throughout this course of instruction, there's more to becoming a professional driver than just obtaining a CDL and hitting the road. This section covers the regulatory qualifications you must meet in order to operate a CMV.

General

Section 391.11 of the FMCSRs states that you must meet certain requirements in order to operate a CMV. You are qualified if you:

- Are at least 21 years old;
- Can read, write, and speak English well enough to:
  - ◆ Speak with the general public,
  - ◆ Understand highway traffic signs and signals,
  - ◆ Respond to official inquiries, and
  - ◆ Make entries on reports and records;

1

- Can drive your truck safely;
- Can pass a DOT physical exam;
- Have only one current CDL;
- Have given your motor carrier a list of any violations you have been convicted of in the last 12 months;
- Are not disqualified to drive a CMV; and
- Passed a road test.

You must also be familiar with methods and procedures for securing cargo so that you can determine whether the cargo you transport is properly loaded, distributed, and secured. We will discuss cargo securement in a later chapter.

Physical qualification and examination

You may not drive a CMV unless you are physically qualified and have been issued a medical examiner's certificate stating you are physically qualified. (See Sec. 391, Subpart E of the FMCSRs.)

You would not be considered physically qualified and may not drive a CMV if you have:

- Lost a foot, leg, hand, or arm and have not been granted a skill performance evaluation (SPE) certificate;
- An impairment of a hand, finger, arm, foot, or leg which interferes with your ability to perform normal tasks associated with driving a CMV and have not been granted an SPE;
- Diabetes requiring insulin for control;
- Heart disease, which causes you chest pain, fainting, or shortness of breath;
- Chest or breathing problems like chronic asthma, emphysema, or chronic bronchitis;
- High blood pressure likely to interfere with driving;
- Loss of movement or feeling in part of your body;
- Any sickness which is likely to cause loss of consciousness or any loss of ability to control a CMV;
- Any mental problems likely to interfere with your ability to drive a CMV safely;
- Poor vision that affects your ability to see objects that are far away (you may use glasses or contact lenses to correct your vision), objects to the side, or traffic signal colors (you may not drive if you see with only one eye);
- Poor hearing (you must be able to hear a loud whispered voice in your better ear at not less than 5 feet with or without the use of a hearing aid or, pass a hearing test on a doctor's testing machine); or
- A current clinical diagnosis of alcoholism.

What is a skill performance evaluation (SPE) certificate? The SPE certificate is a document issued by the FMCSA to a person who is not physically qualified due to the loss or impairment of a foot, leg, hand, or arm that interferes with driving, or impairment of a hand or finger which interferes with grasping. In order to obtain the SPE certificate, a driver and motor carrier must submit an application with the FMCSA.

Also, you are not considered physically qualified and may not drive a CMV if you use of certain drugs and dangerous substances. There is an exception that allows you to use such a substance or drug if the substance or drug is prescribed by a doctor who is familiar with your medical history and assigned duties and who has advised you that the prescribed substance or drug will not adversely affect your ability to safely operate a CMV.

A medical exam is required if you:

- Have not been medically examined and physically qualified to drive a CMV;
- Have not had a medical exam in the past 24 months; or
- Have suffered a disease or injury that affected your ability to drive a CMV.

The medical exam must be performed by a medical examiner that is certified by FMCSA and is listed on the National Registry of Certified Medical Examiners (NRCME). The NRCME may be accessed at: https://nationalregistry.fmcsa.dot.gov.

If the medical examiner finds that you are physically qualified to operate a CMV, you will be given a medical examiner's certificate.

If the medical examiner finds that the determination of whether you are physically qualified to drive a CMV should be delayed pending the receipt of additional information or further examination, the examiner must inform you that the additional information must be provided within 45 days and that the pending status of the examination will be reported to FMCSA.

CDL/Med card merger

When you apply for a CDL, you must turn in a valid copy of your medical examiner's certificate and documentation certifying that you drive under one of four categories (non-excepted interstate, excepted interstate, non-excepted intrastate, or excepted intrastate) to your state driver licensing agency. This information will be maintained on your driving record.

Once you have self-certified, you will not need to self-certify again until you renew, upgrade, add endorsements to, or transfer your CDL.

Prior to your medical examiner's certificate expiring, you will need to go for a new physical and submit your new medical examiner's certificate to your state driver licensing agency. Failure to do so will result in your CDL being downgraded to a non-CDL class.

*Most states are not sending notices to drivers to remind them that their medical certificate is about to expire. It is your responsibility to keep track of the expiration date of your medical certificate, go to a certified medical examiner, and turn in the new medical certificate **before** it expires. If you do not do this, your license will be downgraded to a non-CDL class.*

Driver qualification (DQ) file

Section 391.51 of the FMCSRs requires a motor carrier to maintain a driver qualification (DQ) file for each driver it employs. The following documents must be included in your DQ file:

- Application for employment;
- Motor vehicle record from each state;
- Road test form and certificate (or a copy of the license or certificate accepted in lieu of a road test);
- Medical exam certificate — original or copy (non-CDL drivers);

1

- Motor vehicle record that includes current medical certification status and self-certification information (CDL drivers);

- SPE certificate, medical exemption, or medical variance document (if applicable);

- Motor vehicle record from each state agency for the annual review of driving record inquiry;

- Note relating to the annual review of your driving record;

- List of violations; and

- Note certifying that the medical examiner who issued your medical examiner's certificate is listed on the NRCME.

Your DQ file must be kept by your employer for the entire time you are employed and for 3 years after you leave the employer.

Driver disqualification

A driver holding a CLP or CDL can be disqualified from driving a CMV if convicted of certain offenses while driving any type of vehicle; this includes a personal vehicle. (See Sec. 383.51 of the FMCSRs.)

Major offenses

You are disqualified from operating a CMV if convicted of any of the following major offenses while driving a CMV or non-CMV:

- Being under the influence of alcohol as prescribed by state law;

- Being under the influence of a controlled substance;

- Refusing to take an alcohol test as requested by a state or jurisdiction under its implied consent laws or regulations;

- Leaving the scene of an accident;

- Using a vehicle to commit a felony; or

- Using a vehicle in the commission of a felony involving the manufacturing, distributing, or dispensing of a controlled substance.

As a professional driver, disqualification is a serious issue. One conviction for a violation in any type of vehicle can disqualify you from operating CMVs for one year. This means that even one DUI/DWI on your time off can prevent you from operating CMVs for one year.

You are disqualified from operating a CMV if convicted of any of the following major offenses while driving a CMV:

- Having an alcohol concentration of 0.04 or greater;

- Driving a CMV when, as a result of prior violations committed operating a CMV, your CDL is revoked, suspended, or cancelled, or you are disqualified from operating a CMV; or

- Causing a fatality through the negligent operation of a CMV.

The disqualification period for the first conviction (with the exception of using a vehicle in the commission of a felony involving the manufacturing, distributing, or dispensing of a controlled substance) is one year, provided you are not transporting hazardous materials.

If you are transporting hazardous materials, the disqualification period is three years.

The disqualification period for a second conviction is life.

If you are convicted of using a vehicle in the commission of a felony involving the manufacturing, distributing, or dispensing of a controlled substance, you are disqualified for life and not eligible for reinstatement.

Serious traffic violations

You are disqualified from operating a CMV if convicted of any combination of two or more of the following serious traffic violations while operating any vehicle (CMV or non-CMV):

- Excessive speeding, 15 mph or more above the posted speed limit;
- Reckless driving;
- Making improper or erratic traffic lane changes;
- Following the vehicle ahead too closely; or
- Violating a state or local law relating to motor vehicle traffic control (other than a parking violation) arising in connection with a fatal accident.

You are disqualified from operating a CMV if convicted of any combination of two or more of the following serious traffic violations while operating a CMV:

- Driving a CMV without obtaining a CLP or CDL;
- Driving a CMV without a CLP or CDL in your possession;
- Driving a CMV without the proper class of CLP or CDL and/or endorsements for the specific vehicle group being operated or for the passengers or type of cargo being transported;
- Violating a state or local law or ordinance on motor vehicle traffic control prohibiting texting while driving a CMV; or
- Violating a state or local law or ordinance on motor vehicle traffic control restricting or prohibiting the use of a hand-held mobile telephone while driving a CMV.

A driver convicted of two or more serious traffic violations while operating a non-CMV is disqualified only if the conviction results in the revocation, cancellation, or suspension of the driver's driving privileges.

If you are convicted of two serious traffic violations in separate incidents during any three year period, you are disqualified for 60 days.

If convicted of three serious traffic violations in separate incidents during any three year period, you are disqualified for 120 days.

Out-of-service violations

During a trip, you may be placed out of service by an enforcement officer for a certain period of time or until a given problem has been corrected. This typically happens at a weigh station and/or during a roadside inspection.

Conviction for violating such an out-of-service order subjects you to a fine and disqualification period. The disqualification period ranges from 180 days to 5 years with penalties for drivers of vehicles carrying hazardous materials being more severe. Fines for violating an out-of-service order range from $2,750 to $5,500.

1

Railroad-highway grade crossing violations

You are disqualified from driving if you are convicted of operating a vehicle requiring a CDL in violation of a federal, state, or local law or regulation pertaining to one of six offenses at a railroad-highway grade crossing. (See Sec. 383.51(d) of the FMCSRs.)

If you are convicted of a railroad-highway grade crossing violation, you are subject to a disqualification period of between 60 days and 1 year.

▌ Alcohol and drug testing

The regulations in Part 382 of the FMCSRs address alcohol misuse and drug use by drivers of commercial motor vehicles. The purpose of the regulations is to prevent accidents and injuries that are the result of driver misuse of alcohol and/or abuse of drugs.

Alcohol misuse and drug use

Alcohol misuse that could affect the performance of a safety-sensitive function is prohibited. A safety-sensitive function is defined as all time from the time you begin work or are required to be ready to work until the time you are relieved from work and all responsibilities for performing work. (See Sec. 382.107 of the FMCSRs.) Prohibited alcohol use includes:

- Use while performing safety-sensitive functions;
- Use during the 4 hours before performing safety-sensitive functions;
- Reporting for duty or remaining on duty to perform safety-sensitive functions with an alcohol concentration of 0.04 or greater;
- Use during the 8 hours following an accident, or until you undergo a post-accident test; or
- Refusal to take a required test.

If you have an alcohol concentration of 0.02 or greater but less than 0.04, you may not perform, or be permitted to perform, safety-sensitive functions for at least 24 hours.

Drug use that could affect performance of safety-sensitive functions is prohibited, including:

- Use of any drug, except by doctor's prescription, and then only if the doctor has advised you that the drug will not adversely affect your ability to safely operate a CMV;
- Testing positive for drugs;
- Having an adulterated or substituted drug test result; or
- Refusal to take a required test.

An employer may require you to inform your company of any therapeutic drug use.

Failing an alcohol test, testing positive for drugs, or refusing to take a required alcohol and/or drug test will result in you being removed from all safety-sensitive functions until you go through a return-to-duty process. This is a very serious issue, as under the regulations, you are prohibited from operating a CMV until this process is complete. Also, many motor carriers have a strict policy when it comes to this issue. You could lose your job.

Types of tests

There are six types of tests that are required by the regulations. Drivers of CMVs are subject to the following tests:

Pre-employment test — Before you perform any safety-sensitive functions, you must submit to a drug test. Your motor carrier must receive a negative result prior to allowing you to drive or perform other safety-sensitive functions. A pre-employment alcohol test is not required by the regulations, but an employer may conduct this type of test if certain criteria are met. (See Sec. 382.301 of the FMCSRs.)

Post accident test — A post-accident **alcohol** test is required following an accident when:

- Any person involved in the accident dies; or
- You are cited within 8 hours of the accident for a moving traffic violation **and** any person involved in the accident is injured and is immediately taken away from the accident scene for medical treatment; or
- You are cited within 8 hours of the accident for a moving traffic violation **and** the accident resulted in the towing of one or more vehicles from the scene.

Post-accident alcohol testing should be done within 2 hours of the accident. If the test cannot be performed within 2 hours, the motor carrier must prepare a record stating why the test wasn't given. If the test cannot be performed within 8 hours, the motor carrier should not give the test and must prepare a record stating why the test could not be given within that time.

A post-accident **drug** test is required when:

- Any person involved in the accident dies; or
- You are cited within 32 hours of the accident for a moving traffic violation **and** any person involved in the accident is injured and is immediately taken away from the accident scene for medical treatment; or
- You are cited within 32 hours of the accident for a moving traffic violation **and** the accident resulted in the towing of one or more vehicles from the scene.

Post-accident drug testing must be performed within 32 hours of the accident. If the test cannot be performed within 32 hours, the motor carrier should not give the test and must prepare a record stating why the test could not be given within that time.

Your motor carrier must provide you with necessary post-accident information, procedures, and instructions before you operate a CMV.

If you are subject to post-accident testing you must remain available for testing. Not remaining available for testing is considered a refusal to test. A refusal to test is treated the same as failing an alcohol test or testing positive for drugs.

Nothing in the regulations should delay medical attention for those who are injured or prohibit you from leaving the scene of the accident to get help in responding to the accident.

Random testing — Unannounced random testing is required for a certain percentage of drivers each year. Random tests must be unannounced and spread reasonably throughout the year. When you are

1

informed of being selected for random testing you must immediately go to the testing site.

Random testing for alcohol must be conducted while you are performing, immediately prior to performing, or immediately after performing a safety-sensitive function. Random testing for drugs may be performed at any time while you are at work for your motor carrier.

Selection of drivers for all random testing must be done using a scientifically valid method. The DOT only recognizes a random number table or a computer-based random number generator that is matched with drivers' Social Security numbers, payroll identification numbers, or other comparable identifying numbers as scientifically valid. Drawing names out of a hat is not considered scientifically valid.

Once you are randomly tested for drugs and/or alcohol during a calendar year, your name must be returned to the random pool for each new selection. Each driver must be subject to an equal chance of being tested during each selection process.

Reasonable suspicion testing — Reasonable suspicion testing is required if your supervisor has reason to believe that your behavior or appearance may indicate alcohol abuse or drug use. The supervisor's suspicion must be based on specific, clearly stated observations of your appearance, behavior, speech, or body odors. Indications of the chronic and withdrawal effects of drugs may also be considered when determining reasonable suspicion for drug testing.

Alcohol testing is authorized only if the observations are made during, just before, or just after you perform safety-sensitive functions. The person who makes the determination that reasonable suspicion exists may not conduct the alcohol test.

If reasonable suspicion is observed, but a reasonable suspicion test has not yet been administered, you must not perform safety-sensitive functions until an alcohol test is administered and your alcohol concentration measures less than 0.02, or 24 hours have elapsed following the determination of reasonable suspicion.

Your motor carrier may require you to submit to a drug test at any time reasonable suspicion exists while you are on duty.

The regulations do not give a motor carrier authority to take any action, other than stated above, against you based solely on your behavior and appearance with no test result. However, the motor carrier may take action independent of the regulations.

Testing for reasonable suspicion must be based on the observations of a trained supervisor. The supervisor's training must include 60 minutes of training on alcohol abuse and an additional 60 minutes of training on controlled substances use. It must also include the physical, behavioral, speech, and performance indicators of probable misuse of alcohol and use of controlled substances.

Return-to-duty/follow-up testing — If you fail an alcohol test, test positive for drugs, or refuse an alcohol and/or drug test, you must be evaluated by a substance abuse professional (SAP) and participate in the education and/or treatment program prescribed by the SAP.

You must successfully comply with the education and/or treatment program prescribed by the SAP and undergo a **return-to-duty** test with the results indicating an alcohol concentration of less than 0.02 and/or a verified negative drug test.

You are then subject to **follow-up** testing. The number and frequency of the tests are determined by the SAP, but must consist of at least six tests during the first 12 months following your return to duty.

Follow-up testing may be done for up to 60 months (5 years).

Follow-up testing for alcohol can only be performed when you are performing a safety-sensitive function, or immediately before or after performing a safety-sensitive function.

The commercial motor vehicle — an overview

There are many types of commercial motor vehicles you could be called upon to operate throughout your driving career. The following is a brief summary of some of the basic terms. This will be addressed in more detail in later chapters.

Tractor — The tractor is the power unit. It is used to pull a vehicle or vehicles (trailers, semi-trailers, tankers, flatbeds, etc.).

There are two cab styles that are most common, the conventional tractor and the cab-over-engine (COE) tractor.

Conventional tractor — The engine is located under the hood of the tractor. Like passenger vehicles, the engine is in front of the driver.

Cab-over-engine (COE) — The cab is over the engine. The driver is over the front wheels and the front of the tractor is flat.

The following are other vehicle-related terms that will be used throughout the text.

Steering axle — The front axle, responsible for controlling the vehicle direction.

Drive axle — The axle or axles that are powered and actively pull the load.

Tandem axle — An assembly of two axles (could be on the tractor or the trailer).

1

Duals — A pair of wheels and tires mounted together on the same side of one axle.

Trailer — The trailer is what stores and carries the cargo. There are two types of trailers, the full trailer and the semitrailer.

- **Full trailer** — A full trailer is supported by its own axles. No part of its weight rests on the towing vehicle.

- **Semitrailer** — The front of a semitrailer rests on the tractor, specifically the tractor's fifth wheel. When a semitrailer is disconnected from the tractor, its front end rests on legs commonly referred to as landing gear.

Fifth wheel — The fifth wheel is a coupling device located at the tractor's rear frame that is used to join the front of the trailer to the tractor. It looks like a flat rounded plate with a v-shaped notch.

Combination vehicle — When a trailer is attached to a tractor it is called a combination vehicle. We will cover several types of combination vehicles later in this text.

Summary

In this chapter, you have learned about the first steps you must take to become a professional driver. As you can see, it takes more than just getting a license and driving down the road. You must meet certain qualifications and have an understanding of the industry. You must also understand what your responsibilities are to your company, the regulatory agencies, yourself, your family, and the motoring public.

ORIENTATION QUIZ

Directions: *Read each statement carefully and mark the response that best answers the question.*

1. Trucking is exempt from government regulations.
    A. True
    B. False

2. You must pass a knowledge test obtain a CLP.
    A. True
    B. False

3. Which of the following is a type of vehicle that requires an endorsement on your CDL?
    A. Double trailer
    B. Passenger
    C. Tank
    D. All of the above

4. According to the FMCSRs, you are qualified to operate a commercial motor vehicle if you:
    A. Are at least 16 years old
    B. Passed an IQ test
    C. Have only one current CDL
    D. All of the above

5. You may not drive a commercial motor vehicle if you have been disqualified.
    A. True
    B. False

6. The air-brake endorsement is necessary to operate a commercial motor vehicle equipped with air brakes.
    A. True
    B. False

7. _____ is a major disqualifying offense.
    A. Jaywalking
    B. Following the vehicle ahead too closely
    C. Leaving the scene of an accident
    D. All of the above

8. A_____ is supported by its own axles and has no part of its weight resting on the towed vehicle.
    A. Semitrailer
    B. COE
    C. Full trailer
    D. Conventional tractor

9. The driver of a commercial motor vehicle, subject to the CDL standards, is not subject to drug and alcohol testing.
    A. True
    B. False

10. The engine of a _____ is located under the hood of the tractor.
    A. Cab-over engine
    B. Conventional tractor
    C. Full trailer
    D. All of the above

GENERAL KNOWLEDGE CDL PRE-TEST

The General Knowledge Test must be taken by all applicants for a commercial driver's license. Read each question carefully and then choose the answer that is most correct.

1. While driving you are looking ahead of your vehicle. How should you be looking?

   A. Look to the right side of the roadway
   B. Look back and forth and near and far
   C. Stare straight ahead at all times
   D. All of the above

2. When you are driving at night, you should:

   A. Always use your high beam headlights
   B. Watch the solid white line on the left side of the roadway
   C. Adjust your vehicle speed so as to keep your stopping distance within your sight distance
   D. Keep your high beams on at all times

3. Most serious skids are a result of:

   A. Driving too fast for conditions
   B. Improper loading of the vehicle
   C. Not braking hard enough
   D. All of the above

4. If you drive through heavy rain or standing water, your brakes may get wet. What can this cause when you apply the brakes?

   A. Trailer jackknife
   B. Your brakes to heat up
   C. Hydroplaning
   D. Hydroplaning if you were traveling faster than 30 mph when you applied brakes

5. Which of the following is true about the use of reflective emergency triangles?

   A. The regulation requires they be placed within 10 minutes of stopping
   B. You do not need to use them if you break down as long as your 4-way flashers are working
   C. You do not need to use them as long as you have pulled your vehicle completely off the traveled portion of the roadway
   D. You do not need to use them if you stop on a hill or curve

Control systems

OBJECTIVES

Upon completion of this chapter, you should have a basic understanding of tof your commercial motor vehicle's (CMV) controls and systems. You should be able to:

- Identify and describe the engine controls

- Identify and describe the function of the primary controls

- Identify and describe the function of the secondary controls

- Identify and describe the acceptable operating range for the instruments required to monitor vehicle oil, coolant, and electrical systems

- Identify and describe warning devices

2 Control systems

- ENGINE CONTROLS
- PRIMARY VEHICLE CONTROLS
- SECONDARY VEHICLE CONTROLS
- VEHICLE INSTRUMENTS
- SUMMARY

INTRODUCTION

As a professional driver, it is important that you understand the function of all controls and instruments of any vehicle you operate. Commercial motor vehicles (CMVs) are nothing like your personal vehicle. CMVs have numerous systems, controls, and instruments that you usually do not see in a personal vehicle.

This chapter will introduce you to the controls and instruments found in CMVs.

Engine controls

The engine controls are what you use to start and shut down the commercial motor vehicle's (CMV) engine. Though similar in most vehicles, they do vary somewhat based on the type of engine and engine manufacturer.

For safety's sake, you should never operate a CMV until you have familiarized yourself with its instruments and controls.

Engine control switch — The engine control switch starts the engine. It must be on in order to start the engine.

Starter button — Some trucks have a starter button. If the truck you are operating has a starter button, you must turn the engine key to the on position and then push the starter button. Normal cranking time should be about 3 to 5 seconds.

Cruise control — Cruise control allows the vehicle to maintain a steady, constant speed without depressing the accelerator.

Primary vehicle controls

The primary controls are the controls required for steering, accelerating, braking, and parking a CMV.

Steering wheel and accelerator pedal

Steering wheel — The steering wheel is used to steer the CMV. It has a larger diameter than your car's steering wheel.

Accelerator pedal — The accelerator pedal controls the CMV's speed. It is operated the same way on a CMV as on a car. During your training, you may also hear this referred to as the throttle. You push the throttle down to increase speed and release it to reduce speed. Proper use of the throttle allows you to safely control the vehicle's speed, avoiding excessive use of the vehicle's service brakes.

CHAPTER 2

Clutch pedal

The clutch pedal is used to engage and disengage the clutch and to shift gears. There are four basic clutch positions.

1. **Engaged** — When the clutch is engaged, the pedal is fully released (your foot isn't depressing the pedal). The engine and drive train are connected, if the vehicle is in gear.

2. **Free play** — Free play is the amount of movement possible without engaging or disengaging the clutch. Free play is necessary to prevent excessive clutch wear. Normal free play is about one to two inches.

> Extensive damage can be caused to the transmission or drive train if the clutch pedal isn't operated properly.

3. **Disengaged** — The clutch is disengaged when the pedal is depressed about three to eight inches. In this position, the engine and drive train are separated. The clutch must be disengaged in order to start the engine or shift gears.

4. **Clutch brake** — When disengaged, the transmission of a CMV spins. Because of this, the use of the clutch brake will stop the transmission from turning. This is done while at a stop, not while moving. By depressing the clutch pedal to the floor, the clutch brake will be engaged, bringing the transmission to a stop, which makes it possible to shift into the desired starting gear (forward or reverse).

Transmission controls

The transmission controls vary depending on the type of transmission in the truck.

A manual transmission uses a clutch and a gear shift lever. You have to manually change gears.

The gear shift lever may include a range selector lever, allowing you to switch between high and low ranges. The down position includes the low range of gears and the up position includes the high range of gears. A splitter valve or button allows you to split gears on 13 and 18 speed transmissions.

A semiautomatic transmission includes a clutch and gear shift lever. There could also be a control pad with push-buttons on it, instead of a gear shift lever. Some gear changes are done by an on-board computer and some are done manually.

An automatic transmission only has a gear shift lever, or touch pad. A clutch may not be needed in some models. All gear changes are done by an on-board computer and hydraulics.

Brake controls

The brakes are used to slow or stop the vehicle. The air brake control system is complex and involves a number of separate controls.

Foot brake control valve — The foot brake control valve (also called the service brake, foot valve, or treadle valve) operates both the tractor's and trailer's service brakes. When depressed, it supplies air pressure to all brake chambers.

Trailer brake hand-control valve — The trailer brake control valve (also called the hand valve, trolley valve, or independent trailer brake) operates the service brakes on the trailer only. It is only used in special situations. It shouldn't be used to hold equipment in place while parked or to slow the vehicle. Improper use could cause the trailer to skid or jackknife.

Parking brake control valve — The parking brake control valve is a yellow four-sided knob (diamond shaped) that allows the driver to activate the parking brake. The parking brake should only be used when the vehicle is completely stopped. The parking brake should always be engaged before you leave the driver's seat or turn the engine off. Failure to engage (set) the parking brake could cause the vehicle to roll, even if it is assumed that the vehicle is on level ground.

Trailer air supply valve — The trailer air supply valve, the red eight-sided button, controls air supply to trailer brakes. It must be released (pushed in) for normal operation with a trailer and applied (pulled out) for operation on a tractor without a trailer. It closes automatically in the event that the airlines to the trailer are broken.

Antilock brakes

Since 1998, the National Highway Traffic Safety Administration (NHTSA) has required that all newly manufactured truck tractors be equipped with an antilock braking system (ABS). When used properly, antilock brakes help prevent wheels from locking and losing traction, which can cause a loss of vehicle control.

The biggest difference between ABS and other brake systems is how you use the brake pedal to stop the vehicle. With traditional brakes, you would normally pump the brake pedal. With ABS, a firm and continuous pressure on the pedal is needed to make the brakes work properly.

Auxiliary brakes and retarders

Auxiliary brakes and retarders reduce the vehicle's speed without using the service brakes. They keep service brakes from being overused and becoming overheated. They should only be used on dry road surfaces. There are four basic classes of auxiliary brakes and retarders.

Exhaust brakes — Exhaust brakes are considered the simplest form of heavy vehicle retarder. A valve is installed in the exhaust manifold that keeps exhaust gasses from escaping. This builds up back pressure in the engine, preventing it from increasing speed. Exhaust brakes are usually controlled by an on/off switch in the cab or an automatic control switch on the accelerator or clutch.

Engine brakes — Engine brakes are built into the head of the engine and alter valve timing, turning the engine into an air compressor. They're operated using a switch mounted on the dashboard and when your foot leaves the accelerator and clutch.

Hydraulic retarders — Hydraulic retarders are a type of driveline retarder. They are usually mounted between the engine and flywheel. They reduce a vehicle's speed by directing a flow of oil against the stantor vanes. They may be activated by a hand lever or accelerator switch.

Electric retarders — Electric retarders contain electromagnets which slow the rotors attached to the drive train. They're operated by a switch in the cab.

Few trucks have all four types of auxiliary brake systems. Most trucks only have one. It is important that you know which type your truck has and how it operates.

Interaxle differential lock

An interaxle differential lock unlocks and locks the rear tandem axles. In the unlocked position, the axles turn independently of each other on a dry surface. In the locked position, power to the axles is equalized to prevent wheels lacking traction from spinning. Interaxle differential locks should never be employed any longer than is absolutely necessary.

Secondary vehicle controls

Secondary vehicle controls assist you in safely operating your vehicle. Some are similar to the secondary controls in your car. Others are unique to trucks. The number and type of controls vary from vehicle to vehicle, but typically fall within the following major categories.

Seeing:

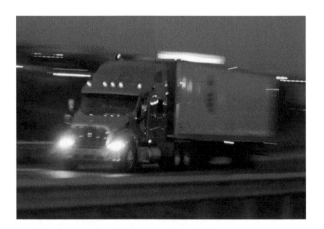

- Lights
- Remote mirrors
- Mirror heaters
- Windshield wipers and washers
- Defroster

Communication:

- Horns
- Lights (turn signals, four-way flashers, high beams, fog lamps, brake lights, etc.)

Climate/Comfort controls:

- Heater
- Air conditioner
- Air vents
- Steering wheel adjustment
- Seat position and adjustment control

Driver safety:

- Bunk restraints
- Seat belts
- Door locks
- Fire extinguisher(s)
- Warning devices (triangles, flares, fusees)

*Make sure you are familiar with and know how to operate all secondary vehicle controls **before** you hit the road.*

▌ Vehicle instruments

Vehicle instruments monitor and report on the operating condition of your vehicle. They warn you of potential problems. Basic instruments are listed below.

Note that this is a representation of the common instruments that you will find in a CMV. There can be variations. Always make sure you are familiar with the instruments in your vehicle.

Speedometer — A speedometer is required under Sec. 393.82 of the Federal Motor Carrier Safety Regulations (FMCSRs). The speedometer shows the speed of the vehicle in miles per hour (mph) and/or kilometers per hour.

Odometer — The odometer indicates the total number of miles (or kilometers) traveled by a vehicle.

Tachometer — The tachometer shows engine speed in hundreds of revolutions per minute (rpm). It serves as a guide for shifting into the appropriate transmission gear. It also assists you in effectively using the engine and transmission when accelerating and decelerating and for fuel efficiency.

Fuel gauge — The fuel gauge shows how much fuel is left in the vehicle's fuel tank(s). Since fuel gauges aren't always accurate, you should check the fuel tank(s) visually before you start a trip.

Ammeter — The ammeter measures the amount of battery being charged or discharged. A normal reading is slightly to the charged side. A continuous high charge or continuous discharge are signs of problems. Ammeters are not found on all CMVs. If your vehicle does not have one, refer to the voltmeter for charging issues.

Voltmeter — The voltmeter measures battery output in volts. The vehicle's operator's manual should be consulted to determine a normal reading for the vehicle you are operating. In most vehicles, a normal reading is between 13 and 14.5 volts. Higher or lower than normal voltage can shorten the life of a battery.

Air pressure gauge — The air pressure gauge measures pressure of air in the reservoir, or tanks in pounds per square inch (psi). A truck may be equipped with one or two air pressure gauges. These gauges are referred to as the primary and secondary air pressure gauges. The air pressure gauge is required on every CMV equipped with air brakes.

When the engine starts, air pressure starts building. It continues to build until maximum pressure is reached (about 120 psi). If pressure drops below 60 psi, a low pressure warning device (light or buzzer) will activate, indicating that continued operation of the vehicle is unsafe. At 20 to 45 psi, the tractor protection valve closes, shutting off the air supply to the trailer. A vehicle without sufficient air pressure shouldn't be operated.

Oil pressure gauge — The oil pressure gauge tells you if the engine is being properly lubricated. In warm weather, oil pressure should register on the oil pressure gauge within a few seconds after the vehicle is started and gradually rise to normal operating range. Normal operating range is 30 psi to 50 psi. In cold weather it could take 30 to 60 seconds to get a reading.

Normal range varies from vehicle to vehicle based on engine speed and oil viscosity. If pressure is low or doesn't register, the engine isn't being lubricated properly. This can cause the engine to be ruined within a short time period. You should know the operating range of your vehicle and stop and investigate anytime there's a loss in pressure or pressure doesn't register.

Coolant temperature gauge — The coolant temperature gauge measures the temperature of water and coolant in the engine block. The cooling system protects the engine from damage caused by heat.

Normally, an engine operates at about 170°-195°F. This can vary, so consult your vehicle's operator's manual for specifics.

If the gauge registers above the normal range, the engine may be overheating. You should immediately turn off the engine.

Oil temperature gauge — The engine oil temperature gauge indicates the temperature of the engine oil. The normal engine oil temperature is between 180°-225°F. This can vary, so consult your vehicle's operator's manual for specifics.

A high oil temperature can cause thinner oil, decreasing oil pressure. This can result in engine damage.

Exhaust pyrometer gauge — The exhaust pyrometer gauge shows the temperature of the exhaust gasses in the manifold. If the vehicle has an exhaust pyrometer, it could be used to determine when the vehicle has cooled enough to shut down the engine.

Axle temperature gauge — The axle temperature gauge measures the temperature of the front and rear drive axles. Above normal readings may indicate bad bearings.

Warning devices

CMVs are also equipped with warning devices. They let you know when pressures or temperatures reach a dangerous level. Some of the more common warning devices are listed below.

Low pressure warning alarm/light — The low pressure warning alarm/light indicates inadequate pressure in the air brake system.

Coolant level alarm — The coolant level alarm lights up when the level starts dropping, indicating a probable leak.

Oil level alarm — The oil level alarm lights up when the oil level drops below what is normal for operation.

It is important that you understand what these warning indicators mean, and what you should do if an indicator light, buzzer, or alarm comes on while driving.

Coolant temperature warning light — The coolant temperature warning light indicates when the temperature is too high for normal operation.

Oil pressure warning light — The oil pressure warning light indicates when oil pressure drops too low for safe operation.

Pyrometer warning light — The pyrometer warning light indicates when exhaust temperatures are abnormal.

Differential warning — The differential warning may stay illuminated when the interaxle differential is in the locked position.

ABS light — This light indicates that the ABS function is not operating.

▌ Summary

This chapter has introduced you to the basics when it comes to vehicle controls and systems. As we have been stressing throughout this chapter, it is important that you are familiar with these components before operating a CMV.

Also, it is important to include a check of the instrument panel as part of your constant scanning motion when behind the wheel. We will discuss scanning in later chapters. This continual awareness of your vehicle's controls and systems will help you detect issues long before they become serious problems that could lead to a breakdown or accident.

Directions: Read each statement carefully and mark the response that best answers the question.

1. You should always familiarize yourself with a vehicle's controls before starting a trip.

    A. True
    B. False

2. Primary vehicle controls include:

    A. Clutch pedal
    B. Accelerator pedal
    C. Transmission controls
    D. All of the above

3. In order to engage the clutch, you push the clutch pedal all the way to the floor.

    A. True
    B. False

4. A manual transmission uses:

    A. Only a gear shift lever
    B. An on-board computer for some gear changes
    C. A clutch and gear shift lever
    D. All of the above

5. An automatic transmission uses an on-board computer and hydraulics to change gears.

    A. True
    B. False

6. The parking brake should only be used when the vehicle is stopped.

    A. True
    B. False

7. Auxiliary brakes reduce the vehicle's speed by using the service brakes.

    A. True
    B. False

8. Which of the following is *not* a secondary vehicle control?

    A. Lights
    B. Heater
    C. Seat belts
    D. Steering wheel

9. Vehicle instruments:

    A. Monitor and report on the operating condition of your vehicle
    B. Slow or stop the vehicle
    C. Control the vehicle's speed
    D. All of the above

10. Warning devices let you know when the vehicle's temperature or pressure level reaches a dangerous level.

    A. True
    B. False

Read each question carefully and select the most correct answer.

1. When you are driving through construction zones, you should:
   A. Speed up and hurry through them so you aren't in them any longer than necessary
   B. Stop before entering them, get in low gear and proceed through
   C. Watch for uneven surfaces
   D. Reduce your speed only if construction workers are near the roadway

2. If you break down on a level, straight, four-lane, divided highway, where should you place the reflective warning triangles?
   A. One 10 feet from the rear of the vehicle, one approximately 100 feet from the rear of the vehicle and another one about 100 feet to the front of the vehicle
   B. One 10 feet from the rear of the vehicle, one approximately 100 feet from the rear of the vehicle, and one about 200 feet from the rear of the vehicle
   C. One 100 feet from the rear of the vehicle, one approximately 200 feet from the rear of the vehicle, and one about 300 feet from the rear of the vehicle
   D. One 50 feet from the rear of the vehicle, one about 100 feet from the rear of the vehicle, and one about 200 feet from the front of the vehicle

3. According to the Commercial Driver's manual, why should you limit the use of your vehicle's horn?
   A. If your vehicle has air brakes, the air horn may not work while you are applying your brakes
   B. It may startle other drivers
   C. You should keep both hands on the steering wheel at all times
   D. The Driver's Manual does not say that a driver should limit the use of the horn

4. Which of the following should you do when dealing with a tailgater?
   A. Increase your following distance
   B. Avoid quick changes
   C. Avoid tricks such as flashing your brake lights
   D. All of the above

5. The proper way to load a vehicle is:
   A. Keep the load balanced in the cargo area
   B. Place the load at the front of the trailer to give your drive wheels better traction
   C. Place the load at the rear of the trailer so your rear tires have better traction
   D. It makes no difference where the cargo is placed as long as you are not over the allowable gross weight

OBJECTIVES

Upon completion of this chapter, you should have a basic understanding of vehicle construction and systems including:

- Identification of the key parts of a tractor-trailer
- How the key parts of a tractor-trailer function
- How the key parts function together in vehicle operation

3 Vehicle systems

- FRAME
- SUSPENSION SYSTEM
- AXLES
- ENGINE
- FUEL SYSTEM
- AIR INTAKE AND EXHAUST SYSTEM
- LUBRICATION SYSTEM
- COOLING SYSTEM
- ELECTRICAL SYSTEM
- DRIVE TRAIN
- BRAKE SYSTEM
- WHEELS AND TIRES
- STEERING SYSTEM
- COUPLING SYSTEM
- SUMMARY

INTRODUCTION

As with any vehicle, a tractor-trailer is made up of many parts. Though these parts have individual jobs or functions, they work together to effectively and efficiently operate the tractor-trailer.

It is important that you understand the basics of vehicle construction and vehicle systems. This will help you maintain a safe vehicle and help you spot problems early on, before they become major, and potentially cause a breakdown or accident.

▌Frame

The frame is the structure around which the vehicle is assembled. It is the vehicle's foundation. The frame includes left and right side frame rails and cross members connecting the frame rails. This provides strength and support to the frame. The frame is connected directly or indirectly to all parts of the truck.

The engine is secured to the frame by engine mounts. Axles and wheels are connected to the suspension system through the frame.

Some types of vehicles, including many cargo tanks and van trailers do not have a frame. The exterior of the vehicle carries the vehicle's weight.

As you review this chapter, keep in mind that vehicle construction varies and that the parts covered may not be included on all vehicles.

█ Suspension system

The suspension system supports the body and frame of the truck. It is made up of springs, air bags, torque arms, and mounting brackets or hangers. The front and rear axles are attached to the suspension system and the frame rests on it.

The suspension system allows the axles to move up and down in response to ground changes without seriously affecting the load. Securing the suspension system at points spread throughout the frame allows the stress of road shocks to be distributed evenly throughout the frame.

The strength and durability of the system is determined by the size and weight of the vehicle as well as the size and weight of the cargo being hauled.

Characteristics necessary for a good suspension system include:

- Capacity to support the load;
- Ability to transmit full brake effort to the chassis frame;
- A cushioned ride for the driver and cargo (laden or unladen);
- Secure axles to assure correct driveline alignment; and
- Easy maintenance and lightweight parts.

In some cases, both leaf spring and air bag suspension systems are combined to provide the best of both systems.

There are two main types of suspension systems, leaf spring and air bag suspension systems.

Leaf spring suspension

This type of suspension system uses metal strips of different lengths that are connected and attached to the spring mounts or hangers.

Air bag suspension

Bags of air are placed between the axle and the frame in this type of suspension system. This system is most often used on trailers and truck tractors. This type of system provides a smooth ride whether the vehicle is loaded or empty.

Shock absorbers

As the vehicle's wheels move over uneven surfaces, shock absorbers reduce the motion of the vehicle body. They are used in both the leaf spring and the air bag suspension systems.

Axles

In general, the axles connect the wheels to the rest of the vehicle and help support the weight of the vehicle and its cargo. Individual axles perform specific functions.

Front tractor axle

This axle is the steering axle. It connects the steering mechanism and brakes.

Rear tractor axles

These axles are the power or drive axles. They transfer power from the engine and drive train to the wheels and serve as the connecting point for the brakes.

Axle types/categories

Axles fall into two types or categories, dead axles and live axles.

Dead axles do not transmit power. They are used to support the load.

Live axles transmit power from the drive shaft to the wheels through a differential gear housing. The live axle(s) contain the necessary components to transmit power to the wheels.

Engine

The engine supplies the vehicle's power. It is fueled by either diesel or gasoline. In today's engines, you may also find the use of propane or natural gas as fuel.

The engine on a truck-tractor is an internal combustion engine. This means the engine burns fuel within closed chambers inside the engine. The enclosed chambers are called cylinders. It is within the cylinders where the power comes from to operate the vehicle.

The engine has five basic parts:

- Engine block;
- Cylinders;
- Pistons;
- Connecting rods; and
- Crank shaft.

Gas vs. diesel

Gas engines may have a carburetor and spark plugs or they may have fuel injectors similar to a diesel engine.

The diesel engine has a series of fuel injectors. Fuel and air are mixed during compression. The compression in a diesel engine is much higher and the compression pressure actually causes ignition of the fuel/air mixture.

Diesel vs. Gasoline Engines	Diesel	Gasoline
Carburetor		x
Spark plug		x
Injector	x	x
Fuel/air mix *before* compression		x
Fuel/air mix *after* compression	x	

Fuel system

The fuel system provides fuel for engine operation. It controls the amount of fuel sent to the engine and determines when the fuel is injected into the cylinders.

The fuel pump draws fuel from the fuel tanks through the fuel lines and fuel filters to the fuel injectors. The fuel injectors are operated by an injector pump and spray a fine mist of fuel into the engine cylinders.

Cleanliness is very important when it comes to the fuel system. Even the smallest amount of dirt or other particles can damage the engine. A properly operating fuel system will eliminate many impurities, but it is also important that you use great care when fueling your vehicle.

Fuel tank

The fuel tank is where the fuel is held. There may be one or two fuel tanks depending on the size and type of vehicle. Additional tanks may carry fuel for heaters and reefers.

Keep the fuel cap area clean. This prevents dirt or other particles from entering the fuel tank.

Fuel filters

A series of filters clean the fuel throughout the fuel system. These filters remove dirt, water, and rust from the fuel system.

Fuel system heaters

Fuel system heaters are especially important for vehicles operated in cold weather. In general, there are three types of heaters:

- In-tank units which heat fuel in the tank;
- In-line units which heat fuel when it is going from the tank to the injector system; and
- Filter heaters which help heat the fuel as it passes through the injection system.

Some diesel trucks do not have fuel heaters. In very large engines, some of the fuel that goes through the engine is not actually burned, but is returned to the fuel tanks by way of a fuel return line. This process heats the fuel and some companies count on this as their "fuel heating" system.

Air intake and exhaust system

Fresh air is important in the operation of a diesel engine. The air intake and exhaust system are responsible for assuring that the engine processes enough fresh air to function properly.

Air intake system

The air intake system filters out dust, dirt, and water and delivers a large amount of fresh air to the cylinders.

Exhaust system

After combustion, the exhaust system collects the used gasses, passes them through the turbo charger, and then expels them through a tailpipe or exhaust stack.

Turbocharger

The turbocharger converts the power it gets from the exhaust gasses into power that can be used by the engine.

Aftercooler

The aftercooler cools the intake air from the turbocharger returning it to a safe temperature level.

Pyrometer

The pyrometer is an instrument that measures the temperature of exhaust gasses. The normal temperature is between 600° F and 1,000° F depending on the vehicle. If the exhaust temperature is too high, the engine and the turbocharger can be damaged.

Lubrication system

The lubrication system has three purposes. It lubricates, cools, and cleans the engine.

- The lubrication system delivers clean oil to parts of the engine. This allows the engine parts to move without rubbing together (friction). This increases engine efficiency and prevents damage.

- The moving parts of the engine create a great deal of heat. Oil flowing through the engine absorbs some of this heat and removes it from the engine, keeping engine temperature at a safe level.

- Oil helps keep the engine clean. As it travels through the engine it picks up dirt and other particles that can damage the engine. These particles are filtered out of the engine. Oil also prevents rust and corrosion by coating surfaces that do not move within the engine.

Maintaining the lubrication system

Proper preventive maintenance can go a long way in making sure your vehicle's engine operates efficiently and effectively. It is important that the oil is changed on a regular basis according to the vehicle manufacturer's recommendations.

As part of the oil change, the condition of the oil filter should be assessed. The oil filter is where dirt and particles that the oil removes from the engine are deposited. A clean filter allows clean oil to flow through the engine.

It is also important to check the oil level in the engine on a daily basis. This can be done by using the dipstick. The dipstick is found at the side of the engine.

To measure the engine's oil level:

- Turn off the engine;
- Put on gloves (the engine may be hot and you need to protect your hands);
- Remove the dipstick and wipe it off with a rag;
- Reinsert the clean dipstick; and
- Again remove the dipstick.

If the dipstick reads "low" or "add oil" do so before operating the vehicle again.

At this point, you should be able to determine the level of the oil in the engine, which is measured in gallons. If the reading isn't clear, wipe off the dipstick, reinsert, remove, and read again.

Oil filter system

The oil filter can help prolong the life of the engine by removing contaminants as oil passes through. There are three types of oil filter systems:

- Full flow systems;
- Bypass systems; and
- Combination bypass/full flow systems.

If you are going to check your oil when stopped during a trip, wait a few moments. Fuel your vehicle, clean your windows, and then check your oil. This will give the oil plenty of time to settle in the engine, providing a more accurate reading.

Cooling system

Though heat is important to engine operation, too much heat can damage an engine. The cooling system lowers the heat level of an operating engine.

Coolant (a combination of water and antifreeze) is stored in the radiator and circulated through engine water jackets by the water pump. At this point, the coolant is collecting some of the engine's heat and then returns to the radiator. In the radiator, the heated coolant travels through tubes which cool the coolant. The cooled coolant then recirculates, repeating the process.

Always follow the engine manufacturer's requirements for selecting coolant. Make sure the radiator is filled with the proper amount of coolant. Too much or too little coolant can damage the engine. Also keep in mind that different operating conditions (weather, etc.) require different levels of water to antifreeze mixture.

If you are going to check your coolant when stopped during a trip, wait a few moments after stopping. Then, be careful when removing the radiator cap, as the engine may be hot and you could be splashed or sprayed with hot engine coolant.

3

Electrical system

The electrical system serves many purposes. It is used to crank or start the engine and operate the vehicle's electrical equipment including lights and instruments.

The electrical system is comprised of four parts (circuits); charging, cranking, ignition, and lighting and accessory.

Charging circuit

The charging circuit produces electricity. This keeps the battery charged and runs the electrical circuits. The charging circuit is comprised of the following major parts.

- **Battery** — The battery is an electrochemical device for storing and supplying electrical energy. The battery's energy is what activates the starter.

- **Alternator or generator** — Most vehicles on the road today are equipped with an alternator, but some still use a generator. These devices are responsible for recharging the battery. When the engine is running, the alternator creates electricity. Most of the electricity the vehicle needs is supplied by the alternator.

- **Ammeter** — An ammeter is a gauge on the vehicle's instrument panel that shows the amount of current flowing from the alternator. It shows whether the battery is being charged or is discharging.

- **Voltmeter** — The voltmeter is another gauge on the vehicle's instrument panel. It shows if the electrical system is charging properly.

- **Voltage regulator** — The voltage regulator is the device that controls the voltage output of the alternator or generator. The voltage regulator keeps the electrical system voltage from getting too high. If the voltage is too high, the battery and other components could overcharge and damage could occur.

Cranking circuit

The cranking circuit moves electricity from the battery to a starter motor. Depressing the starter switch inside the vehicle gets this process started.

Ignition circuit

The ignition circuit is the electrical circuit that provides sparks for each cylinder, igniting the fuel and air mixture in a gasoline engine. An ignition circuit is not needed in a diesel engine.

Lighting and accessory circuits

These circuits provide electricity for the vehicle's lights, horn, instrument lights, windshield wipers, etc.

▍Drive train

The drive train is a series of connected mechanical parts which take the power generated by the engine and applies it to the tractor's drive wheels.

The drive train is comprised of the clutch, transmission, drive shaft, universal joints, and differential. These parts modify the torque/twist and engine speed produced by the engine, turning it into power to move the vehicle down the road.

Clutch

The clutch is the part of the power train that allows the driver to connect or disconnect the engine from the power train. The clutch allows the driver to shift gears. The clutch is composed of six major parts:

- Clutch housing;
- Flywheel;

- Clutch disc(s);
- Pressure plate;
- Release assembly; and
- Controls.

In most trucks the clutch has three plates; one plate is squeezed tightly between two other plates. The plate in the middle is the driven member (clutch disk), which is connected to the shaft leading to the transmission. The other two plates are driving members which are connected directly to the engine. A strong spring or springs, force the two driving members together. This tightens their grip on the middle plate until they all turn as one unit.

The engine flywheel is used for the first driving member. It has a smooth surface where the pressure plate pushes up against it.

The other driving member is called the pressure plate. It is a heavy cast iron ring which is smooth on one side. It is fastened to the cover, which is bolted to the flywheel, so they all turn together. It is fastened so it can slide back and forth.

The driven plate is a flat disk of steel with friction facing on each side. The plate is fastened by splines to a shaft going to the transmission. It fits into grooves on the shaft so they can turn together, but the plate can slide backward and forward on the shaft. This disc is softer than the other plates. This allows the disc to wear out, preventing damage to other parts of the drive train.

Transmission

The transmission basically is a box/case of various sized gears. It is located behind the clutch and is fastened to the clutch housing.

The transmission adjusts the power generated by the engine. This provides the correct speed and torque needed. It transmits this power from the engine to the drive or powered axle(s) in order to propel the vehicle.

The transmission's gears control the speed of the vehicle. Though the engine moves at only one speed, the gears allow the vehicle to move at different speeds.

Another property of the transmission is torque. This is what makes something rotate. The torque of the gears in a transmission is related to the amount of power a vehicle exhibits. The gears let the driver vary the speed and force (torque) that the engine delivers to the wheels. When selecting gears, keep in mind that the more torque, the less speed there is and the more speed, the less torque there is.

By manipulating the gears in the transmission, you can change the ratio between the engine and the rear wheels to produce more speed or torque as needed.

Drive shaft and universal joints

Behind the transmission is a propeller which runs to the rear of the vehicle. This is called the drive shaft. The drive shaft is a hollow or solid steel shaft that connects the transmission to the rear of the vehicle.

At the front and rear of the shaft are universal joints. They are (in most cases) made up of two U-shaped pieces at right angles to each other and fastened together by a cross having arms of equal length.

The drive shaft transfers the twisting motion of the engine to the rear axle. The universal joints connect the shaft to the transmission and the rear axle.

The U-shaped pieces pivot on the arms of the cross. Since there are two pivots, the two shafts can be at an angle to one another and still turn around and transmit power. They do not have to be in a straight line. This is important because they become somewhat misaligned with each bump in the road. The rear axle moves up and down with the wheels, while the transmission moves very little as it is fastened to the frame. The universal joints allow the drive shaft to keep on turning smoothly even though its two ends are not always directly in line with each other.

Differential

The differential is the part of the drive train that splits the drive axle in half, allowing one wheel to turn at a different rate of speed than another. This helps a vehicle when turning. When performing a turn, the outside wheel must rotate faster than the inside wheel so your right wheel is actually turning at a different speed than your left wheel.

Brake system

The braking system is what slows down and stops the vehicle. It is made up of three major elements, service, emergency, and parking brakes.

- **Service brakes** — Service brakes slow down and stop the vehicle. The service brakes are regulated by the driver by using the foot and trolley valves. There are two types of service brakes, drum and disc.
  - ◆ **Drum brakes** — This metal cylinder looks like a drum that is bolted to each end of an axle. The braking mechanism is located inside the drum. To stop, the brake shoes and linings are forced/pushed against the inside of the drum. This causes friction which slows the vehicle and creates heat. When too much heat is created the brakes can stop working, making it harder, and, in some cases, impossible to stop.

- ◆ **Disc brakes** — Disc brake systems have a fixed disc attached to the inside of the wheel which rotates with the wheel. To stop, the linings are squeezed against the side of the disc which creates friction to stop the vehicle.

- **Emergency brakes** — Emergency brakes slow down and stop the vehicle when there is a failure in the air system. The red, eight-sided button on the dash controls the emergency brakes.

- **Parking brakes** — Parking brakes prevent vehicle movement when parked. The yellow, four-sided button on the dash controls the parking brakes.

Air brakes

Air brakes use compressed air to maximize braking force. The parts which make up an air brake system are listed below.

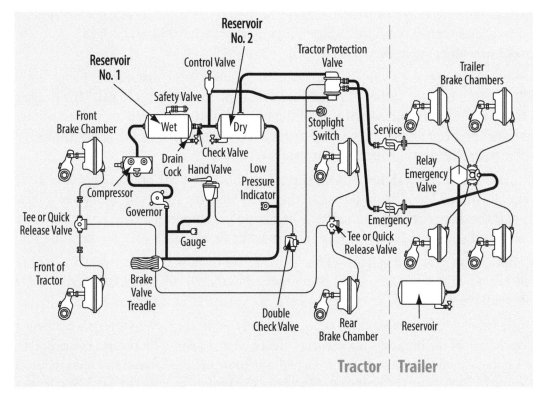

- **Compressor** — This device is designed to build up and maintain required air pressure in the brake system reservoir. The compressor is run by the vehicle's engine. It runs when the engine runs. The compressor may use belts and pulleys or shafts and gears, which are lubricated by the engine's lubrication system. The normal operating range is 90-125 pounds per square inch (psi). The compressor runs until the pressure in the air reservoir reaches 125 psi. It then stops until needed.

- **Governor** — The governor regulates the compressor. This allows the compressor to maintain appropriate pressure by opening and closing inlet valves.

- **Air tanks** — Air tanks hold the compressed air. There are three tanks which hold air; a wet tank, dry tank, and trailer reservoir. The wet tank removes most of the moisture and delivers the air to the dry tank. The trailer reservoir holds compressed air close to the trailer brake

The number of tanks on a vehicle may vary. Some tractors have one tank, which is a combined wet and dry tank. There also may be one or two tanks on the trailer.

chambers for use in normal and emergency situations. The sizes of the tanks vary based on the number of tanks and the size of the brake chambers.

- **One-way check valve** — This valve prevents air from getting back into the compressor from the air reservoirs. If air flows back, the brakes will not work.

- **Safety valves** — Safety valves, also called pressure relief valves, keep air pressure from reaching a dangerous level. A safety valve opens (usually when pressure reaches 150 psi) and releases the air into the atmosphere, lowering the pressure in the system. If the safety valve activates often or continuously, the air governor may need servicing. This should only be done by a qualified mechanic. Never make these adjustments on your own. You have probably heard the occasional release of air while standing next to a big truck. This is the safety valve releasing and is normal.

- **Drain cocks** — Drain cocks release moisture from air brake system reservoirs. The braking system could be damaged if this moisture is not removed, especially in winter, when the moisture could freeze. To prevent damage, you should drain the moisture daily. This should be done on a level surface, with the vehicle properly chocked. Allow all of the air pressure to escape to make sure all of the moisture is released.

- **Air pressure gauge** — The air pressure gauge is located on the instrument panel. It tells you how much pressure is in the system. The normal operating range is 90-120 psi. This gauge should always be included in your visual scan of the vehicle's instruments. This will help you detect a malfunction before it becomes an emergency. Remember, this could be one gauge with two needles or two separate gauges; primary and secondary.

- **Low-pressure warning signal** — This signal warns you that air pressure has dropped to a potentially unsafe level (below 60 psi). Either a red warning light will light up or a buzzer will sound. If this happens, stop immediately. If you do not stop immediately, you may lose more pressure and your brakes will lock up. This must be fixed before you can continue your trip.

- **Air application pressure gauge** — This gauge shows the amount of air pressure being applied to the brakes. When pressure is not being applied to the service brakes, the gauge will read 0 psi. (Not on all trucks.)

- **Treadle valve** — The treadle valve (also called the foot brake or brake pedal) controls the air for the operation of the brakes. This valve is controlled by pushing (depressing) the brake pedal. The further down the brake pedal is pushed, the more air the system will receive, until it is at full capacity. Releasing the brake pedal releases the brakes by letting air exhaust from the brakes.

- **Independent trailer brake** — The independent trailer brake (also called the trolley valve or hand valve) is a hand-operated control that applies the trailer brakes by regulating the airflow to the trailer unit. This brake should never be used for slowing down or parking. (Not on all trucks.)

- **Tractor parking valve** — This hand controlled knob can be pushed in to release the tractor parking brake and pulled out to set the parking brake. It also operates the spring brakes.

- **Glad hands** — Glad hands are connectors mounted on the front of the trailer for connecting air lines from the tractor. When the glad hands lock, the connection is secure. An O-ring seals the coupling, preventing dirt and debris from entering and air from escaping. You should check the O-ring for damage or dirt and debris before connecting the air lines. These O-rings are color coded. The service line is usually blue and the emergency line is usually red. When the air lines are unhooked, they should be sealed with protector plates to keep out dirt and debris. Keeping the air lines clean reduces your chances of brake failure.

- **Quick release valve** — This valve (located near the brake chambers) allows the brakes to release in a short amount of time. When you remove your foot from the valve, the pressurized air in the chambers escapes quickly into the atmosphere. This allows the brake shoes to release quickly.

- **Relay valve** — This valve is used to speed up the application and release of the rear wheel brakes. In other words the relay valve is responsible for making sure that all brakes apply at the same time.

- **Emergency relay valve** — The emergency relay valve is installed either on the trailer reservoir or on the trailer frame close to the brake chambers. This valve controls brake application and also provides for automatic trailer brake application should the trailer become disconnected from the tractor. The emergency relay valve can also release the trailer brakes quickly.

- **Brake chamber** — The brake chambers are chambers of air that are installed close to each wheel. They are attached to the brakes by either a pushrod and slack adjuster (cam brake) or simply a pushrod (wedge brake). Air enters the chamber from the brake lines. From the chamber to the brake shoe and drum, the force is applied mechanically.

Air brake system operation

So how does a basic air brake system work? The following steps outline the process.

- The pressurized air is pumped by the compressor to the wet tank where moisture is removed.

- The air then passes through the one-way check valve to the dry reservoir.

- When you put your foot on the brake, the air flows through the service air lines to the tractor brake chambers (both front and rear). At the same time, air travels through the tractor protection valve, through the service glad hand, to the trailer brake chambers.

- When you release the brake pedal, air escapes through the foot valve or relay valve in the tractor and the quick release valve in the trailer.

Antilock brake systems

The purpose of the antilock system (ABS) is to control wheel lock-up, which can cause a vehicle to skid and possibly jackknife. This is accomplished by an electronic system which senses the speed of each wheel.

In 1995, the National Highway Traffic Safety Administration (NHTSA) issued rules requiring manufacturers to install ABS on truck-tractors, trucks, trailers, and buses. The majority of the vehicles you will be operating (those manufactured in the mid- to late-1990s and later) will be equipped with ABS.

When the wheel speed sensor detects an imminent lock-up, a valve is opened and air in the chamber is released. As the wheel speed increases, the valve is closed and air is reapplied. All of this occurs automatically if the vehicle is stopping and a lock-up is sensed.

The antilock system activates when you apply pressure to the brake pedal sharply enough to lock the wheels. The computer system senses the potential for lock-up and "pumps" the brakes at a rate three to five times faster than a human could. You should never pump the brakes when operating a vehicle with an antilock brake system. Let the computer do the work for you.

Most ABS-equipped vehicles have a warning light on the dashboard. This light will turn on for a few seconds when starting your vehicle. If the light stays on or suddenly turns on while you are driving, the ABS may not be working. Though you still have properly working brakes, the antilock function may not be working. Get this checked out as soon as possible. The light also turns on for a short period of time when the brakes are applied.

Wheels and tires

Wheels

Spoke and disc wheels are the two types of wheels found on most trucks.

- **Spoke wheels** — Spoke wheels are made up of two pieces. They are heavier and more difficult to align and balance.
- **Disc wheels** — Disc wheels are made of aluminum or steel. They are easier to align because they are fastened together with one locking stud and nut that runs through both rims.

There are two types of wheel mounting systems used on most trucks, stud piloted and hub piloted.

- **Stud piloted** — A stud piloted mounting system uses the studs on the wheel hub to guide and center the wheel.
- **Hub piloted** — A hub piloted mounting system uses the wheel hub to guide and center the wheel.

The wheels are fastened by either ball-seat nuts or flange nuts.

Tires

There are three types of tires used on most trucks; radial, bias ply, and belted bias tires.

- **Radial tires** — The body plycords run around the tire perpendicular to the tread. Radial tires also have belt plies that run circumferentially around the tire, under the tread. This type of tire construction allows for better traction and fuel mileage.

  The tread on radial tires lasts 40 to 100 percent longer because when the surface area of radials comes in contact with the road, they have greater traction while creating less friction and less heat.

  This gives your vehicle greater fuel mileage and better performance.

- **Bias ply tires** — The body plycords run diagonal across the tire. The tire may also have breakers or narrow plies under the tread.
- **Belted bias tires** — The body ply cords run diagonal across the tread and belted plies run circumferentially around the tire under the tread. The belts on this tire are of heavier construction.

Mixing radial and bias ply tires — Generally, radial and bias ply tires should not be mixed. All tires on your vehicle should be the same size and type. The differences in traction and turning capabilities among the different types of tires can cause problems if the types of tires are improperly mixed. There are ways to properly mix the tires. Consult the tire manufacturer for guidelines/instructions.

Tire tubes — Some tires have tubes that fit between the tire and the rim. The air that keeps the tire inflated is kept in the tire tube. Flat tires are more prone to tire fires because the underinflated tube spins inside the tire, creating excessive heat.

Tubeless tires — Tubeless tires are mounted onto a single-piece wheel. The tire (instead of a tube) holds the air. Tubeless tires are lighter and easier to mount.

3

Tire maintenance — Proper tire inflation is important. Underinflation can increase tread wear and reduce the life of the tires. Overinflation can damage the tires and reduce stopping efficiency. Consult the vehicle's owner's manual for inflation guidance.

Tire pressure should be checked regularly. This should be done with an accurate gauge when the tire is cool.

Tire pressure should be checked and adjusted when the tire is cool. If the tire is hot, the pressure reading will be higher. If you do check a heated tire, and the pressure is higher than recommended, do not release any air. Wait until the tire is cool and check again.

Tread design — There are two basic truck tire tread designs; rib and lug tread.

- **Rib tread** — The open groove design of this tread allows for a high degree of control, helping you avoid skids. This type of tread is recommended for the front wheel positions on tractors.

- **Lug tread** — In over the road high-torque service, lug treads provide maximum protection from wear and greater traction. This type of tread is recommended for drive wheels. Generally the vehicle gets better mileage with this tread than rib tread.

Proper tire inflation and care

Proper tire inflation has many benefits including increased fuel efficiency, a smoother ride, and a reduced chance of blow out or tire fire. Inspect your tires often and check the pressure with a tire gauge. Refer to the manufacturer's specifications for correct pressure.

When inflating a tire, keep in mind the maximum pressure for the load you are carrying, making sure you do not exceed the rim or wheel rating.

During regular operation of your vehicle, the pressure of the tires should increase, as the tires get warmer. Expect increases of 10-15 psi. Greater increases, which can create an abnormal amount of heat, may indicate under inflation, excessive speed, and/or incorrect tire size. If this happens, you should stop, investigate, and correct the problem.

Underinflation — When a tire is underinflated, the following can happen:

- The tread wears down more quickly;
- The temperature within the tire increases, possibly causing the separation of the tread from the body or belt ply; and
- Deflation can occur, weakening the tire's body cords, potentially causing a blowout.

If you operate duals and one is under inflated or flat a fire can start.

Overinflation — An overinflated tire becomes rigid, making it easier for the tire to be cut or punctured by objects on the road. Overinflation also makes the ride less smooth, as the tires are unable to absorb shock.

Tire care — Tires should be rotated periodically based on manufacturer recommendations. This will help in evenly distributing wear.

As well as being a good, safe practice, inspecting tires is required by the Federal Motor Carrier Safety Regulations (FMCSRs). Section 392.7 states that a driver must be satisfied that certain vehicle parts and accessories are in good working condition prior to driving his/her vehicle. This includes tires.

Appropriate tire condition and tread depth is also addressed in the FMCSRs. Section 393.75 states that you may not drive your vehicle if a tire has any of the defects listed below:

- Body ply or belt material exposed through the tread or sidewall;
- Any tread or sidewall separation;
- The tire is flat or has an audible leak; or
- The tire has a cut that exposes the ply or belt material.

Section 393.75 also states that any tire on the front wheels must have a tread groove pattern depth of at least $4/32$ of an inch when measured at any point on a major tread groove. All other tires must have a tread groove pattern depth of at least $2/32$ of an inch when measured in a major tread groove.

Matching and spacing of duals — If two tires of differing diameters are positioned together, the larger tire will begin to overheat and bulge out at the sides due to taking more of the load on its own. The smaller tire will wear irregularly because it doesn't have proper contact with the road, possibly causing the tread to separate. If the larger tire bulges too far, it will begin to touch the other tire, increasing friction and heat between the two, which can cause a blowout in one or both of the tires.

To be on the safe side, allow no more than ¼ inch difference between the diameters, no matter what the tire size. Also keep the spacing between the tires at the recommended distance to prevent the tires from touching, creating a heat build-up.

▌ Steering system

The steering system is what gives you directional control of your vehicle. The components that make up the steering system include:

- **Steering wheel** — The steering wheel controls the direction of the vehicle. It is connected to and turns the steering shaft.

- **Steering shaft** — The steering shaft connects the steering wheel to the steering gear box.

- **Gear box** — The gear box transfers the turning of the steering shaft to the Pitman arm.

- **Pitman arm** — This component is connected to the steering gear box and moves the drag link.

- **Drag link** — The drag link transfers movement from the Pitman arm to the left steering arm.

- **Steering arm** — The right side attaches the tie rod to the wheels, the left side attaches to the drag link.

- **Tie rod** — The tie rod connects the front wheels to together and adjusts their operating angle.

3

All of the parts listed must be correctly aligned. Incorrect alignment can cause difficulty in steering and improper tire wear.

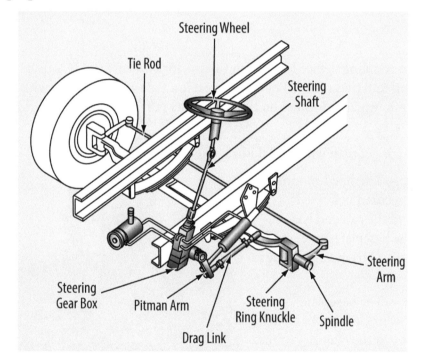

Wheel alignment

The following alignment characteristics are built into the axle by the manufacturer. They may be changed as necessary.

- **Caster** — The caster of an axle is the amount of tilt it has. This is measured in degrees and it is recommended that the axle have positive caster (it tilts forward). When set this way, the vehicle will want to naturally move straight ahead and will recover from turns more easily. Positive caster makes it easier for you to steer.

- **Camber** — The camber of the wheels is the degree of tilt they have with respect to the road. It is best when the truck's wheels have a positive camber to support the load. In other words, the distance across the top of the wheels is greater than the distance across the bottom.

When a heavy load is placed on the truck, it straightens out the tires with the road.

Other alignment characteristics are the result of wear and damage. The most notable of these are toe-in and toe-out.

- **Toe-in** — The wheels on the same axle are closer on the front than the back.
- **Toe-out** — The wheels on the same axle are closer in the back than the front.

Power steering

Power steering allows you greater control of your vehicle with less effort. There are many advantages to power steering; it takes less effort, reducing driver fatigue, road shocks are better absorbed, and it is easier to maneuver the vehicle in difficult situations.

Coupling system

The coupling system is what connects the tractor and trailer. Two main components make up the coupling system, the fifth wheel and kingpin.

Fifth wheel

The fifth wheel is a coupling device located on the tractor's rear frame. It is used to join/couple the front end of the trailer to the tractor. The fifth wheel is a flat, rounded plate with a V-shaped notch in the rear. The kingpin, which is located on the trailer, fits into the fifth wheel, allowing the tractor to pull the trailer.

There are several types of fifth wheels including fixed-mount and sliding/adjustable.

- **Fixed-mount** — The fixed-mount fifth wheel is secured in a fixed position behind the cab and has three parts, the baseplate, bracket subassemblies, and frame mounting members.

  - **Baseplate** — The baseplate includes the locking mechanism. It also takes on the majority of the stress of coupling.
  - **Bracket subassemblies** — The bracket subassemblies keep the baseplate in place.
  - **Frame mounting** — The frame mounting members are structural steel angles bolted to the fifth wheel.

- **Sliding/adjustable** — The sliding or adjustable fifth wheel slides backward and forward to accommodate different types of loads. The sliding fifth wheel may be locked into place with pins that fit into holes in the slider track or by a plunger that fits into a row of slotted holes.

Adjustment of the slider may be done by hand or by a control in the cab. When adjusted by hand, the driver manually moves the pins or plunger and adjusts the fifth wheel by moving it forward or backward. When adjusted from the cab, activating a switch unlocks the locking device. The driver then sets the trailer brakes and moves the tractor forward and backward until the fifth wheel is in the correct position.

Proper maintenance of the fifth wheel is important. This includes making sure the fifth wheel has the right amount of grease so it functions properly.

Kingpin

The kingpin is attached to the upper fifth wheel plate, under the front of the trailer. It is a two inch steel pin that attaches to the fifth wheel to couple the tractor to the trailer.

Landing gear

Landing gears support the front end load weight of the trailer when uncoupled. They are usually cranked up or down. Landing gears have either wheels or skid feet attached to the bottom.

3

▌ Summary

This chapter has covered the basics of vehicle construction and systems. This information will help you maintain a safe vehicle and help you spot problems early on, before they become major, and potentially cause a breakdown or accident.

VEHICLE SYSTEMS QUIZ

Directions: *Read each statement carefully and mark the response that best answers the question.*

1. The wheels are the vehicle's foundation.
   A. True
   B. False

2. The _____ supports the body and frame of the truck.
   A. Engine
   B. Lubrication system
   C. Suspension system
   D. All of the above

3. _____ transmit power from the drive shaft to the wheels.
   A. Dead axles
   B. Live axles
   C. Secondary axles
   D. All of the above

4. Which of the following is not part of the engine?
   A. Cylinders
   B. Pistons
   C. Service brakes
   D. Crank shaft

5. Cleanliness is not important when it comes to the fuel system.
   A. True
   B. False

6. Heat is important to engine operation, but too much heat can damage an engine.
   A. True
   B. False

7. Which of the following is not part of the drive train?
   A. Clutch
   B. Drive shaft
   C. Kingpin
   D. Transmission

8. The braking system is made up of two major elements: service brakes and travel brakes.
   A. True
   B. False

9. The driver should check his/her oil immediately after stopping the engine to avoid a false reading.
   A. True
   B. False

10. Air brakes use compressed air to maximize braking force.
    A. True
    B. False

GENERAL KNOWLEDGE CDL PRE-TEST

Read each question carefully and select the most correct answer.

1. If you aren't sure that you have safe space to pass under an object, you should:
   A. Assume all clearances are of sufficient height
   B. Height clearance is not a concern as long as you stay on state or federal roadways
   C. Take another route
   D. All of the above

2. Controlled braking is:
   A. Applying brakes hard enough for the wheels to lock up
   B. Pressing the brakes hard enough to lock-up the wheels, then releasing and then reapplying again
   C. Applying firm brake pressure, but not to the point of lock-up
   D. Only used if the vehicle does not have anti-lock brakes

3. You are driving on a straight and level roadway at 60 mph and suddenly a tire blows out on your vehicle. What should you do first?
   A. Immediately begin light, controlled braking
   B. Immediately begin stab braking
   C. Grip steering wheel firmly with both hands and stay off the brakes until the vehicle has slowed down
   D. Immediately begin emergency braking

4. Which of the following is true?
   A. Tires with tread separation or cuts should not be used on a vehicle
   B. Tires which are mismatched sizes should be used on a vehicle
   C. $\frac{1}{32}$ inch tread depth is allowed on drive tires
   D. $\frac{1}{32}$ inch tread depth is permissible for steering tires

5. Why do hazardous materials regulations exist?
   A. To provide for safe drivers and equipment
   B. To communicate a risk
   C. To contain the product
   D. All of the above

Vehicle inspection

OBJECTIVES

Upon completion of this chapter, you should have a basic understanding of the vehicle inspection process. You should know how to:

- Inspect and check the condition of critical components of the tractor-trailer

- Perform accurate and efficient pre-trip inspections

- Perform en-route inspections

- Perform post-trip inspections, including completion of a driver vehicle inspection report (DVIR)

4 Vehicle inspection

- THE IMPORTANCE OF INSPECTIONS
- TYPES OF INSPECTIONS
- CONDUCTING AN INSPECTION
- PRE-TRIP INSPECTION
- EN-ROUTE INSPECTION
- POST-TRIP INSPECTION
- SPECIAL RIGS
- SUMMARY

INTRODUCTION

As well as being a regulatory requirement, proper vehicle inspections can go a long way in ensuring your vehicle's safe and efficient operation.

Vehicle inspections can help in finding mechanical problems before they cause a breakdown or accident. This can help in avoiding costly on the road repairs as well as delays in deliveries.

▌ The importance of inspections

In addition to preventing accidents and breakdowns, a solid vehicle inspection program can play a role in avoiding citations and/or out-of-service orders during an inspection. Vehicle maintenance violations are frequently cited during roadside inspections.

Such importance is placed on vehicle maintenance, that it is one of seven categories that a motor carrier is rated on under the Federal Motor Carrier Safety Administration's Compliance, Safety, Accountability (CSA) program.

For more information on the CSA program, turn to Chapter 33 of this text.

▌ Types of inspections

Three types of inspections are mandated by the Federal Motor Carrier Safety Regulations (FMCSRs), pre-trip, on-the-road (en-route), and post-trip inspections.

Pre-trip inspection (Sec. 396.13)

This inspection is performed before taking your vehicle on the road. Doing a pre-trip inspection allows you to identify problems that could cause a breakdown or accident.

On-the-road (en-route) inspection (Sec. 392.9)

Watch your vehicle's gauges for signs of problems. Check all critical items each time you stop, including tires, wheels and rims, brakes, lights, electrical and air connections to the trailer, trailer coupling devices, and cargo securement devices.

Post-trip inspection (Sec. 396.11)

A post-trip inspection is conducted at the end your day's work on the vehicle you are operating. This inspection includes filling out a driver vehicle inspection report (DVIR) if defects or deficiencies are discovered. This report helps a motor carrier make necessary repairs before the vehicle returns to the road.

▌ Conducting an inspection

As well as being a regulatory requirement, conducting vehicle inspections on a regular basis can prevent costly and time-consuming breakdowns and can prevent possible accidents due to vehicle failure. The following are critical items and issues that should be addressed regularly.

Fluid leaks

A fluid leak (oil, fuel, coolant) can lead to serious engine damage.

Fluid levels should be routinely checked as part of the vehicle inspection process. Also, as part of your vehicle inspection, watch for fluid loss (drips, puddles) underneath the vehicle.

Fluid levels should also be checked when your vehicle's gauges indicate unusual readings.

Tire defects

A tire problem can cause a blowout, resulting in handling problems, loss of control, or even an accident. A tire blowout can also result in downtime, costing both you and your company money.

Watch for too much or too little air pressure as well as excessive wear.

Tread depth should measure at least ⁴⁄₃₂ inch in the major grooves on the front tires. Tread depth should measure at least ²⁄₃₂ inch on other tires. No fabric should show through the tread or sidewall.

Look for cuts, bulges, tread separation, mismatched sizes, and cut or cracked valve stems.

Wheel and rim defects

A damaged rim could cause a tire to lose pressure or come off, causing downtime and potentially causing an accident. Watch for:

- Rust around lug nuts;
- Tightness of lug nuts;
- Missing clamps, spacers, or lugs;
- Mismatched, bent, or cracked lock rings;
- Unsafe or illegal welding repairs;
- Dented rims; and
- Loose rims.

Braking system defects

Brake system air pressure checks are critical. You should not be able to hear any air leaks or observe a loss of air pressure on the air pressure gauge.

Air pressure should not leak more than 3 pounds per minute with the engine off and brakes released, and no more than 4 pounds per minute with the engine off and brakes fully applied (after initial application).

Check for defective gauges and low air warning devices. Section 393.51 of the FMCSRs requires that all trucks and truck tractors be equipped with a properly working warning device.

Brake drums should be checked for cracks. Shoes or pads need to be inspected for proper thickness, signs of oil or grease, and wear. Brake chambers should be securely mounted. Slack adjusters should be inspected for missing and loose parts and proper adjustment.

Brake lines (hoses) must be properly secured. They shouldn't show signs of hardening, swelling, or excessive wear or damage. They shouldn't be bent or folded over, causing possible air flow restriction.

The air reservoir should be properly attached to the vehicle and shouldn't contain excessive water. It should be bled daily to check for moisture.

Air lines to the trailer shouldn't be tangled, restricted, or damaged. They should be correctly attached and supported. They shouldn't rub on the frame or catwalk.

Steering system defects

Steering system defects include missing parts (nuts, bolts, cotter pins, etc.) and bent, loose, or broken parts including the steering column, steering gear box, tie rods, drag link, pitman arm, and steering arm.

Inspect the hoses, pumps, and fluid level, and keep an eye out for leaks. Check the power steering fluid.

Watch the steering wheel for looseness or "play." Steering wheel play of more than 10 degrees can make it hard to steer.

Section 393.209 of the FMCSRs states that steering wheel lash may not exceed the following parameters:

Steering wheel diameter	Manual steering system	Power steering system
16" or less	2"	4 ¼"
18"	2 ¼"	4 ¾"
20"	2 ½"	5 ¼"
22"	2 ¾"	5 ¾"

Frame

The frame is the vehicle's foundation. It is directly or indirectly connected to all parts of the truck. Making sure it is in good repair is mandated by Sec. 393.201 of the FMCSRs.

Make sure the frame isn't cracked, loose, sagging, or broken. The bolts securing the cab or body of the vehicle to the frame must not be loose, broken, or missing.

Suspension system defects

The suspension system supports the vehicle and its load and keeps axles in place. A broken or faulty suspension can, among other things, allow sudden shifts in cargo or steering, which can lead to an accident. Inspect for:

- Cracked, loose, or broken spring hangers;
- Cracked, loose, or damaged torque rods;
- Cracked, loose, or damaged U-bolts;
- Missing, misaligned, or broken leaves in any leaf spring;

- Damaged air bags;
- Loose or damaged air bag mounts;
- Shock absorber leaks; and
- Loose, cracked, broken, or missing frame members.

Exhaust system defects

An exhaust system defect can allow poisonous fumes into the cab or sleeper berth. Check for loose, leaking, cracked, broken, or missing:

- Exhaust pipes;
- Mufflers;
- Exhaust stacks;
- Mounting brackets;
- Clamps; and
- Nuts and bolts.

Exhaust system parts should not rub against fuel system parts, tires, or other vehicle parts. Also look for leaks in the exhaust system. Soot around the clamping indicates a leak.

Coupling system defects

A coupling system defect can cause a serious accident or damage to cargo.

Check for excessive slack or damage in the fifth wheel mechanism. Inspect the fifth wheel assembly for cracks, breaks, and security. Also make sure the fifth wheel is greased appropriately.

Inspect the area around the pivot pin for cracks or wear. Check the release arm and safety latch, making sure they are not bent or damaged.

The fifth wheel sliding mechanism pins should be securely locked in place and be free of any other damage.

Check kingpin for excessive cracking, bending, or wear.

Missing U-bolts, cracked or broken welds, or other defects in fifth wheel mounting devices should be repaired or replaced.

Emergency equipment

Section 393.95 requires that a vehicle carry emergency equipment including:

- Fire extinguisher(s);
- Spare electrical fuses (unless equipped with circuit breakers); and
- Warning devices.

Cargo problems

Inspect cargo for overloading, correct balance, and securement. If the cargo containins hazardous materials, inspect for proper paperwork and placarding.

▌ Pre-trip inspection

A pre-trip inspection is performed before each trip to identify problems that could cause a breakdown or accident. Section 396.13 of the FMCSRs states that before driving a motor vehicle you must:

- Be satisfied that the vehicle is in safe operating condition;
- Review the last vehicle inspection report (see post-trip inspection); and
- Sign the report, only if defects or deficiencies were noted by the driver who prepared the report, to acknowledge that the report has been reviewed and that there is certification that the repairs have been performed.

The seven-step pre-trip inspection

By doing a pre-trip inspection the same way every time, you are less likely to forget to check an important vehicle component. The following seven-step routine is recommended.

1. Vehicle overview

Walk around the vehicle and note its overall condition. Look for body damage or any fluids leaking from the vehicle.

Look for leaning, door securement, cargo security, license plates, and annual inspection stickers/documentation.

Also check the area around the vehicle for potential hazards (pedestrians, overhead wires, other vehicles)

Review the last vehicle inspection report. Make sure any damage or defects noted on the report have been corrected/fixed.

2. Engine compartment

Make sure the parking brakes are on and the wheels are chocked. Open the vehicle hood, tilt the cab, or open the engine compartment hood and check the following:

- All fluid levels (oil, coolant, power steering, transmission (if applicable), windshield washer);
- All hoses for leaks, wear, or looseness;
- All belts for wear or looseness;
- The alternator, water pump, and air compressor;
- The engine compartment for leaks; and
- The electrical wiring insulation for cracks or wear.

4

Also check the wheels and tires, brakes, steering system, suspension, exhaust, and frame at this point.

Although these items are not part of the engine compartment check, this is where these parts are most accessible.

3. Inside the cab

Make sure the parking brake is on and the vehicle is in neutral (or if an automatic transmission in park). Depress the clutch and start the vehicle. Listen for unusual noises and check all gauges for normal readings including the following:

- Oil pressure (read within 15 seconds; 30-45 seconds in cold weather);
- Ammeter (should register positive);
- Voltmeter (should register positive);
- Coolant temperature (will rise); and
- Air pressure (85-100 psi within 45 seconds).

Also check the following controls for looseness, sticking, damage, or improper setting:

- Steering wheel;
- Clutch;
- Accelerator;
- Brakes;
- Transmission control;
- Horn;
- Windshield wipers; and
- Lights.

Inspect mirrors and windshield for cracks, dirt, and other obstructions. Clean and adjust mirrors if necessary.

Make sure all safety equipment is on the vehicle and in good condition. This includes a fully charged fire extinguisher, spare fuses (if applicable), and three emergency triangles.

4. Lights

With the parking brake set, turn off the engine and turn on the lights and emergency flashers. Get out of the vehicle, go to the front and check all lights. Also make sure the headlights' high beam and low beam settings are operational.

Turn off the headlights and emergency flashers. Turn on the vehicle's parking, clearance, side-marker, and identification lights. Turn on the right turn signal and then start the walk around inspection on the driver's side (left front side) of the vehicle.

5. Walk around

Left front side — Make sure the window and mirror on the driver's door is clean and that all door latches and locks work properly.

Inspect the left front wheel including the condition of:

- **Wheel and rim** — Look for missing, bent, broken studs, clamps or lugs as well as signs of misalignment. Check for cracked wheels.
- **Tires** — Make sure they are properly inflated, that the valve and stem are in good condition, and that all valve caps are in place. Check for cuts or bulges. Watch for excessive tread wear.
- **Hub oil seal** — Not leaking.
- **Lug nuts** — Pay special attention to rusted lug nuts.

Inspect the left front suspension checking the condition of the springs, spring hangers, shackles, U-bolts, and shock absorbers.

When inspecting the left front brake, check the condition of the brake drum, hoses, brake chamber, slack adjuster, and push rod.

Front — Inspect the condition of the front axle and steering system. When checking the steering system watch for loose, worn, bent, damaged, or missing parts. Also test the steering mechanism for looseness.

Check the condition of the windshield. Look for damage and clean it if it is dirty. Also inspect the windshield wipers. Check the wiper arms for proper spring tension and the wiper blades for damage.

Make sure the parking, clearance, and identification lights as well as all reflectors are clean, operating properly, and are the correct color.

Also inspect the right front turn signal light, making sure it is clean, operating properly, and is the correct color.

Right side — At the right front of the vehicle, repeat the inspection of all of the items you checked on the left front (windows, door, wheels, tires, suspension, brake, etc.).

If the vehicle is a cab-over engine design make sure the primary and safety cab locks are engaged.

Inspect the right fuel tank, making sure it is securely mounted and is not damaged or leaking. The fuel crossover line should be secure and not leaking. The tanks should contain enough fuel, and the cap(s) should be secured.

Check the condition of visible parts including the:

- Rear of the engine for leaks;
- Transmission for leaks;
- Exhaust system, making sure it's secure, not leaking, and not touching wires, fuel, or air lines;
- Frame and cross members for bends or cracks;
- Drive shaft;
- Air lines and electrical wiring, making sure they're secured against snagging, rubbing, or wearing;
- Spare tire carrier or rack for damage;

4

- Spare tire/wheel, making sure it is the proper size, properly inflated, and securely mounted in its rack; and

- Header board.

Coupling system area — Check the fifth wheel (lower), making sure it is securely mounted to the frame and that all mounting bolts are tight. Look for missing or damaged parts. Make sure it has enough grease and that there isn't any visible space between the upper and lower fifth wheel. The locking jaws should be around the shank and not the head of the kingpin. Also make sure the release arm is properly seated and the safety latch/lock is engaged, if so equipped.

Make sure the glide plate is securely mounted to the trailer frame and the kingpin is not damaged when checking the fifth wheel (upper).

Inspect the air and electrical lines to the trailer. Inspect at both the rear of the tractor and the front of the trailer. The air and electrical lines should not drag or rub along the catwalk. The electrical cord should be firmly plugged in and secured. The air lines should be properly connected to the glad hands.

There shouldn't be any air leaks and there should be enough slack for turning.

Check the sliding fifth wheel. The slide shouldn't be damaged or have any parts missing. It should be properly greased and all locking pins must be present and locked in place. If the sliding fifth wheel is air powered, there shouldn't be any air leaks. Also make sure the fifth wheel isn't so far forward that the tractor frame will hit the landing gear, or that the trailer will hit the cab when turning.

Right rear — Check the condition of the wheels and rims. Make sure there aren't any missing, bent, or broken spacers, studs, clamps, or lugs.

Check the condition of the tires. Make sure they are properly inflated, that the valve and stems are in good condition, and that all valve caps are in place. Check for cuts or bulges. Watch for excessive tread wear. The tires shouldn't rub together and nothing should be stuck between them. They should be of the same type and of the same size (evenly matched).

Also check the wheel bearings/seals for leaks.

Inspect the suspension, checking the condition of the springs, spring hangers, shackles, and U-bolts.

The axle should be secure and the powered axles shouldn't leak.

Check the condition of the torque rod, arms, bushings, and shock absorbers.

If the vehicle is retractable axle equipped, check the condition of the lift mechanism and if it is air powered, check for leaks.

Inspect the brakes, including:

- Brake drums, shoes, and pads;

- Hoses;

- Slack adjusters; and

- Brake chambers.

Inspect all lights and reflectors including side marker lights and reflectors. They should be clean, properly operating, and the correct color. This includes:

- Rear clearance and identification lights;
- Reflectors;
- Tail lights; and
- Rear turn signals.

Check all door hinges. Make sure the license plate is clean and secured and that splash guards are in good condition, properly fastened, and not dragging on the ground.

The landing gear should be fully raised and not have any missing or damaged parts. The crank handle should be in place and secured. If it is power operated, check for air or hydraulic leaks.

Left side — In addition to the items you checked on the right side (fuel tank, engine, transmission, exhaust, frame, air lines, etc.), check the battery (if not mounted to the engine compartment) making sure it is properly secured and isn't broken or leaking.

6. Signal Lights

Get in the vehicle and turn off all lights, then turn on the stop lights (apply the trailer hand brake or have a helper put on the brake pedal). Also turn on the left turn signal lights.

Get out of the vehicle and look at the left front turn signal light. It should be clean, operating, and the proper color. Then look at the left rear turn signal light and both stop lights. Make sure they are clean, operating, and the proper color.

7. Brake System

All brake systems should be tested, making sure they are operating properly.

Tractor parking brake — Charge the air brake system. Apply the tractor's parking brakes. Release the trailer's emergency brakes. Pull gently on the trailer (in a low gear) with the tractor to test that the tractor brake will hold.

Trailer emergency brakes — Charge the air brake system. Apply the trailer emergency brakes. Release the tractor brakes. Pull gently on the trailer with the tractor to test the trailer emergency brakes.

Service brakes — Wait for normal air pressure, release the parking brake, slowly move the vehicle forward, and then firmly apply the brakes (brake pedal). Watch for the vehicle pulling to one side or delayed stopping action.

Trailer service brakes — Check for normal air pressure, release the parking brake, slowly move the vehicle forward, and then apply the trailer brakes. You should be able to feel the brakes operate. (Note: Not all trucks have a way to do this.)

Trailer service brakes are often referred to as the hand valve, trolley brake, Johnson bar, or Johnny bar.

Air leakage rate — Chock the vehicle, then with a fully charged air system, turn off the engine, release all of the brakes, and time the air pressure drop after the initial drop. The loss rate should be less than two pounds per square inch (psi) in one minute for a single vehicle and less than three psi in one minute for combination vehicles. Apply normal brake pressure. After the initial pressure drop, if the air pressure falls more than three psi in one minute for single vehicles and more than four psi for combination vehicles, the air loss is too great. Check for leaks before operating the vehicle.

Low pressure warning signal — Once the vehicle has enough air pressure, shut off the engine and release the brakes. Turn on the electrical power and step on and off the brake pedal to reduce air tank pressure. The low air pressure warning signal must come on before the pressure drops to less than 60 psi in the air tank. This signal can be audible or visual. If the signal isn't working, you could lose air pressure and not know it.

Tractor protection valve — Build up normal air pressure in the air brake system and push the air supply knob in. Shut the engine off. Pump on the brake pedal several times to reduce the air pressure in the tanks. The tractor protection valve control (also called the trailer air supply control) should go from normal to the emergency position (pop out) when the air pressure falls into the pressure range specified by the manufacturer. This should be when the air pressure drops to between 20 and 45 psi. If the tractor protection valve doesn't work right, an air hose or trailer brake leak could drain all the air from the tractor. This would cause the emergency brakes to come on, possibly causing loss of control.

Rate of air pressure buildup — With the engine at operating rpm, the pressure should build up from 85-100 psi within 45 seconds in dual air systems. (This may vary, check manufacturer's specifications.) If air pressure doesn't build up fast enough, the vehicle's pressure may drop too low, requiring an emergency stop or activating the spring brakes.

Air compressor governor cut-in and cut-out pressures — Pumping by the air compressor should start at about 90-100 psi and stop at about 125 psi. (Check manufacturer's specifications for details.) Run the engine at a fast idle. The air governor should cut out the air compressor at the manufacturer's specified pressure. The reading on the air pressure gauge should stop rising. With the engine idling, step on and off the brake to reduce the air tank pressure. The governor should cut in and the compressor will start building air pressure. Once the tank pressure reaches 125 psi, the governor will cut out and the process starts again. If the air governor doesn't work as described above, it may need to be fixed. A governor that doesn't work right may not maintain enough air pressure in the system for safe driving.

En-route inspection

There are several items you should be checking regularly while on the road including:

- Vehicle gauges;
- Air pressure gauges;
- Engine temperature gauges;
- Pressure gauges;
- Ammeter;
- Voltmeter;
- Mirrors;
- Tires; and
- Cargo including covers and restraints.

Checking these items can help you detect a problem before the problem results in a breakdown or accident.

From a regulatory standpoint, Sec. 392.9 of the FMCSRs requires the driver to follow certain inspection rules while on the road.

The vehicle's cargo and load-securing devices must be checked within the first 50 miles of a trip. Any necessary adjustments must be made at this time.

After the first 50 miles of the trip, the vehicle's cargo and load-securing devices must be reexamined:

- When the driver makes a change of duty status; or
- After the vehicle has been driven for 3 hours; or
- After the vehicle has been driven 150 miles — whichever occurs first.

Inspection of the cargo and load securing devices is not required if your vehicle is sealed and you have been ordered not to open the vehicle. Also, you are not required to inspect the cargo and load securing devices if the vehicle is loaded in a way that makes inspection of the cargo impossible.

Though you may not be able to inspect the cargo and load securing devices, this does not give you a pass on reviewing your vehicle's condition while on the road.

4

Post-trip inspection

At the end of your day's work on the vehicle you operated, you need to review the condition of your vehicle.

If during this post-trip inspection of your vehicle, you discover any defects or deficiencies which could affect the safe operation of your vehicle or cause a mechanical breakdown, you must complete a written report, commonly referred to as a driver vehicle inspection report (DVIR).

Section 396.11 of the FMCSRs requires that the DVIR include at least the following parts and accessories:

- Service brakes including trailer brake connections;
- Parking brake;
- Steering mechanism;
- Lighting devices and reflectors;
- Tires;
- Horn;
- Windshield wipers;
- Rear vision mirrors;
- Coupling devices;
- Wheels and rims; and
- Emergency equipment.

Though a driver is not required by the FMCSRs to complete a DVIR when no defects or deficiencies are discovered during a post-trip inspection, many motor carriers do require a driver to complete a DVIR at the end of each day's work on a vehicle. This best practice and safety management control aids the motor carrier in minimizing the risk of operating unsafe vehicles and aids in protecting the motor carrier's Vehicle Maintenance BASIC score under the FMCSA's CSA program (see Chapter 33 for more information on CSA).

After completing the inspection and listing all defects and/or deficiencies, you must sign the DVIR.

On two driver operations, only one driver needs to sign the DVIR, provided both drivers agree with what is written in the report.

Before the vehicle can be operated again, any items listed as being defective or deficient that may affect the safe operation of the vehicle must be repaired. The following criteria must be met:

- The motor carrier must certify (on the DVIR) that the defect or deficiency has been corrected or that correction is not necessary to safely operate the vehicle; and
- The motor carrier must retain the original copy of each DVIR and certification of repairs for at least three months from the date it was completed.

Intermodal equipment — If you are hauling intermodal equipment and it has a defect or deficiency, you must complete a DVIR and turn it in to the intermodal equipment provider. The DVIR must cover at least the following parts and accessories:

- Brakes;
- Lighting devices, lamps, markers, and conspicuity marking material;
- Wheels, rims, lugs, tires;
- Air line connections, hoses, and couplers
- King pin upper coupling device;
- Rails or support frames;
- Tie down bolsters;
- Locking pins, clevises, clamps, or hooks; and
- Sliders or sliding frame lock.

The DVIR must include the name of the motor carrier responsible at the time the defect or deficiency was discovered, the motor carrier's and intermodal equipment provider's USDOT numbers, a unique identifying number for the intermodal equipment, the date and time the report was submitted, a list of defects or deficiencies, and your signature.

Before the intermodal equipment can be transported again, any defect or deficiency that affects the safety of operation of the equipment must be repaired. The intermodal equipment provider must certify on the DVIR that the defects or deficiencies were repaired or that repair is unnecessary.

The intermodal equipment provider must retain the original copy of each DVIR and certification of repairs for at least 3 months.

▌ Special rigs

Special rigs require additional, and in some cases unique inspection procedures. A summary of the additional procedures for three types of vehicles (multiple trailers, tankers, and refrigerated units) follows.

Multiple trailers

Special attention should be given to:

- Air lines, valves, and glad hands between the two trailers;
- Valve positions;
- Brake operation;
- Hook up of emergency lines and glad hands; and
- Pintle hook latches and safety chains.

See Chapter 19 for additional information regarding special rigs.

Tankers

Special attention should be given to:

- Dome covers to tank compartments;
- Hoses and pumps (fastened and secured);
- Emergency shut off valves;
- Condition of the tank; and
- Proper display of hazardous materials placards (if applicable).

Refrigerator Units (Reefers)

Special attention should be given to the condition of the trailer, including looking for:

- Holes in the walls, ceiling, or floor;
- Cleanliness;
- Damaged cold air circulation ducts;
- Proper locks and seals on the doors; and
- Proper securement of rails or racks on the ceiling.

The water, oil, and coolant levels should be checked in the refrigerator unit and the thermostat should be set to the appropriate temperature. The refrigeration unit should be run before loading (amount of time varies).

▌ Summary

In this chapter, you have learned about the vehicle inspection process. This includes inspecting critical vehicle components and performing accurate and efficient pre-trip, en-route, and post-trip inspections.

VEHICLE INSPECTION QUIZ

Directions: *Read each statement carefully and mark the response that best answers the question.*

1. What type of inspection is mandated by the Federal Motor Carrier Safety Regulations (FMCSRs)?
   A. Pre-trip
   B. En-route
   C. Post-trip
   D. All of the above

2. Inspecting cargo for overloading, correct balance, and securement is part of a good pre-trip inspection program.
   A. True
   B. False

3. A _____ step pre-trip inspection routine is recommended to make sure you examine all critical parts and components every time you conduct an inspection.
   A. One
   B. Five
   C. Seven
   D. Twelve

4. A pre-trip inspection is not required if a post-trip inspection was performed in the past 48 hours.
   A. True
   B. False

5. When inspecting the engine compartment, you should check:
   A. The voltmeter
   B. The steering wheel
   C. All fluid levels
   D. All of the above

6. Section 392.9 of the FMCSRs requires you to inspect the vehicle's cargo and load-securing devices within the first 50 miles of a trip.
   A. True
   B. False

7. After the initial inspection of the vehicle's cargo and load-securing devices, they must be reexamined:
   A. When you make a change of duty status
   B. After the vehicle has been driven for 3 hours
   C. After the vehicle has been driven 150 miles
   D. When whichever of the above occurs first

8. At the beginning of each day's work on each vehicle operated, Sec. 396.11 of the FMCSRs requires you complete a driver vehicle inspection report (DVIR).
   A. True
   B. False

9. Lighting devices and reflectors, tires, and mirrors are all items that must be covered in the post-trip inspection.
   A. True
   B. False

10. Special rigs, such as tankers, require additional and in some cases unique inspection procedures.
    A. True
    B. False

GENERAL KNOWLEDGE CDL PRE-TEST

Read each question carefully and select the most correct answer.

1. Which of the following statements about backing a commercial motor vehicle is NOT true?

   A. Since you can't see behind you, you should back quickly until you bump the dock
   B. Use mirrors on both sides of your vehicle
   C. You should always back toward the driver's side when possible
   D. Both A and C

2. Alcohol use impairs:

   A. Muscle coordination
   B. Reaction time
   C. Depth perception
   D. All of the above

3. Which of the following is true concerning cold weather driving?

   A. Exhaust system leaks are not of concern during cold weather
   B. If the temperature is below 32 degrees Fahrenheit, the engine cannot overheat
   C. Using bleach on tires will provide increased traction
   D. You should use windshield washer fluid which contains an anti-freeze

4. _____ are signs put on the outside of a vehicle which identify the hazard class of the cargo.

   A. Labels
   B. Shipping papers
   C. Placards
   D. All of the above

5. Controlled braking is used when:

   A. The goal is to keep the vehicle in a straight line while braking
   B. You must stop as quickly as possible
   C. Is only used with hydraulic brakes
   D. Is only used when the vehicle is equipped with anti-lock brakes

Basic control

OBJECTIVES

Upon completion of this chapter, you should have a basic understanding of:

- Starting, warming up, and shutting down the engine of a tractor-trailer

- How to put a tractor-trailer into motion and how to stop a tractor-trailer

- How to straight line back a tractor-trailer

- How to turn a tractor-trailer

5 Basic control

- STARTING, WARMING UP, AND SHUTTING DOWN
- PUTTING THE VEHICLE IN MOTION AND STOPPING
- STRAIGHT LINE BACKING
- TURNING
- SUMMARY

Operating a tractor-trailer is very different from operating car or pickup truck. Everything about a tractor-trailer, from starting the engine to backing and turning, requires a new set of knowledge and skills. This chapter will address basic control issues. It is important that you have a good understanding of these issues, as many of the skills covered in this chapter are the foundation for future lessons.

▍Starting, warming up, and shutting down

There is a specific procedure that must be followed when starting and shutting down the engine of a tractor-trailer. This section will address the proper procedure for starting a four-cycle diesel engine.

Starting the engine

1. Apply the parking brake (if not already applied).
2. Depress the clutch pedal completely to the floor, and make sure the truck is in neutral.
3. Turn the ignition switch/key on.
4. Operate the starter (push the button). If the engine doesn't start in 15-20 seconds, turn the ignition switch/key off for at least one minute and try again.
5. Once the engine has started, and the transmission is in neutral, ease off the clutch.
6. Check all instruments and gauges. Pay extra attention to the oil pressure gauge. In warm weather, the oil pressure should come up to operating level in 3 to 5 seconds. If it does not, you should immediately shut the vehicle off, as severe damage could result.

It is important that you understand these procedures so you can prevent damage to your vehicle's engine.

Engine warm-up

Engine warm-up is generally done at a low revolution per minute (rpm) level (800-1,000 rpm). This allows the oil to warm and circulate, and oil pressure to build up.

During warm-up, the cylinder walls become coated and bearings are lubricated. Coolant temperature increases and air pressure builds up as well.

Usually, a short period of idling time is required/recommended. Check the operator's manual for specific details on the vehicle you are driving.

When driving during warm-up, keep rpm low and avoid high rpm when accelerating in first gear. Shift to the next highest gear as soon as possible. Keep all acceleration smooth and easy.

Engine warm-up is complete when the water temperature reaches 170°F – 195°F. You will not typically reach this temperature by just sitting and idling so you need to proceed slowly at low rpm, until this temperature range has been reached.

Engine shutdown

1. Depress the clutch and move the gear shift to neutral.
2. Set the parking brakes.
3. Turn the engine (key or switch) off.
4. If the engine has a stop control, move it to off.

Engine cool down can be as important as a proper warm-up. Engine damage can occur if there isn't a sufficient cool down period. Engine cool down allows heat generated during normal operation to dissipate. The appropriate cool down period will vary based on engine type as well as the nature of the trip and cargo hauled.

Excessive idling

Avoid excessive idling. Most recently manufactured engines don't need to idle for more than a few minutes. This can waste fuel and cause unnecessary wear on the engine.

Also, several states and municipalities have laws and/or regulations limiting the amount of time an engine is allowed to idle. Make sure you are aware of any laws and/or regulations that may limit or prohibit you from idling your vehicle's engine.

Putting the vehicle in motion and stopping

Putting in motion and stopping a tractor-trailer requires more specific skills and driver expertise than those required to do the same tasks in your personal vehicle. This includes:

- Testing the tractor-trailer hook-up;
- Putting the tractor-trailer in motion; and
- Stopping the tractor-trailer.

This section addresses manual transmission vehicles. If you operate an automatic transmission, consult the manufacturer's manual for details.

Testing the tractor-trailer hook-up

The coupling must be tested every time a trailer is connected to a tractor or dolly. For vehicles with an independent trailer brake control (hand valve/trolley valve):

1. Release the tractor (parking) and trailer (emergency) brakes.
2. Depress the clutch, and move the gearshift to the lowest gear.
3. Engage the independent trailer brake control to apply the trailer brakes.
4. Release the clutch to the friction point.
5. Pull gently against the locked trailer brakes. Stop as soon as you feel the engine start to drag down.
6. Disengage the clutch.

For vehicles without an independent trailer brake control (hand valve/trolley valve):

1. Release the tractor (parking) brake.
2. Depress the clutch and move the gearshift to the lowest forward gear.
3. Release the clutch to the friction point.

4. Pull gently against the locked trailer brakes. Stop as soon as you feel the engine start to drag down.

5. Disengage the clutch.

Putting a tractor-trailer in motion

1. Release the tractor and trailer parking brakes.

2. Depress the clutch fully, engaging the clutch brake, and place the transmission in the lowest gear.

3. Release the clutch to the friction point. This is the point where the clutch engages. A decrease in the rpm is a sign that the friction point has been reached. Then gradually release the clutch until it's fully engaged. As you engage the clutch, a slight increase in engine rpm may be needed to avoid stalling the engine (100-300 rpm is normal).

4. When the vehicle starts to move, gradually increase engine rpm to increase vehicle speed, by depressing the throttle.

5. When the vehicle is in motion with the clutch fully engaged, take your foot off the clutch until you are ready to shift again or stop.

6. Try to avoid excessive clutch slipping. Engage the clutch as smoothly as possible without stalling the engine. To avoid slipping the clutch, use very little additional fuel until the clutch is completely engaged.

Steering a tractor-trailer

Hold the steering wheel firmly with both hands. Your hands should be on opposite sides of the wheel. If you don't have a firm hold, the wheel could pull away from your hands if you hit a curb or pothole.

Stopping a tractor-trailer

1. Release the accelerator pedal.

2. Depress the brake pedal gradually. The amount of brake pressure you will need to stop will depend on how quickly you need to stop.

3. As the vehicle begins to slow, downshift to the appropriate gear (if operating a vehicle with an automatic transmission, you will not need to complete this step).

4. As the vehicle slows, release some brake pressure. When the engine is almost at idle, depress the clutch (the truck should be stopped within the next 50-75 feet).

5. After stopping, maintain enough brake pressure to keep the vehicle stationary. If you're parking the truck, put the gearshift lever in neutral, set (apply) the parking brakes, and release the clutch.

▍ Straight line backing

Though backing is a basic tractor-trailer maneuver, it is one of the most difficult to master. The information in this chapter is a basic overview of and introduction to straight line backing, the simplest of all backing maneuvers. More difficult backing maneuvers will be covered in Chapter 7.

5

When executing a straight line backing maneuver:

1. **Position the vehicle properly** — Put the vehicle in position by moving forward until the tractor and trailer are straight in front of one another and the front (steering) wheels are straight.

2. **Clear the area**— Make sure the area behind your vehicle is clear of other vehicles, people, and other obstacles. Get out and walk around the vehicle. Check:

   - To the rear of the vehicle;
   - Above, under, and to the sides of the vehicle;
   - In front of the vehicle; and
   - For adequate swing clearance.

   Once you have completed your safety checks, you shouldn't delay moving the vehicle. Any delay could allow time for a hazard to move into your vehicle's path. If there is a delay, you should conduct the safety checks a second time.

3. **Watch speed** — Turn on your vehicle's four-way flashers and then put the vehicle in reverse. Using an idle speed, back as slowly as possible, but don't ride the clutch or brakes. Backing slowly makes it easier to correct errors or stop quickly if necessary.

4. **Check behind** — Constantly check behind when backing. Make sure all doors are closed and continually check all mirrors. If you are unsure as to what may be behind your vehicle, stop, get out of your vehicle, and check your path.

5. **Steering** — Keep the vehicle on path and don't over steer. If drifting starts, try to correct it by turning the steering wheel in the direction of the drift as soon as it occurs. Try not to over steer. Only slight movement is required if the drift is caught right away.

   Use the push-pull method of steering to keep the trailer in line. When the trailer gets bigger in your mirror (a sign that it is drifting), turn the top of the wheel toward the side that is bigger in the mirror. Once the drift has stopped, return the wheel to its original position and realign the tractor in front of the trailer.

The biggest error when using this method is not returning the wheel to the straight-ahead position immediately.

6. **Pull up and start again** — If your vehicle is too far out of position, pull up and start again. It is easier and safer to start over than reposition the vehicle while backing.

Turning

There are four basic rules when it comes to turning:

- Know the vehicle;
- Plan in advance;
- Allow for off-tracking; and
- Watch your mirrors.

Off-tracking

Off-tracking is something that happens to all vehicles with more than one set of wheels. Put simply, the term means the rear wheels don't follow the same track as the front wheels when moving through a turn or curve. They follow a shorter path.

Factors that determine off-tracking in a tractor-trailer unit include:

- Distance between the kingpin and rear trailer wheels (the greater the distance between the kingpin and rear trailer wheels, the more off-tracking occurs);
- Amount of sideways drag of the rear tires (the more sideways drag, the greater the off-tracking); and
- Radius of the curve.

Right turns

Good judgment, proper speed control, and accurate steering are all important in executing safe right turns.

When approaching an intersection, adjust your vehicle's speed. The sharper the turn, the slower the vehicle should be moving. This allows you to use all available space.

Shift into the correct gear before the turn and complete the turn in the same gear. This allows you to keep both hands on the wheel during the turn.

Keep in mind is that due to its length, a tractor-trailer must pull further into the intersection than a smaller vehicle in order to avoid hitting the curb. One basic rule of thumb is to get about one-half of the rig past the corner before beginning the turn. Once the vehicle has reached that point, turn the steering wheel to the right and complete the turn. Accelerate slightly to smooth out the turn.

Before, during, and after the turn, check both the right and left mirrors for the position of the trailer wheels.

When approaching a corner for a right turn, position your trailer so that no vehicles can come between your trailer and the curb.

Immediately after the turn is complete, turn the steering wheel back to straighten out the wheels.

The following are some of the most common errors made when executing a right turn:

- Not sizing up the corner properly;
- Approaching the intersection too fast;
- Forgetting to gear down before beginning the turn;
- Accelerating in the turn;
- Shifting gears while turning;
- Leaving too much space between the trailer and the curb;
- Forgetting to allow for off-tracking; and
- Not watching the mirrors before, during, and after the turn.

Left turns

As with a right turn, reduce vehicle speed when approaching the intersection.

Shift into the correct gear, keep the vehicle's wheels straight before starting the turn, and complete the turn in the same gear.

When executing this maneuver, turn from as far right as possible to allow plenty of room for the tractor.

If you turn too soon or too tightly, off-tracking may cause the left side of the vehicle to hit another vehicle, curb, light pole, or safety island.

Watch your mirrors before, during, and after the turn. Turn the steering wheel back to the right immediately upon completion of the turn.

The most common errors made when executing a left turn are the same as those for right turns, except the errors are made from the other side.

If you are on a road with two lanes for turning left, use the outside (right most) lane.

Curves

Positioning is important. When approaching a right traveling curve (not a corner), keep the vehicle close to the center of the road without crossing the center line. Failure to keep toward the center could result in the rear of your vehicle running off the road, on to the shoulder, or hitting something on the right side.

When approaching a left traveling curve, keep the front of the vehicle as close to the outer edge of the road as possible. This will keep your trailer from running over the center line on a curve.

Look ahead and recognize upcoming curves. Keep in mind that there may be times that you have to stop and yield to traffic before proceeding.

5

▍ Summary

As you now know, basic operation of a tractor-trailer varies from that of your personal vehicle. There are certain, specific procedures for starting and shutting down a tractor-trailer as well as for backing and negotiating corners. Remember that maneuvers such as backing and turning require practice, patience, planning, and skill.

BASIC CONTROL QUIZ

Directions: Read each statement carefully and mark the response that best answers the question.

1. Operating a tractor-trailer is different than operating your personal vehicle.

   A. True
   B. False

2. A specific procedure should be followed when starting a tractor-trailer engine.

   A. True
   B. False

3. The first step you should take when starting any type of tractor-trailer engine is:

   A. Depress the clutch
   B. Pump the accelerator
   C. Apply the parking brake
   D. All of the above

4. Engine warm-up is generally done at a low rpm level.

   A. True
   B. False

5. When starting to put a tractor-trailer in motion you should depress the clutch fully and place the transmission in the lowest forward gear.

   A. True
   B. False

6. An engine cool down period isn't necessary.

   A. True
   B. False

7. When backing in a straight line, you should:

   A. Position the vehicle properly
   B. Constantly check behind the vehicle
   C. Not over steer
   D. All of the above

8. When turning, shift into the proper gear before the turn and stay in that gear until the turn is complete.

   A. True
   B. False

9. Which of the following is a common right turn error?

   A. Not shifting gears while turning
   B. Allowing for an adequate amount of space for off-tracking
   C. Approaching the intersection too slowly
   D. Approaching the intersection too fast

10. If you are on a road with two left turn lanes, you should use the inside lane.

    A. True
    B. False

GENERAL KNOWLEDGE CDL PRE-TEST

Read each question carefully and select the most correct answer.

1. What is hydroplaning?

   A. An emergency situation created when an aircraft must make an emergency landing on a highway
   B. Excessive heat built up in the radiator
   C. Something that only occurs at high vehicle speeds
   D. When water or slush collects on the road, and your vehicle's tires lose contact with the road

2. If you are being tailgated you should:

   A. Motion for the tailgater to pass you when it is safe
   B. Increase your following distance
   C. Turn your 4-way flashers on
   D. Slam on the brakes

3. Which of the following conditions may produce a skid?

   A. Driving too fast for conditions
   B. Overbraking
   C. Oversteering
   D. All of the above

4. When fighting a fire, which is most correct?

   A. Get as close to the fire as possible
   B. Aim the fire extinguisher at the base of the fire
   C. Aim the fire extinguisher at the top of the fire
   D. All of the above

5. If a state or federal inspector determines that your vehicle is unsafe, it will be put out of service:

   A. For 24 hours
   B. For 48 hours
   C. Until you can contact your carrier and make arrangements for repair
   D. Until it is fixed

Shifting

OBJECTIVES

Upon completion of this chapter, you should have a basic understanding of the procedures and skills required to shift a vehicle including:

- The key elements required to properly shift a manual transmission
- Basic shift patterns and procedures of a manual transmission
- The basics of automatic and semiautomatic transmissions

6 Shifting

- KEY ELEMENTS OF SHIFTING
- SHIFTING GEARS
- SHIFTING PATTERNS
- SUMMARY

INTRODUCTION

Shifting gears is one of the more difficult skills you will learn as you work toward becoming a professional driver. Mastering this skill takes coordination, patience, and practice. This chapter will address the knowledge and skills it takes to shift safely and efficiently.

▌ Key elements of shifting

Shifting controls

There are three controls used in shifting a manual transmission, the accelerator, shift lever, and clutch.

Accelerator — The accelerator controls the flow of fuel to the engine. That, in turn, determines the speed or revolutions per minute (rpm) of the engine in any one gear.

Shift lever — The shift lever controls what gear the transmission is in. The gear selected determines the amount of power supplied by the engine which then transfers into road speed.

A low gear provides a great deal of power with little road speed. Lower gears supply the power needed to build up momentum.

A high gear provides less power, but much more road speed. Higher gears allow the vehicle to obtain and maintain higher road speeds once momentum is developed.

Clutch — The clutch transfers power from the engine to the transmission. Put simply, it allows you to shift gears.

When the clutch pedal is depressed, it disengages the transmission from the engine, and gears may be safely shifted. When the clutch pedal is fully released, the transmission and engine are engaged, and gears generally can't be safely shifted.

Successful shifting takes coordination and precise timing. Improper timing or a lack of coordination can cause over revving of the engine and gear grinding. As well as causing damage to the vehicle's components, improper shifting can cause problems in controlling the vehicle. Coordinating the use of the clutch and the shift lever is a simple process; first depress the clutch, and then shift gears.

When should you shift? Driving conditions and vehicle needs will determine when you will upshift or downshift.

Upshifting

As mentioned earlier, low gears provide a great deal of power. This power is needed to get a stopped vehicle moving.

Select the highest gear possible that will allow the vehicle to move without slipping the clutch or lugging the engine. As vehicle speed increases, upshift to a higher gear to gain additional speed. The purpose of upshifting is to allow a vehicle to increase speed. Higher gears also keep rpms low, and fuel mileage may increase with lower rpms.

Downshifting

Downshifting aids in slowing a vehicle. It acts as a braking force. Downshifting can also provide more power to the vehicle when needed. Never downshift earlier than necessary. Early downshifting can cause the vehicle's engine to rev at a high level, possibly causing engine damage.

The speedometer, tachometer, and governor are all necessary tools when it comes to safe shifting.

> *Patience and practice are how you become proficient at shifting. The more you practice, the better you will become at performing this skill. With enough practice, this skill will become a habit.*

Speedometer — The speedometer displays the speed of a vehicle in miles per hour (mph) and/or kilometers per hour. For each gear, there is a range of road speed which corresponds (matches). This varies based on the type of vehicle you are operating. When your vehicle reaches the maximum speed for a gear, you must upshift. When your vehicle reaches the minimum speed for a gear you must downshift.

Tachometer — The tachometer displays engine speed in hundreds of revolutions per minute (rpm). It serves as a guide for shifting into the appropriate gear. When your vehicle reaches the maximum rpm for a gear, you must upshift. When your vehicle reaches the minimum rpm for a gear you must downshift.

Note: Electronic fuel pumps also limit the amount of fuel supplied to the engine, requiring you to shift to a higher gear to gain more speed.

Governor — The governor prevents the engine from excessively revving while downshifting.

Shifting gears

Most heavy vehicles with manual transmissions require double clutching to change gears. When double clutching is done properly, the gears do not grind. The following is the basic method when upshifting and downshifting.

Upshifting

To successfully upshift, follow these steps:

1. Release the accelerator, depress the clutch, and shift to neutral at the same time.

2. Release the clutch.

3. Let the engine reach the rpm required for the next gear.

4. Depress the clutch and shift to the next higher gear at the same time.

5. Release the clutch and press the accelerator.

Downshifting

To successfully downshift, follow these steps:

1. Release the accelerator, depress the clutch, and shift to neutral at the same time.

2. Release the clutch.

3. Press the accelerator, increasing engine speed to reach the rpm required for the lower gear.

4. Depress the clutch and shift to the lower gear at the same time.

5. Release the clutch and press the accelerator.

It is important to maintain correct engine speed when either upshifting or downshifting.

Experience also plays a part in successful shifting. Veteran drivers are often able to tell when to shift gears by using their senses and instincts. They can tell by the sound of the engine and the feel of the vehicle.

Consult the vehicle's owner's manual for recommendations. One rule of thumb (in absence of manufacturer's recommendations) is when changing gears, change the rpm by about 500 rpm.

Hitting/hunting a gear

There is a third shifting skill that is required when operating a vehicle with a manual transmission. Often called hitting a gear or hunting a gear, this skill is used when your vehicle is rolling and you must get the transmission into the proper gear. When performing this skill, follow these steps:

1. Think about how the engine should feel at that speed in that gear. Experienced drivers also take into account the vehicle's speed. For each speed, there's a specific gear you should hunt for.

2. Depress the clutch and push the shift lever lightly against the gear you think is the correct gear.

3. Continue this until the shift lever goes in without excessive grinding.

If this doesn't work, move the shift lever and feel how changing the engine rpm changes the shift lever vibrations.

If the rpm is too high, you will hear a high pitched grinding noise. If the rpm is too low, you will hear a deep and hollow grinding noise. If the engine is close to the correct rpm, the shift lever vibrations are larger and farther apart. If you reach the correct rpm, the shift lever will fall into gear. When this happens, depress the clutch and push the shift lever into place. Once you have done this, you can release the clutch and press the accelerator.

Good shifting skills

There is no exact science when it comes to the art of shifting. Again, experience may be the best aid in successfully performing this skill.

Good shifting skills are the trademark of an accomplished, professional driver. This includes:

- Good timing and coordination;
- Knowing what gear your vehicle is in at all times;

6

- Knowing what the top mph and rpm is for each gear on your vehicle;
- Making shifts without forcing, raking, or grinding gears;
- Never riding the clutch;
- Always using the clutch when shifting;
- Always using the proper gear for best fuel economy; and
- Anticipating changes in terrain and/or traffic.

▌ Shifting patterns

Not all transmissions have the same shifting patterns. This section will address some of the most common shift patterns currently being used.

Eaton® Fuller® Nine Speed

This transmission has a low range and high range of gears. The low range has five forward gears (low through fourth) and the high range has four gears (fifth through eighth). The range control lever must be lifted or lowered to reach the high or low gears.

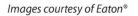

Images courtesy of Eaton®

Upshifting — To successfully upshift, follow these steps:

1. Depress the clutch.
2. Make sure the range lever is in the low range (down).
3. Move the shift lever to first gear.
4. When shifting to second through fourth gear, double clutch.
5. To shift from fourth to fifth gear (from low to high range), lift the range control lever up before moving the gear lever.
6. Shift from fifth through eighth gear using normal double clutching.

Downshifting — To successfully downshift, follow these steps:

1. Shift from eighth through fifth gear by double clutching (make sure you are matching engine speed to road speed before shifting).
2. To shift from fifth to fourth gear, push the range control lever down before moving the gear lever.
3. Shift from fourth through first gear by double clutching (make sure you are matching engine speed to road speed before shifting).

Eaton® Fuller® Super Ten

This transmission has five gear positions that are split. This cuts gear lever movement in half.

Upshifting — To successfully upshift, follow these steps:

1. Depress the clutch.
2. Move the gear shift lever to first gear.
3. To make a splitter shift (first to second, third to fourth, etc.), move the splitter button forward, take your foot off the accelerator, wait for the gear to engage, then accelerate.
4. To make a lever shift (second to third, fourth to fifth, etc.) move the splitter button back, double clutch, and shift normally.

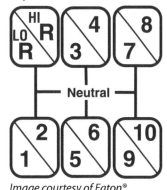

Image courtesy of Eaton®

Downshifting — To successfully downshift, follow these steps:

1. To make a splitter shift down (tenth to ninth, eighth to seventh, etc.) move the splitter button back, take your foot off the accelerator, wait for the gear to engage, then accelerate.
2. To make a lever shift down, move the splitter button forward, double clutch, and shift normally.

Rockwell Ten Speed

This transmission system has a low (first through fifth gear) and high (sixth through tenth gear) range of gears. A range control lever is used to reach the high range of gears.

Upshifting — To successfully upshift, follow these steps:

1. Depress the clutch.
2. Make sure the range lever is in the low range (down).
3. Move the shift lever to first gear (top left).
4. When shifting through fifth gear, double clutch.
5. To shift from fifth to sixth gear (from low to high range), lift the range control lever up before moving the gear lever.
6. Shift from sixth through tenth gear using normal double clutching.

Downshifting — To successfully downshift, follow these steps:

1. Shift from tenth through sixth gear by double clutching (make sure you are matching engine speed to road speed before shifting).
2. To shift from sixth to fifth gear, push the range control lever down before moving the gear lever.
3. Shift from fifth through first gear by double clutching (make sure you are matching engine speed to road speed before shifting).

Eaton® Fuller® Thirteen Speed

This transmission has a low range and a high range. The high range has four direct ratios and four overdrive ratios with the overdrive ratios being engaged by using a splitter switch.

Image courtesy of Eaton®

Upshifting — To successfully upshift, follow these steps:

1. Depress the clutch.
2. Move the shift lever to first gear.
3. When shifting through fourth gear, double clutch.
4. To shift from fourth to fifth gear (from low to high range), lift the range control lever up before moving the gear lever.
5. Shift from fifth through eighth gear using normal double clutching.

6. To go from direct to overdrive, flip the splitter switch, release the accelerator, push down and release the clutch, and accelerate.

7. To go from overdrive to direct in the next higher gear, move the gear lever to the next gear and flip the splitter switch before releasing the clutch.

Downshifting — To successfully downshift, follow these steps:

1. To go from overdrive to direct in the same gear, flip the splitter switch, release the accelerator, push down and release the clutch, and accelerate.

2. To shift from direct in one gear to overdrive in the next lower gear, flip the splitter switch to overdrive and make a normal downshift.

3. Shift from fifth to fourth gear by pushing the range lever down, double clutching, and making a normal downshift.

Semiautomatic transmission

A semiautomatic transmission uses electronic controls to help you shift. Like a manual transmission, a semiautomatic transmission has a clutch and gearshift lever. What is different is that the top gears automatically change.

Autoshift transmission

An autoshift transmission has a clutch and gear select lever or button control. The clutch is used for starting and stopping the vehicle to disengage the transmission and engine. Once the vehicle is rolling, the transmission will shift according to the position you placed the control.

Automatic transmission

An automatic transmission uses a torque converter instead of a clutch to shift gears. A lever or button is used to change gears. The following are the range selector positions found on an automatic transmission.

Neutral — Neutral is used for starting, standing, and parking the vehicle. Never coast in neutral. This can damage the transmission as well as cause you to lose control of your vehicle.

Reverse — Reverse is used for backing. The vehicle must be stopped before shifting into reverse.

Drive (2-5) — Drive is used for normal driving conditions. It begins in second and automatically upshifts to five as you accelerate. It also automatically downshifts as you slow the vehicle.

Lower range (2-3/2-4) — This range provides engine braking and should be used when road and/or traffic conditions warrant use of a lower gear.

Low gear (2) — This gear is used when driving up a steep grade or operating in snow or mud.

Creeper gear (1) — This gear provides the greatest amount of traction and should only be used in off-road situations.

▌ Summary

This chapter has covered the basics of shifting. Keep in mind that exact shifting patterns vary from manufacturer to manufacturer and that you should always consult the owner's manual prior to using an unfamiliar type of shifting pattern. Also remember that coordination, practice, and patience are key to mastering this professional driving skill.

Directions: *Read each statement carefully and mark the response that best answers the question.*

1. Which of the following is used when shifting a manual transmission?

   A. Accelerator
   B. Shift lever
   C. Clutch
   D. All of the above

2. A low gear provides little power or road speed.

   A. True
   B. False

3. A high gear allows a vehicle to obtain and maintain higher road speeds once momentum is developed.

   A. True
   B. False

4. The purpose of upshifting is to:

   A. Allow a vehicle to maintain speed
   B. Allow a vehicle to decrease speed
   C. Allow a vehicle to increase speed
   D. All of the above

5. The speedometer, tachometer, and governor are all tools that assist in safe shifting.

   A. True
   B. False

6. When done properly, double clutching causes a vehicle's gears to grind.

   A. True
   B. False

7. Good shifting skills include:

   A. Riding the clutch
   B. Grinding gears
   C. Never riding the clutch
   D. All of the above

8. A semiautomatic transmission does not have a clutch or gear shift lever.

   A. True
   B. False

9. A lever or button is used to change gears on an automatic transmission.

   A. True
   B. False

10. Good shifting skills are the trademark of an accomplished, professional driver.

    A. True
    B. False

Read each question carefully and select the most correct answer.

1. Shifting gears properly is important because:

   A. Doing so helps you maintain control of the vehicle
   B. It helps to keep the oil flowing through the crankcase
   C. It keeps the radiator cool
   D. It keeps the engine at the proper operating temperature

2. The braking effect of the engine is greatest when:

   A. It is above the governed rpms and the transmission is in the high gears
   B. It is near the governed rpms and the transmission is in the lower gears
   C. It is above the governed rpms and the transmission is in the lower gears
   D. It is near the governed rpms and the transmission is in the high gears

3. Water will extinguish which of the following fires?

   A. Electrical
   B. Diesel fuel
   C. Gasoline
   D. Tire

4. Convex (curved) mirrors will:

   A. Make objects appear to be larger than they really are
   B. Make objects appear to be closer than they really are
   C. Make objects appear closer and larger than they really are
   D. Show a wider area than flat mirrors

5. The Driver's Manual says you should use your horn:

   A. To make the deer standing alongside the road to move further away
   B. When a car gets in the way
   C. If it may help you to avoid a collision
   D. When you begin to change lanes

Backing

OBJECTIVES

Upon completion of this chapter, you should have an understanding of:

- Backing principles and rules
- Basic backing maneuvers

7 Backing

- BACKING PRINCIPLES AND RULES
- SIGHT SIDE AND BLIND SIDE BACKING
- BASIC BACKING MANEUVERS
- SUMMARY

INTRODUCTION

Though backing is a basic tractor-trailer maneuver, it is one of the most difficult a professional driver performs. Successfully backing a tractor-trailer requires skill, practice, patience, and good judgment.

This chapter focuses on the basics of backing including safe backing and the types of backing maneuvers commonly used.

Backing principles and rules

Steering principles

The techniques/procedures used for backing a tractor-trailer are very different from those used to back your personal vehicle. In most personal vehicles, the front axle serves as the steering axle. In the case of a tractor-trailer, the rear tractor axle steers the trailer.

The amount of turning or movement of the trailer is proportional to the angle between the tractor and trailer. The greater the angle, the more the trailer will pivot and the less rearward movement there will be.

When backing a tractor-trailer, if you turn the steering wheel to the right, the trailer drifts to the left, and if you turn to the left, the trailer drifts to the right.

Rules for safe backing

All backing maneuvers have the potential to become dangerous. In most backing situations, even a second or two is enough time for someone or something to get in the path of a vehicle.

Before starting any backing maneuver, get out of your vehicle and check:

- To the rear of the vehicle;
- Above, under, and to the sides of the vehicle;
- For adequate swing clearance; and
- In front of your vehicle.

Also, make sure you warn others that the truck is backing.

Once the safety checks have been made, don't delay in moving the vehicle. Any delay could allow time for another potential hazard. If there is a delay, conduct the safety checks a second time.

Proper position is essential to successful backing. The easiest and safest position to start from is straight. However, keep in mind that most backing situations do not give the room needed to line up in a completely straight manner. When it comes to all backing maneuvers:

- Be patient;
- Back as slowly as possible, using the lowest reverse gear;
- Don't accelerate (use idle speed) or ride the clutch;
- Don't oversteer;

- Back to the left side (sight side) whenever possible;
- Use your vehicle's mirrors;
- Use your vehicle's horn and flashers;
- Turn off the radio and keep the windows open to listen for noises;
- Watch for obstacles that can tilt the trailer (curbs, ramps);
- Look out for overhead objects (wires, tree limbs); and
- Restart the backing maneuver instead of backing poorly.

Use of a helper — Depending on company policy, you may have the option of using a helper to complete a backing maneuver.

When using a helper, you and the helper must agree on signals, with the most important signal being stop. The helper should be in front of the tractor, walking from side-to-side so you can see the helper at all times. If you can't see your helper, stop immediately.

Even though you are using a helper, you must continue to take full responsibility for your actions. You can't neglect your responsibility because a helper is available.

Sight side and blind side backing

Sight side backing

This means you are backing toward the left side of the vehicle. You can see along the intended path of the trailer. Sight side backing is preferred, as you have maximum visibility.

Blind side backing

This means you are backing toward the right side of the vehicle. You can only see where you are going in your rear view mirrors. Blind side backing is more difficult and dangerous than sight side backing. You have limited visibility and have more of a chance of hitting something. Blind side backing should be avoided when possible.

Basic backing maneuvers

The following are the basic backing maneuvers you need to master in order to safely perform your job:

- Straight line backing;
- Alley dock backing;
- Parallel parking.

Straight line backing

As previously stated, this is the simplest of the backing techniques and is fundamental in learning all other backing maneuvers. Straight line backing should be mastered before attempting other backing maneuvers.

When executing a straight line backing maneuver, your vehicle should be positioned straight and shouldn't drift to either side. Keep in mind that the earlier the drift is detected, the less steering input will be needed to correct for the drift. If drifting can't be easily corrected, start the maneuver over. It is easier to start over than to reposition the vehicle while backing.

While backing, frequently check both mirrors. Select a reference point about 100-200 feet to the rear of the trailer. This will help you recognize when the vehicle is drifting.

Alley dock backing

This maneuver involves backing while turning into a space that is 90 degrees to the truck. It most often occurs at loading docks when you must back in from off the street or between two vehicles.

This maneuver combines sight side backing and straight line backing. This maneuver requires patience and extreme caution. Continually check vehicle clearance and watch for vehicles, pedestrians, or other objects that may move into the path of your vehicle after the start of the backing maneuver.

The following steps should be followed when alley dock backing:

1. Pull forward, in a straight line near the loading dock or parking space. Check the mirrors for obstructions (people, animals, objects). When the front of the trailer is in line with the left side of the loading dock or parking space, turn hard to the right.

2. Continue to move forward (slowly, at idle speed). When the tractor is positioned at about 12 o'clock, turn to the left to a 45 degree angle.

3. Continue to move forward (slowly) until the trailer is at a 45 degree angle. When you can see the dock or parking space in your left mirror, straighten your vehicle and stop.

4. Once you have stopped, set the vehicle's brakes, exit the vehicle, and do a visual check before starting the backing maneuver. This includes the safety checks mentioned earlier in the chapter. Also check vehicle positioning. The steering tires should be straight. If you are making a delivery or picking up a load, open the trailer's doors.

5. Get back into the vehicle and start backing (slowly). Keep in mind that there may be situations in which you may have to stop the vehicle and recheck your path. Straighten out the vehicle as you proceed. Use your mirrors. Keep a close watch for drift and correct it as necessary.

6. Do not try to salvage a poor set up. It is safer to start over than to make a correction while moving backward.

Though technique is the same for all vehicles, there are some variables based on the vehicle. For example, a vehicle's overhang may cause the trailer to hit something to the side.

Parallel parking

This maneuver involves backing into a space along a curb or dock. While the principle is the same as parallel parking a car, it is one of the more difficult to learn and execute with a tractor-trailer. Practice, skill, and patience are required to successfully complete this maneuver.

The following steps should be followed when parallel parking:

1. Your vehicle should be positioned next to the other parked vehicles. Leave about three feet of space between the vehicles.

2. Pull forward, in a straight line, near the parking space.

3. When the rear tandem axles of the trailer are about eight feet in front of the parking space, stop. Set the vehicle's brakes, exit the vehicle and do a visual check before starting the backing maneuver. This includes the safety checks mentioned earlier in the chapter. Also check vehicle positioning. Your vehicle should be positioned in a straight line with about three feet between your vehicle and other parked vehicles. The rear tandem axles should be about eight feet in front of the parking space.

4. Get back into the vehicle and start backing (slowly) with the steering wheel turned to the left. The trailer should be entering the space at about a 15 degree angle.

5. Turn the steering wheel sharply to the right and continue backing until the tractor and the trailer are in a straight line. The middle of your vehicle should be in the parking space. Continue to back until the front of the trailer is even with the front of the parking space.

6. Turn the steering wheel sharply to the right and keep backing until the trailer is parallel in the parking space.

7. When the trailer is almost parallel to the parking space, turn the wheel all the way to the left and follow the trailer into the space. Any corrections can be made by pulling forward to straighten out the units.

Should your vehicle be out of position at any time while backing, remember, it is easier to restart the backing maneuver than it is to try and correct what is wrong.

▍ Summary

In this chapter, you have learned about backing principles and rules and basic backing maneuvers. Remember backing is one of the most difficult maneuvers performed by the professional driver. Practice, skill, and patience all play a part in successful backing.

7

BACKING QUIZ

Directions: *Read each statement carefully and mark the response that best answers the question.*

1. Backing a tractor-trailer is one of the most difficult maneuvers performed by a professional driver.
   A. True
   B. False

2. Which of the following is a basic backing maneuver?
   A. Alley dock backing
   B. Straight line backing
   C. Parallel parking
   D. All of the above

3. Prior to backing, you should get out of your vehicle and check above, under, to the sides, and to the rear of the vehicle.
   A. True
   B. False

4. One of the keys to successful backing is:
   A. Riding the vehicle's clutch
   B. Backing to the right whenever possible
   C. Starting in the proper position
   D. Using extreme acceleration

5. Another key to successful backing is:
   A. Oversteering to compensate for the backward motion
   B. Avoiding the use of mirrors because they distort objects
   C. Backing as slowly as possible using the lowest reverse gear
   D. All of the above

6. This backing maneuver is the easiest to learn and execute:
   A. Alley dock backing
   B. Parallel parking
   C. Double parallel parking
   D. Straight line backing

7. You should back to the right side whenever possible.
   A. True
   B. False

8. It is best to restart a backing maneuver instead of backing poorly.
   A. True
   B. False

9. If you are able to use a helper when backing:
   A. You and the helper must agree on signals prior to backing
   B. The helper must be in a position so you can see the helper at all times
   C. You must still take full responsibility for your actions
   D. All of the above

10. Straight line backing should be mastered before attempting other backing maneuvers.
    A. True
    B. False

GENERAL KNOWLEDGE CDL PRE-TEST

Read each question carefully and select the most correct answer.

1. Before entering a curve, you should:
    A. Slow down to a safe speed
    B. Increase your speed to increase vehicle stability
    C. Come to a complete stop and proceed as slowly as possible
    D. All of the above

2. Which of the following happens when a tire blows at highway speed?
    A. You will experience an immediate and dramatic drop in speed
    B. You will feel a vibration
    C. You will hear a hissing sound
    D. The high air pressure signal device will come on

3. What is the purpose of a pre-trip inspection?
    A. To add an additional 15 minutes of time to your log book
    B. To aid you in being cited by a law enforcement official
    C. To help you find problems that could lead to a breakdown or accident
    D. To see if an additional 1,000 pounds of freight can be added to maximize revenue

4. When you see a hazard in the road in front of you, you should:
    A. Steer and counter steer around it
    B. Stop quickly and get off the roadway if possible
    C. Stop quickly, stay in the roadway, and go to the rear of your vehicle to flag down traffic
    D. Turn on your 4-way flashers or flash your brakes lights to warn others

5. When driving in fog, you should:
    A. Increase your vehicle's speed
    B. Stop on the side of the road
    C. Use low-beam headlights
    D. All of the above

Coupling and uncoupling

OBJECTIVES

Upon completion of this chapter, you should have an understanding of the procedures and skills necessary for safe coupling and uncoupling of tractor-trailer units, including:

- Tractor alignment
- Backing procedures
- Trailer securement
- Tractor/trailer connections
- Landing gear retraction and securement

8 Coupling and uncoupling

- COUPLING TRACTOR-TRAILERS
- UNCOUPLING TRACTOR-TRAILERS
- COUPLING TWIN TRAILERS
- UNCOUPLING TWIN TRAILERS
- OTHER COMBINATIONS
- SUMMARY

INTRODUCTION

Proper coupling and uncoupling skills are vital for safe tractor-trailer operations. Incorrect coupling and uncoupling can be very dangerous, resulting in trailers being dropped, air and electrical lines being torn, cab damage, freight damage, and other serious consequences.

This chapter will present the step-by-step procedures that must be followed and help you develop the skills necessary for safe coupling and uncoupling of tractor-trailer units.

▮ Coupling tractor-trailers

The following is a general 16-step approach to coupling.

Step 1: Inspect the fifth wheel and kingpin

To help ensure a safe connection, the tractor's fifth wheel and the trailer's kingpin must be inspected *before* attempting to couple the tractor to the trailer. When inspecting the fifth wheel and kingpin, you should:

The process can vary based on the type of vehicle being coupled/ uncoupled, as well as the policies/ procedures set in place by your motor carrier. Always consult with your motor carrier when it comes to this process.

1. Check for damaged, loose, or missing parts.
2. Make sure the mounting of the fifth wheel to the tractor is secure. Make sure there are no cracks in the frame or in any of the weld points and that all attached bolts are secure.
3. Grease the fifth wheel plate, if necessary. The result of an improperly greased fifth wheel will be steering problems caused by increased friction between the tractor and trailer. This is especially noticeable in turns.
4. Ensure that the fifth wheel is in the proper position for coupling. It should be tilted down toward the rear of the tractor, with the jaws open, and the release handle in the released or unlocked position.
5. If you have a sliding fifth wheel, make sure that the fifth wheel is in the locked position and that all pins are seated correctly to prevent movement of the fifth wheel.
6. Make sure the position of the fifth wheel will not allow the tractor to strike the landing gear or the trailer to strike the back of the tractor cab.
7. Check the trailer kingpin to ensure that it's not loose, bent, or broken.

Step 2: Check area and secure trailer

The coupling procedure must be done in a location that provides enough space to maneuver safely. In addition, the trailer should be secured against movement before backing up to it, in the event your tractor makes contact with it.

1. Make sure the area around the vehicle is clear.
2. Check the cargo, if any, to make sure it will not shift when the tractor and trailer are coupled.
3. Chock the trailer wheels, or if the trailer has spring brakes, make sure they are applied.

Step 3: Position the tractor

Get into the tractor. Position the tractor squarely and directly in front of the trailer, not at an angle. Also, the kingpin should be aligned with the throat of the fifth wheel.

Backing under the trailer at an angle might push the trailer sideways and damage or break the landing gear, potentially causing the trailer to fall or hit something. If you must back at an angle, get out of the cab frequently to check the alignment of the fifth wheel to the kingpin.

When positioning the tractor, use your outside mirrors to look along both sides of the trailer and your drive axle tires. It is important that you frequently check both the left and right mirrors in order to get a true picture of the alignment between the units.

If the trailer is 8 feet (96 inches) wide, the outside edge of the drive axle tires and the edge of the trailer should form a straight line. If the trailer is wider (many are now 8-½feet (102 inches) wide), adjust your position accordingly, so the tractor tires are inside the outside edge of the trailer by a few inches.

Step 4: Back slowly into position

Begin backing the tractor up towards the front of the trailer, *slowly*. Stop just as the fifth wheel touches the trailer. Don't bump the trailer or lift it up onto the fifth wheel. At this point, you should be able to compare the fifth wheel height with the trailer height.

Step 5: Secure the tractor

Shift the transmission into neutral and engage the parking brake before exiting the cab.

Step 6: Check the trailer height

Check the height of the trailer in relation to the fifth wheel. The trailer should be low enough that it will make contact with the middle of the fifth wheel and will be raised slightly by the tractor when the tractor is backed under it.

If the trailer is too low, the tractor may strike and damage the nose of the trailer. If the trailer is too high, it may not couple correctly or completely miss the pin, possibly striking the rear of the cab.

Raise or lower the trailer as needed by cranking the landing gear up or down, and/or raise or lower the fifth wheel using the tractor's adjustable air suspension, if so equipped. Secure the landing gear crank when desired height is reached.

Never go under a trailer that is not supported by a tractor.

Finally, check that the kingpin and fifth wheel are aligned, and make sure the jaws are open if the tractor has been moved any distance.

Step 7: Connect the air lines

Before connecting the tractor to the trailer, check your trailer brakes. Most trailers will already have the brakes set, but if your trailer was manufactured prior to 1975, you may need to assure that the brakes are set by supplying air to them before backing under the trailer. The connection must be done properly for the brakes to work correctly. It's a good idea to connect the air lines at this stage, even if the trailer is equipped with spring brakes.

There are two air lines to be connected: the "service" line and the "emergency" line. There are several ways the lines may be distinguished from one another:

- They may be stamped with the words "Service" and "Emergency."

- They may be color coded, with blue or black for the service line and red for the emergency line.

- The glad hands may be coded by shape, with square glad hands for the service line and round glad hands for the emergency line.

Check all four glad hand seals (rubber grommets) for cracks or other damage, and then connect the tractor's emergency air line to the trailer's emergency glad hand (usually on the right side when facing the trailer). Make sure the connection is firm, and then engage the safety latch or other mechanism to keep the lines together. Connect the service line in the same manner.

Make sure air lines are safely supported where they won't be crushed or caught while the tractor is backing under the trailer, and make sure there is enough slack in the lines so the glad hands won't uncouple.

Step 8: Supply air to the trailer

This step should only be done if you have determined that the brakes are not already set (pre-1975 trailer), or if you can't tell whether they are set or not. From the cab, with the engine off, push in the air supply knob or move the tractor protection valve control from the "emergency" to the "normal" position to supply air to the trailer brake system.

Wait until the air pressure is normal. Check the air brake system pressure gauge for signs of major air loss and listen for escaping air (a sign that a problem exists).

Apply and release the trailer brakes and listen for the sound of the trailer brakes. You should hear the brakes activate when they are applied, and hear air escape when they are released.

Step 9: Start the engine and set the trailer brakes

When you're sure the trailer brakes are working, start the engine. Make sure the air pressure is up to normal.

Apply the trailer brakes (if they are not already applied) by pulling out the air supply knob or moving the tractor protection valve control from normal to emergency.

8

Step 10: Back under the trailer

At this point in the process, it's time to make the main connection. Put the tractor into the lowest reverse gear and release the tractor's parking brake.

Back the tractor slowly under the trailer. The trailer apron should contact the fifth wheel, lifting the trailer onto the tractor. Stop when you hear and/or feel the fifth wheel's jaws close around the kingpin.

Hitting the kingpin too hard could cause extensive damage to the kingpin, fifth wheel, landing gear, and/or cargo.

Step 11: Check the connection

Put the tractor in low gear and gently pull forward, while the trailer brakes are still locked, to check that the trailer is locked onto the tractor. Stop as soon as you feel resistance from the trailer, and repeat the test once more.

Step 12: Secure the vehicle

Once the connection is solid, put the transmission in neutral and apply the tractor parking brakes. Shut off the engine and take the key with you so someone else won't move the truck while you're under it.

Step 13: Inspect the coupling

In this step, you'll make sure the coupling is safe and secure. This will require you to go under the trailer to inspect the coupling, so bring a flashlight if necessary. Check the following:

- Make sure there's no space between the upper (apron) and lower (platform) fifth wheel. The trailer apron and fifth wheel plate should be in full contact. If there is space, something is wrong. Fix the problem before doing anything else (the ground may be uneven, or the kingpin may be on a ridge inside the jaws or on top of the closed fifth wheel jaws, which would allow the trailer to come loose very easily).

- Go under the trailer and look into the throat of the fifth wheel using a flashlight. Make sure the fifth wheel jaws have closed and locked around the shank of the kingpin, not the head.

- Check that the release arm is in the locked position.

- Check that the safety latch is in position over the release arm, if there is one. (On some fifth wheels, the latch must be put in place by hand.)

If the coupling isn't right, don't move the vehicle.

Step 14: Connect the electrical cord and check the air lines

If you haven't already done this, plug the electrical cord into the trailer and fasten the safety latch. Don't force the connection if it doesn't fit.

Check both the air lines and electrical cord for proper securement and signs of damage. A good way to do this is to set your tractor brakes, release the trailer brakes, and listen for any air leakage.

Make sure the air lines and electrical cord won't snag any moving parts of the vehicle or rest on the catwalk.

Step 15: Raise trailer supports and remove chocks

Most landing gear cranks have two speeds, low and high. Use the low speed to begin raising the landing gear. Once the landing gear is free of weight, switch to high speed.

Raise the landing gear all the way up, making sure both legs are up. Never drive with your landing gear only partially raised, as it may catch on railroad tracks or other obstructions.

After raising the landing gear, secure the crank handle safely.

When the full weight of the trailer is resting on the tractor, do the following:

1. Check for enough clearance between the rear of the tractor frame and the landing gear. This is especially important with a tandem axle tractor and/or a sliding fifth wheel. If there isn't enough clearance, the tractor may hit the landing gear during sharp turns.

2. Check that there's enough clearance between the top of the tractor tires and the nose of the trailer.

To make sure you have completed this procedure correctly, set your trailer brakes, release your tractor brakes, and give a gentle tug against the trailer.

Step 16: Remove chocks

Finally, remove and store the wheel chocks in a safe place.

▌Uncoupling tractor-trailers

The following 12-step approach to uncoupling will help protect you, your vehicle, your cargo, and others from damage and injury.

Step 1: Position the rig

The first step is to make sure the surface of the parking area is level and that it can support the weight of the trailer. Dirt, sand, and gravel surfaces can cause problems, as can hot blacktop. If necessary, use trailer supports, such as boards to prevent the trailer from sinking.

Align the tractor with the trailer. Pulling out at an angle can damage the landing gear.

Step 2: Secure the trailer and ease pressure on locking jaws

Pull out the trailer air supply button to lock the trailer brakes.

Ease pressure on the fifth wheel locking jaws by backing up gently. This will help you release the pressure of the locking jaws against the kingpin.

Put the tractor parking brakes on while the tractor is pushing against the kingpin. This will hold the rig with pressure off the locking jaws. Place the transmission in neutral and turn off the engine.

8

Step 3: Chock the trailer wheels

Chock the trailer wheels if the trailer doesn't have spring brakes, or if you're not sure. (The air could leak out of the trailer air tank, releasing its emergency brakes. The trailer could then move if it didn't have the wheels chocked.)

Step 4: Lower the landing gear

Check the landing gear for damage, excessive rust, cracks, broken welds, or other problems. Lower the landing gear until it makes firm contact with the ground.

Make sure both supports are firmly touching the ground. If they are not, find more level ground before dropping the trailer.

If the trailer is loaded, after the landing gear makes firm contact with the ground, turn the crank in low gear a few extra turns to lift some weight off the tractor. This will make it easier to unlatch the fifth wheel and to couple next time. Do not lift the trailer off the fifth wheel.

Step 5: Disconnect air lines and electrical cord

Disconnect the air lines from the trailer. Connect the air line glad hands to the dummy couplers on the back of the cab, or couple them together.

Hang the electrical cord with the plug facing down to prevent moisture from entering it. Make sure the lines are supported so they won't be damaged while driving the tractor.

Step 6: Unlock the fifth wheel

Lift the fifth wheel release handle lock or safety latch (if so equipped). If necessary, use a hook or extension handle to reach the lock/latch.

Pull the release handle to open position.

Keep your legs and feet clear of the rear tractor wheels to avoid serious injury in case the vehicle moves.

Step 7: Lower the air suspension

Before lowering the air suspension (if your tractor has air suspension), slowly drive forward (about one foot) to clear the kingpin. Do not pull the fifth wheel out from under the trailer at this point.

If your tractor has air suspension, release pressure from the air bags and wait for them to drain so the rear of the tractor doesn't jump when pulling clear of the trailer.

Step 8: Pull the tractor partially clear

Release the tractor's parking brake and pull the tractor forward until the fifth wheel just begins to clear the trailer's apron plate. Stop with the tractor frame still under the trailer, to prevent the trailer from falling to the ground if the landing gear should collapse or sink.

Step 9: Secure the tractor

Apply the parking brake, place the transmission in neutral, and exit the cab.

Step 10: Inspect the trailer supports

Make sure the ground is supporting the trailer. Make sure the landing gear isn't damaged. If necessary, use a trailer safety jack to support the trailer.

Step 11: Pull the tractor clear

Release the parking brakes, check the area, and slowly drive the tractor clear of the trailer.

Step 12: Raise the air suspension

If your tractor has an air suspension, reinflate the air bags (see Step 7 above).

Coupling twin trailers

The procedures for coupling twin trailers are a bit more complicated than those for single trailers. The following steps should be followed when coupling twin trailers.

Step 1: Secure the rear trailer

If the second trailer doesn't have spring brakes (pre-1975), drive the tractor close to the trailer, connect the emergency air supply line, charge the trailer air tank, and disconnect the emergency line. This will set the trailer emergency brakes (if the slack adjusters are correctly adjusted). Chock the wheels.

Step 2: Couple the tractor and first trailer

Using the procedures for coupling tractor-trailers discussed previously, couple the tractor and the first trailer.

For safe handling on the road, the more heavily loaded trailer must always be in first position behind the tractor. The lighter trailer should be in the rear.

Step 3: Position the converter dolly

Release the dolly brakes by opening the air tank petcock. Or, if the dolly has spring brakes, use the dolly parking brake control.

If the distance is not too great, roll the dolly into position by hand so it's in line with the rear trailer's kingpin. Otherwise, use the tractor and first trailer to pick up the converter dolly. Position the combination as close as possible to the dolly.

A converter gear or dolly is a coupling device of one or two axles and a fifth wheel by which a semi-trailer can be coupled to the rear of a tractor-trailer combination.

Move the dolly to the rear of the first trailer and couple it to the trailer.

Lock the pintle hook.

Secure the dolly support in the raised position.

Pull the dolly into position as close as possible to the nose of the second trailer.

8

Lower the dolly support.

Unhook the dolly from the first trailer.

Wheel the dolly into position in front of the second trailer in line with the kingpin.

Step 4: Connect the dolly to the front trailer

Back the first trailer into position in front of the dolly tongue.

Hook the dolly to the front trailer.

Lock the pintle hook.

Secure the converter gear support in the raised position.

Step 5: Connect the dolly to the rear trailer

Make sure the trailer brakes are locked and/or the wheels chocked.

Make sure the trailer height is correct. It must be slightly lower than the center of the fifth wheel, so the trailer is raised slightly when the dolly is pushed underneath.

Back the converter dolly under the rear trailer. Raise the landing gear slightly off the ground to prevent damage if the trailer moves.

Test the coupling by pulling against the pin of the number two trailer.

Make a visual check of the coupling. There should be no space between the upper (apron) and lower (platform) fifth wheel, and the locking jaws should be closed around the kingpin.

Connect safety chains, air hoses, and electrical cord.

Close the converter dolly air tank petcock and the shut-off valves at the rear of the second trailer (service and emergency shut-offs).

Open the shut-off valves at the rear of the first trailer (and on the dolly, if so equipped).

Raise the landing gear completely on the second trailer.

Charge the trailers (push the trailer air supply knob in) and check for air at the rear of the second trailer by opening the emergency line shut-off. If air pressure isn't there, something is wrong and the brakes won't work. A valve may be closed or possibly an air line is crossed.

▌ Uncoupling twin trailers

Like coupling twin trailers, the procedures for uncoupling twin trailers are a bit more complicated than those for single trailers. The following steps should be followed when uncoupling twin trailers.

Step 1: Uncouple the rear trailer

Park your rig in a straight line on firm, level ground.

Apply the parking brakes so the rig won't move.

Chock the wheels of the second trailer if it doesn't have spring brakes.

Lower the landing gear of the second trailer enough to remove some weight from the dolly.

Close the air shut-offs at the rear of the first trailer (and on the dolly if so equipped).

Disconnect all dolly air and electric lines and secure them.

Release the dolly brakes.

Release the converter dolly fifth wheel latch.

Slowly pull the tractor, first trailer, and dolly forward to pull the dolly out from under the rear trailer.

Never unlock the pintle hook with the dolly still under the rear trailer. The dolly tow bar may fly up, possibly causing injury, and at the very least, making it very difficult to recouple.

Step 2: Uncouple the converter dolly

Lower the dolly landing gear.

Disconnect the safety chains.

Apply the converter gear spring brakes or chock the wheels.

Release the pintle hook on the first trailer.

Slowly pull clear of the dolly.

▌ Other combinations

The methods and procedures described in this chapter apply to the most common tractor-trailer combinations. However, there are additional types of combinations, as well as other ways of coupling and uncoupling them. While they won't be covered here, it's your responsibility to learn the right way to couple and uncouple the vehicle(s) you'll drive.

▌ Summary

The coupling/uncoupling procedure is a skill required of everyone operating a tractor-trailer combination. This chapter has covered the step-by-step procedures used to couple and uncouple most common tractor-trailer combinations. Following the 16 coupling and 12 uncoupling steps, in order, should allow you to perform the coupling/uncoupling procedure safely in most situations.

For your own safety and the safety of your equipment and the motoring public, you should practice the procedures until they become second habit and you are able to easily, correctly, and safely couple and uncouple your tractor-trailer every time.

8

Directions: *Read each statement carefully and mark the response that best answers the question.*

1. After coupling, there should be no space between the upper and lower fifth wheel.
   A. True
   B. False

2. Failing to grease the fifth wheel plate could result in steering problems.
   A. True
   B. False

3. If you must back up to a trailer at an angle, you should:
   A. Rely on your mirrors alone to line up the fifth wheel and kingpin
   B. Lock the fifth wheel to the kingpin before connecting the air lines
   C. Get out of the cab frequently to check the alignment of the fifth wheel and kingpin
   D. Complete the maneuver as quickly as possible

4. Before driving, the landing gear should be stowed inside the trailer.
   A. True
   B. False

5. Air should be supplied to the trailer brakes:
   A. Only after connecting the tractor to the trailer
   B. Before backing under the trailer
   C. If wheel chocks are not available
   D. After the trailer supports have been removed

6. When backing the tractor into position in front of the trailer, you should stop before the fifth wheel touches the trailer.
   A. True
   B. False

7. Before backing under the trailer, what should the height of the fifth wheel be in relation to the nose of the trailer?
   A. The trailer nose should be higher than the fifth wheel, so the kingpin goes directly into the locking jaws
   B. The trailer nose should be lower than the fifth wheel
   C. The trailer nose should be aligned with the middle of the fifth wheel, so the trailer is lifted upward when the tractor is backed under it
   D. The height of the fifth wheel is not important

8. In a set of doubles, the heaviest trailer should be positioned toward the rear.
   A. True
   B. False

GENERAL KNOWLEDGE CDL PRE-TEST

Read each question carefully and select the most correct answer.

1. Your vehicle is 40 feet long and you are traveling at 50 mph. The safe following distance is:

   A. 5 seconds
   B. 6 seconds
   C. 4 seconds
   D. 3 seconds

2. Drinking alcohol can affect your:

   A. Judgment
   B. Vision
   C. Coordination and reaction time
   D. All of the above

3. Aggressive driving is:

   A. Operating in a selfish, bold, or pushy manner, without regard for the rights or safety of others
   B. Acceptable during rush hour in a metropolitan area
   C. Operating in a cautious and courteous manner
   D. All of the above

4. Which of the following is true about rear drive wheel braking skids?

   A. The vehicle's front wheels will slide sideways
   B. It is not a cause of jackknifing
   C. The locked wheels have more traction than the wheels that are rolling
   D. If it occurs with a vehicle towing a trailer, the trailer can push the towing vehicle sideways

5. Which of the following statements is true?

   A. Hazards are easier to see at night than during the day
   B. Hazards are easier to see during the day than at night
   C. Most drivers are more alert at night than during the day
   D. It is recommended that you use your high beams at all times during the period from 7:00 P.M. to 7:00 A.M.

CHAPTER 8

Visual search

OBJECTIVES

Upon completion of this chapter, you should have a basic understanding of:

- The importance of continually scanning your entire sight area
- How to properly adjust and use your vehicle's mirrors
- The importance of monitoring the space behind your vehicle

9 Visual search

- SEEING AHEAD AND TO THE SIDES
- USE OF MIRRORS
- ADJUSTING MIRRORS
- SEEING TO THE REAR
- SUMMARY

INTRODUCTION

A safe driver is aware of what is going on all around his/her vehicle. The purpose of this chapter is to introduce you to the skills required to conduct an effective visual search.

▌ Seeing ahead and to the sides

A tractor-trailer covers more distance than your personal vehicle when stopping, changing lanes, or reacting to problems on the road. Because of this, it is important that you continually scan your entire sight area. This includes focusing on:

- The road, vehicles, and other problems ahead;
- Vehicles and other problems to the left and right; and
- Vehicles behind.

Distance scanning

Looking ahead can help you travel safely. Always look far enough ahead to:

- Give yourself time to spot a problem;
- Give yourself time to decide on the best way to avoid a problem;
- Check for adverse traffic conditions; and
- Give yourself enough time to maneuver away from a potential problem situation.

As a general rule, look about 12-15 seconds ahead of your vehicle. In the city, 12-15 seconds is equal to about two to three blocks. On the highway, 12-15 seconds is equal to just over one quarter of a mile. If you can't see that far ahead, you should slow down.

As well as looking ahead, you should be scanning to the sides and behind your vehicle. Watch road signs and check your vehicle's instruments. Your eyes should be continually moving from far to near. When scanning ahead, pay special attention to anything that could affect your path of travel including:

- Other vehicles;
- Road signs;
- Traffic signals;
- Debris;
- Animals;
- Weather-related hazards (ice, rain, snow);
- Intersections;

- Work/construction zones;
- Stopped vehicles;
- Emergency vehicles; and
- Accidents.

There are several benefits to distance scanning including being able to identify hazards early, and having additional time to react/respond to situations including finding ways to avoid the situation. Distance scanning helps you avoid abrupt stops and radical speed changes. Also, effective scanning can help reduce fatigue. Your eyes are continually moving and are not fixed on a single object.

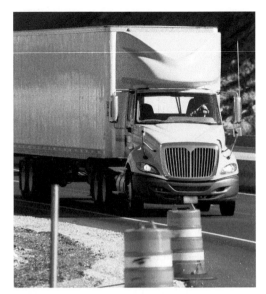

Scanning to the sides

When on the road, you should be periodically scanning to the sides, but there are certain situations where scanning to the sides is critical including crosswalks, intersections, and school zones.

At crosswalks you should use extra caution. As well as watching the entire area, you should pay additional attention to what is happening to your right. Pedestrians, bicycles, etc. are often hidden from your line of sight when closest to your vehicle. Also, remember to yield the right of way to pedestrians when turning on green.

At intersections, move your vehicle forward slowly. Look left, right, and left again. Start to pull into the intersection, continuing to scan as you pull through the intersection.

School zones are another place where you need to be especially careful. Watch for children, bikes, balls, etc. darting into traffic.

In cities, scanning to the sides is crucial to your safety and the safety of others. Cars parked along the shoulder create increased hazards that may not be seen if you are not constantly scanning. Often, people will walk between cars or will open their door into traffic without even looking. By scanning you can avoid a possible accident or injury caused by the inattentiveness of others.

▋ Use of mirrors

Mirrors provide your only view of the rear of your vehicle. You must check your mirrors before changing speed or position in traffic. You should check your mirrors about every four seconds. Also, use mirrors to assist in checking your vehicle's blind spots.

Most tractors are equipped with two types of mirrors:

- Plane or west coast; and
- Convex.

Plane/west coast

A plane or west coast mirror assists you in seeing down the sides and toward the rear of your trailer and the roadway behind. It doesn't give as wide a view as the convex mirror does, but it does allow for better visibility down the length of the trailer. The left mirror is closer and reflects a larger image which means you have a greater field of view from that mirror.

Remember that mirrors do not allow you to see everything. There are blind spots on both sides of your vehicle. This makes lane changes, passing, and other maneuvers risky. Tight turns can also pose a problem. You can't see smaller vehicles or pedestrians that are next to the vehicle. Along with using your mirrors, signal and wait a moment before changing direction or lanes.

Images in your side mirror will appear to be similar to those when you are driving your personal vehicle. When using your plane mirror in this situation, you should be able to judge the speed and distance of overtaking vehicles.

Convex

Convex mirrors are designed with an outward curvature to provide a wide-angle view. They give a broader view than plane mirrors and, if adjusted correctly, eliminate much of the blind area. Convex mirrors provide the best close-up view of the sides of your vehicle.

One negative aspect of convex mirrors is that they show a distorted image. Overtaking vehicles appear smaller and farther away than they really are. When using this mirror, you need to gain a solid understanding of what you are looking at. This will take practice as this view is not something you are used to in your personal vehicle.

9

A combination of plane and convex mirrors work best. They provide maximum side and rear vision. The drawback is that the combination can be a bit confusing at first. Frequently making sure the mirrors are clean and properly adjusted can be a great aid in reducing any confusion.

Adjusting mirrors

Proper adjustment is important. It ensures that you have the best view possible to the sides and rear of your vehicle.

Mirror adjustment should be checked on a regular basis. Make sure your vehicle is straight before making any adjustments.

Left side plane/west coast

You should see the trailer body on the inside vertical edge of the mirror. The rest of the mirror should show what is next to and behind the trailer. You should be able to see a point on the ground about 30 feet away on the bottom, horizontal edge of the mirror.

Left side convex

You should see part of the trailer on the inside vertical edge of the mirror. The top, horizontal edge of the mirror should show a point on the ground that is about 35 feet away. The bottom, horizontal edge should show a point on the ground that is about 7 feet away.

Right side plane/west coast

You should see the trailer body on the inside vertical edge of the mirror. The rest of the mirror should show what is next to and behind the trailer. You should be able to see a point on the ground about 60 feet away on the bottom, horizontal edge of the mirror.

Right side convex

You should see part of the trailer on the inside vertical edge of the mirror. The top, horizontal edge of the mirror should show a point on the ground that is about 65 feet away. The bottom, horizontal edge of the mirror should show a point on the ground that is about 8 feet away

Some vehicles also make use of fender mirrors, which are mounted on the right and left corners of the front fenders. Companies have also started exploring the use of certain types of collision avoidance systems. Although these two types of visual aids are not on every commercial motor vehicle, they do provide an additional level of sight around the vehicle which adds to safer driving operations in many instances.

Seeing to the rear

Continually use your mirrors to monitor the rear of your vehicle.

Check load and cargo security. Watch for loose or falling cargo. If operating a flatbed, watch for loose straps, ropes, chains, or tarps.

Keep an eye on your tires. Look for potential problems including flat or damaged tires or tire fires.

Use your mirrors to check for vehicles beside your tractor and trailer. Be alert. Know what is going on at all times.

Use your mirrors when changing lanes. Check your mirrors:

- Before you change lanes (making sure there's room to change lanes);
- After you signal (making sure no one/nothing moved into your blind spot);
- Right after you begin the lane change (making sure your path is still clear); and
- After you complete the lane change.

Use of your mirrors is just one part of the scanning process. Check your mirrors quickly, and don't focus on them for too long. The more time spent focusing on a mirror is more time away from focusing on the road ahead.

Also check your mirrors when you slow down, merge, or turn.

Use of mirrors is also important when approaching alleys and intersections. Mirrors must be used more frequently when in traffic tie-ups and when approaching or driving alongside parked or stopped vehicles.

▌ Summary

In this chapter, you have learned about the skills required to conduct an effective visual search. This includes seeing ahead, to the sides, and behind your vehicle as well as proper use and adjustment of mirrors.

9

VISUAL SEARCH QUIZ

Directions: Read each statement carefully and mark the response that best answers the question.

1. A good driver continually scans his/her entire sight area.
   A. True
   B. False

2. As a general rule, you should always look about _____ seconds ahead of your vehicle.
   A. 8-10
   B. 10-12
   C. 12-15
   D. 30-40

3. When behind the wheel, your eyes should be continually moving, scanning ahead and to the sides.
   A. True
   B. False

4. There aren't any benefits to distance scanning.
   A. True
   B. False

5. When on the road, you should be periodically scanning to the sides.
   A. True
   B. False

6. The two types of mirrors most tractors are equipped with are:
   A. Concave and convex
   B. Concave and straight
   C. Large and small
   D. Plane/west coast and convex

7. Mirrors enable you to see everything to the sides and rear of your vehicle.
   A. True
   B. False

8. Even with the use of mirrors, there are still blind spots around your vehicle.
   A. True
   B. False

9. When using mirrors to monitor the rear of your vehicle, watch for:
   A. Tire problems
   B. Cargo security
   C. Both A and B
   D. None of the above

10. Use your mirrors when:
   A. Changing lanes
   B. Merging
   C. Turning
   D. All of the above

Read each question carefully and select the most correct answer.

1. Can federal inspectors inspect your truck or bus?

    A. Yes, and they have the authority to place your vehicle out of service
    B. Yes, but they have no authority to place your vehicle out of service
    C. Yes, but only at a port of entry
    D. No

2. Bridge formulas are designed to:

    A. Determine the total gross vehicle weight of a vehicle
    B. Permit the same maximum axle weight for any axle spacing
    C. Permit less maximum axle weight for axles that are closer together
    D. Permit less maximum axle weight for axles that are further apart

3. When traveling down a long downgrade, you should always:

    A. Apply trailer brakes to reduce speed or maintain speed
    B. Use the braking effect of the engine
    C. Downshift when you exceed a safe speed
    D. Exceed the posted speed limit

4. What three factors add up to the total stopping distance for a commercial motor vehicle?

    A. Perception distance, reaction distance, and braking distance
    B. Eye lead time, reaction distance, and braking distance
    C. Perception distance, reaction distance, and response distance
    D. Response distance and braking distance

5. Which of the following is a sign of drowsy driving?

    A. You can't stop yawning
    B. You drift between lanes
    C. Your eyes close or go out of focus by themselves
    D. All of the above

Communication

OBJECTIVES

Upon completion of this chapter, you should have a basic understanding of:

- Communicating intent
- Communicating presence
- What is considered misuse of communications
- Communication from others

- COMMUNICATING INTENT
- COMMUNICATING PRESENCE
- COMMUNICATION FROM OTHERS

INTRODUCTION

In this chapter, you will be introduced to the basic principles of communication. This includes the appropriate processes and procedures on your part when it comes to communicating with others as well as developing the skills to understand the communications of others.

▌ Communicating intent

Like you, other drivers are not mind readers. They can't know what you are going to do if you don't communicate appropriately. Clear communication of your intentions is important. Basic methods of visibly communicating your intent include:

- Turn signals;
- Headlights;
- Four-way emergency flashers;
- Flashing brake lights; and
- Altering vehicle position.

Turn signals

Turn signals communicate your intent to change direction. Signal anytime you plan to:

- Turn;
- Change lanes;
- Pass another vehicle;
- Merge;
- Exit;
- Parallel park; or
- Pull into traffic from the curb.

Always use turn signals in these situations, even if you don't see any other vehicles around. Remember, your vehicle does have blind spots. The most dangerous vehicles are the ones you can't see. The following are standard turn signal guidelines you should follow.

Signal early — Signal well in advance of turning or changing lanes. In city traffic, signal one-half block before turning. On the highway, signal about 500 feet in advance. Your turn signal should blink at least three times before attempting to turn or change lanes.

Signal continuously — Keep both hands on the wheel to turn safely. Don't cancel the signal until your maneuver is complete. Remember to cancel the signal after completing the turn or lane change.

Slowing down

There will be times that you will need to let other drivers know that you are slowing down. Other drivers may not expect you to be slowing down, especially when approaching a steep grade, setting up for a turn, or stopping to load, unload, or park. A few light taps on the brake pedal (causing your brake lights to flash) should warn drivers following your vehicle. If you are driving very slowly or are stopped, use your four-way emergency flashers.

Because of the size of your vehicle and the difficulty other drivers may have seeing in front of it, it is important that you communicate early when traffic is slowing or stopping. There are many situations in which other drivers don't expect you to slow or stop, such as on the highway or in the middle of a block.

Directing traffic

One thing you should *never* do is direct traffic. Some drivers will try to help others by signaling when it is safe to pass or pull out by flashing lights, blowing the horn, or using hand signals. This could cause an accident, resulting in injury, damage, and potential liability. You could very easily be found at fault for the mistake of someone else if you signaled them to move.

▋ Communicating presence

Others may not notice your vehicle, even when it is in plain sight. Communicating your presence can help prevent an accident.

Whenever you're about to pass a pedestrian or bicyclist, assume they don't see you and could suddenly move in front of your vehicle. When it is safe and legal to do so, move your vehicle to the left of your lane, tap the horn lightly or, at night, flash your headlights off and on (if it is safe and legal). Tap the horn or flash your lights from a distance, if possible, so you don't startle the pedestrian or bicyclist.

From dusk to dawn your headlights should be turned on. They should also be turned on when it is raining, snowing, or foggy. As well as helping you see the road, this helps other drivers see you. Keep in mind that some states have laws requiring the use of headlights if weather conditions warrant the use of windshield wipers.

If you have to pull off the road and stop, immediately turn on the four-way emergency flashers.

Warning devices

Section 392.22 of the Federal Motor Carrier Safety Regulations (FMCSRs) addresses when and how warning devices must be set out on the highway.

When a vehicle is stopped on the traveled portion of the highway or the shoulder of the highway you must immediately activate your vehicle's hazard warning flashers. You then have 10 minutes to set out emergency warning devices.

When placing the devices, you should hold them in front of you, and if possible wear a high-visibility vest, to help you be clearly visible to traffic.

The placement of devices varies depending on where the vehicle is stopped. See Chapter 28 for complete details.

You should remain alert for vehicles that may not see you along the roadway.

Using your horn

Your vehicle's horn informs others of your presence. Only use your horn when necessary, for example to help in preventing an accident. When used unnecessarily it can be dangerous. Remember, a light tap sends a much different message than a long blast.

In general, use only your vehicle's electric horn. The air horn is extremely loud and can distract or frighten others. The horn should be used for communicating your presence and to warn of immediate danger. It isn't a toy and should only be used for appropriate purposes.

CB radio

The citizen's band (CB) radio can be a good communication tool if used safely and legally. When used appropriately, CBs can provide information about weather and traffic conditions and provide a way for you to notify authorities of an accident or other road hazard.

Avoid using your CB to obtain directions. Because you are broadcasting "over the air" anyone can be listening, including cargo thieves.

Like your vehicle's horn, the CB isn't a toy and should be used appropriately. Avoid idle chatter and never use offensive language over the CB.

Cell phone

Like the CB, a cell phone (mobile telephone) can be a good communication tool if used safely and legally.

Section 392.82 of the FMCSRs prohibits a driver from using a hand-held mobile telephone while driving a commercial motor vehicle. Use of a hand-held mobile telephone includes:

- Using at least one hand to hold a mobile telephone to conduct voice communication;
- Dialing or answering a mobile telephone by pressing more than a single button; or
- Reaching for a mobile phone in a manner that requires a driver to maneuver so he/she is no longer in a seated driving position, restrained by a seat belt.

Use of a hand-held mobile telephone is allowed when necessary to communicate with law enforcement officials or other emergency services.

Texting

Texting is another form of communication that is prohibited while driving a commercial motor vehicle (Sec. 392.80).

Texting is defined as manually entering text into, or reading text from an electronic device. This includes (but is not limited to):

- E-mailing;
- Instant messaging;
- Short messaging;
- A command or request to access a webpage; and
- Engaging in any other form of electronic text retrieval or electronic text entry for future or present communication.

Texting is allowed when necessary to communicate with law enforcement officials or other emergency services.

In addition to the mobile telephone and texting bans in the FMCSRs, many states and some municipalities have laws or regulations prohibiting the use of these devices while behind the wheel.

∎ Communication from others

As a safe and professional driver, you must effectively communicate your intentions and it is just as important that you watch for and understand the communications of other drivers.

As well as the obvious means of communication (turn signals, lights, horn), there are other, more subtle communications you need to watch for when on the road.

For example, driver movement in a vehicle, such as shifting around in the seat or looking in the mirror, may indicate possible directional changes.

Observing other vehicles can give you clues as to a driver's intentions. Sudden slowing or a slight position change in a lane may indicate a direction change. Turned front wheels or visible exhaust from a parked car may indicate the vehicle is going to pull out of a parking space.

Be alert to the obvious, and sometimes not so obvious, communication of others as ways to anticipate and avoid potential problems.

▌ Summary

In this chapter, you have learned the importance of communication when it comes to highway safety. This includes appropriately communicating your intentions to others and understanding how others may communicate with you.

10

Directions: *Read each statement carefully and mark the response that best answers the question.*

1. Which of the following is a way you can visibly communicate your intent when operating a tractor-trailer?
   A. Use of turn signals
   B. Use of warning flashers
   C. Flashing the vehicle's brake lights
   D. All of the above

2. If you don't see any other vehicles, you don't have to use a turn signal when changing lanes.
   A. True
   B. False

3. In city traffic, you should signal_____ before turning.
   A· ¼ block
   B· ½ block
   C. 1 block
   D. 2 blocks

4. On the highway, you should signal about _____ before turning.
   A. 100 feet
   B. 250 feet
   C. 500 feet
   D. 1,000 feet

5. A few light taps on your vehicle's brakes can be used to alert other drivers that you are slowing down.
   A. True
   B. False

6. If you are driving very slowly or are stopped, you should use the vehicle's four-way flashers.
   A. True
   B. False

7. According to the FMCSRs, if your vehicle is stopped on the traveled portion of the highway or the shoulder of the highway, you have _____ to set out emergency warning devices.
   A. 5 minutes
   B. 10 minutes
   C. 15 minutes
   D. 30 minutes

8. It is acceptable to text while driving if you need help with directions.
   A. True
   B. False

9. Turned front wheels or visible exhaust from a parked car may indicate the vehicle is going to pull out of a parking space.
   A. True
   B. False

10. A driver shifting around in his seat or looking in the mirror may indicate that he may be changing direction.
    A. True
    B. False

COMBINATION VEHICLE CDL PRE-TEST

Read each question carefully and select the most correct answer.

1. You are hooking a tractor to a semi-trailer and have backed up but are not under it. What should you do before backing under the trailer?

   A. Hook up the electrical service cable
   B. Hook up the emergency and service air lines
   C. Connect the ground cable
   D. Nothing, back up and secure the fifth wheel to the trailer

2. After pushing in the trailer supply valve, you should not move the tractor until the whole air system is:

   A. Charging
   B. At normal pressure
   C. Bled down to half the maximum pressure
   D. Between 50 and 60 psi

3. There are two things that a driver can do to prevent a rollover. They are (1) Keep the cargo as close to the ground as possible, and:

   A. Make sure that the brakes are adjusted properly
   B. Keep both hands firmly on the steering wheel
   C. Drive slowly around turns
   D. Keep the fifth wheel free-play loose

4. When pulling a trailer, you should:

   A. Make sudden movements with your steering wheel
   B. Steer gently and smoothly
   C. Slow down to a safe speed after entering a turn
   D. All of the above

5. The fifth wheel locking lever is not locked after the jaws close around the kingpin. This means that:

   A. The trailer will not swing on the fifth wheel
   B. You cannot set the fifth wheel for proper weight distribution
   C. The hand valve is released and you may drive away
   D. The coupling is not correct and should be corrected before driving the coupled unit

OBJECTIVES

Upon completion of this chapter, you should have a basic understanding of:

- The science of speed and stopping distance
- The role road conditions play in speed management
- Adjusting speed for curves and grades
- The relationship between speed and visibility
- The influence of speed on traffic management
- The hows and whys of obeying the speed limit

11 Speed management

- STOPPING DISTANCE
- ROAD CONDITIONS
- ROAD SHAPE
- SPEED AND VISIBILITY
- SPEED AND TRAFFIC FLOW
- USE OF CRUISE CONTROL
- OBEYING THE SPEED LIMIT
- SUMMARY

Proper speed management means operating at the appropriate speed for all road conditions. This includes taking into account the condition of the road, visibility, and traffic speed and flow.

This chapter focuses on the importance of managing your vehicle's speed in order to stop safely.

Stopping distance

In order to manage speed, you need to understand the four factors involved in stopping a vehicle:

- Perception distance;
- Reaction distance;
- Brake lag distance; and
- Braking distance.

All times and distances discussed in this example are estimates based on ideal conditions. Total stopping distance can be affected by many factors including fatigue, distractions, and weather/road conditions.

Perception distance

Perception distance is the distance a vehicle travels from the time you see a hazard until your brain recognizes it. The perception time for an alert driver is approximately ¾ of a second. At 55 mph, a vehicle travels about 60 feet in ¾ of a second.

Reaction distance

Reaction distance is the distance a vehicle travels from the time your brain tells your foot to move from the accelerator until your foot hits the brake pedal. The average driver has a reaction time of ¾ of a second. At 55 mph, that accounts for another ¾ of a second and another 60 feet traveled.

Brake lag distance

When operating a vehicle with air brakes, it takes about ½ second for the mechanical operation to take place.

Braking distance

Braking distance is the distance it takes a vehicle to stop once the brakes are applied. Braking distance is affected by weight, length, and speed of the vehicle as well as road condition. A heavy vehicle's components (brakes, tires, springs, etc.) are designed to work best when a vehicle is fully loaded. At 55 mph on dry pavement with good brakes, a heavy vehicle travels about 170 feet and can take about 5 seconds to stop.

Total stopping distance

When you add together the perception, reaction, brake lag, and braking time and distance, at 55 mph it will take between 6 and 7 seconds to stop, and the vehicle will travel about 290 feet (almost the length of one football field) in ideal conditions. Higher speeds increase the stopping distance.

◼ Road conditions

Traction is necessary for vehicle control. The less friction between a vehicle's tires and the road, the less traction. Certain road conditions reduce traction and lower speeds are necessary.

Rain

Rain can affect a vehicle's traction. As rain begins to fall, it mixes with oils on the road, causing the oils to rise to the road's surface.

Until additional rain breaks down and washes away these oils, there is a layer of slippery oil between a vehicle's tires and the road. This condition can last anywhere from a few minutes to a few hours.

New pavement is more slippery when wet than old pavement. New pavement has a greater concentration of oils that have yet to be washed away by years of rain. White foam on the road is an indication of oil and water mixing, a clue that the road surface is slippery.

A heavy rain that results in standing water on the road can cause a vehicle's tires to lose traction and skim along the water's surface. This is called hydroplaning. The faster a vehicle travels on standing water, the greater the chance of hydroplaning.

When a vehicle hydroplanes, its tires are not in contact with the road and traction is lost, resulting in a loss of vehicle control.

Even a fully load tractor-trailer can hydroplane on very little water.

When it rains, vehicle speeds should be reduced by at least one-third.

Snow

Snow causes reduced traction and limited visibility. Slowing down is required for both visibility and vehicle control purposes.

A light, powdery snow often blows off the road causing few problems. If there is enough powder to cover the road, it will form a slick, smooth surface.

A heavier, slushy snow can affect vehicle control. If the snow becomes hard packed, it can cause an ice hazard.

Vehicle speeds should be reduced by at least one-half in snowy conditions. Remember, when determining vehicle speed in snowy conditions, you must be confident that you can safely stop and maneuver based on road conditions.

Ice

An icy road can present more dangers than a snowy road. When temperatures are near freezing, you have to be alert to the potential for black ice.

Black ice forms when temperatures drop rapidly and moisture on the road freezes into a smooth, nearly invisible, slippery surface. In black ice conditions, the road appears to be wet, when actually it is icy.

To check for ice formation, feel the front of the vehicle's mirrors or antenna. If ice is forming there, it is also forming on the road. Also watch the spray off of other vehicles. If the spray stops, ice may be forming.

At the very least, you should slow your vehicle by one-half in icy conditions. As with snowy conditions, when determining vehicle speed, you must be confident that you can safely stop and maneuver based on road conditions. If the road is very slippery, get off the road as soon as safely possible

Shady portions of the road can remain slippery for a long time after ice on sunny areas of the road has melted and the pavement is dry. Slow down on shade-covered roads.

When conditions warrant, you will need to slow your vehicle to a safe speed. The speeds covered in this text are suggested guidelines. Only you, the professional driver, based on your knowledge of the situation and experience can determine a safe speed in adverse driving conditions.

11

When the temperature drops, bridges can freeze before the road does. If slippery conditions are likely, avoid any change (acceleration, shifting, or braking) in driving habits while crossing the bridge. Maintain a smooth and steady speed.

Road shape

Curves

The posted speed limits on curves are designed with cars in mind. Driving a tractor-trailer through a curve too fast (at or above the posted speed limit) can cause several problems including skidding off the road or vehicle roll over.

Slow to a safe speed before entering a curve, at least 5 mph below the posted speed limit. Slow down as needed, but keep in mind that braking in a curve can be dangerous. It is easier to lock your vehicle's wheels and cause a skid.

Never exceed the posted speed limit in a curve. Also, to help maintain vehicle control, be in a gear that will let you accelerate slightly through the curve.

Grades

Gravity and vehicle weight play a part in speed management when driving on upgrades and downgrades.

On an upgrade, your vehicle has to work harder to fight the pull of gravity and maintain its speed. To maintain speed, you must place more pressure on the accelerator, and/or possibly shift to a lower gear.

The procedures for dealing with uphill/downhill driving will be covered in Chapter 14.

On a downgrade, your vehicle is working with gravity, resulting in an increase in speed. Vehicle weight also has an impact on truck speeds going down a grade. Heavier trucks want to accelerate faster than lighter ones. You must use care in maintaining a safe and even speed.

▌ Speed and visibility

You should always be able to stop within your field of vision. In other words, you should be able to stop within the distance you can see ahead.

When driving at night or in poor weather conditions such as rain, fog, or snow, you will need to slow down so you can stop your vehicle within your field of vision.

▌ Speed and traffic flow

When driving in heavy traffic, the safest speed is generally the speed of the other vehicles on the roadway, provided you can maintain an adequate following distance and you are not violating the posted speed limit. If you are unable to maintain a safe following distance, slow your vehicle to 3 mph to 4 mph less than the flow of traffic.

Often, drivers believe that exceeding the speed limit can save (or make up) time. When operating in traffic, this isn't always the case. If you are traveling faster than the speed of other traffic, you will have to pass other vehicles. This increases your chances of being involved in an accident. This type of driving can also add to your level of fatigue which can also increase your chances of being involved in an accident.

It is best to go with the flow of traffic when safe and legal to do so.

▌ Use of cruise control

Due to safety concerns, many motor carriers have policies that limit or prohibit the use of cruise control.

When used in appropriate situations, cruise control allows a driver to maintain a uniform vehicle speed. This in turn assists with fuel conservation.

If your motor carrier allows use of cruise control, it should only be used in good driving conditions, during daylight hours, on roads that have light traffic, few curves or hills, and a consistent speed limit.

Cruise control should never be use in the following situations:

- When operating in adverse driving conditions including wet, icy, or slippery roads;
- During rush hour, in heavy traffic, or on congested highways;
- At night;
- When you are tired or fatigued.

Adaptive/intelligent cruise control

Truck manufacturers are starting to install adaptive or intelligent cruise control systems on their vehicles.

Use of cruise control can contribute to a driver becoming less engaged or even potentially falling asleep at the wheel. Do not use cruise control during your body's "down time," when you are most fatigued.

An adaptive/intelligent cruise control system differs from a standard cruise control system by requiring speed and following distance settings.

The system uses forward looking sensors to monitor closing speed and warn the driver of a potential collision with the vehicle ahead.

Obeying the speed limit

Speed limits are based, in part, on the principles of good speed management. They take into account several issues including sight distance limitation, road conditions, and traffic volume. There are many reasons why you should not speed. Some of these reasons are outlined in this section.

Accidents

Accidents are more likely to occur at higher speeds. There's less reaction time and you aren't able to have as much control of your vehicle.

Penalties

Two or more convictions for excessive speeding (15 mph or more over the speed limit) in either a commercial or non-commercial vehicle (including your personal vehicle) can disqualify you from operating a commercial motor vehicle. Section 383.51 of the Federal Motor Carrier Safety Regulations (FMCSRs) states that you can be disqualified for a period of 60-120 days for excessive speeding violations.

All speeding convictions (whether they prompt disqualification or not) become part of your permanent driving record. Your driving record must be reviewed by your employer each time you begin work for a new motor carrier and then at least once each year.

Also, speeding convictions can be costly. As well as incurring fines, speeding convictions may be tracked by your insurance carrier, prompting higher premiums.

Maintenance costs

Higher speeds can affect maintenance costs. Tires and brakes wear out faster at higher speeds. As speed increases, so does overall wear.

Fuel economy

Your speed has a direct and substantial effect on your fuel economy. By adjusting your speed, even a couple miles per hour, you can positively affect your fuel mileage and save thousands of dollars over the course of a year.

If you are getting five miles per gallon at 70 miles per hour and six miles per gallon at 60 miles per hour, how much can you save by traveling at the slower speed? If you drive 130,000 miles per year and fuel averages $2.50 per gallon, you'll save over $10,000 in fuel costs alone.

Summary

In this chapter, you were introduced to the factors involved in stopping a tractor-trailer and the part speed plays in safe operation.

SPEED MANAGEMENT QUIZ

Directions: Read each statement carefully and mark the response that best answers the question.

1. Perception distance, reaction distance, brake lag, and braking distance are the four factors involved in stopping a vehicle.
   A. True
   B. False

2. _____ is the distance a vehicle travels from the time you see a hazard until your brain recognizes it.
   A. Perception distance
   B. Reaction distance
   C. Braking distance
   D. All of the above

3. _____ is the distance a vehicle travels from the time your brain tells your foot to move from the accelerator until your foot hits the brake pedal.
   A. Perception distance
   B. Reaction distance
   C. Braking distance
   D. All of the above

4. _____ is the distance it takes a vehicle to stop once the brakes are applied.
   A. Perception distance
   B. Reaction distance
   C. Braking distance
   D. All of the above

5. The more friction between a vehicle's tires and the road, the less traction.
   A. True
   B. False

6. A heavy rain that causes water to stand on a road can cause a vehicle to:
   A. Metroplane
   B. Deplane
   C. Hydroplane
   D. All of the above

7. You should slow to at least 5 mph below the posted speed limit when entering a curve.
   A. True
   B. False

8. You should always be able to stop your vehicle within your field of vision.
   A. True
   B. False

9. When driving in heavy traffic, it is best to travel at 5 - 10 mph faster than the surrounding vehicles.
   A. True
   B. False

10. It is best to go with the flow of traffic when it is safe and legal to do so.
    A. True
    B. False

COMBINATION VEHICLE CDL PRE-TEST

Read each question carefully and select the most correct answer.

1. A driver crosses the air lines when hooking up to an old trailer. What will happen?

    A. The hand valve will apply the tractor brakes instead of the trailer brakes

    B. The brake pedal will work the trailer spring brakes instead of the trailer brakes

    C. If the trailer has no spring brakes, the driver could drive away but wouldn't have trailer brakes

    D. The brake lights will not come on when the brake pedal is pressed

2. After coupling a semi-trailer, you should crank up the front trailer supports (dollies) how?

    A. Raised ½ way with the crank handle secured

    B. Raised ¾ way with the crank handle removed

    C. Fully raised with the crank handle secured

    D. Three turns off the top with the crank handle secured in its bracket

3. Air brake equipped trailers made before 1975:

    A. Are not required to have spring brakes

    B. Are easier to stop than newer trailers because they are heavier

    C. Usually need a glad hand converter

    D. Cannot be operated on interstate highways

4. The trailer hand valve should only be used:

    A. When you park at loading docks

    B. When you are parking for less than one hour

    C. When parking on a step grade

    D. To test the trailer brakes

5. Air lines on a combination vehicle are often colored to keep from getting them mixed up. The emergency line is _____.

    A. Red

    B. Black

    C. Blue

    D. Orange

CHAPTER 11

Space management 12

OBJECTIVES

Upon completion of this chapter, you should have a basic understanding of:

- The importance of space management
- The concept of maintaining an appropriate cushion of space
- Managing the space needed to execute a safe turn

12 Space management

- MANAGING SPACE
- TURNING SPACE
- SPACE WHEN CROSSING AND ENTERING TRAFFIC
- SUMMARY

Proper space management means maintaining enough space around your vehicle to operate safely.

◼ Managing space

When operating a tractor-trailer, you need to manage your cushion of space. This includes the space ahead, behind, to the sides, above, and below your vehicle. There must be enough space to allow you to adjust when traffic conditions change, for example, when a vehicle brakes suddenly or pulls into your lane of travel without warning.

Ahead

The space ahead of your vehicle is the most important, and one of the easiest to monitor and adjust as needed.

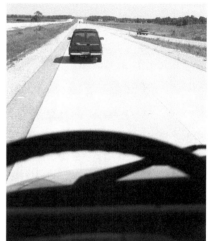

The amount of space needed depends on the speed of your vehicle and road conditions.

One rule of thumb to follow (in good driving conditions) is to allow at least one second for each 10 feet of vehicle length at speeds below 40 mph. At greater speeds, add an additional second.

In poor driving conditions, such as rain, ice, snow, or fog, allow for a greater stopping distance.

To determine how much space you have, wait until the vehicle ahead passes a clear landmark (pavement marking, road sign). Then count off the seconds until you reach the same spot. Compare your count with the rule of one second for every 10 feet of length and add one additional second if traveling at over 40 mph.

For example, if you are driving a 60 foot vehicle at 55 mph (in good weather conditions), and only counted three seconds you are following too closely. You should have at least seven seconds of space ahead.

After some practice, and experience on the road, you'll be able to easily determine how far back you should follow.

All times and distances discussed in this example are estimates based on ideal conditions.

Behind

It is impossible to keep other drivers from following too closely (tailgating), but there are some things that can be done to make it safer. Stay to the right, slow down, and give the tailgater plenty of chances to pass.

The following are steps you can take to help prevent an accident if you find that you are being tailgated.

- **Avoid quick changes** — If you have to slow down or turn, signal early and gradually reduce your vehicle's speed.

- **Increase your following distance** — Opening up room in front of you will help you to avoid making sudden speed or direction changes. This also makes it easier for the tailgater to get around you.

- **Don't speed up** — It's safer to be tailgated at a low speed than a high speed.

- **Avoid tricks** — Don't turn on your taillights or flash your brake lights.

To the sides

Commercial motor vehicles often take up most of a lane. There are several things you should try to avoid to ensure that there is plenty of space between your vehicle and other road users.

- **Don't hug the center line** — It becomes very easy to drift across the center line into oncoming traffic.

- **Avoid hugging the right side of the road** — A soft shoulder can cause control problems.

- **Avoid traveling alongside other vehicles** — Another driver may change lanes suddenly, turning into your vehicle, or your vehicle may be trapped, unable to change lanes. Also, try to avoid driving alongside others in strong winds, especially cross winds. The problem is most prevalent for empty or light trucks.

Above

Adequate space above is needed to clear bridges, overpasses, trees, and wires. Never assume the heights posted on bridges and overpasses are correct. Repaving or packed snow may reduce the clearances since the heights were posted.

The weight of a vehicle's cargo can also change its height. An empty vehicle is higher than a loaded one.

Know the height of your vehicle and never assume that all posted heights are correct.

Be aware of how a road is graded. Road grade can cause a high vehicle to tilt, which can be a clearance problem.

If you have doubts about whether there is enough overhead space to proceed, take another route.

Below

It's very easy to forget the space under your vehicle. That space can be very small when the vehicle is heavily loaded.

Driveways, railroad tracks, dirt roads, and unpaved lots can be a challenge. Slow and steady is the rule in these cases. This is also one of the reasons why you should always crank the landing gear up all the way.

Turning space

Correct procedures are important when making turns. Because of wide turning and off-tracking, commercial motor vehicles run the risk of hitting other vehicles or objects during turns.

Right turns

When making a right turn, proceed slowly. This gives you as well as others time to avoid trouble. Also, scan ahead to identify potential problems.

If you are unable to make the right turn without swinging into another lane, turn wide as you complete the turn. Keep the rear of your vehicle close to the curb. Though you can position your vehicle to make it hard for drivers to pass you on the right, never assume you blocked traffic completely. Keep an eye on the right side of the vehicle, assuming that smaller vehicles may try to pass on the right.

Don't turn wide to the left as you start the turn. A driver who is following may think you are turning left and try to pass on the right.

Remember to use your mirrors. Before, during, and after the turn, you should be checking both the right and left mirrors.

If you must cross into the oncoming lane to make a turn, watch for vehicles approaching. Give them room to go by or stop, but never back up. You might hit someone behind your vehicle.

Left turns

When executing a left turn, make sure the vehicle has reached the center of the intersection before starting the turn. Starting it too soon will lead to the trailer taking a shorter path. Anything in that path will be run over (light poles, traffic signs, other vehicles).

If there are two turning lanes, always take the lane furthest to the right. Don't start on the inside lane, as you may have to swing right to make the turn.

Space when crossing and entering traffic

Because of slow acceleration and the length of your vehicle, you will need a larger gap to enter traffic than you would in your personal vehicle. Also keep in mind that acceleration varies with the load. Allow more room if your vehicle is heavily loaded.

Before starting across a road, make sure you can get all the way across before traffic reaches you. It can take 7-15 seconds to clear an intersection. If you miss a gear or cross a large intersection, it could take longer.

Summary

This chapter has covered the importance of managing all of the space around your vehicle and how to develop a safety cushion. In combination, speed and space management play an important role in safe vehicle operation.

SPACE MANAGEMENT QUIZ

Directions: *Read each statement carefully and mark the response that best answers the question.*

1. Proper space management includes taking into account space ahead, behind, to the sides, above, and below your vehicle.
   A. True
   B. False

2. The space _____ your vehicle is most important, and one of the easiest to monitor and adjust as needed.
   A. Behind
   B. To the sides of
   C. Above
   D. Ahead of

3. In good driving conditions, you should allow at least one second for each 10 feet of vehicle length at speeds below 40 mph.
   A. True
   B. False

4. Which of the following is a step you should take to prevent an accident if you are being tailgated?
   A. Slam on the brakes
   B. Speed up
   C. Increase your following distance
   D. All of the above

5. When managing your vehicle's space to the sides, you should:
   A. Hug the center line
   B. Avoid traveling alongside other vehicles
   C. Hug the right side of the road
   D. All of the above

6. Never assume that heights posted on bridges and overpasses are correct.
   A. True
   B. False

7. If you have doubts about whether there is enough space overhead to proceed, you should:
   A. Empty the vehicle's cargo and reload the vehicle after passing under the bridge/overpass
   B. Increase your vehicle's speed
   C. Take another route
   D. All of the above

8. Fast and quick is the rule when driving on an unpaved lot or dirt road.
   A. True
   B. False

9. Because of wide turning and off-tracking, tractor-trailers run the risk of hitting other vehicles or objects during turns.
   A. True
   B. False

10. Because a tractor-trailer is able to accelerate at a quicker rate, you need a smaller gap than other types of vehicles to enter traffic when at an intersection.
    A. True
    B. False

COMBINATION VEHICLE CDL PRE-TEST

Read each question carefully and select the most correct answer.

1. How do you supply air to the air tank on the trailer? You supply air to the trailer tank by:
   A. Pushing in the trailer air supply knob/valve
   B. Pulling out the trailer air supply knob/valve
   C. Connecting the emergency line glad hand
   D. Applying the trolley valve

2. In normal driving, some drivers use the trolley (hand) valve before the brake pedal. Which of these statements is true?
   A. It should never be done
   B. It results in less skidding than using the brake pedal alone
   C. It lets the driver steer with both hands
   D. It is the best way to brake in a straight line

3. When backing under the trailer, you should:
   A. Use the lowest reverse gear
   B. Back the tractor slowly under the trailer
   C. Stop when the kingpin is locked into the fifth wheel
   D. All of the above

4. When backing up under a trailer, you should line up:
   A. About 15 degrees off the line of the trailer
   B. The right mirror along the right edge of the trailer
   C. Directly in front of the trailer
   D. To the far left of the trailer

5. _____are coupling devices used to connect the service and emergency air lines from a truck or tractor to the trailer.
   A. Clamps
   B. Shut-off valves
   C. Hand valves
   D. Glad hands

CHAPTER 12

Night driving

OBJECTIVES

Upon completion of this chapter, you should have a basic understanding of:

- The factors that affect night driving including the driver, roadway, and vehicle
- Procedures for driving at night

13 Night driving

- NIGHT DRIVING FACTORS
- NIGHT DRIVING PROCEDURES
- SUMMARY

Drivers who work the overnight hours trade the hazards of busy, congested roadways for another set of hazards including reduced visibility and impaired drivers. This chapter will address night driving factors and procedures for safely traveling at night.

▌ Night driving factors

Driving at night presents several challenges for the professional driver. Potential hazards include poor lighting, reduced visibility, and impaired drivers. There are three major factors you need to focus on when driving at night; driver, roadway, and vehicle.

Driver factors

The major factors that affect you when operating at night are vision, glare, fatigue, and driver inexperience.

Vision — Put simply, we do not see as well at night as we do during the day. At night, visual acuity is reduced, side vision is poorer, and the eyes have a difficult time adjusting to abrupt changes from darkness to light and back to darkness.

Glare — Glare is another problem. The bright light of oncoming headlights can temporarily blind you. It can take several seconds for your eyes to recover from the effects of glare. This can be dangerous. At 55 mph, a vehicle covers about 150 to 160 feet in two seconds. That is a substantial distance to drive with impaired vision.

Avoid looking directly into bright lights. Look toward the right side of the road and/or right lane edge marking when bright lights approach.

Fatigue — Fatigue is a factor when it comes to safe driving; especially at night. Fatigue can reduce your reaction time to hazards and cause blurred vision. Some of fatigue's warning signs include:

- Drowsiness;
- Frequent or repeated yawning;
- Loss of visual focus;
- Fighting to keep your eyes open;
- Heavy/drooping head;
- Stiff or sore neck muscles;
- Lack of alertness;

More information on the causes of and how to fight fatigue can be found in Chapter 30.

- Poor memory recall;
- Dozing off for a few seconds at a time;
- Weaving from lane-to-lane;
- Making bad driving decisions;
- Erratic speed control;
- Erratic shifting;
- Intermittent shifting; and
- Following vehicles ahead too closely.

Driver inexperience — Inexperience with operating a tractor-trailer under nighttime conditions is also a factor. As with all other aspects of driving this type of vehicle, the more practice and experience you have, the better you will be able to deal with the challenges of driving at night.

Roadway factors

Roadway hazards you face at night include poor visibility, lack of familiarity with your route and its hazards (road construction, curves), impaired drivers, and other road users.

Poor visibility — At night, hazards aren't as easy to see and may not be recognized as quickly as during daylight hours.

In rural areas, you need to depend on your vehicle's headlights for lighting.

In urban areas, lighting levels can vary. Since levels vary, your eyes are required to adjust to different levels of lighting.

Familiarity with route — Though caution should be used on all roads (familiar or unfamiliar) when driving at night, slow down and use extra caution on unfamiliar roads. Make sure you have enough stopping distance.

Impaired drivers — Impaired drivers are a hazard to everyone on the road. Extra caution should be used around closing times for bars and taverns. Keep an eye out for vehicles that weave from lane-to-lane, stop without reason, have trouble maintaining a constant speed, or show other signs of impaired or erratic driving.

Other road users — In many cases, darkness impairs your view of other road users including those who jog, walk, or bike along the side of the road. Pay special attention to roadways that are lined by woods and/or tall grass. Deer, raccoons, and other animals are often on the move at night and can dart into the roadway.

Vehicle factors

Vehicle condition plays a part in safe night driving. A vehicle's lights, turn signals, windshield, and mirrors should be kept clean and in good working condition.

Lights — At night, headlights are the main way to see and be seen on the highway. In good weather, low beams allow you to see about 250 feet ahead and high beams about 350-500 feet ahead. Speed may need to be adjusted so the vehicle can be stopped within the range of the headlights.

All of your vehicle's lights and signals should be clean, in proper working order, and in proper adjustment.

Always drive within the range of the headlights. Driving outside the range of the headlights (over driving the headlights) can adversely affect your ability to recognize hazards.

Other lights that must be clean and work properly include:

- Marker lights;
- Reflectors;
- Clearance lights;
- Taillights; and
- Identification lights.

Turn signals and brake lights — The importance of communicating your intention to turn, change lanes, or stop is multiplied at night. Other drivers may have a hard time seeing your vehicle and understanding your intent. The turn signals and brake lights may be the only way to communicate this information.

Windshield and mirrors — A clean windshield and mirrors are very important at night. Bright lights hitting dirt on a windshield or mirror can create a glare. Dirt on the windshield can also cause problems if driving into a sunrise or sunset.

▮ Night driving procedures

Preparing to drive at night

Being prepared to drive at night can go a long way when it comes to safety. A prepared driver is focused on the task ahead and doesn't have to be concerned with issues such as route planning or whether the vehicle's headlights are working appropriately.

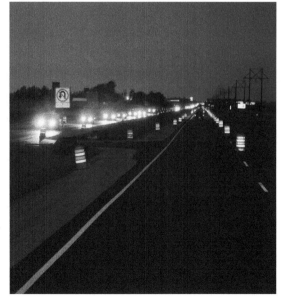

Get yourself ready — Make sure you are rested and alert. The cover of darkness can magnify the effects of fatigue, making night driving more dangerous.

If you wear eyeglasses, make sure they are clean and free of scratches. Scratches can magnify glare, reducing your ability to see clearly. Never wear sunglasses at night.

Plan your route — Know where you are going. Know where you may have to exit or enter a roadway and where construction zones are located. Know where rest stops are located. If you are familiar with your route, keep in mind where hazards are located.

13

Get your vehicle ready — Do a complete pre-trip inspection of your vehicle. When conducting this inspection, pay special attention to the lights, reflectors, and windshield. Clean and replace as needed.

When driving at night

There are additional issues you need to consider when driving at night compared to driving during daylight hours.

Avoid blinding others — Glare from your vehicle's headlights can cause problems for drivers coming toward you. They can also bother drivers going in the same direction as you are, when your vehicle's lights shine into their rearview mirrors. If you are using high beams, dim them before they pose a glare problem for others. This includes dimming your lights within at least 500 feet of an oncoming vehicle and when following another vehicle within 500 feet.

Don't blind yourself — Don't look directly at the lights of an oncoming vehicle. As mentioned earlier in this chapter, look toward the right side of the road and/or right lane edge marking when bright lights approach.

Maximize visibility — Use high beams when it is safe and legal to do so. Remember, high beam headlights should be dimmed within 500 feet of an oncoming vehicle or within 500 feet of a vehicle you are following.

Turn off the vehicle's dome light and adjust the brightness of the instrument lights. This makes it easier to see outside the vehicle.

Also, don't forget to scan your mirrors. As well as maximizing visibility, this helps fight fatigue by helping you avoid staring at one point for a period of time.

Communication — At night, communication is limited to your vehicle's lights and horns. Signal all stops, slowdowns, and direction changes a bit earlier than you would in daylight. Avoid blinding others with lights as a way of signaling. Use the horn sparingly.

Speed and space — Increase following distance at night by at least one second. This will give you extra time and space to spot and react to hazards.

As previously mentioned in this chapter, drive within the range of the headlights. Over driving the headlights can adversely affect visibility as well as your ability to stop for hazards.

When rounding a curve, headlights shine straight ahead (off the road) reducing vision. Reducing vehicle speed is the best way to deal with curves.

▌ Summary

In this chapter, you have learned about the special issues and challenges associated with night driving. This includes the factors that contribute to the increased danger of night driving and the procedures that need to be followed in order to complete a safe nighttime trip.

13

NIGHT DRIVING QUIZ

Directions: *Read each statement carefully and mark the response that best answers the question.*

1. At night, visual acuity is reduced, side vision is poorer, and the eyes have a difficult time adjusting to abrupt changes from darkness to light and back to darkness.
    A. True
    B. False

2. Drowsiness, repeated yawning, and lack of alertness are all signs of_____.
    A. Driver inexperience
    B. Poor visibility
    C. Fatigue
    D. All of the above

3. At night, hazards may not be recognized as quickly as during daylight hours.
    A. True
    B. False

4. A vehicle that weaves from lane-to-lane or has trouble maintaining a constant speed may indicate:
    A. There is fog ahead
    B. Nothing in particular
    C. An impaired driver is behind the wheel
    D. All of the above

5. In good weather, low beam headlights allow you to see about _____.
    A. 150 feet
    B. 250 feet
    C. 500 feet
    D. 1,000 feet

6. In good weather, high beam headlights allow you to see about _____.
    A. 150 to 200 feet
    B. 200 to 250 feet
    C. 250 to 300 feet
    D. 350 to 500 feet

7. To avoid blinding others, high beam headlights should be dimmed within at least _____ of an oncoming vehicle.
    A. 250 feet
    B. 300 feet
    C. 500 feet
    D. All of the above

8. To avoid being blinded by the headlights of another vehicle, you should:
    A. Look directly at the oncoming vehicle's lights
    B. Look slightly to the right
    C. Look slightly to the left
    D. All of the above

9. At night, you should signal all stops, slowdowns, and direction changes later than you would in daylight.
    A. True
    B. False

10. Over driving your vehicle's headlights can adversely affect visibility.
    A. True
    B. False

COMBINATION VEHICLE CDL PRE-TEST

Read each question carefully and select the most correct answer.

1. After hooking up, you should check the fifth wheel connection by:

   A. Driving away at 20 mph and pulling down the trailer hand valve
   B. Backing up with the trailer brakes released
   C. Pulling the tractor ahead sharply to release the trailer brakes
   D. Pulling the tractor ahead gently with the trailer brakes locked

2. How often should you drain your vehicle's trailer air tanks?

   A. Daily
   B. Weekly
   C. Monthly
   D. Yearly

3. The emergency air line supplies air to the trailer air tanks and:

   A. Supplies air to the cab
   B. Controls the emergency brakes on combination vehicles
   C. Are coded with the color green to keep them from getting mixed up with other lines
   D. All of the above

4. How much space should be between the upper and the lower fifth wheel plates?

   A. About 1 inch
   B. About ½ inch
   C. About ¼ inch
   D. None

5. When not pulling a trailer, why is it a good idea to lock the glad hands together or to a dummy coupler?

   A. It keeps air from escaping
   B. The brake circuit becomes a secondary air tank
   C. It keeps dirt and water out of the lines
   D. All of the above

CHAPTER 13

Extreme driving conditions

OBJECTIVES

Upon completion of this chapter, you should have a basic understanding of:

- Operating in adverse driving conditions including snow, ice, and cold temperatures
- Operating in hot weather conditions
- The challenges of mountain driving

14 Extreme driving conditions

- VEHICLE PREPARATION
- EMERGENCY EQUIPMENT
- TIRE CHAIN INSTALLATION
- COLD WEATHER STARTING
- DRIVING HAZARDS
- SKIDDING AND JACKKNIFING
- SLIPPERY SURFACES
- WET BRAKES
- FREEING A STUCK VEHICLE
- BREAKDOWNS
- MOUNTAIN DRIVING
- SUMMARY

Extreme driving conditions demand increased preparation and awareness. Both you and your vehicle must be in top form. This chapter will introduce you to the challenges of operating a tractor-trailer in extreme driving conditions.

▍ Vehicle preparation

Adverse weather conditions (including snow, ice, rain, and fog) demand increased preparation for you and your vehicle. Reduced traction increases stopping distances and decreases vehicle maneuverability and control. Reduced visibility decreases your ability to clearly see hazards.

During the winter months, conditions can change quickly. Being prepared is key to successfully operating in snow, ice, and extreme cold. In addition to your regular vehicle inspections, pay close attention to the items listed below.

Coolant level and antifreeze concentration

Make sure the cooling system is full and that there's enough antifreeze in the vehicle's system. A low coolant level can affect the engine's performance as well as the operation of the vehicle's defroster and heater. Antifreeze concentration can be checked with a tester designed for this purpose.

Defrosting and heating equipment

Make sure the vehicle's defrosters and heater are working and that you know how to operate this equipment. Also check the heaters for the mirrors and fuel tank(s).

Windshield wipers and washers

Make sure the wiper blades are in good condition. The wiper blades need to press against the window hard enough to wipe the windshield clean. This is important in keeping snow off of the windshield. Also make sure the windshield washer works and that there's an appropriate type and amount of washer fluid (fluid that will not freeze in cold weather) in the reservoir. Also check the reservoir for cracks or other damage.

Tires

Check tire tread depth. The drive tires must provide enough traction to operate on wet pavement and snow. The steering tires must have enough traction to steer the vehicle. The front wheels must have a tread depth of at least ⁴⁄₃₂ inch on every major groove to be legal. Other wheels must have a tread depth of at least ²⁄₃₂ inch to be legal. Also check tire mounting and inflation.

Tire chains

You may be faced with conditions which require the use of chains (per state or local law). Prepare for this possibility by carrying the proper size and number of chains as well as extra cross-links. Check the chains for broken hooks, worn or broken cross-links, and bent or broken side chains. Make sure chain slack adjusters are also available if you need them.

Brakes

Brake balance should be checked. The brakes should apply pressure equally at the same time. Check adjustment, and take up any slack. Be careful when setting your brakes in very cold weather. If there is a lot of moisture on them, they could freeze together and you may not be able to release them. One way to avoid this is to lightly ride your brake when exiting the highway or while going through the parking lot. This will help warm the brakes and get rid of moisture.

Also, keep air tanks as moisture-free as possible. Drain both tractor and trailer tanks daily. Moisture in the air lines can cause the vehicle's brakes to freeze. If your vehicle has other moisture-control equipment (alcohol evaporators, spitter valves), make sure they are working properly.

Lights and reflectors

Visibility of lights and reflectors is very important in poor weather conditions. Make sure the vehicle's lights and reflectors are clean (free of dirt, snow, ice, road salt) and check them often. In poor weather, the condition of your lights and reflectors play a big part in determining your range of sight and how well others can see your vehicle.

Windows and mirrors

Remove all ice, snow, and debris from the windshield by using a snow brush and/or scraper and the windshield defroster.

Hand holds, steps, and deck plates

Reduce your chances of slipping and falling by removing all ice and snow from the handholds, steps, and deck plates.

Exposed wiring and air lines

Remove ice and snow from wiring and air lines. At or below zero degrees, plastic air lines can become brittle and can brake very easily. Snow and ice build-up can cause them to sag and possibly get snagged on the tractor, trailer, or the tires.

Fuel tank

Make sure the fuel tank is full before starting out and kept topped off regularly if bad weather is expected. This will help keep water out of the fuel, which can freeze in fuel lines and filters. This is also a good precautionary measure to make sure you don't run out of fuel and are stranded in a dangerous situation. It's also a good idea to always know where your next fuel stop is, even if it's not where you plan on stopping.

Exhaust system

Loose exhaust system connections can cause carbon monoxide to leak into your vehicle. Carbon monoxide is poisonous. It can kill you if you are exposed to it, especially if you are in an area with poor ventilation, like a truck cab with the windows rolled up.

Coupling devices

Before coupling, remove all snow and ice. In below freezing temperatures, the jaws of the coupling device may not lock if the grease is frozen. Double check the locking mechanism and make sure the fifth wheel is lubricated with a winter-grade lubricant. This will help prevent binding and help steering on slippery roads.

Emergency equipment

When it comes to your vehicle you should have the following items:

- Windshield scraper;
- Snow brush;
- Extra windshield washer fluid;
- Small shovel;
- Flashlight;
- Spare batteries;
- Jumper cables; and
- Warning devices.

As for your protection and safety, you should have the following items:

- Drinking water;
- Extra food;
- Medicine (as needed);
- Hats;
- Boots;
- Gloves;
- Extra clothes and blankets; and
- Proper outerwear (heavy jacket, heavy coveralls).

Always stay up to date on the latest road and weather conditions. States provide road reports via the internet and/or toll-free phone numbers. The National Weather Service and other media outlets provide weather forecasts and radar services via the internet as well. Also stay in contact with your dispatcher, as he/she may be able to provide up-to-date information from various sources.

Tire chain installation

Tire chains are constructed to grip the tire around the sides and provide traction across the tread. Installed on the drive wheels, they improve uphill traction. On trailer wheels, they improve

14

traction for downhill braking. Chains help keep your vehicle on the road, and they decrease your chances of getting stuck.

Chains are most effective in heavy snow. In light, dry snow they provide little traction advantage, but do provide some stability. Most chains are not effective on glare ice.

When installing chains, they should be snug, but not too tight. They are designed to creep or move on the tires to prevent gouging or breakage. Chains should be regularly checked and retightened as necessary to prevent slap against the trailer or catching on to the suspension or fuel tank.

Use extreme caution when installing chains:

- Pull well off the road (most areas that require chains have "chain-up" areas);
- Park on a level surface;
- Work facing traffic;
- Know where you are going if confronted by an out of control vehicle;
- Watch your footing; and
- Watch your own vehicle, making sure it doesn't slide.

Many states have laws and/or regulations addressing the type and number of chains that must be used on certain highways and the dates in which they must be carried in the vehicle and used if necessary. Make sure you understand state and local laws for the states in which you travel.

Cold weather starting

The colder it is, the harder it is to start any type of engine. There are a number of devices that can help in starting your vehicle's engine.

Ether and ether-based fluids

There are both good and bad points to using ether to help start your vehicle in cold temperatures. On the good side, ether has a very low flash point and can ignite easily at cold temperatures. On the bad side, if ether is not used properly, it can damage the engine. Also, it can be dangerous to use as it is highly volatile. Too much either could crack your engine block, cause vapor lock, or cause other serious internal damage. Should you spill some on your clothes, stay away from cigarettes, lighters, and heaters and change immediately.

Ether and ether-based fluids come in a variety of forms including:

- Aerosol sprays;
- Pressurized cylinders; and
- Driver-controlled, automatic injection systems.

Aerosol sprays and pressurized cylinders are used manually and require the placement of ether into the air intake. The automatic injection system is activated by either the driver turning on a switch in the cab or the vehicle automatically injecting ether when the vehicle is started.

No matter what form of ether you may use, always use extreme caution to prevent an accident and/or injury.

Glow plugs

Glow plugs are electric heating elements that warm air coming into the engine from the air intake. Consult your vehicle's owner's manual for specific operating instructions.

Preheaters

Preheaters keep the engine warm while your vehicle is parked for an extended period of time. Most truck tractors use an in-block type of preheater. In-block heaters fit into the freeze plug holes in the lower water jacket. They are then plugged into an electrical outlet. Coolant is heated to 160°F and the heated coolant is circulated throughout the engine. This eliminates warm-up, allowing you to use normal starting procedures.

In extremely cold areas, coolant heaters are frequently supplemented with battery box heaters, oil sump heaters, and fuel heaters. Consult your vehicle's owner's manual and maintenance personnel for proper operation.

If your engine doesn't start

If your vehicle's engine won't start with the use of starting aids, check the fuel and electrical systems. To make sure your vehicle is getting enough fuel, watch the exhaust stack while cranking your engine. If you don't see vapor or smoke, the engine may not be getting fuel. Don't continue to crank the engine, as this will run down the battery. Check the fuel tank and fuel lines for ice blockage. Also check the fuel tank vent.

Never crank the engine for more than 15 seconds. If the engine is getting fuel, but isn't starting, there could be a problem in the electrical system. Check the battery for terminal corrosion, loose connections, cracks in cables, and moisture on cables.

If your vehicle has an air starter, it needs an air supply to start. If there is no air, you'll need to resupply air from either an air compressor or another tractor. Check the vehicle's owner's manual for specific procedures.

14

▌ Driving hazards

There are two main hazards when driving in adverse winter weather conditions, reduced visibility and reduced traction.

Reduced visibility

When snow and ice buildup on your vehicle's lights, windows, and mirrors your visibility is reduced in all directions (front, side, and rear). If operating properly, your vehicle's defroster and windshield wipers will keep the windshield clean and clear. However, you will need to stop to clean off the side windows and mirrors. Never drive if you cannot see in all directions.

As mentioned earlier in this chapter, snow, ice, and dirt can build up on your vehicle's lights and reflectors. This reduces your visibility and the ability of other drivers to see your vehicle. Frequently clean all lights and reflectors.

Snow and ice can greatly reduce your visibility. Adjust your speed in bad weather to compensate for limited visibility. If you are unable to see, do not continue driving. Pull off the road at the nearest safe place and stop until conditions improve.

A trip in adverse conditions will take longer than in good driving conditions. As well as having to slow down due to reduced visibility and/or traction, more stops should be made to clean off windows, lights, and mirrors. Make sure you account for this extra time when planning a trip.

Reduced traction

Different surfaces have a different amount of traction. For example, a snow-packed or ice-covered surface will have only one-fifth (20 percent) of the traction that the same surface does when it's wet.

Slippery surfaces reduce traction, causing a vehicle's drive wheels to spin easily. This impairs your ability to maneuver the vehicle. Proper tire inflation and tread as well as proper weight on the drive wheels increases traction and improves maneuverability.

Traction is needed for accelerating, turning, and braking. As vehicle speed increases, more traction is needed. If traction is poor, you must reduce your speed.

On a wet surface, you may need to reduce your speed by one-fourth or more. For example, if you normally travel at 65 mph on a stretch of road, you will need to reduce your speed to about 45-48 mph.

As a general rule, you can drive about one-half your normal speed on packed snow. If you usually travel at 65 mph, you should cut your speed to about 30-32 mph.

Note that these are suggested guidelines. Only you, the professional driver can determine a safe speed when it comes to traveling in adverse conditions.

On ice, cut your speed to about one-third of your normal speed. Again, if traveling at 65 mph, slow to about 18-20 mph.

Black ice is one of the most dangerous road conditions, as most drivers aren't aware of black ice until it is too late. Black ice forms when temperatures drop rapidly and hover around the freezing mark (32°F).

Any moisture on the road freezes into a smooth, nearly invisible, slippery surface.

On cold days, when the road is wet, pay extra attention to the spray thrown from other vehicles. If the spray suddenly stops, black ice may be forming.

The most common places for black ice to form include:

- Bridges;
- Beneath underpasses;
- Dips in the road where water can collect and freeze;
- Shaded areas from buildings, trees, hills, and embankments; and
- The lower side of banked curves.

Also, watch for rain turning into freezing rain as temperatures drop. Listen for a change in the sound of your tires on the road. Watch for spray from other vehicles suddenly disappearing. Feel for ice on the front of your outside mirror. Watch the vehicle's antenna for signs of ice formation.

Skidding and jackknifing

There are three basic causes of skidding and jackknifing: overacceleration, overbraking, and oversteering.

Overacceleration — Too much acceleration sends too much power to the drive wheels, causing them to spin.

Overbraking — Braking too hard for conditions causes wheels to lock-up.

Oversteering — Turning the steering wheel too quickly can cause the front wheels to slide, the drive tires to slide, or the trailer to skid or swing out.

Driver error is a major contributor when it comes to skidding and jackknifing.

Slippery surfaces

Drive slowly and deliberately on slippery roads. If the road is so slippery that it is unsafe to proceed, stop at a safe place and wait for conditions to improve. Take the following steps when operating on what could be a slippery road:

- Don't hurry. Give yourself plenty of time to get a feel for the road.
- Make turns as gently as possible.
- Don't brake any harder than necessary.
- Don't use the engine brake or speed retarder.
- Never pump antilock brakes (if your vehicle is so equipped).
- Don't pass slower vehicles unless necessary.
- Go slow and steady. Avoid having to slow down and speed up.
- Take curves at slower speeds and don't brake while in curves.

- Know that roads become more slippery as temperatures rise to the point where ice begins to melt.
- Road temperatures and air temperatures can vary widely.
- Don't drive next to other vehicles.
- Keep a larger following distance.
- If you see a traffic jam ahead, slow down or stop until it has cleared.
- Try to anticipate stops so you can slow down gradually.

Wet brakes

When driving in heavy rain or deep standing water, your vehicle's brakes will get wet. Water in the brakes can reduce their effectiveness. This can cause a lack of braking power, wheel lock-ups, pulling to one side or the other, and vehicle jackknife (if pulling a trailer).

If possible, avoid driving through deep puddles or flowing water. If you can't avoid this, take the following steps:

1. Slow down.
2. Place the vehicle transmission in a low gear.
3. Increase engine speed (rpm).
4. Cross the water while keeping light pressure on the brakes.

When out of the water, keep light pressure on the brakes for a short distance. This heats up and dries out the brakes. Make a test stop if it is safe to do so. Check behind you to make sure no one is following, then apply the brakes to make sure they work correctly. If they aren't working correctly, again apply light pressure on the brakes and travel a short distance. Do not apply too much brake pressure and accelerate at the same time. This can cause the brake drums and linings to overheat.

Freeing a stuck vehicle

The best way to deal with freeing a stuck vehicle is by not getting stuck in the first place. The best way to prevent getting stuck is by avoiding soft shoulders, deep snow, muddy roads, and icy/slippery surfaces.

If you do get stuck, don't panic, and take the following steps:

1. Avoid spinning the drive wheels and rocking. This digs the vehicle in deeper. On ice or snow, spinning wheels warm the ice or snow under the tires, reducing traction even more.
2. Use traction aids. Dig out from in front of the wheels. Scatter sand or gravel in the wheel path. Lay loose chains in front of the vehicle's tires.
3. When ready to try pulling out, start with the steering wheel facing straight ahead. Don't turn the wheels until the vehicle is moving.
4. Start in second or third gear, using very little power. This keeps the wheels from spinning and gives a smoother application of force.
5. Accelerate smoothly and gently. Ease off at the first sign of spinning or slipping. Allowing the wheels to continue spinning can cause you to dig in deeper and/or cause a spin out.

Towing

If all of the procedures to free your vehicle fail, you may need to call a tow truck. Remember, even if towing is necessary, you are still responsible for your vehicle and cargo. You need to stay in charge of the situation, not the tow truck operator. Supervise the operation. If the tow truck operator does something wrong or unsafe, stop the operation, and correct the problem.

The tow chain or cable should be hooked to the vehicle following these steps:

1. Make sure there's enough chain or cable, so once freed, your vehicle doesn't lurch into the tow truck.

2. In hooking up, pass the chain or cable through the hole in the bumper, but do not hook it to the bumper.

3. Attach the chain or cable to a solid portion of the frame or a frame cross member. (Some vehicles are equipped with tow hooks protruding from the frame.) Be careful not to get the chain around the steering tie-rod or spring shackles along with the axle.

Before towing, agree on a procedure to be followed. Know the direction the tow truck will pull and the direction your vehicle is to be steered. Agree on a signal that you can both clearly hear or see for stopping (if you run into problems) or for when your rig is clear. Also, make sure all bystanders are out of the way just in case a chain or cable snaps.

As the towing procedure starts, accelerate the tractor gently, just enough to turn the wheels slowly. When you have been pulled clear, signal the tow truck driver to stop accelerating immediately. Apply the tractor-trailer brakes. This prevents your vehicle from rear ending the tow truck.

▌ Breakdowns

A vehicle breakdown can be dangerous at any time, but it is especially dangerous in adverse weather conditions. Exposure to wind and cold can cause frostbite. Blowing and drifting snow can be disorientating. If your vehicle breaks down in adverse conditions, stay in the cab.

Put on extra clothing to stay warm. Use your food and beverage supply cautiously. Depending on weather conditions and the amount of traffic on the road, you could be stranded for a while. If the vehicle's engine is able to run, idle the engine to keep the truck warm.

Don't try to walk for help unless it is absolutely necessary. If you must leave your vehicle, leave a note on the steering wheel stating when you left, where you were headed, and when you think you may return.

14

▮ Mountain driving

In mountain driving, gravity plays a major role on both upgrades and downgrades. Because of this, it is important that your vehicle's brakes are in top condition. If your vehicle is equipped with an air brake system, you should check for the following:

- Compressor maintaining full reservoir pressure;
- Pressure drop on full application within limitations;
- Slack adjusters for full push rod travel, within specifications;
- Audible air leaks, applied and released;
- Drums for overheating; and
- Trailer protection valve operation.

> *There are several ways to address the topic of mountain (uphill/downhill) driving. The approach that will be taken in this text is the one recommended in the commercial driver's license manual distributed by state driver licensing agencies.*

Upgrades

The force of gravity causes all vehicles to slow down on upgrades, making it difficult to maintain a constant speed.

The steepness and length of the grade, as well as the weight of the load on the vehicle, all play a part in which gear you select to safely travel on an upgrade. The steeper and/or longer the grade and the heavier the load, the lower the gear you should select. If you select a gear that is too high for conditions, your vehicle could overheat and possibly stall.

The vehicle's gauges should also be monitored as the vehicle heads uphill. The task of traveling uphill causes all of the vehicle's components to work harder than when traveling on a flat roadway.

This additional work causes the engine to create more heat. If the vehicle's gauges indicate high temperatures, a decrease in engine oil pressure, or if water and exhaust gas temperature readings are abnormal, pull over in a safe area and allow the engine to cool down.

When traveling uphill on a multi-laned road, travel in the right lane. This will allow smaller, faster vehicles to pass safely. Continue to pay attention to the traffic surrounding your vehicle. Especially to the left and rear.

Downgrades

Gravity's pull forces all vehicles to speed up on downgrades. To help combat the forces of gravity when traveling downhill, select:

- An appropriate speed;
- A low gear; and
- Proper braking technique.

An appropriate speed is one that is slow enough to allow a vehicle's brakes to hold the vehicle without the brakes overheating and fading. If you have to continually increase the pressure applied to the brakes to get the same stopping power, the brakes will eventually fade until there's little to no stopping control.

When selecting an appropriate speed, consider the total weight of the vehicle and its cargo, the grade's steepness and length, and weather and road conditions.

As with upgrades, stay to the right, allowing other vehicles to pass. Also be aware of any warning signs along the roadway. The signs may indicate maximum vehicle size or safe rate of speed for handling the grade.

The braking effect of the engine should be used as the primary way to control the vehicle's speed. The engine's braking effect is greatest when it is near the governed RPMs and the transmission is in the lower gears.

Before starting down a grade, shift the transmission into a low gear. Once a vehicle's speed has been built up, it will be difficult, if not impossible to downshift.

If you attempt to downshift with a manual transmission, the vehicle may get stuck in neutral. This can cause a vehicle to coast downhill and lose all braking effect, creating what can be a very dangerous situation.

Forcing an automatic transmission to shift into a lower gear can damage the transmission and can cause the vehicle to lose all braking effect.

How brakes can fail

Anytime a brake is used, heat is created. The rubbing of the brake pad against the brake drum or disc is what creates this heat. Excessive heat, caused by excessive braking can cause brakes to fail.

All brakes must be adjusted and operating properly to safely and efficiently control a vehicle.

If some brakes are out of adjustment, others may become overworked, causing them to overheat and fade, leaving a driver with little or no braking control.

As with all vehicle components, brake adjustment should be checked often, but it should be given even more attention when you are ready to head downhill.

Braking technique

The following is proper braking technique for a vehicle traveling in the proper, low gear.

1. Identify a safe speed for the load and grade. In most cases, this speed will be less than the posted speed limit. Keep in mind that posted speed limits are meant for cars.

2. When that speed is reached, apply the brakes hard enough to feel a definite slowdown.

3. Once the vehicle's speed has been reduced by 5 mph below the vehicle's safe speed, release the brakes. The application of the brakes should last about 3 seconds.

4. When the vehicle's speed increases back to or above the safe speed, repeat the first two steps.

14

For example, if the vehicle's safe speed is 30 mph, don't apply the brakes until the vehicle's speed has reached 30 mph. Then, the brakes should be applied just hard enough to gradually reduce the vehicle's speed to 25 mph. Once at 25 mph, the brakes may be released.

Pay close attention to the signs posted at the top of the grade. Take note of the steepness of the grade, the total miles to descend the grade, the posted speed limit, and the distance to the next escape ramp.

Escape ramps

Escape ramps are found on steep mountain downgrades. They are designed to help in safely stopping a runaway vehicle. These ramps can help save lives when a vehicle's brakes fail. There are four basic types of escape ramps.

Gravity ramps — Gravity ramps are found on steep ascending grades. They are constructed of a pea gravel surface with mounds of sand or gravel at the end of the ramp.

Always be prepared for the worst. Know the location of the escape ramps and have a plan on how you use the escape ramp if your vehicle has an equipment failure.

Sand piles — Sand piles contain mounds or ridges tall enough to drag the undercarriage of a vehicle.

Arrester beds — Arrester beds have large masses of loose material (at least 18 inches deep), causing a vehicle to sink.

Ramp and arrester bed combinations — This combination relies on both loose surface material and long grades to slow a vehicle.

▍ Summary

In this chapter, you have been introduced to the challenges of and how to handle extreme driving conditions.

14

EXTREME DRIVING CONDITIONS QUIZ

Directions: *Read each statement carefully and mark the response that best answers the question.*

1. When operating in winter driving conditions, you should pay close attention to _____ when conducting vehicle inspections.
   A. Coolant level
   B. Windshield wipers and washers
   C. Coupling devices
   D. All of the above

2. Tire chains are most effective on:
   A. Glare ice
   B. Light, dry snow
   C. Heavy snow
   D. All of the above

3. A windshield scraper, snow brush, and small shovel are just some of the emergency items you should carry in your vehicle.
   A. True
   B. False

4. _____ occurs when moisture on the road freezes into a smooth, nearly invisible, slippery surface.
   A. Brown ice
   B. Black ice
   C. Blue ice
   D. Plaid ice

5. The three basic causes of skidding and jackknifing are:
   A. Dry powdery snow, rain, and wind
   B. Underacceleration, underbraking, and understeering
   C. Overacceleration, overbraking, and oversteering
   D. All of the above

6. When driving on a slippery surface:
   A. Get the feel of the road
   B. Go slow
   C. Watch far enough ahead to keep a steady speed
   D. All of the above

7. If you believe a road is too slippery to safely proceed, you should:
   A. Stop at the first safe place and wait for conditions to improve
   B. Reduce your vehicle's speed to 5 mph
   C. Pass other vehicles with extreme caution
   D. Keep on driving so you aren't late in making your delivery

8. Water in the brakes can cause a lack of braking power.
   A. True
   B. False

9. When operating in hot weather conditions, you should pay close attention to _____ when conducting vehicle inspections.
   A. Coolant level
   B. Windshield wipers and washers
   C. Coupling devices
   D. All of the above

10. _____ plays a major role in mountain driving.
    A. Amount of sunshine
    B. Temperature
    C. Gravity
    D. All of the above

GENERAL KNOWLEDGE CDL PRE-TEST

Read each question carefully and select the most correct answer.

1. While driving, you are looking ahead of your vehicle. How should you be looking?

   A. Look to the right side of the roadway
   B. Look back and forth and near and far
   C. Stare straight ahead at all times
   D. All of the above

2. When you are driving at night, you should:

   A. Always use your high beam headlights
   B. Watch the white line on the left side of the roadway
   C. Adjust your vehicle speed so as to keep your stopping distance within your sight distance
   D. Keep your high beams on at all times

3. Most serious skids are a result of:

   A. Driving too fast for conditions
   B. Improper loading of the vehicle
   C. Not braking hard enough
   D. All of the above

4. If you drive through heavy rain or standing water, your brakes may get wet. What can this cause when you apply the brakes?

   A. Trailer jackknife
   B. Your brakes to heat up
   C. Hydroplaning
   D. Hydroplaning if you were traveling faster than 30 mph when you applied brakes

5. Which of the following is true about the use of reflective emergency triangles?

   A. The regulation requires they be placed within 10 minutes of stopping
   B. You do not need to use them if you break down as long as your 4-way flashers are working
   C. You do not need to use them as long as you have pulled your vehicle completely off the traveled portion of the roadway
   D. You do not need to use them if you stop on a hill or curve

Hazard perception

OBJECTIVES

Upon completion of this chapter, you should have a basic understanding of:

- Hazard recognition
- Road hazards
- User hazards
- The importance of planning ahead

15 Hazard perception

- HAZARD RECOGNITION
- ROAD HAZARDS
- USER HAZARDS
- PLAN AHEAD
- SUMMARY

Any road user or road condition can be a potential hazard. Learning to recognize hazards is a skill that you should continually work on and will continually develop as you proceed in your professional driving career. This chapter will introduce you to the nature of hazards, and the clues to recognizing them.

Hazard recognition

A hazard is any road condition or road user that can pose a potential danger to the motoring public. Being aware of and anticipating potential hazards is key to effective hazard perception which, in turn, helps in preventing accidents.

In some ways, hazard perception is like doing detective work. You should be continually looking for clues; signs that you could be dealing with a potential hazard. This includes scanning the road ahead and the area around your vehicle. The clues or signs you are looking for fall into two major categories, road hazards and user hazards.

Road hazards

Road hazards appear in many different forms. They may be naturally occurring, man-made, or a combination.

Road hazards are outstanding characteristics of the road surface that could adversely affect your ability to control your vehicle or see clearly.

Road hazards include:

- Pavement drop-offs;
- Road construction/work zones;
- Road debris;
- Off-ramps; and
- On-ramps.

Pavement drop-offs

Sometimes, the pavement drops off sharply near the edge of the road. Driving too close to the edge can cause a vehicle to suddenly tilt. This can cause a vehicle to hit roadside objects (tree limbs, signs). Also, it can be hard to steer when crossing a drop-off.

Road construction/work zones

Traveling through a work zone can present several challenges. There may be narrow lanes, sharp turns, poor visibility, unclear lane markings, or uneven surfaces. Other drivers are often distracted and may drive unsafely. Workers and construction vehicles may get in the way.

Road debris

Foreign objects (debris) can be a road hazard. Debris can be a danger to tires and wheel rims, damage electrical and brake lines, and get caught between dual tires causing severe damage.

Some obstacles which appear harmless can be very dangerous. A box or bag that appears to be empty may contain a heavy material, causing damage.

It is very important to keep an eye out for objects in the road, and see them early enough in order to avoid them without making unsafe, sudden moves.

Off-ramps

Freeway and turnpike exits can be particularly dangerous. Off-ramps often have speed limit signs posted, but the posted speed is the recommended speed for an automobile, and may not be safe for a larger vehicle. Exits that go downhill and turn at the same time can be especially dangerous. The downhill grade makes it difficult to reduce speed.

On-ramps

A driver entering a freeway or turnpike may not be paying attention. He/she may not notice a vehicle approaching from behind or the side. In some cases, on-ramps have a short upgrade. This makes it difficult for a heavy vehicle to get up to speed and merge.

User hazards

Anticipating a situation is key to avoiding a user hazard. The following are considered user hazards:

- Intersections;
- Blocked vision;
- Parked vehicles;
- Children and animals;
- Disabled vehicles;
- Inattentive/distracted drivers;
- Confused drivers; and
- Accidents.

Intersections

Vehicles may be hidden by a blind intersection or alley. A driver may not have a clear view of traffic and may pull into the intersection or roadway. Always be prepared to stop.

Blocked vision

People who can't see others can be a danger. It is important to be alert for drivers whose vision is blocked. Vans and cars with rear windows blocked are a couple of examples. Rental trucks should also be watched carefully. In many cases, rental truck drivers aren't used to the limited vision they have to the sides and rear of the truck. In winter, vehicles with ice or snow covered windows are a hazard.

Parked vehicles

A parked vehicle can be hazardous when it is starting to pull out into traffic or is suddenly starting up and driving into traffic. Watch for movement inside the vehicle or movement of the vehicle itself that shows people are inside. Keep an eye out for brake lights, backup lights, exhaust, or other clues that a driver is about to move.

Children

Children tend to act quickly without checking traffic. They may dart into the road or between parked vehicles to retrieve a ball or chase another child. Pay extra attention when traveling through school zones and at bus stops.

Disabled vehicles

Drivers changing a tire or working on an engine may not pay attention to traffic. Jacked-up wheels or raised hoods are hazard clues.

Inattentive drivers

People who are distracted can be a hazard. Texting, cell phone use, eating, and drinking are all common driver distractions. Pay attention to where other drivers are looking. If they are looking elsewhere, they can't see you.

Confused drivers

Confused drivers often change direction or stop without warning. Confusion is common near freeway or turnpike interchanges and major intersections.

Tourists unfamiliar with an area can be hazardous. Clues to watch for when looking for tourists include car top luggage, trailers, and out-of-state license plates.

Hesitation is another sign of confusion. Keep an eye out for vehicles driving very slowly, frequent use of brakes, or drivers looking at signs or maps.

Accidents

People involved in an accident may not look for traffic. Passing drivers tend to look at the accident. People often run across the road without looking and vehicles may slow down or stop suddenly.

▌ Plan ahead

Strong observation skills as well as the ability to think fast and quickly develop a plan are important. A hazard can easily turn into an emergency situation. Good preparation can improve safety for everyone on the road. You should:

- Stay alert;
- Aim high (scan at least 12-15 seconds ahead of your vehicle);
- Scan, see the whole picture, use your mirrors;
- Identify your options; and
- Execute (carry out your plan).

▌ Summary

In this chapter, you have learned about the types of hazards that can pose a potential danger to the professional driver as well as ways to identify these hazards well in advance. These skills are important when it comes to accident prevention and keeping you and your vehicle safe.

15

HAZARD PERCEPTION QUIZ

Directions: *Read each statement carefully and mark the response that best answers the question.*

1. A hazard is any road condition or road user that can pose a potential danger to the motoring public.
   A. True
   B. False

2. _____ hazards are outstanding characteristics of the road surface that could adversely affect your ability to control your vehicle or see clearly.
   A. User
   B. Pedestrian
   C. Road
   D. All of the above

3. _____ is a road hazard.
   A. Children
   B. Pavement drop-offs
   C. Disabled vehicles
   D. All of the above

4. An object which appears to be harmless (paper bag or box) can actually pose a danger to you and your vehicle.
   A. True
   B. False

5. The speed limit posted on an off-ramp is the safe, recommended speed for all vehicles.
   A. True
   B. False

6. Blocked vision, parked vehicles, and disabled vehicles are _____.
   A. User hazards
   B. Pedestrian hazards
   C. Road hazards
   D. All of the above

7. _____ is a user hazard.
   A. An inattentive driver
   B. A confused driver
   C. An accident
   D. All of the above

8. Driver hesitation, changing direction, or stopping without warning are signs of a confused driver.
   A. True
   B. False

9. When it comes to hazard perception, strong observations skills are not important.
   A. True
   B. False

10. Good preparation on your part can improve safety for all road users.
    A. True
    B. False

Read each question carefully and select the most correct answer.

1. When you are driving through construction zones, you should:
   A. Speed up and hurry through them so you aren't in them any longer than necessary
   B. Stop before entering them, get in low gear and proceed through
   C. Watch for uneven surfaces
   D. Reduce your speed only if construction workers are near the roadway

2. If you break down on a level, straight, four-lane, divided highway, where should you place the reflective warning triangles?
   A. One 10 feet from the rear of the vehicle, one approximately 100 feet from the rear of the vehicle and another one about 100 feet to the front of the vehicle
   B. One 10 feet from the rear of the vehicle, one approximately 100 feet from the rear of the vehicle, and one about 200 feet from the rear of the vehicle
   C. One 100 feet from the rear of the vehicle, one approximately 200 feet from the rear of the vehicle, and one about 300 feet from the rear of the vehicle
   D. One 50 feet from the rear of the vehicle, one about 100 feet from the rear of the vehicle, and one about 200 feet from the front of the vehicle

3. According to the Commercial Driver's manual, why should you limit the use of your vehicle's horn?
   A. If your vehicle has air brakes, the air horn may not work while you are applying your brakes
   B. It may startle other drivers
   C. You should keep both hands on the steering wheel at all times
   D. The Driver's Manual does not say that a driver should limit the use of the horn

4. Which of the following should you do when dealing with a tailgater?
   A. Increase your following distance
   B. Avoid quick changes
   C. Avoid tricks such as flashing your brake lights
   D. All of the above

5. The proper way to load a vehicle is:
   A. Keep the load balanced in the cargo area
   B. Place the load at the front of the trailer to give your drive wheels better traction
   C. Place the load at the rear of the trailer so your rear tires have better traction
   D. It makes no difference where the cargo is placed as long as you are not over the allowable gross weight

Railroad crossings

OBJECTIVES

Upon completion of this chapter, you should understand the importance of and methods for:

- Determining when stopping is required
- Stopping at and crossing tracks safely
- Recognizing crossing signs, gates, and signals
- Emergency procedures

16 Railroad crossings

- THE REGULATIONS
- TYPES OF WARNING DEVICES
- SIGNS AND SIGNALS
- SAFETY TIPS
- SUMMARY

With over 200,000 highway-rail grade crossings in the United States, every driver must know how to cross railroad tracks safely. That is especially true for drivers of long, heavy vehicles like tractor-trailer combinations.

This chapter will address safely crossing railroad tracks including regulatory requirements, emergency procedures, and recognition of safety devices and signs.

▌ The regulations

A highway-rail grade crossing is the area where a roadway (highway, road, street) crosses a railway at grade. In other words, where both the roadway and the railway are at the same level at the crossing point, as opposed to grade-separated overpasses or underpasses.

Highway-rail grade crossing regulations for commercial motor vehicles (CMVs) are addressed in Part 392 of the Federal Motor Carrier Safety Regulations (FMCSRs).

Section 392.10 requires that certain types of CMVs stop within 50 feet of, and no closer than 15 feet to the railroad tracks. CMVs that must stop include:

In 2014, there were 2,287 collisions at railroad crossings in the United States. According to Federal Railroad Administration data, these incidents resulted in 269 deaths and 849 injuries.

- Buses transporting passengers;
- CMVs transporting any quantity of a Division 2.3 chlorine;
- CMVs required to be marked or placarded with one of the following classifications:

  - ◆ Division 1.1;
  - ◆ Division 1.2 or Division 1.3;
  - ◆ Division 2.3 Poison gas;
  - ◆ Division 4.3;
  - ◆ Class 7;
  - ◆ Class 3 Flammable;
  - ◆ Division 5.1;
  - ◆ Division 2.2;
  - ◆ Division 2.3 Chlorine;

  - ◆ Division 6.1 Poison;
  - ◆ Division 2.2 Oxygen;
  - ◆ Division 2.1;
  - ◆ Class 3 Combustible liquid;
  - ◆ Division 4.1;
  - ◆ Division 5.1;
  - ◆ Division 5.2;
  - ◆ Class 8; or
  - ◆ Division 1.4.

- Cargo tank CMVs, whether loaded or empty, used for the transportation of any hazardous material; and
- Cargo tank CMVs transporting commodities under specific circumstances (see Sec. 392.10).

When at a railroad crossing, you must listen and look in each direction along the tracks for an approaching train and make certain a train is not approaching. Do not shift gears when crossing the tracks.

There are also certain instances when stopping at railroad tracks isn't required. This includes:

- A streetcar crossing, or railroad tracks used exclusively for industrial switching purposes, within a business district, as defined in Sec. 390.5 of the FMCSRs;

- A railroad grade crossing when a police officer or crossing flagman directs traffic to proceed;

- A railroad grade crossing controlled by a functioning highway traffic signal transmitting a green indication which, under local law, permits the CMV to proceed across the railroad tracks without slowing or stopping;

- An abandoned railroad grade crossing which is marked with a sign indicating that the rail line is abandoned; and

- An industrial or spur line railroad grade crossing marked with a sign reading "Exempt."

If the CMV is not required to stop, Sec. 392.11 of the FMCSRs requires that the vehicle travel at a rate of speed that is slow enough to stop before reaching the tracks.

Your CMV may not cross the tracks until you are certain the crossing is clear.

Also, Sec. 392.12 of the FMCSRs states that you must ensure that you have sufficient space to drive completely through a highway-rail grade crossing without stopping.

Driver disqualification

A conviction for any one of six highway-rail grade crossing offenses while operating a CMV requiring a commercial driver's license will disqualify a driver from operating a CMV. The offenses, which are listed in Sec. 383.51 of the FMCSRs include:

> *Disqualification is a very serious issue for the professional driver. A driver who is disqualified may not drive, and his/her motor carrier may not require/allow the driver to drive a CMV for the disqualification period.*

- Failing to stop or slow down when required;

- Failing to have enough space to completely cross without stopping;

- Failing to obey a traffic control device; and

- Failing to negotiate a crossing because the CMV has insufficient undercarriage clearance.

The disqualification period ranges from 60 days for the first conviction to one year for three or more convictions in a three year period.

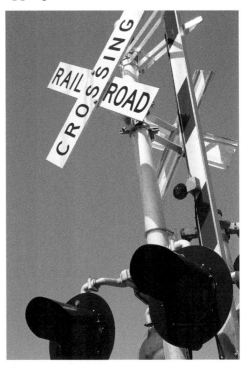

Types of warning devices

There are two basic types of warning devices at railroad crossings, passive and active.

Active warning devices

Active warning devices activate automatically when a train approaches a highway-rail grade crossing. They include gates, bells, lights, traffic signals, and other physical barriers. Active devices offer greater protection than passive devices.

Passive warning devices

Passive warning devices are not electronic and do not give notice of the approach of a train. Passive devices are intended to direct the driver's attention to the crossing so the driver may exercise caution. These devices include crossbuck signs, stop signs, yield signs, pavement markings, and constantly flashing lights.

Signs and signals

It is important to know and understand the various signs and signals that are posted to alert you to an upcoming crossing. The following are a few of the most commonly used signs and signals.

Crossbuck signs

A crossbuck sign is one of the oldest warning devices. It is a white, regulatory, X-shaped sign with the words "Railroad Crossing" in black lettering. It is located alongside the highway prior to the railroad tracks.

In most cases, the crossbuck sign is installed on the right-hand side of a public roadway on each approach to the highway-rail grade crossing. A crossbuck sign is a passive yield sign and is considered the same as a "Yield" sign. The crossbuck sign is required at all public highway-rail grade crossings.

Advance warning sign

An advance warning sign is a round, yellow warning sign with a black "X" and "RR." These signs are located alongside the highway in advance of the crossing, and serve to alert motorists to the crossing.

The advance warning sign is usually the first sign you see when approaching a highway-rail grade crossing.

Flashing light signal

This is a device installed on a standard mast which, when activated, displays red lights flashing alternately. Flashing light signals activate upon the approach or presence of a train at a highway-

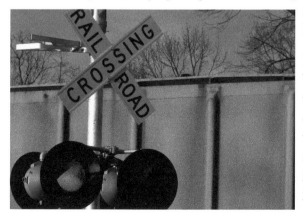

rail grade crossing and require a complete stop by the highway user.

Flashing light signals are mandatory with gates. When both are activated, the gate arm light nearest the tip will be illuminated continuously and the other two lights shall flash alternately in unison with the flashing light signals. The typical flashing light signal assembly on a side-of-the-roadway location includes a standard crossbuck sign and, where there is more than one track, an auxiliary "number of

16

tracks" sign, all of which indicate a highway-rail grade crossing ahead. A bell may be included in the assembly and operated in conjunction with the flashing lights.

Flashing light signals are found at all types of public highway-rail grade crossings. They normally are placed to the right of the approaching highway traffic on all roadway approaches to a crossing.

Standard bell

A standard bell is a device which, when activated, provides an audible warning. It may be used with flashing light signals and gates, and is most effective as a warning to pedestrians and bicyclists.

A standard bell is designed to ring loudly when a train is approaching, to warn people in the surrounding area. When used, the bell is usually mounted on top of one of the signal support masts. The bell is usually activated whenever the flashing light signals are operating.

Standard gates

A standard gate assembly is an active traffic control device used with flashing lights and normally accompanied by a crossbuck sign, flashing light signals, and other passive warning signs. It consists of a drive mechanism and a fully reflectorized red and white striped gate arm with lights, which in the down position extend across the approaching lanes of highway traffic about four feet above the top of the pavement. The flashing light signal may be supported on the same post with the gate mechanism or separately mounted.

When no train is approaching or occupying the crossing, the gate arm is in an upright, vertical position. In a normal sequence of operation, the flashing light signals and the lights on the gate arm in its normal upright position are activated immediately upon detection of a train. The gate arm is designed to start its downward motion not less than three seconds after the signal lights start to operate, reach its horizontal position before the arrival of any train, and remain in that position as long as the train occupies the crossing. When the train clears the crossing, and no other train is approaching, the gate arm ascends to its upright position.

Exempt sign

This sign is placed in advance of and at crossings authorized by state law or regulation to inform placarded hazardous materials vehicles, buses, and other highway users that a stop is not required, except when a signal, train crew member, or uniformed police officer indicates that a train, locomotive, or other railroad equipment is approaching the crossing.

Yield sign

The yield sign assigns right-of-way. Vehicles controlled by a yield sign need to avoid interference with other vehicles, including trains, which are given the right-of-way.

Do not stop on tracks sign

This sign is a black and white regulatory sign placed at a crossing when an engineering study or experience determines there is a high potential for vehicles stopping on the tracks.

Stop sign

A standard, red regulatory stop sign with lettering is intended for use where motor vehicle traffic is required to stop. This sign can be added to the crossing, requiring all vehicles to come to a complete stop before crossing the railroad tracks.

Tracks out of service sign

This sign is for use at a crossing in lieu of the crossbuck when a railroad track has been abandoned or its use discontinued.

Parallel track sign

This sign is a diamond-shaped yellow advance warning sign located on a roadway parallel to the railroad tracks, indicating the road ahead will cross the tracks. This sign is intended to warn motorists making a turn that there is a highway-rail grade crossing immediately after the turn.

Low ground clearance sign

Of particular importance to truck drivers is the "low ground clearance" sign. This sign is used at railroad grade crossings where conditions are sufficiently abrupt to create hang-up of long wheelbase vehicles or trailers with low ground clearance.

Number sign

At multiple-track crossings, a sign indicating the number of tracks will be on the post below the crossbuck.

Pavement markings

The white letters "R&R" can be set into the surface of, applied to, or attached to, the pavement in advance of a crossing, to advise, warn, or guide traffic.

▮ Safety tips

On a level road, with good surface conditions, it takes about 14 seconds for an 80,000 pound 53-foot rig to cross a single track, and more than 15 seconds to cross a double track. The following are safety practices that should be followed when it comes to railroad crossings.

- When you see an advance warning sign you should begin slowing down so you can stop if necessary.
- Check for traffic behind you and make sure they know your intentions.

16

- When approaching a crossing, you should always expect to encounter a train.

- Freight trains do not travel at fixed times, and passenger train schedules can vary.

- Trains have the right of way 100 percent of the time.

- Look and listen carefully in each direction for the sight and/or sound of a train.

- It is extremely difficult to judge a train's speed as well as its distance from the crossing. If you are unsure that you can safely cross, wait until the train has passed.

- Never race a train to the crossing.

- Never drive around lowered gates. As well as being dangerous, it is illegal.

- Use a pull-out lane, if available. Turn on your flashers in traffic, if necessary.

- If the warning lights at the crossing begin to flash after you have started to cross the tracks, keep going and don't back up.

- Don't begin to cross until you are sure you can completely cross the tracks without stopping. Remember, in addition to being unsafe, stopping on the tracks is illegal.

- Never shift gears when crossing tracks.

- If the vehicle has a low ground clearance, select another route to make sure you don't get stuck on the tracks.

- When crossing multiple tracks, watch for a second train.

Stuck on the tracks

If you get stuck on the tracks, you should follow these steps:

1. Get out of the vehicle immediately. Take your cell phone (if available).

2. Move far away from the vehicle in the direction of any approaching train, to avoid being near the point of impact.

3. Look for an emergency telephone number posted at the crossing and call it. If you don't have a phone, flag someone down.

4. Give your exact location, using landmarks and the DOT number from the crossing.

5. If there is no posted emergency number, call law enforcement or 911 immediately.

▌ Summary

In this chapter, you learned about the serious dangers associated with crossing highway-rail grade crossings, the regulations addressing this issue, and the "best practices" you should use to safely approach and cross railroad tracks.

16

RAILROAD CROSSINGS QUIZ

Directions: Read each statement carefully and mark the response that best answers the question.

1. It's up to you, the truck driver, to avoid an accident because:
   A. Trains can't stop quickly
   B. Trains always have the right of way
   C. Trains cannot swerve to avoid collisions
   D. All of the above

2. When approaching a railroad crossing, if you are not required to stop, you should slow down and proceed with caution.
   A. True
   B. False

3. If there are multiple tracks, it's okay to shift gears while crossing.
   A. True
   B. False

4. If you are required to stop at railroad crossings, you should stop:
   A. Within 15 feet of the nearest rail
   B. Between 15 and 50 feet from the nearest rail
   C. At least 50 feet from the nearest rail
   D. None of the above

5. A round, yellow sign with a large "X" and the letters "RR" tells you:
   A. There is a railroad yard nearby
   B. There is a train approaching
   C. There is only one railroad track ahead
   D. To slow down, because you are approaching a railroad crossing

6. A sign with the words "Railroad Crossing" on two crossed white boards is called a crossbuck.
   A. True
   B. False

7. As you start driving over some tracks, the red lights begin to flash and the gates start to come down. You should stop and abandon the vehicle.
   A. True
   B. False

8. If your vehicle gets stuck on the tracks, you should stay in the vehicle and call 911.
   A. True
   B. False

9. Why shouldn't you cross the tracks when an approaching train appears to be far away?
   A. The train may be closer and faster than it appears
   B. The train may unexpectedly slow down
   C. You may not be able to clear the tracks in time
   D. Both A and C

10. A driver who holds a CDL can be disqualified if convicted of certain highway-rail grade crossing violations.
    A. True
    B. False

Read each question carefully and select the most correct answer.

1. If you aren't sure that you have safe space to pass under an object, you should:
   A. Assume all clearances are of sufficient height
   B. Height clearance is not a concern as long as you stay on state or federal roadways
   C. Take another route
   D. All of the above

2. Controlled braking is:
   A. Applying brakes hard enough for the wheels to lock up
   B. Pressing the brakes hard enough to lock-up the wheels, then releasing and then reapplying again
   C. Applying firm brake pressure, but not to the point of lock-up
   D. Only used if the vehicle does not have anti-lock brakes

3. You are driving on a straight and level roadway at 60 mph and suddenly a tire blows out on your vehicle. What should you do first?
   A. Immediately begin light, controlled braking
   B. Immediately begin stab braking
   C. Grip steering wheel firmly with both hands and stay off the brakes until the vehicle has slowed down
   D. Immediately begin emergency braking

4. Which of the following is true?
   A. Tires with tread separation or cuts should not be used on a vehicle
   B. Tires which are mismatched sizes should be used on a vehicle
   C. $\frac{1}{32}$ inch tread depth is allowed on drive tires
   D. $\frac{1}{32}$ inch tread depth is permissible for steering tires

5. Why do hazardous materials regulations exist?
   A. To provide for safe drivers and equipment
   B. To communicate a risk
   C. To contain the product
   D. All of the above

Emergency maneuvers

OBJECTIVES

Upon completion of this chapter, you should have a basic understanding of:

- The role of emergency maneuvers
- Evasive steering
- Emergency stopping
- Off-road recovery
- How to handle brake failure
- How to deal with a tire blowout

17 Emergency maneuvers

- THE ROLE OF EMERGENCY MANEUVERS
- EVASIVE STEERING
- EMERGENCY STOPPING
- OFF-ROAD RECOVERY
- BRAKE FAILURE
- BLOWOUTS
- SUMMARY

INTRODUCTION

Emergencies occur when one or more drivers fail to observe safe operating practices. As a professional driver, you can reduce the likelihood of being involved in an emergency situation by practicing safe driving skills. Unfortunately, even the safest and most conscientious professional drivers face emergency situations during their careers. This chapter will address the importance of recognizing an emergency situation and the methods and techniques for safely dealing with the situation.

■ The role of emergency maneuvers

The safest and best way to avoid an emergency is to prevent it from happening in the first place. Proper driving skills, hazard perception technique, and preventive maintenance can go a long way in preventing many emergencies.

■ Evasive steering

Generally, steering to avoid an emergency is safer than trying to stop. If an escape path is available, evasive steering provides a better chance of avoiding a collision than attempting to stop. Constant scanning for hazards, adequate following distance, and good driver and vehicle preparation are key.

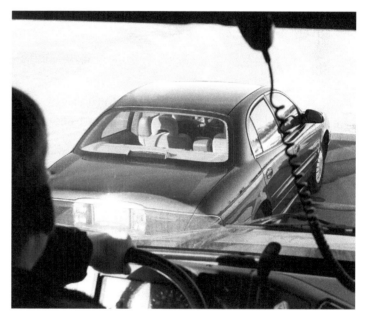

The two most common escape routes are another lane of traffic and the shoulder of the road. If a lane is available, a quick lane change is the best escape route. If a lane change is impossible or dangerous, the shoulder of the road provides an alternate escape route.

Evasive steering, when done correctly, is generally safe. A number of factors can affect the outcome of an evasive steering maneuver. Be aware of these factors. React accordingly.

The best results are achieved when you are hauling stable cargo with a low center of gravity and are able to steer onto a firm road or shoulder.

General procedures

When evasive steering, minimize the amount of turning necessary. Start the maneuver as soon as possible; as soon as you see the emergency/hazard. The earlier an evasive maneuver starts, the less steering input is needed to avoid the emergency/hazard.

Turn only as much as needed. Avoid over steering. Keep in mind that the larger the steering input, the greater the chance of a jackknife or rollover.

Turn as quickly as possible. Use hand-over-hand steering. Each turn of the wheel should be about 180 degrees. Placing your hands in the 9:00 and 3:00 positions while driving allows you to turn 180 degrees without letting go of the steering wheel.

Ease your foot off of the accelerator to gradually reduce vehicle speed.

Avoid braking while turning. Braking could cause the tractor and trailer wheels to lock-up, which can result in a loss of control.

Brake before turning. A firm braking application reduces your speed before turning. This allows your vehicle to turn more sharply and reduces the chance of a jackknife or rollover.

After making the evasive turn, be prepared to countersteer immediately. Smooth, quick countersteering is required to keep your vehicle from going outside its escape path; off the shoulder or into another lane of traffic. Begin to countersteer as soon as your vehicle clears the obstacle.

Though important at all times (and required per the regulations) the use of a seat belt is extremely important when involved in an evasive maneuver. A quick turn could cause you to slide out of the driver's seat, causing you to lose control of your vehicle if you are not wearing a seat belt.

Details of how an evasive maneuver is performed depend on the specific situation. These special maneuvers may be needed for emergencies involving oncoming, stopped, and merging vehicles.

Oncoming vehicle

Evade an oncoming vehicle by steering to the right. Sound your horn to get the driver's attention. This may startle the driver, causing him/her to correct his/her action. Don't steer to the left. Entering the left lane may cause a head-on collision .

Stopped vehicle

If the left lane is clear, turn into that lane. Swerving to the right could cause you to sideswipe a vehicle next to you. The height of your cab should allow you to see ahead to determine if the left lane is clear. Also be aware of what is next to your vehicle. Check your mirrors when determining if is safe to make a lane change.

If you're next to a clear shoulder, you may be able to go to the right if the left lane is blocked.

If you're in the middle lane of a multi-lane road, choose to steer into the lane which presents the least danger. Otherwise, evade to the right. It is better to force a vehicle onto the shoulder than to force another vehicle into oncoming traffic.

Merging vehicle

When another vehicle converges (merges) causing an emergency situation, sound your horn. This generally gets the other driver's attention, causing him/her to stop or correct his/her action. This can minimize the amount of evasive steering you will have to do. Remember, though a horn sounding may frighten or annoy another driver, it will communicate your presence, warning the other driver of a problem.

If the vehicle continues to converge (merge), swerve away from the vehicle. Don't try to steer behind it. If the other vehicle should stop, this would cause a collision.

Never steer away from a converging (merging) vehicle if it puts you into the path of oncoming traffic. It's better to collide at an angle with the merging vehicle than to swerve into the path of an oncoming vehicle.

Emergency stopping

Over application of the brakes will lock-up your vehicle's wheels, causing your vehicle to skid and possibly jackknife. You could also lose control of your vehicle. Proper emergency braking allows you to bring your vehicle to a stop within a minimum distance while allowing you to maintain control of the vehicle.

There are two emergency braking techniques that can be used to safely stop your vehicle, controlled and stab braking.

Controlled braking

In controlled braking, you maintain a steady pressure on the brakes, applying them just short of lock-up. Keep in mind that it is difficult to precisely anticipate the point of lock-up. Developing this skill requires practice in the vehicle you're operating.

Stab braking

When stab braking, fully apply the brakes. Then release the brake pedal partially when the wheels lock. Applying the brakes achieves maximum braking. Releasing or backing off the brakes avoids a skid. When the wheels roll again, reapply the brakes. Make sure you allow time for the wheels to roll again between each stab. Reapplying the brakes too quickly will cause a skid. Repeat the stab braking sequence until your vehicle has slowed enough for a safe stop or turn maneuver.

Off-road recovery

17

In many emergencies, the roadside provides the best escape path. As previously stated, the use of the roadside is better than colliding with another vehicle.

Drivers are often fearful of leaving the roadway. Many fear that an accident/crash will be the result of their using the roadside for an evasive maneuver. The fact is that many of the reported roadside crashes are the result of fatigued or impaired driving. Keep in mind that many evasive maneuvers are successful and are never reported.

Successful off-road recovery often requires leaving the roadway immediately. Too often drivers react too late. Most crashes/accidents that involve off-road recovery are due to incorrect technique.

Off-road recovery is generally safe when the roadside is wide enough to accommodate the vehicle and firm enough to support the vehicle.

General procedures

If you need to leave the road to avoid a collision, brake before turning, reduce speed as much as possible, and use controlled or stab braking to prevent loss of control. If you are operating a vehicle with an antilock braking system (ABS), keep braking until a safe speed is achieved.

Steering control is important. Avoid braking while turning, as the vehicle is more likely to skid during braking, unless you have full ABS. With full ABS you can brake and steer at the same time without losing control of your vehicle.

Minimize turning. Keep one set of wheels on the pavement if possible. This will aid in traction and help you maintain control. Maintain as straight a course as possible. Remember, each turn creates the danger of a skid.

If the roadside is clear, fight the tendency to return to the roadway. Grasp the steering wheel firmly and concentrate on steering.

Stay on the roadside until your vehicle comes to a complete stop. Allow engine compression to slow and help stop the vehicle. Apply your brakes only after speed has been reduced. When the situation has passed, signal and check your mirror before returning to the travel lane.

If the roadside is blocked by a parked vehicle, sign, or other obstacle, you'll need to return to the road more quickly. If this happens, allow your vehicle to slow as much as possible before returning to the road. Then turn the steering wheel sharply toward the roadway. Attempting a gradual return to the roadway can cause you to lose control of your vehicle. Turning sharply allows you to determine the point of return to the road and allows you to countersteer.

Upon returning to the roadway, countersteer. Turn quickly in the direction of the roadway. Turn as soon as the right front wheel (steering axle) rides up onto the surface. Both turning back onto the roadway and countersteering should be executed as a single, integrated steering maneuver.

Often, if a truck is too close to the edge of the roadway, the wheels will drop off the pavement. If this happens, avoid immediate return to the roadway. You can maintain control easily with one side of the rig on the pavement. The vehicle may overturn or veer across the roadway if you try to return to the road too quickly.

When your vehicle's wheels drop off the pavement, follow the same procedure as off-road recovery.

Brake failure

A well-maintained brake system rarely fails completely. Despite this, brake failures do occur. The result of brake failure is a vehicle that is not under your control. Like all other emergency situations, keeping your cool is key to bringing your vehicle under control in this situation.

There are four common causes of brake failure:

- Loss of air pressure;
- Air blockage;
- Brake fade; and
- Mechanical failure.

Loss of air pressure

A warning buzzer will sound and/or a light will illuminate on the instrument panel when air pressure is too low. Stop immediately. Continued loss of air pressure could cause your brakes to completely fail. This will lock-up your brakes and not allow your vehicle to move.

Your brakes should apply automatically when air loss reaches a critical level (between 20-40 psi). This happens when there is still enough air in the system to stop your vehicle. Do keep in mind that even when everything works as designed, air loss could happen too quickly, and the air could be exhausted before the vehicle is stopped. Also, the independent trailer brake valve won't activate the trailer brakes, as they also depend on the air system.

The brakes will activate automatically on a vehicle equipped with spring-loaded parking brakes when air pressure fails. This will generally bring the vehicle to a stop.

Air blockage — A blockage can prevent air from reaching the brakes. This is commonly caused by water freezing in the air system or dirt through the glad hands.

Brake fade — On long downgrades, brakes may overheat and fade. The brakes will lose their ability to stop wheel rotation. The brakes won't cool quickly.

Mechanical failure — Brake failure can result from a failure in the mechanical linkage. Rarely are all brakes affected at once. Usually, in this situation, the vehicle can be stopped.

General procedures

The following steps should be followed if your vehicle's brake system fails:

Downshift — If on a relatively flat road, putting a vehicle into a lower gear will help to slow it down. Continue to downshift until your vehicle has slowed to a point that you can apply the parking brake. Do not try to downshift if you are on a downgrade.

17

Escape route — While slowing your vehicle, look for an escape route. A safe escape route may include an open field, side street, or escape ramp. Turning uphill is another way to slow and stop your vehicle. If you do use a hill to slow your vehicle, make sure it doesn't start rolling backward after stopping by applying the parking brake.

Downgrade procedures

If your vehicle's brakes fail on a downgrade, you will have to look outside your vehicle for something to help slow and stop. One option is the use of an escape ramp. Escape ramps are intended to safely stop a runaway vehicle. Escape ramps use a soft material such as gravel or sand to slow and stop a vehicle.

If an escape ramp isn't available, an open field or side road that is flat or turns uphill are options.

Make a move to slow your vehicle as soon as you are aware that your brakes aren't working. The longer you wait, the greater the vehicle's speed and the harder it is to stop.

▌Blowouts

The term "blowout" refers to a sudden loss of tire inflation. Blowouts can result from worn tires, cracks in the tire casing, or damage from debris, potholes, or nails. Remember, a careful pre-trip inspection can prevent blowouts caused by wear.

A blowout of a front tire disrupts steering and can cause the vehicle to veer in the direction of the blowout. With a rear tractor tire blowout, you may feel the rear of the tractor slide from side-to-side. A trailer tire blowout is harder to detect. You may hear the tire blowing out, see it in your mirrors, or you may experience some difficulties in handling the vehicle.

The sooner you are aware of a tire blowout, the more time you have to react. The major signs of tire failure are sound, vibration, and feel.

Sound —The loud bang of a blowout is an easily recognizable sign. Any time you hear a tire blow, assume it is one of your vehicle's tires.

Vibration — If your vehicle thumps or vibrates heavily, it may be a sign that one of the tires has gone flat.

Feel — If steering feels heavy, it's probably a sign that one of the front tires has failed. At times, rear tire failure will cause a vehicle to fishtail or slide back and forth.

Procedure — There are five steps to follow to safely handle tire failure.

1. Be aware the tire has failed.

2. Accelerate to overcome drag.

3. Hold the steering wheel firmly. If a front tire fails, it can twist the steering wheel out of your hands.

4. Stay off the brake. Braking when a tire has failed can cause loss of control. Unless you're about to collide with something, stay off the brake until the vehicle has slowed down. Then brake gently, pull off the road, and stop.

5. After stopping, get out of the vehicle and check all tires. If one of your dual tires goes, a visual check may be the only way to discover this problem.

▌ Summary

In this chapter, you have learned about the importance of properly executing emergency maneuvers including evasive steering, emergency braking, and off-road recovery. You have also learned the common techniques to apply when dealing with brake failure and tire blowouts.

17

EMERGENCY MANEUVERS QUIZ

Directions: Read each statement carefully and mark the response that best answers the question.

1. The best way to avoid an emergency is to prevent it from happening in the first place.
   A. True
   B. False

2. Attempting to stop provides a better chance of avoiding a collision than evasive steering.
   A. True
   B. False

3. The best way to evade an oncoming vehicle is by:
   A. Braking hard
   B. Steering to the left
   C. Steering to the right
   D. All of the above

4. _____ braking are two emergency braking techniques that can be used in an emergency situation.
   A. Jacking and chasing
   B. Controlled and stab
   C. Steer and countersteer
   D. All of the above

5. Successful off-road recovery often requires leaving the roadway immediately.
   A. True
   B. False

6. A common cause of brake failure is:
   A. Loss of air pressure
   B. Brake fade
   C. Mechanical failure
   D. All of the above

7. When air is low in a vehicle's brake system, a warning buzzer or alarm should sound.
   A. True
   B. False

8. If your vehicle's brakes fail, you should:
   A. Find an escape route
   B. Increase the vehicle's speed
   C. Jump from the vehicle
   D. All of the above

9. A front tire blowout can disrupt steering.
   A. True
   B. False

10. If a tire fails, you should:
    A. Hold the steering wheel firmly
    B. Stay off the brake
    C. After stopping, check all of the tires
    D. All of the above

GENERAL KNOWLEDGE CDL PRE-TEST

Read each question carefully and select the most correct answer.

1. Which of the following statements about backing a commercial motor vehicle is NOT true?

   A. Since you can't see behind you, you should back quickly until you bump the dock
   B. Use mirrors on both sides of your vehicle
   C. You should always back toward the driver's side when possible
   D. Both A and C

2. Alcohol use impairs:

   A. Muscle coordination
   B. Reaction time
   C. Depth perception
   D. All of the above

3. Which of the following is true concerning cold weather driving?

   A. Exhaust system leaks are not of concern during cold weather
   B. If the temperature is below 32 degrees Fahrenheit, the engine cannot overheat
   C. Using bleach on tires will provide increased traction
   D. You should use windshield washer fluid which contains an anti-freeze

4. _____ are signs put on the outside of a vehicle which identify the hazard class of the cargo.

   A. Labels
   B. Shipping papers
   C. Placards
   D. All of the above

5. Controlled braking is used when:

   A. The goal is to keep the vehicle in a straight line while braking
   B. You must stop as quickly as possible
   C. Is only used with hydraulic brakes
   D. Is only used when the vehicle is equipped with anti-lock brakes

Skid control and recovery

OBJECTIVES

Upon completion of this chapter, you should have a basic understanding of:

- The factors that affect vehicle control
- The major causes of skids
- Common types of tractor-trailer skids, how they are caused, and prevention
- Skid recovery technique

18 Skid control and recovery

- SKID DYNAMICS
- CAUSES OF SKIDS
- TRACTOR-TRAILER SKIDS
- SKID RECOVERY
- SUMMARY

Put simply, a skidding vehicle is an out of control vehicle. It is much easier to prevent a skid than to correct a skid. This chapter will address what causes a vehicle to skid, types of vehicle skids, and techniques for safely dealing with the situation.

▌ Skid dynamics

A skid happens when a vehicle's tires lose their grip on the road.

Factors that affect vehicle control include traction, wheel load, and force of motion. If there is an imbalance among these vehicle control factors, a skid will occur.

Traction

Traction is the grip your tires have on a road surface. Traction plays a part in determining how much control you have over your vehicle. If traction is poor, control of your vehicle is poor, which can lead to a skid.

Wheel load

Wheel load is the downward force of weight on a wheel. Weight of the vehicle and load distribution determine wheel load. Keep in mind the fact that although wheel load can increase downward force and the amount of tire tread on the road, this may not improve traction.

Force of motion

Force of motion is determined by the weight and speed of the vehicle. The heavier the vehicle and its cargo, and the faster it travels, the greater the force. Speeding up, braking too quickly, or changing direction too quickly can affect the force of motion.

▌ Causes of skids

The major causes of skids include overbraking, oversteering, overacceleration, and driving too fast for road conditions.

- **Overbraking** occurs when you are braking too hard, resulting in the vehicle's wheels locking up.
- **Oversteering** happens when you are turning the wheels more sharply than the vehicle can turn.
- **Overacceleration** means your are supplying too much power to the drive wheels, causing them to lose traction.
- The most serious skids are the result of **driving too fast for conditions.**

▌ Tractor-trailer skids

Tractor-trailer skids are classified based on what occurs during the skid. There are four major kinds of skids:

- Trailer jackknife;
- Tractor jackknife;
- Front wheel skid; and
- All-wheel skid.

Trailer jackknife

Overbraking or oversteering can cause a trailer jackknife. When a trailer jackknife occurs, the trailer's tires are locked, causing it to skid.

When overbraking, the trailer will continue to move forward at a higher speed than the tractor. Not being able to move forward, it will slide around.

When taking a curve too fast for surface conditions, the rear of the trailer may continue in the same direction as it was originally heading while the tractor and the front of the trailer turn.

To prevent a trailer jackknife:

- Inspect your air system and check brake adjustments;
- Adjust your speed to suit conditions;
- Read the road ahead;
- Avoid braking in curves (brake before entering the curve); and
- Avoid hard braking.

Tractor jackknife

A tractor jackknife occurs when the drive wheels lose traction. This can be caused by wheel lock-up or overacceleration. In this situation, the drive wheels attempt to take over the front wheels, causing the rear of the tractor to swing out. The tractor follows the path of least resistance while the trailer continues in its original direction. Then, as the trailer pivots, it pushes the rear of the tractor outward, resulting in a jackknife.

To prevent a tractor jackknife:

- Avoid overbraking, overacceleration, and sudden downshifts;
- Load your cargo properly, making sure it is secure; and
- Pay special attention to the brake system and tire tread when performing your pre-trip inspection.

Front wheel skids

Front wheel skids are caused by reduced front wheel traction. Reduced front wheel traction can be caused by an excessive load on the fifth wheel, lack of tread on the front tires, hydroplaning, oversteering, or brake system malfunction.

In a front wheel skid, the front end tends to go in a straight line regardless of how much you turn the steering wheel. On a very slippery surface, you may not be able to steer around a curve or a turn.

18

A good inspection of the following vehicle components can aid in preventing front wheel skids:

- Tires;
- Front wheel alignment;
- Suspension system; and
- Fifth wheel lubrication.

A reduction of vehicle speed on wet or slippery pavement can also help in preventing skids.

All-wheel skids

In an all-wheel skid, all wheels are locked. Friction/traction changes from rolling to sliding as the wheels are not turning. Usually, during an all-wheel skid, your vehicle continues in a straight line in spite of your efforts to steer. The main cause of this is over braking on slippery surfaces.

The best way to prevent an all-wheel skid is by avoiding excessive speed and braking, especially on slippery surfaces.

Skid recovery

The following technique can be used to recover from the majority of tractor skids.

1. **Stop braking or accelerating** — Disengage the clutch and steer. If you have an automatic transmission, shift it into neutral. This allows the drive wheels to roll again, keeping them from sliding any further.

2. **Turn quickly** — When your vehicle begins to slide sideways, quickly steer in the direction you want the vehicle to travel.

3. **Countersteer** — As your tractor turns back on course, it has the tendency to keep turning. Countersteering prevents your vehicle from skidding in the other direction.

Skid recovery is a skill that is not easy to perform. Learning to follow the skid recovery steps takes lots of practice. The best way to recover from a skid is to not put yourself in this situation. Proper inspection and safe driving technique can go a long way when it comes to preventing a skid.

Once your vehicle is again traveling in a correct path, you can use your brakes to stop. A light, steady application is the preferred technique.

Front wheel skids

Most front wheel skids are caused by driving too fast for conditions. Other causes include lack of tread on the front tires and improper loading of cargo (not enough weight on the front axle).

When a front wheel skid occurs, the only way to stop the skid is to let the vehicle slow down. Stop turning and do not brake hard. Slow down as quickly as safely possible.

Summary

In this chapter, you have learned about the causes of skids and skid prevention. You have also learned about the common techniques used to recover from a skid.

18

SKID CONTROL AND RECOVERY QUIZ

Directions: *Read each statement carefully and mark the response that best answers the question.*

1. The factors that affect vehicle control include traction, wheel load, and forces of motion.
   A. True
   B. False

2. The major cause(s) of skids include:
   A. Overbraking
   B. Overacceleration
   C. Oversteering
   D. All of the above

3. One way to avoid a trailer jackknife is by adjusting your speed to suit conditions.
   A. True
   B. False

4. Another way to avoid a trailer jackknife is by using a hard braking technique at all times.
   A. True
   B. False

5. A tractor jackknife occurs when the drive wheels lose traction.
   A. True
   B. False

6. To prevent a tractor jackknife, you should overbrake and overaccelerate when road conditions are icy or snowy.
   A. True
   B. False

7. Front wheel skids are caused by reduced front wheel traction.
   A. True
   B. False

8. _____ can help in preventing front wheel skids.
   A. Use of hard braking technique
   B. Increasing speed on wet or slippery pavement
   C. Reducing speed on wet or slippery pavement
   D. None of the above

9. In an all-wheel skid, _____ of the vehicle's wheels are locked.
   A. None
   B. 3 to 4
   C. 5 to 6
   D. All

10. The best way to recover from a skid is to:
    A. Do nothing
    B. Stop braking, turn the steering wheel, disengage the clutch, and countersteer
    C. Brake hard, hold the steering wheel tightly, and engage the clutch
    D. None of the above

GENERAL KNOWLEDGE CDL PRE-TEST

Read each question carefully and select the most correct answer.

1. What is hydroplaning?

   A. An emergency situation created when an aircraft must make an emergency landing on a highway
   B. Excessive heat built up in the radiator
   C. Something that only occurs at high vehicle speeds
   D. When water or slush collects on the road, and your vehicle tires lose contact with the road

2. If you are being tailgated you should:

   A. Motion for the tailgater to pass you when it is safe
   B. Increase your following distance
   C. Turn your 4-way flashers on
   D. Slam on the brakes

3. Which of the following conditions may produce a skid?

   A. Driving too fast for conditions
   B. Over braking
   C. Over steering
   D. All of the above

4. When fighting a fire, which is most correct?

   A. Get as close to the fire as possible
   B. Aim the fire extinguisher at the base of the fire
   C. Aim the fire extinguisher at the top of the fire
   D. All of the above

5. If a state or federal inspector determines that your vehicle is unsafe, they will put the vehicle out of service

   A. For 24 hours
   B. For 48 hours
   C. Until you can contact your carrier and make arrangements for repair
   D. Until it is fixed

Special rigs

OBJECTIVES

Upon completion of this chapter, you should be able to identify various types of special rigs and their unique operating characteristics and hazards, including:

- Multiple articulation vehicles (doubles, triples, and B-trains)
- Oversize, low-clearance, and high center-of-gravity vehicles
- Unstable loads (tankers and livestock haulers)
- Reefers (refrigerated trailers)
- Other special rigs

19 Special rigs

- MULTIPLE ARTICULATION VEHICLES
- OVERSIZE VEHICLES
- HIGH CENTER-OF-GRAVITY VEHICLES
- SPECIAL CARGO VEHICLES
- SUMMARY

INTRODUCTION

A "special rig" is any combination vehicle that differs from the standard tractor and dry freight trailer with five axles and up to 18 wheels.

This chapter will describe the most common special rigs, their handling characteristics, and the special skills required to operate them.

◼ Multiple articulation vehicles

Multiple articulation vehicles, also known as longer combination vehicles (LCVs), have several joints or points at which two parts of the vehicle are joined. A typical tractor-trailer unit has only one joint, located at the connection between the kingpin and fifth wheel. Multiple articulation vehicles, as the name implies, have two or more joints and include various types of doubles and triples.

Doubles

Federal and state regulations often restrict operation of special rigs in some way. These restrictions should be well known to motor carriers that use special rigs.

Doubles consist of a tractor and two semi-trailers, with the second trailer converted to a full trailer using a converter gear (a set of wheels with a fifth wheel, called a converter dolly). The converter dolly is connected to the first trailer by one or two drawbar(s) with an eye(s) connected to a pintle hook(s) on the back of the first trailer.

A dolly with a single drawbar (the most common type) is known as an A-dolly, and a rig equipped with an A-dolly is known as an **A-train**. A dolly with two parallel drawbars is called a B-dolly, and a rig equipped with a B-dolly is called a **C-train**. Being equipped with two drawbars, a C-train eliminates the rear trailer's ability to rotate at the hitch point.

While a standard tractor-trailer unit has one point of articulation or joint, doubles have three:

- Front trailer kingpin and fifth wheel;
- Pintle hook and eye; and
- Converter gear fifth wheel and kingpin of the second trailer;

Following are some defining characteristics and handling requirements of several types of doubles.

Before operating a CMV hauling doubles, you'll need a double/triple trailers endorsement on your commercial driver's license (CDL). In order to obtain this endorsement, you will need to successfully complete a doubles/triples knowledge test.

Western doubles — A Western double is a standard A-train with two equal-length trailers, typically 24-31 feet long, and an overall length of 60-75 feet. The trailers may be dry vans, tankers, flatbeds, or dumps.

There are several special handling concerns when pulling Western doubles:

Many states limit or prohibit the operation of doubles, depending on the weight and length involved. You may need to obtain state permits before driving in certain states.

- Avoid backing. This typically difficult maneuver is made even more difficult with a double trailer unit not designed to be backed.
- Smooth steering is required. Jerking or aggressively moving the steering wheel is greatly magnified in the second trailer. (To create a picture in your own mind, think of a group of ice skaters playing "crack the whip.")
- The heaviest trailer must always be ahead of the lighter one. This adds stability for turning and braking.
- Don't apply brakes in a curve, because this will cause the second trailer to dip.
- The greater length of the rig requires the driver to plan further ahead. Additional time is needed for passing, changing lanes, and crossing intersections.
- It's very difficult to make tight turns with close coupled rigs.
- Bumps and potholes may cause the tops of the trailers to strike each other.
- On curves, be aware of the vehicle's tracking so you stay within your lane while going around the curve.

Doubles add steps to the normal coupling and inspection procedures. The drawbar and pintle hook must be properly in place and hooked. Safety chains need to be in place, electrical cords need to be attached, all air lines must be hooked up properly, and valves must be opened or shut as required. These items must be checked closely during pre-trip and en-route inspections as well.

Turnpike doubles — A Turnpike double has longer trailers than a Western double, generally 35-48 feet, with an overall vehicle length of around 100 feet or more. They typically are equipped with nine axles.

A high-output engine and multiple gear range transmission are required for Turnpike doubles.

Other major characteristics, handling, and special requirements are essentially the same as for Western doubles, but magnified somewhat by the additional length.

A. ROCKY MOUNTAIN DOUBLE

40'-53' 26'-29'

B. TURNPIKE DOUBLE

35'-48' 35'-48'

C. TRIPLE TRAILERS

27'-28' 27'-28' 27'-28'

Rocky Mountain doubles — A Rocky Mountain double is composed of a longer trailer in the front and a shorter trailer in the rear. Generally, the front (semi) trailer is 40-53 feet long, and the rear (full) trailer is 26-29 feet long. Overall length is generally 80-100 feet.

Other major characteristics, handling, and special requirements are essentially the same as for Western doubles, though the long front trailer does require extra room for maneuvering.

B-trains — A B-train is composed of two semi-trailers. On the first trailer, tandem rear axles are to the rear of the trailer body so the second axle is under the nose of the second semitrailer. A fifth wheel mounted above the second axle eliminates the need for a converter dolly. This also eliminates one articulation point normally found on a double rig. B-trains have two articulation points rather than three.

Trailer and overall length will vary. Generally, there will be two 40-foot trailers or one 40-foot and one 27-foot trailer.

Again, other major characteristics, handling, and special requirements are essentially the same as for Western doubles, with adjustments for trailer length. Backing is easier with B-trains, though it should still be avoided.

Triples

Triple trailers are made up of three semi-trailers, with the second and third converted to full trailers using converter gear and connected, as with doubles, by drawbar and pintle hook.

CHAPTER 19

There are three kingpin/fifth wheel connections and two eye/pintle hook connections. Trailers are typically 27-28 feet long, with overall lengths of up to 100 feet.

Triple trailers require drivers to have more advanced operating skills. Their length requires additional time and space for making turns, stopping, and performing other maneuvers. Some maneuvers, such as backing, should never be attempted.

Before operating a CMV hauling triples, you'll need a double/ triple trailers endorsement on your CDL. In order to obtain this endorsement, you will need to successfully complete a doubles/ triples knowledge test.

▌ Oversize vehicles

Oversize-vehicle trailer types may include lowboys, drop frames, flatbeds, open-top vans, and extendable trailers. There can be a number of wheel and axle combinations depending on weight, size of cargo, and state regulations. Many oversize vehicles are equipped with outriggers to support oversized loads. Converter dollies may be attached to the trailer or tractor by fifth wheel and kingpin, or to the cargo itself to distribute weight over more axles and support longer loads.

Typically, the cargo that creates or makes necessary an oversize vehicle is over dimensional or overweight. Oversize vehicles are usually operated with special permits and on designated highways. Requirements will vary depending on type of cargo, size, weight, and state regulations.

The following are some examples of oversize trailer types.

Double-drop low bed with two axles — The deck on this semitrailer is at a standard flatbed height over the fifth wheel and dual rear axles, but drops close to the ground in between. These trailers are used to carry large, heavy loads. Outriggers may be used to extend the sides of the trailer to support wider loads.

Removable gooseneck low bed — Typically equipped with 2, 3, or 4 axles, these low-bed trailers have a removable gooseneck, allowing the trailer to rest on the ground for easier loading and unloading of heavy equipment. These trailers are often used for front loaders, bulldozers, and backhoes. Outriggers may be used to extend the sides of the trailer.

Folding gooseneck low bed — This trailer is similar to the removable gooseneck trailer, but the gooseneck folds to the ground to allow loading and unloading.

Hydraulic sliding axle trailer — A sliding axle trailer, as the name implies, has rear axles that can slide forward and a bed that slopes to the ground, allowing for easier loading and unloading of heavy equipment.

Hydraulic tail low bed — This type of trailer, with a fixed gooseneck, has a hydraulically operated ramp in the rear, allowing for the loading and unloading of heavy equipment.

Low bed with jeep dolly — A low-bed semi-trailer can be attached to a multi-axle jeep dolly to increase the trailer's capacity. Part of the cargo rests on the dolly and part on the trailer.

Low-clearance vehicles

Low-clearance vehicles are designed to haul heavy, oversized cargo or to accommodate greater cubic capacity loads. Special training and skills are required before operating these trailers.

There are two basic kinds of low-clearance vehicles, double-drop and single-drop frames.

The double-drop frame drops right behind the kingpin and right in front of the trailer axles, close to the ground.

The single-drop frame has a single drop located right behind the kingpin; it only drops about half as much as a double-drop frame.

Both types of trailers are designed with enough clearance behind the kingpin to prevent the back of the tractor from hitting the dropped portion of the trailer, as long as the unit is properly adjusted. The driver must ensure that the fifth wheel is back far enough to allow for adequate clearance.

Double-drop frames are especially susceptible to bottom clearance problems at curbs, railroad crossings, and other places where the pavement is uneven.

Single-drop frames can handle taller loads than conventional trailers, and bottom clearance problems are not as significant as with double-drop trailers. A single-drop low bed is also called a drop-deck or step-deck trailer.

High center-of-gravity vehicles

In a high center-of-gravity vehicle, the majority of the weight is high off the ground, so the greatest danger is in the vehicle's tendency to tip, especially in curves.

High center–of–gravity vehicles require the driver to plan ahead to avoid abrupt steering and braking. Whenever feasible, this type of vehicle should be loaded with the heaviest material low in the trailer and forward (weight permitting) for improved handling.

Examples of high center-of-gravity vehicles include dry bulk tankers, liquid tankers, livestock trailers, and some reefers (refrigerated units).

Dry bulk tankers

Dry bulk tankers are generally cylindrical in shape and are used to haul dry bulk goods such as cement, limestone, flour, and sugar. They are generally loaded through the top and unloaded through the bottom.

Liquid tankers

Liquid tankers are generally semi-trailers, either oval, round, or occasionally square in shape. There are cold tankers, hot tankers, and pressurized tankers. Liquid tankers may contain one compartment or several, and they may or may not contain baffles.

Before operating a tank vehicle, you'll need a tank endorsement on your CDL. In order to obtain this endorsement, you will need to successfully complete a knowledge test.

Liquid surge is what makes handling this type of vehicle difficult. To avoid rollover, drivers must accelerate and turn slowly, and avoid braking in corners.

Driver inspections must include checking for leaks, checking all hoses, valves, fittings, the emergency valve release, and any special emergency equipment

If you are hauling hazardous materials, in addition to the tank endorsement, you will need a hazardous materials endorsement on your CDL. In order to obtain this endorsement, you will need to successfully complete a knowledge test and pass a federal security threat assessment.

Livestock trailers

Livestock trailers have a flat floor or double-drop frame and are used to carry live animals, including cattle, sheep, and pigs. Slots or holes in the sides allow livestock to breathe. Livestock trailers often have side doors in addition to, or instead of, rear doors.

Trailer length will vary and will have a fixed tandem or spread axle. Smaller animals such as pigs or sheep are often carried in trailers converted to accommodate two or three decks.

Live cargo can create problems. Put simply, animals shift. You need to maintain a speed at which you can safely keep the vehicle under control. When stopping, tap brakes lightly to set the animals, then gradually apply brakes. Never attempt to haul livestock without proper training. Livestock hauling is unique in that the driver is responsible for the animals' health and safety en route.

Refrigerated trailers

Refrigerated trailers, or reefers, come in basically two types, nose mounts and belly mounts.

Nose mounts have the refrigeration unit mounted on the upper front of the trailer.

Belly mounts, as the name implies, have the refrigeration unit mounted under the trailer.

Reefers are most often van- or box-type trailers. Some have racks or rails suspended from the roof, on

which animal carcasses are hung, and which can make them unstable. Handling requires the same care as liquid tankers and livestock transport.

Others have separate compartments to keep some cargo frozen while other cargo is kept cool. Slotted floors allow for air or gas circulation. Floors, walls, and roofs are insulated.

Refrigerated trailers have their own engines powered by diesel fuel or liquefied petroleum gas, and have their own fuel tank.

Special reefer inspection procedures include checking for holes in walls, checking ceiling and floor ducts, and inspecting the doors and door gaskets. Fuel, coolant, oil, and refrigerant levels must also be checked regularly. Trailer temperature must also be maintained to avoid cargo damage.

Special cargo vehicles

A special cargo vehicle is any vehicle designed to haul primarily one particular type of cargo. Two of the most common types of special cargo vehicles are pole trailers and auto transporters.

Cargo securement requirements for these and other special cargo vehicles are addressed in Part 393, Subpart I of the Federal Motor Carrier Safety Regulations (FMCSRs).

Pole trailers

Pole trailers are designed to carry poles, steel girders, logs, and other types of long, narrow cargo. These trailers can be lengthened or shortened as needed to fit the load. Generally, a pole trailer is equipped with two U-shaped cradles (known as bunks) to hold the cargo in place. In some cases, the load itself becomes the body of the trailer; in others, a steel beam forms the body.

Auto transporters

Auto transporters generally hold 6-10 automobiles. Sometimes, a rack holds a car atop the tractor itself. These trailers are equipped with ramps in the rear to be used for loading and unloading. Auto transporters have a very low ground clearance. Overhead clearance may vary with each load of vehicles being transported.

Summary

Merely being able to identify a special rig is not enough to be able to operate one. Adequate driver training is essential for the operation of the special rigs discussed in this chapter. Each has its own unique operating characteristics and hazards, and each may require its own training, endorsements, and permits before being operated.

Directions: *Read each statement carefully and mark the response that best answers the question.*

1. Which of the following qualify as a special rig?
   A. Western doubles
   B. Low-clearance vehicles
   C. Refrigerated trailers
   D. All of the above

2. A refrigerated trailer has its own engine and fuel tank.
   A. True
   B. False

3. A special rig is any combination vehicle that differs from the standard tractor and dry freight trailer.
   A. True
   B. False

4. What do liquid tankers and livestock trailers have in common?
   A. Furnace units are used to heat the cargo
   B. Cargo movement can create serious handling problems
   C. Trailer length is always 45 feet
   D. A removable gooseneck allows for easy loading

5. To operate doubles or triples, you do not need an endorsement on you CDL.
   A. True
   B. False

6. The greatest danger with high-center-of-gravity vehicles is their tendency to tip.
   A. True
   B. False

7. One danger associated with double-drop trailers is:
   A. Their inability to carry heavy loads
   B. Low ground clearance
   C. Their tendency to tip
   D. Their length

8. A double trailer rig in which the front trailer is 45 feet long and the rear trailer is 27 feet long would be known as:
   A. Rocky Mountain double
   B. Western double
   C. B-train
   D. C-train

9. _____ consist(s) of a tractor and two semi-trailers.
   A. A tank vehicle
   B. A passenger vehicle
   C. Doubles
   D. Triples

10. When hauling Western doubles, you should always:
   A. Place the lightest trailer ahead of the heaviest one
   B. Avoid backing
   C. Apply your brakes as you are going through curves
   D. Tap your brakes lightly to "set" the cargo before fully applying the brakes

GENERAL KNOWLEDGE CDL PRE-TEST

Read each question carefully and select the most correct answer.

1. Which of the following statements about causes of vehicle fires is true?

   A. An overheated radiator is the most common type of vehicle fire
   B. Carrying a properly charged and rated fire extinguisher will help to prevent fires
   C. Under-inflated or flat tires will not cause a vehicle fire
   D. Poor trailer ventilation can cause cargo to catch fire

2. If you become so ill that you cannot operate a motor vehicle safely, you should:

   A. Drink extra coffee to stay alert
   B. Drive faster, so you get home quicker
   C. Not drive, or if on the road, drive to the nearest place where you can safely stop
   D. All of the above

3. Can federal inspectors inspect your truck or bus?

   A. Yes, and they have the authority to place you out-of-service
   B. Yes, but they have no authority to place you out-of-service
   C. Yes, but only at a port-of-entry
   D. No

4. How many missing leaves in a leaf spring will cause your vehicle to be placed out-of-service?

   A. One-fourth of the total
   B. One-eighth of the total
   C. One-sixteenth of the total
   D. Any

5. Use of alcohol can cause serious driving errors, including

   A. Decreased reaction time to hazards
   B. Increased reaction time to hazards
   C. Gradual, smooth starts
   D. All of the above

OBJECTIVES

Upon completion of this chapter, you should have a basic understanding of:

- Your role in vehicle inspection and maintenance
- Types of maintenance
- Maintenance requirements under the Federal Motor Carrier Safety Regulations (FMCSRs)
- Preventive maintenance as a cost deterrent

20 Preventive maintenance

- TYPES OF MAINTENANCE
- YOUR RESPONSIBILITY
- REGULATORY REQUIREMENTS
- PITFALLS OF POOR VEHICLE MAINTENANCE
- SUMMARY

In order for a safe, efficient, and economical fleet to exist, vehicles need to be inspected and maintained on a regular basis. As a professional driver, your involvement is key when it comes to a successful preventive maintenance program, as you are often the first to notice a problem or issue.

Types of maintenance

The three kinds of maintenance covered in this chapter are:

- Routine servicing;
- Scheduled preventative maintenance (PM); and
- Unscheduled maintenance and repair.

Routine servicing

There will be times when you need to add oil or coolant, or drain moisture from fuel and air systems. Though these tasks are considered routine, if they are overlooked, it could lead to problems down the road.

Scheduled preventive maintenance

Section 396.3 of the Federal Motor Carrier Safety Regulations (FMCSRs) requires a motor carrier to systematically inspect, repair, and maintain its vehicles. In other words, a motor carrier must have a preventive maintenance program (PM).

PM schedules can be arranged in various ways, including according to mileage, engine hours, or time.

Fully participating in your motor carrier's PM effort can reduce unexpected periods of downtime, saving both money and time.

Worn, failed, or incorrectly adjusted components can cause or contribute to accidents. Preventive maintenance and periodic inspection procedures help to prevent failures from occurring while you are on the road.

Unscheduled maintenance

Unscheduled maintenance is an unexpected expense. Examples would include repairs that are noted on your driver vehicle inspection report (DVIR), and repairs due to accidents and breakdowns.

▌ Your responsibility

You are ultimately responsible for the safe operating condition of your vehicle. As a professional driver, you can do the following to help keep your vehicle's components in good working order:

- Be proficient in detecting maintenance and repair needs as you travel, and refer them to the correct place for handling;

- Be expert at doing good pre-trip and post-trip inspections, making sure you check all pertinent components each time you do an inspection;

- Be certain that an annual vehicle inspection has been conducted on the vehicle; and

Never attempt to repair something you have not been trained to or know how to repair.

- Stop to check out any potential problems you think may be developing with your vehicle.

Don't continue with your trip until you are satisfied that everything is in good operating condition, and it's safe to do so. Federal and state regulations require that you not drive a vehicle unless you are satisfied that it is in safe operating condition.

Your driving behavior can help in getting the most out of your vehicle. We are going to look at four major vehicle areas that can be impacted (either positively or negatively) based in your driving behavior and maintenance practices.

Brakes

Your braking system is one of the "key" safety systems. Sudden failure can lead to loss of control and inability to recover. Progressive brake deterioration, such as brake shoe wear without corresponding adjustment, can be even more troublesome because it may appear harmless during normal driving, but may cause an accident during emergency braking situations. To help assure that your brakes are performing well:

- Test your brakes for stopping performance before heading out on the highway;

- Assure yourself that your brakes are properly adjusted;

- Learn how to determine if the air system is operating correctly;

- Check to be sure that low air warning devices are functioning properly; and

- During a trip, before entering severe downgrades, stop and check your brake adjustment.

Having your brakes adjusted properly is one of your most important maintenance tasks. One thing you can do to keep your brakes functioning well is to check the slack adjusters. Some vehicles are equipped with automatic slack adjusters while others are adjusted manually. Checking slack adjustment is especially important if you do a lot of mountain driving. When you adjust, remember that each brake should be adjusted to the same degree so they are performing the same amount of work when they stop the vehicle.

Tires

The best way to extend the life of your tires is to watch your load weight. Know the load rating of the tires you have on your truck and the weight of the load you are carrying. As well as being illegal, driving overloaded is extremely hard on your tires. Exceeding the load rate on the tires can contribute to a blowout, potentially causing an accident and/or a delay in your schedule.

Reduce the wear and tear on your tires by making sure they are inflated correctly. Ideally, tire pressure should be checked when a tire is cold, but it can be checked during a trip. The heat generated by an under inflated tire at highway speeds can reduce a tire's tread life, or worse yet cause the tread to physically separate from the tire body, causing breaks in the body cords.

You should also make sure you are not overinflating your tires. An overinflated tire doesn't absorb road shocks well, and has more of a chance of being punctured or suffering other damage. Another problem with overinflated tires is traction. Tread doesn't make proper contact with the road surface, and traction is reduced.

Clutch

Good driving practices can help extend the life of your vehicle's clutch. The clutch initially compensates for the difference in rotation between the running engine and a stopped vehicle. When you engage the clutch, you are putting 35 tons or more of equipment and cargo into motion. Proper specifications and good maintenance are important in keeping the clutch operating well. A clutch cannot last forever, but its lifespan can be extended if it is properly spec'ed for the vehicle, properly maintained, and properly treated during operation.

Your experience behind the wheel, combined with good observation skills, can help you avoid downtime when it comes to dealing with clutch problems. Keep your eyes open for problems with the clutch and report them as soon as possible to your maintenance department. Be as detailed as you can be in describing the clutch problem. In many cases, with early detection the problem can be easily handled, and at low cost. Here are some common problems you may encounter with your truck's clutch:

- Unusual noise in the clutch may mean you have been riding or slipping the clutch, but it also could mean poor lubrication;
- Clutch slippage can be a sign of worn facings or a lack of clutch pedal freeplay;
- Clutch drag can be caused by something as simple as poor adjustment or something as serious as a warped disc; and
- There should be 1-2 inches of freeplay at the top of the clutch pedal. If not, it may need to be adjusted.

Overloading can be a problem as well. If the clutch you are dealing with is not spec'ed for the weight you are carrying, burnout is likely, and extensive damage can happen.

To increase the lifespan of your clutch, follow some simple guidelines. Start out in the correct gear, engage the clutch properly, and don't ride the clutch or cause it to slip. Clutch problems can also be caused by improper shifting technique. Don't skip gears or shift up before the vehicle has reached adequate speed. These bad habits force the clutch to work extra hard and also generate excessive heat.

Engine

There are a couple of easy ways to improve the lifespan of your truck's engine. They are progressive shifting and good observation skills.

Progressive shifting — This practice reduces equipment wear and also saves on fuel. Generally, it doesn't take any longer to bring a vehicle up to full speed with progressive shifting than it does with other shifting techniques.

So what is progressive shifting? Normally you shift when you have accelerated up to the governor. In progressive shifting, however, you only accelerate enough to bring engine rpm up to peak torque where you can shift gears. Peak torque is where the engine develops maximum pulling power. This usually occurs in the mid-range of engine rpms.

In the lower gear ranges, you don't need to accelerate up to the governor before shifting. The major advantage of progressive shifting is that the engine doesn't work as hard as in standard shifting, thus extending life of both the engine and the drive train, and increasing fuel mileage.

Good observation skills — Even the best of drivers with well-maintained vehicles occasionally have to deal with engine problems. One of the most obvious signs of engine trouble is oil consumption. If your oil consumption increases to a point where you are getting less than 200 miles per quart, you could very well be dealing with engine problems. Increased oil consumption is often accompanied by loss of power, increased fuel consumption, and reduced compression. In large diesel engines, oil is usually measured and replaced by the gallon, not the quart. Typically, if your engine is running correctly, you may use as little as one gallon every 12,000 to 15,000 miles.

Another indicator of trouble is injectors that become erratic. When you give the engine the throttle, the vehicle will act like it's choking or missing. Many times plugging, poor spray patterns, or over fueling is the culprit. These can all be caused by malfunctioning fuel injectors.

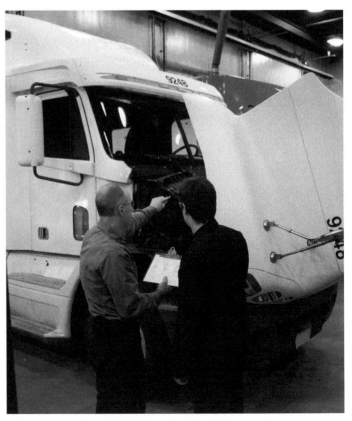

▌ Regulatory requirements

Part 396 of the FMCSRs addresses vehicle inspection and maintenance. The regulations address systematic maintenance, daily inspections, and annual or periodic inspections.

Systematic maintenance

As mentioned earlier in this chapter, Sec. 396.3 of the FMCSRs states that every motor carrier must systematically inspect, repair, and maintain all vehicles in its control or make provisions for systematic inspection, repair, and maintenance.

The term systematic means a regular or scheduled program to keep vehicles in safe operating condition. In other words, a motor carrier must have a preventive maintenance program.

It is up to the motor carrier to determine the time-frame for conducting systematic vehicle inspections as long as they are reasonable and systematic. They may be based on mileage, time, or engine hours.

Pre-trip inspection

Section 396.13 of the FMCSRs states that before driving a motor vehicle you must:

- Be satisfied that the vehicle is in safe operating condition;

- Review the last vehicle inspection report (see post-trip inspection); and

- Sign the report, only if defects or deficiencies were noted by the driver who prepared the report, to acknowledge that the report has been reviewed and that there is certification that the repairs have been performed.

On-the-road inspection (en-route)

Section 392.9 of the FMCSRs requires that you follow certain inspection rules while on the road.

The vehicle's cargo and load-securing devices must be checked within the first 50 miles of a trip. Any necessary adjustments must be made at this time.

After the first 50 miles of the trip, the vehicle's cargo and load-securing devices must be reexamined:

- When you make a change of duty status; or

- After the vehicle has been driven for 3 hours; or

- After the vehicle has been driven 150 miles — whichever occurs first.

These on-the-road inspection rules do not apply if you are driving a sealed vehicle and have been ordered not to open the vehicle to inspect its cargo. Also, the rules do not apply if the vehicle that has been loaded in a way that makes inspection of the cargo difficult or impossible.

Post-trip inspection

A post-trip inspection is conducted at the end your day's work on the vehicle you are operating. This inspection includes filling out a driver vehicle inspection report (DVIR) if defects or deficiencies are discovered. This report helps a motor carrier make necessary repairs before the vehicle returns to the road.

Roadside inspections

A roadside inspection is an examination of a driver and his/her commercial motor vehicle by law enforcement to ensure compliance with the FMCSRs as well as Hazardous Materials Regulations (HMRs). The goal is to ensure that safe drivers and vehicles are on the road.

The majority of roadside inspections occur at weigh stations or scales along the highway. They are conducted by trained law enforcement officers who follow specific guidelines as outlined by the North American Uniform Out-of-Service Criteria, developed by the Commercial Vehicle Safety Alliance (CVSA).

The Out-of-Service criteria identifies critical vehicle inspection items and provides enforcement with criteria for placing a vehicle out of service

Section 396.9 of the FMCSRs is the regulation that grants agents of the Federal Motor Carrier Safety Administration (FMCSA) the authority to perform roadside inspections and declare a vehicle out of service if they believe continued operation of the vehicle is likely to cause an accident or breakdown due to a safety-related defect or deficiency.

If placed out of service, the vehicle cannot be operated again until any and all defects and deficiencies have been repaired. In addition, your company must not allow, permit, or require you to violate an out-of-service order.

The consequences are severe for violating an out-of-service order. Both you and your company can be fined and you can be disqualified from operating CMVs.

20

Pitfalls of poor vehicle maintenance

As we have previously discussed, it is important to report vehicle defects and deficiencies to your motor carrier as soon as they are discovered. Not reporting a problem when it first occurs can have serious consequences for both you and your motor carrier, including potentially a vehicle breakdown or an accident.

Breakdown costs include more than the parts and labor to get the vehicle up and running once again. Every minute a truck is in the shop or placed out of service, it is not being used to bring in revenue to a carrier. An incapacitated vehicle may incur additional expense, such as:

- Cost of towing;
- Driver wages, meals, and lodgings when unable to drive;
- Cost of renting another vehicle;
- Late delivery charges;
- Lost customers; and/or
- Cargo transfer fee.

All of these costs have a bearing on a motor carrier's bottom line, its profitability. This in turn can play a role in your future compensation and benefits with the company.

If a defective part causes an accident, the costs incurred can include insurance deductibles, higher insurance rates, potential litigation, and a tarnished safety record for the carrier. For you it could mean potential citations and fines as well as personal injury.

Summary

In this chapter, you have learned about the importance of preventive maintenance. Preventive maintenance, though an initial expense, can very easily be justified. Even if a breakdown, accident, or out-of-service order does not happen, a vehicle which is not well-maintained will not operate efficiently. Its cost per mile will eat into profits. In addition, a truck which does not stick to a strict preventive maintenance program will wear out sooner and may have to be replaced before its time.

PREVENTIVE MAINTENANCE QUIZ

Directions: *Read each statement carefully and mark the response that best answers the question.*

1. The four major vehicle areas that a driver should keep an eye on include brakes, clutch, tires, and _____.
   A. Rims
   B. Windshield wipers
   C. Engine
   D. All of the above

2. Under the pre-trip inspection requirements in Sec. 396.13 of the FMCSRs, a driver must:
   A. Be satisfied that the vehicle is in safe operating condition
   B. Take the word of the previous driver of the vehicle that everything is working fine
   C. Complete an inspection sometime during the course of the day at the driver's convenience
   D. All of the above.

3. A DVIR is required to be completed in the middle of a driver's shift
   A. True
   B. False

4. A pre-trip inspection only needs to be completed twice a week.
   A. True
   B. False

5. Out-of-service orders are suggestions, and a driver can drive the truck back to the terminal.
   A. True
   B. False

6. Preventive maintenance schedules can be arranged according to:
   A. Mileage
   B. Engine hours
   C. Time
   D. Any of the above

7. A driver should not attempt to repair something he/she has not been trained to or know how to repair.
   A. True
   B. False

8. Breakdown costs include:
   A. Cost of parts and labor
   B. Missed utilization of the truck while in the garage
   C. Lost or dissatisfied customers
   D. Any of the above

9. Progressive shifting reduces engine wear and saves on fuel.
   A. True
   B. False

10. Roadside inspections are conducted by:
    A. Other drivers
    B. Trained mechanics
    C. Trained law enforcement officers
    D. All of the above

GENERAL KNOWLEDGE CDL PRE-TEST

Read each question carefully and select the most correct answer.

1. Shifting gears properly is important because:
   A. Doing so helps you maintain control of the vehicle
   B. It helps to keep the oil flowing through the crankcase
   C. It keeps the radiator cool
   D. It keeps the engine at the proper operating temperature

2. The braking effect of the engine is greatest when:
   A. It is above the governed RPMs and the transmission is in the high gears
   B. It is near the governed RPMs and the transmission is in the lower gears
   C. It is above the governed RPMs and the transmission is in the lower gears
   D. It is near the governed RPMs and the transmission is in the high gears

3. Water will extinguish which of the following fires?
   A. Electrical
   B. Diesel fuel
   C. Gasoline
   D. Tire

4. Convex (curved) mirrors will:
   A. Make objects appear to be larger than they really are
   B. Make objects appear to be closer than they really are
   C. Make objects appear closer and larger than they really are
   D. Show a wider area than flat mirrors

5. The Driver's Manual says you should use your horn:
   A. To make the deer standing alongside the road to move further away
   B. When a car gets in the way
   C. If it may help you to avoid a collision
   D. When you begin to change lanes

Diagnosing and reporting malfunctions

OBJECTIVES

Upon completion of this chapter, you should have a basic understanding of:

- The diagnosis and reporting of vehicle malfunctions
- Troubleshooting
- Procedures for reporting vehicle malfunctions

21 Diagnosing and reporting malfunctions

- DIAGNOSING AND REPORTING MALFUNCTIONS
- TROUBLESHOOTING
- DVIR REQUIREMENTS
- SUMMARY

In this chapter, you will learn about the importance of diagnosing and reporting vehicle malfunctions as well as your role in troubleshooting. You should understand that you know your vehicle best. Diagnosing and reporting problems while they are small/minor can keep you and your vehicle on the road and in service.

Diagnosing and reporting malfunctions

You should be aware of your vehicle's condition at all times. Your ability to spot a potential problem can help in diagnosing a vehicle malfunction. As well as being alert for warning lights and alarms, pay attention to your senses. Sights, sounds, smells, and/or the feel of the vehicle can indicate a potential problem. Report to your company anything that doesn't seem quite right and have it checked out.

Sight — Look at your vehicle's gauges. Know what the proper readings are and what readings indicate a potential problem. Watch for defects in all vehicle components when performing vehicle inspections.

Sound — Listen for unusual or abnormal equipment sounds. Squeaks, squeals, thumps, and rattles can be the first sign of vehicle malfunction.

Catching a problem in the early stages, reporting it to your company, and having the problem checked out will save you and your company time and money. It's cheaper to do this than suffer a breakdown or accident.

Smell — Be aware of unusual smells including burning rubber, hot oil, or fuel.

Feel — Be aware of vibration, swaying, or other movement that isn't normal for your vehicle.

Driver responsibility

As a professional driver, you are responsible for safely operating your vehicle. This responsibility includes reporting any problems with your vehicle to your company and making sure these issues are looked into.

Your responsibilities when it comes to actual maintenance will depend on your company's policy. Most companies expect you to fix simple problems, but do not expect or want you to make other repairs. Never attempt to fix a problem if you do not have the appropriate training, knowledge, or tools.

Mechanic responsibility

The mechanic is responsible for making sure your vehicle is in safe operating condition. When you report a problem with your vehicle, it should be checked out and appropriate repairs should be made.

Driver and mechanic responsibility

Communication between a driver and mechanic is important. Your on-the-road observations can go a long way in diagnosing vehicle problems. Working together can aid in making sure a vehicle is repaired properly and in an efficient manner.

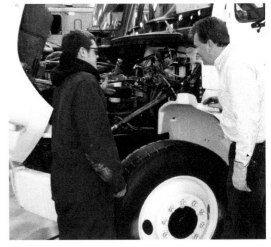

▌ Troubleshooting

Knowing your vehicle can go a long way when it comes to troubleshooting. This includes knowing the vehicle's systems, where they are located, and how they work (both independently and together).

Warning signs

In many cases, a vehicle will give you clues that there could be a problem. Some things to watch for that may signal a possible problem include inconsistent/erratic gauge readings, unusual sounds (rattling, whining, grinding), or a sharp drop in fuel mileage.

Many motor carriers have specific policies and procedures dealing with driver and mechanic communication. This helps in assuring that all parties have the same understanding of the vehicle problem.

Detection of problems

If you notice a problem, stop your vehicle as soon as practical. If you can, try to identify the source of the problem. If the problem is one you can fix based on your knowledge/experience and company policy, do so. If you cannot fix it, report it to your company. Make sure you include a description of what you observed and how the vehicle acted/responded. Get mechanical help as soon as possible.

▌ DVIR requirements

Section 396.11 of the Federal Motor Carrier Safety Regulations (FMCSRs) requires a driver to prepare and sign a written driver vehicle inspection report (DVIR) if vehicle defects or deficiencies are discovered. This report helps a motor carrier make necessary repairs before the vehicle returns to the road.

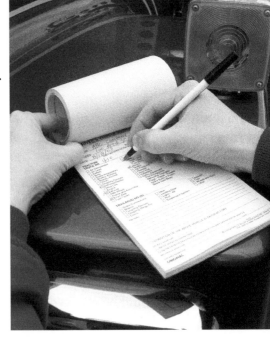

The motor carrier is then required to have the problem checked out and determine whether repairs are warranted. The mechanic who checked out the problem must then certify on this DVIR that either the problem was corrected or that no corrective action was necessary.

When the driver next operates this vehicle, he/she must review the action(s) taken and sign the DVIR indicating the needed repairs were done.

Though this DVIR is required by the regulations, it should not replace direct communication with your company and the mechanic who will be doing any necessary repairs. Knowing what you observed, in addition to what you indicate on the DVIR will help in determining your vehicle's problem.

Summary

In this chapter, you have learned about the importance of diagnosing and reporting malfunctions, your role in troubleshooting, and reporting requirements. Remember, you know your vehicle best. Diagnosing and reporting problems while they are small/minor can keep you and your vehicle on the road and in service. Waiting until the problems become critical can take you off the road for long periods of time, costing both you and your company time and money.

21

Directions: *Read each statement carefully and mark the response that best answers the question.*

1. Your ability to diagnose a vehicle malfunction can prevent a potential problem, reduce downtime, and enhance safety.

   A. True
   B. False

2. Abnormal _____ can indicate a problem with the vehicle.

   A. Smells
   B. Sounds
   C. Feel
   D. All of the above

3. As a professional driver, it is not your responsibility to report vehicle problems.

   A. True
   B. False

4. Communication between a driver and mechanic is important.

   A. True
   B. False

5. Unusual sounds or smells may signal a problem with your vehicle.

   A. True
   B. False

GENERAL KNOWLEDGE CDL PRE-TEST

Read each question carefully and select the most correct answer.

1. Before entering a curve, you should:

   A. Slow down to a safe speed
   B. Increase your speed to increase vehicle stability
   C. Come to a complete stop and proceed as slowly as possible
   D. All of the above

2. Which of the following happens when a tire blows at highway speed?

   A. You will experience an immediate and dramatic drop in speed
   B. You will feel a vibration
   C. You will hear a hissing sound
   D. The high air pressure signal device will come on

3. What is the purpose of a pre-trip inspection?

   A. To add an additional 15 minutes of time to your log book
   B. To aid you in being cited by a law enforcement official
   C. To help you find problems that could lead to a breakdown or accident
   D. To see if an additional 1,000 pounds of freight can be added to maximize revenue

4. When you see a hazard in the road in front of you, you should:

   A. Steer and counter steer around it
   B. Stop quickly and get off the roadway if possible
   C. Stop quickly, stay in the roadway, and go to the rear of your vehicle to flag down traffic
   D. Turn on your 4-way flashers or flash your brakes lights to warn others

5. When driving in fog, you should:

   A. Increase your vehicle's speed
   B. Stop on the side of the road
   C. Use low-beam headlights
   D. All of the above

Handling cargo

OBJECTIVES

Upon completion of this chapter, you should have a basic understanding of:

- The importance of properly handling cargo
- The principles and methods of cargo securement
- The principles of weight distribution
- Safe loading responsibilities
- Common tools used to load/unload a vehicle

22 Handling cargo

- THE IMPORTANCE OF PROPER CARGO HANDLING
- PRINCIPLES AND METHODS OF CARGO SECUREMENT
- PRINCIPLES OF WEIGHT DISTRIBUTION
- SAFE LOADING RESPONSIBILITIES
- LOADING/UNLOADING TOOLS
- SUMMARY

INTRODUCTION

The proper handling of cargo is just one of many tasks the professional driver faces on a daily basis. This chapter will address the importance of proper handling of cargo, cargo securement, and weight distribution principles.

■ The importance of proper cargo handling

As a professional driver, it is your job to safely and efficiently transport cargo to the customer, making sure it arrives on time and damage-free.

Your responsibility for the cargo starts as the cargo is being loaded onto your vehicle and continues until delivery. Follow applicable regulations including state and local requirements in the areas you are traveling.

■ Principles and methods of cargo securement

As cargo is being loaded on your vehicle, you need to ensure that it is properly secured. Shifting cargo can be easily damaged and can pose a hazard to both you and others on the road.

Regulatory requirements

Section 391.13 of the Federal Motor Carrier Safety Regulations (FMCSRs) requires that you know how to properly locate, distribute, and secure cargo. This regulation also requires you to be familiar with the methods and procedures for securing cargo in or on your vehicle.

Section 392.9 of the FMCSRs states that a vehicle may not be driven unless the vehicle's cargo is properly distributed and adequately secured.

The vehicle's tailgate, tailboard, doors, tarpaulins, spare tire, and other equipment used in its operation, and the means of fastening the cargo, must be secured.

In addition, the vehicle's cargo must not:

- Block your view ahead or to the right or left sides;
- Interfere with the free movement of your arms or legs;
- Prevent you from reaching accessories required for emergencies; or
- Prevent you or any other person from exiting the vehicle's cab or driver's compartment.

You must inspect your vehicle's cargo and load-securing devices within the first 50 miles of a trip.

After that initial inspection, your must reexamine the security of your vehicle's load after driving for 3 hours, 150 miles, or when you make a change of duty status (whichever comes first).

You may be exempt from this requirement if your vehicle is sealed and you have been ordered not to open it to inspect, or if your vehicle is loaded in a way that makes it impractical to inspect the cargo.

Part 393, Subpart I of the FMCSRs covers load-securement specifics. The regulations, which begin with Sec. 393.100, apply to:

- Trucks;
- Truck tractors;
- Semi-trailers;
- Full trailers; and
- Pole trailers.

The regulations require a commercial motor vehicle to be loaded and equipped, and the cargo secured, in a way that prevents the cargo from leaking, spilling, blowing, or falling from the vehicle.

All cargo must be contained, immobilized, or secured to prevent shifting that adversely affects the vehicle's stability or maneuverability.

All cargo must be firmly immobilized or secured on or within the vehicle by structures of adequate strength, dunnage or dunnage bags, shoring bars, tiedowns, or a combination of these.

Cargo that is likely to roll must be restrained by chocks, wedges, a cradle, or other equivalent means to prevent rolling. The means of preventing rolling must not be capable of becoming unintentionally unfastened or loose while the vehicle is in transit.

Certain types of cargo have specific securement requirements. These requirements are found in Secs. 393.116 – 393.136 of the FMCSRs. You will need to review the regulations if you haul any of the following:

- Logs;
- Dressed lumber/building products;
- Metal coils;
- Paper rolls;
- Concrete pipe;
- Intermodal containers;
- Automobiles/light trucks/vans;
- Heavy vehicles/equipment/machinery;
- Flattened/crushed vehicles;
- Roll-on/roll-off/hook lift containers; and
- Large boulders.

Securement devices

Tiedowns — Cargo placed beside each other and secured by tiedowns must either:

- Be placed in direct contact with each other; or
- Be prevented from shifting towards each other while in transit.

The aggregate working load limit of tiedowns used to secure cargo against movement must be at least one-half times the weight of the cargo.

Usually, the working load limit of a tiedown is marked on the device by the manufacturer. If it is not listed on the device, the table in Sec. 393.108 must be used.

Section 393.110 of the FMCSRs specifies the minimum number of tiedowns that must be used.

One tiedown is required for cargo that is:

- Five feet or less in length; and
- Weighs 1,100 pounds or less.

Two tiedowns are required if the cargo is:

- Five feet or less in length; and
- Weighs more than 1,100 pounds.

Two tiedowns are required if the cargo is longer than five feet but less than or equal to ten feet in length, regardless of the weight.

Two tiedowns are required if the cargo is longer than ten feet and one additional tiedown is required for every additional ten feet in cargo length or fraction thereof, beyond the first ten feet of length.

If an individual article is blocked, braced, or immobilized to prevent movement in the forward direction by a headerboard, bulkhead, other articles which are adequately secured, or by an appropriate blocking or immobilization method, it must be secured by at least one tiedown for every ten feet of article length, or fraction thereof.

When using tiedowns:

- Always check the rated load limit of the tiedown to make sure it's the proper strength for your load.
- Before using, check the tiedowns for signs of wear or weakness. Don't use tiedowns that have been knotted or repaired.
- Place the tiedowns flat on the load and secure them to the vehicle using hooks, bolts, rails, rings, or other approved devices. The tiedowns should be tight against the load, but not so excessively tight that they damage the load.
- If the trailer you are using has rub rails, all tiedowns and other cargo securement components should be inboard of the rub rails whenever practical.
- Edge protection must be used whenever a tiedown may be subject to damage (abrasion or cutting).
- After use, store tiedowns in a clean, dry space.

22

Blocking and bracing — Blocking is a cargo securement procedure where you fit blocks snugly against the cargo's front, back, or sides to prevent the cargo from sliding. Normally, blocking is secured to the cargo deck or sides. Bracing (putting pressure on a piece of cargo to keep it in place) is generally used between cargo and the trailer ends or sides to keep an object stationary.

Dunnage — Dunnage is filler material used in the empty spaces between cargo. Dunnage keeps the cargo from shifting. Wood, cardboard, airbags, extra pallets, bubblewrap, and plastic are types of material used as dunnage.

Load locking bars — Load locking bars can be used vertically or horizontally. The bars have rubber feet that are placed against the vehicle walls or ceiling and floor. The bars are placed snugly against the cargo and then tightened with a jacking device until they are tightly wedged in place against the cargo.

Tarps — If you carry freight in an open cargo area, you may need to use a tarp. Tarps prevent loose material like sand, gravel, or salt from blowing or falling out of a vehicle. They can also be used to protect cargo from the weather. If you use a tarp, make sure it fully covers your load and is secured at all securing points. While traveling, check your mirrors frequently to make sure the tarp has not become loose, causing a hazard for you and/or others on the road.

Principles of weight distribution

As a professional driver, it is your responsibility to make sure your vehicle is not overloaded. The following are some definitions of weight measurements you should know.

Gross vehicle weight (GVW) — The total weight of a single vehicle, plus its load.

Gross combination weight (GCW) — The total weight of a powered unit, plus trailer(s), plus load.

Gross vehicle weight rating (GVWR) — The value specified by the manufacturer as the loaded weight of a single vehicle.

Gross combination weight rating (GCWR) — The value specified by the manufacturer as the loaded weight of a combination (articulated) motor vehicle.

Axle weight — The amount of gross weight that rests on any one axle.

Tire load — The maximum safe weight a tire can carry at a specified pressure. The rating is usually stated on the side of the tire.

Coupling device capacity — Coupling devices are rated for the maximum weight they can pull or carry.

Legal weight limits

Your vehicle must stay within legal limits. Federal requirements outlined in 49 CFR 658.17 are as follows.

The maximum gross vehicle weight (GVW) is 80,000 lbs. except where a lower GVW is dictated by the bridge formula.

The maximum gross weight on any one axle, including any one axle of a group of axles, or a vehicle, is 20,000 lbs.

The maximum gross weight on tandem axles is 34,000 lbs.

Vehicles are not allowed on Interstate highways if the gross weight on two or more consecutive axles exceeds the limitations prescribed in the Bridge Gross Weight Formula, described below.

$$W = 500\left[\frac{LN}{N-1} + 12N + 36\right]$$

W = the maximum weight in pounds that can be carried on a group of two or more axles to the nearest 500 pounds.

L = the distance in feet between the outer axles of any two or more consecutive axles.

N = the number of axles being considered.

This formula limits the weight on groups of axles in order to reduce the risk of damage to highway bridges. Allowable weight depends on the number of axles a vehicle has and the distance between those axles. However, the single- or tandem-axle weight limits supersede the Bridge Formula limits for all axles not more than 96 inches apart.

Each state has its own weight limitations. Be aware of the regulations for the states you travel through.

22

Overloading

Overloading can adversely effect a vehicle's steering, braking, and speed control. An overloaded truck moves slowly on upgrades and can gain too much speed on downgrades. Stopping distance increases and brakes can fail if worked too hard.

Keep in mind that in bad weather or when traveling through a mountainous area, it may not be safe to operate at the legal maximum weight.

Top-heavy loads

The height of a vehicle's center of gravity is important for safe handling. A high center of gravity (heavy cargo on top or cargo piled too high) makes it easier for your vehicle to tip over. A high center of gravity is also dangerous when in a curve or when you have to swerve to avoid a hazard. Load your vehicle so the heaviest cargo is on the bottom and the lightest on top. Also, distribute cargo so it's as low as possible.

Weight balance

Poor weight distribution can make vehicle handling unsafe.

Too much weight on a steering axle can cause hard steering and cause damage to the steering axle and tires.

Under loaded front axles (cargo weight is too far to the rear) can make the weight on the steering axle too light to steer safely. Too little weight on the driving axles can cause poor traction. The drive wheels may spin easily.

▉ Safe loading responsibilities

You are responsible for making sure your vehicle is loaded safely and legally. It must meet all cargo securement and weight distribution requirements.

Know what you are hauling and the amount you are hauling. Make sure the commodity and amount on your vehicle matches your bill of lading or shipping papers. Report any discrepancies to the shipper and document this on your bill of lading or shipping papers. If you have any questions about accepting the shipment, call your supervisor.

Also check and document the condition of the cargo. Report any damages to the shipper and document this on your bill of lading or shipping papers. Again, if you have any questions about accepting the shipment, call your supervisor.

Resolve any cargo discrepancies before signing the bill of lading or shipping papers.

▉ Loading/unloading tools

When loading or unloading your vehicle, set the parking brake, turn off the vehicle, put the keys in your pocket, and chock the vehicle's wheels. (You may not need to chock the vehicle's wheels if loading/unloading from a dock equipped with a dock lock.) The following are just some of the tools you may use when loading or unloading your vehicle.

Forklift

A forklift is a mechanical device used for moving materials. It is powered by an electric motor or internal combustion engine. A forklift may only be operated by an individual who has successfully completed a training program as mandated by the Occupational Safety and Health Administration (OSHA) under 29 CFR 1910.178.

Pallet jacks

When you must move cargo on pallets, you may use a pallet jack.

Hand pallet jacks are best for short distances and on low grades.

Powered pallet jacks are useful for heavier loads or when you have to move cargo greater distances. A powered pallet jack may only be operated by an individual who has successfully completed a training program as mandated by OSHA under 29 CFR 1910.178.

Although relatively easy to use, pallet jacks must be used carefully. When using a pallet jack:

- Always check the pallet jack for any defects that might affect its operation or safe use.
- Make sure the items on the pallet are properly balanced and secured. Heavier items should be on the bottom with lighter ones on the top.
- Position the forks well into the pallet before raising the load. If the load is too heavy, take some of the items off.

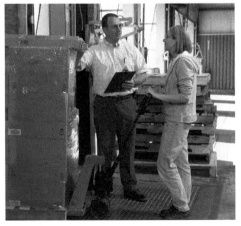

Two-wheel dolly

A dolly is a simple piece of equipment that will let you haul several items at one time or move heavier items with greater ease. Although it's a simple device, if not used carefully, it can crush toes, injure ankles, strain backs, and damage cargo.

To use a dolly properly:

- Make sure the load is securely stacked and balanced. If so, tip the load forward slightly and push the "tongue" of the dolly completely under the load.
- The load should not limit your view. If you cannot see above and around the items, split the load and make multiple trips.
- Test the load by moving it a short distance. You want to be sure it can be moved without shifting or falling.
- Once you're certain you can move the load safely, check your path to make sure no people or obstacles are in your way.
- Use your leg muscles to move the dolly. Keep your back straight and use one hand to steer and the other to balance the load.
- Do not try to push the dolly too fast.
- Make sure the floor is clean and flat before lowering the load.
- When lowering the load, use your leg muscles, not your back, to set the load on the floor.

22

▌ Summary

In this chapter, you have learned about the proper handling of cargo, cargo securement, and basic weight distribution principles. All play an important part in safely and efficiently getting a shipment to its destination.

HANDLING CARGO QUIZ

Directions: Read each statement carefully and mark the response that best answers the question.

1. The Federal Motor Carrier Safety Regulations (FMCSRs) require you to examine your vehicle's load and load securing devices within _____ of the start of your trip.
   A. 20 miles
   B. 25 miles
   C. 50 miles
   D. 75 miles

2. The FMCSRs do not require periodic examination of your vehicle's cargo.
   A. True
   B. False

3. According to the FMCSRs, you are not required to check the cargo on a sealed load that is not to be opened, or if checking the cargo is impractical.
   A. True
   B. False

4. _____ is a filler material used in empty spaces between cargo to keep cargo from shifting.
   A. Tiedown
   B. Dunnage
   C. Tarps
   D. All of the above

5. _____ is a cargo securement procedure where you fit blocks snugly against the cargo (front, back, and/or sides) to prevent it from sliding.
   A. Tarps
   B. Dunnage
   C. Tiedown
   D. Blocking

6. Never use tiedowns that have knots or have been repaired.
   A. True
   B. False

7. Dunnage prevents loose material like sand or gravel from blowing or falling out of a vehicle.
   A. True
   B. False

8. Overloading a vehicle can adversely effect a vehicle's steering, braking, and speed control.
   A. True
   B. False

9. A high center of gravity makes it harder for a vehicle to tip over.
   A. True
   B. False

10. Too little weight on a vehicle's driving axles can cause poor traction.
    A. True
    B. False

GENERAL KNOWLEDGE CDL PRE-TEST

Read each question carefully and select the most correct answer.

1. Your vehicle is 40 feet long and you are traveling at 50 mph. The safe following distance is:

   A. 5 seconds
   B. 6 seconds
   C. 4 seconds
   D. 3 seconds

2. Drinking alcohol can affect your:

   A. Judgment
   B. Vision
   C. Coordination and reaction time
   D. All of the above

3. Aggressive driving is:

   A. Operating in a selfish, bold, or pushy manner, without regard for the rights or safety of others
   B. Acceptable during rush hour in a metropolitan area
   C. Operating in a cautious and courteous manner
   D. All of the above

4. Which of the following is true about rear drive wheel braking skids?

   A. The vehicle's front wheels will slide sideways
   B. It is not a cause of jackknifing
   C. The locked wheels have more traction than the wheels that are rolling
   D. If it occurs with a vehicle towing a trailer, the trailer can push the towing vehicle sideways

5. Which of the following statements is true?

   A. Hazards are easier to see at night than during the day
   B. Hazards are easier to see during the day than at night
   C. Most drivers are more alert at night than during the day
   D. It is recommended that you use your high beams at all times during the period from 7:00 P.M. to 7:00 A.M.

Cargo documentation · 23

OBJECTIVES

Upon completion of this chapter, you should have a basic understanding of:

- The terms/definitions most commonly used in conjunction with cargo documentation

- The basic forms used to document cargo movement

- Pickup and delivery procedures

23 Cargo documentation

- BASIC DEFINITIONS
- BASIC DOCUMENTS
- PICKUP AND DELIVERY PROCEDURES
- SUMMARY

INTRODUCTION

As a professional driver, you will be dealing with some form of freight documentation. You need to know what documents are required and what your responsibility is in handling them. This chapter will cover the basics of cargo documentation including a general overview of the bill of lading and freight bill and procedures you should follow when making pickups and deliveries.

▌ Basic definitions

There are many terms associated with freight documentation that you need to understand so you can effectively read and interpret bills of lading and freight bills.

Carrier — An individual, partnership, or corporation engaged in the business of transporting goods or passengers.

Shipper (consignor) — The person or company (usually the owner) that ships goods to customers.

Receiver (consignee) — The person who receives goods shipped from the owner.

Freight broker — An individual or company who arranges, for compensation, the truck transportation of cargo belonging to others, utilizing authorized for-hire carriers to provide the actual truck transportation. A broker does not assume responsibility for the cargo and usually does not take possession of the cargo.

Freight forwarder — An individual or company that accepts small shipments from various shippers and combines them into one larger shipment.

Originating (pickup) carrier — The carrier who picks up a shipment from a shipper.

Connecting carrier — The carrier that interchanges trailers/freight with another carrier to complete shipments.

Terminal carrier (agent) — The line haul motor carrier making delivery of a shipment at its destination. Terminal carrier means the last or final carrier.

Bill of lading — A written transport contract between the shipper and carrier. It identifies the freight, who it is consigned to, place of delivery, and terms of agreement.

Straight bill of lading — Provides that goods be delivered to the consignee indicated. The consignee doesn't have to surrender his copy to receive the goods.

Through bill of lading — Covers a shipment by more than one carrier at a fixed rate for the entire service.

Manifest — A document describing the contents of an entire shipment on a vehicle.

Packing slip — A detailed list of packed goods prepared by the shipper.

Delivery receipt — A receipt signed by the customer receiving the goods indicating acceptance of the goods from the driver.

Warehousing receipt — A receipt for goods placed in a warehouse.

Charges and services

Both goods and transportation services have to be paid for. Payment for goods is usually arranged between the shipper and consignee. In rare cases, the carrier is required to collect. When this occurs, the driver can't deliver or relinquish possession of freight unless these charges are paid. Because of this, it is important for you to understand the following terms.

Prepaid — The transportation charges are paid for or will be paid at the shipping point.

COD — The payment for goods is made at the delivery point. The driver must collect payment before the cargo is unloaded. Policies regarding this vary from company-to-company.

Order notify shipment — The payment of goods on an Order Notify Bill of Lading. The driver must collect a copy of the bill of lading from the person receiving the goods as payment for the goods.

Basis of rates — Rates are charges based on the value of the transportation and additional services performed by the carrier. Mileage rates are determined by a fee per mile. Class rates are set by grouping goods into classifications according to characteristics such as density, stability, ease of handling, and liability.

Value of cargo — Cargo is valued as either actual valuation or released valuation.

Actual valuation — The actual value of goods shown on the bill of lading when the rate applied is dependent on that fact.

Released valuation — The value of goods set by the shipper as limits of carrier liability and as the basis of rates charged.

Weight and distance — The primary determiner of shipping charges. Rates are expressed in terms of per pound of cargo and per mile traveled.

Services performed by carrier — A list of services that a carrier performs and the rates for those services.

Tariffs — Rates on transportation charges based on the type of service.

Minimum rate — The lowest lawful rate that may be charged.

Maximum rate — The highest rate that can be charged for a specific type of shipment.

Duties — Government tax on imports and exports which must be collected.

Services and surcharges

Basic rates, services, and duties are determined in advance by rules and agreements between the shipper and carrier. Services and surcharges are based on such things as type of cargo (valuation), weight, destination, and type of service. Additional services and rates may be specified on the bill of lading. It is important to know and understand what each of the following terms mean so you can perform the services indicated as required.

Inside delivery — The freight is unloaded and delivered inside instead of at curbside.

Tailgate delivery — The freight is unloaded and delivered at the truck's tailgate (back of truck).

Helper service (lumper) — The arrangement and compensation for loading/unloading should appear on the bill of lading, but seldom does. Usually what is listed is that the load is either shipper/receiver "load and count" or it is driver "load and count." A driver may hire a helper service (lumper) to load/unload if there is one available. This is usually paid for by the driver's company and is included in the freight rate.

Residential delivery — The freight is to be delivered to a residential address. The bill of lading will specify the conditions of delivery and method of collection of payment.

Dunnage and return of dunnage — Dunnage is cardboard, lumber, or other material used to stabilize and secure a shipment. It is not packaging. The bill of lading should list the weight of dunnage. Usually there is no charge for dunnage weight. If return of dunnage is specified, the driver must keep the dunnage and return it to the carrier or shipper as indicated.

Storage and delay charges — Additional charges are made for storage or if the carrier is delayed from making a delivery.

Demurrage (detention) — The detention of a vehicle beyond a specified time. Payment is made to the carrier for this delay (detention time).

Basic documents

As a professional driver, there are two basic documents you will deal with on a regular basis when picking up and delivering cargo. These documents are the bill of lading and freight (expense) bill.

Bill of lading

The bill of lading is the document used in transactions between a shipper and common carrier. The front or face of the bill of lading is where the required information for transportation of the freight must be entered. The reverse side or back of the bill of lading usually contains the terms and conditions of carriage.

There are three distinct and important functions served by the bill of lading:

1. It is a receipt issued by the carrier to a shipper for goods received for transportation. The bill of lading:

    ◆ States the place and date of shipment;

    ◆ Describes the goods' weight, dimensions, identification marks, condition; and

    ◆ Sometimes the goods' quality and value.

2. It is a contract naming the:

    ◆ Parties involved;

    ◆ Specific rate or charge for transportation; and

    ◆ Agreement and stipulations regarding the limitations of the carrier's common law liability in the case of loss or injury to the goods.

3. It also lists other obligations assumed by the parties or to matters agreed upon by them.

Certain bills of lading provide documentary evidence of title to the goods being transported. The "Order" or "Negotiable" bill of lading designates the consignee as the owner of the freight and the carrier may only deliver the cargo to the person in possession of the bill of lading. When a bill of lading is negotiated, the person to whom it is negotiated receives title to the cargo. Use of this bill of lading is very limited.

23

Bills of lading must be legibly written in ink, indelible pencil, or preferably, typed. It is important that all information be written or typed in the exact space provided for it.

The following information must be included on the bill of lading.

Name of consignor — The person or company (usually the owner) that ships goods to customers.

Name of consignee — The person who receives goods shipped from the owner (consignor).

Address — The street address of the consignee should always be listed in the space provided. A post office box is not acceptable for delivery.

Destination — The destination must be accurate. An error of illegibly written or misspelled destination can cause a great deal of trouble and expense. If there are two destinations of the same name within a state, insert the name of the county to indicate the correct destination clearly.

Date — This should be the exact date of delivery of the merchandise to the carrier. This can help prevent misunderstandings regarding what rate of tariff applies to the shipment.

Description of goods — The description of goods covered by the bill of lading should be complete and exact regarding quality and quantity. Other information may be necessary to allow the carrier to classify and properly rate the shipment.

Special marking and instructions — Special marks shown on the shipping units should be reproduced on the bill of lading. Special instructions (freezable, transit privileges, pick-up allowances, etc.) should be included.

Payment of freight charges — Carriers may require prepayment of freight charges on certain commodities or on freight consigned to certain points, and they have the right under law to require prepayment on all freight as long as they avoid discrimination. Generally, it is the option of the shipper to determine who will pay the charges and at what point.

Bill of lading forms must indicate who is responsible for transportation charges. The charges may be "prepaid" or "collect."

Section 7 — The box on the face of the bill of lading referring to "Section 7 of conditions," sometimes known as the "no recourse clause," deals with the payment of freight charges. It is explained in Section 7 of the terms and conditions on the back of the bill of lading, and basically provides that the shipper/consignor is primarily responsible for payment of the freight and other lawful charges, unless the shipper stipulates in writing in the space provided, that the carrier makes delivery without requiring pre-payment.

Shippers who leave the Section 7 area blank, or unsigned, in effect are telling the carrier that if they do not, or are unable to collect the charges from the consignee, the carrier may return to the shipper (consignor) for payment of the freight charges, even though the terms for payment of freight charges on the bill of lading are collected on delivery.

Whether Section 7 is executed or not, this clause has a direct impact on the carrier's ability to collect freight charges from the consignor when the charges are due and uncollectible from the consignee.

© Copyright 2010 J. J. KELLER & ASSOCIATES, INC.®, Neenah, WI • USA • 800-327-6868 • jjkeller.com • Printed in the United States

STRAIGHT BILL OF LADING – ORIGINAL – NOT NEGOTIABLE

Shipper's No. _____

Carrier's No. _____

Carrier		SCAC	Date

TO:
Consignee

FROM:
Shipper

Street

Street

Destination | Zip | Origin | Zip

Route | Vehicle Number | U.S. DOT Hazmat Reg. No.

Number and Type of Packages	HM	Description of Articles	Total Quantity (mass, volume, or activity)	Weight (subject to correction)	Class or Rate

Remit COD to:
Address:
City: _____ State: _____ Zip: _____

NOTE: Where the rate is dependent on value, shippers are required to state specifically in writing the agreed or declared value of the property. The agreed or declared value of the property is hereby specifically stated by the shipper to be not exceeding $ _____ Per _____

Subject to Section 7 of conditions, if this shipment is to be delivered to the consignee without recourse on the consignor, the consignor shall sign the following statement: The carrier shall not make delivery of this shipment without payment of freight and all other lawful charges.

COD AMT:
$ _____

TOTAL CHARGES:
$ _____

(Signature of Consignor)

COD FEE:
Prepaid ☐
Collect ☐ $

FREIGHT CHARGES:
☐ Prepaid ☐ Collect

RECEIVED, subject to individually determined rates or contracts that have been agreed upon in writing between the carrier and shipper, if applicable, otherwise to the rates, classifications and rules that have been established by the carrier and are available to the shipper, on request; and all applicable state and federal regulations; the Property described above, in apparent good order, except as noted (contents and condition of contents of packages unknown), marked, consigned, and destined as indicated above which said company (the word company being understood throughout this contract as meaning any person or corporation in possession of the property under the contract) agrees to carry to delivery at said destination, if on its route, or otherwise to deliver to another carrier on the route to said destination. It is mutually agreed as to each carrier of all or any of said Property over all or any portion of said route to destination and as to each party at any time interested in all or any of said Property that every service to be performed hereunder shall be subject to all the conditions not prohibited by law, whether printed or written, herein contained, including the conditions on the back hereof, which are hereby agreed to by the shipper and accepted for himself and his assigns.

NOTE: Liability Limitation for loss or damage in this shipment may be applicable. See 49 U.S.C. 14706(c)(1)(A) and (B).

This is to certify that the above-named materials are properly classified, described, packaged, marked, and labeled, and are in proper condition for transportation according to the applicable regulations of the Department of Transportation   PER:

SHIPPER: _____

CARRIER: _____

PER: _____ DATE: _____

PER: _____ DATE: _____

EMERGENCY RESPONSE
TELEPHONE NUMBER:

NAME OR CONTRACT NUMBER
OR OTHER UNIQUE IDENTIFIER:

30-BLS-C4 994
(REV. 9/10)

23

Bill of lading unilateral amendments

Amendments, or changes, to the bill of lading contract made by only one party to the contract are not binding upon the parties. Any changes or amendments must be accomplished by both parties, with amended copies of the contract provided.

Bill of lading retention period

To satisfy Federal Motor Carrier Safety Administration (FMCSA) requirements, a bill of lading must be retained by a motor carrier, broker, household goods freight forwarder, or water carrier for a period of one year from the date of the document, or until any claim or dispute involving the transportation of freight based upon the document is resolved.

Basis of rates

Rates are charged based on the value of the transportation and additional services performed by the carrier. Mileage rates are determined by a fee per mile. Class rates are set by grouping goods into classifications according to characteristics such as density, stability, ease of handling and liability.

Freight (expense) bill

Every motor common carrier must issue a freight or expense bill for each shipment transported.

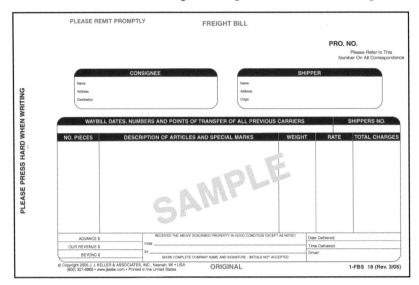

The freight or expense bill must include:

- Names of consignor and consignee;
- Date of shipment;
- Origin and destination points;
- Number of packages;
- Description of freight;
- Weight, volume, or measurement of freight (if applicable to the rating of the freight);
- Exact rate(s) assessed;
- Total charges due, including the nature and amount of any charges for special service and the points at which such service was rendered;
- Route of movement and name of each carrier participating in the transportation;
- Transfer point(s) through which shipment moved; and
- Address where remittance must be made or address of bill issuer's principal place of business.

No person shall cause a motor carrier to present false or misleading information on a document for payment about the actual rate, charge, or allowance to any party to the transaction.

The shipper or receiver owing the charges shall be given the original freight or expense bill and the carrier shall keep a copy as prescribed in 49 CFR 379.

▮ Pickup and delivery procedures

Before signing the bill of lading, make sure the freight is properly described.

Freight pickup

By signing the bill of lading, you are stating that your company accepts the contract terms. Since you are acting as your company's agent, your signature legally binds the company. It also means that you accept responsibility for the freight and that the actual freight matches the type and amount listed on the bill of lading.

Always count, inspect, and determine, in general, that the freight is properly described before signing the bill of lading. You should refuse or note in writing, on the bill of lading, if the freight is short, damaged, or poorly packed.

Freight delivery

There are several things you need to keep in mind when delivering freight.

- Make sure the delivery is made to the right person (consignee);
- Handle payment for merchandise correctly;
- Handle freight changes correctly;
- Get the proper signatures on the bill of lading (and freight bill if applicable); and
- Always follow your company's policy dealing with short shipments, damages, or any other freight problems.

If another party is unloading the freight, observe/supervise the unloading process (if possible). Remember, the freight is yours until the consignee signs for it.

Split shipments

A split shipment is one in which cargo is picked up at more than one address. A receipted bill of lading must be furnished at each address. The bill of lading must also contain the address for each delivery.

When dealing with a split shipment, be especially careful. Check each piece against the bill of lading and/or freight bill very carefully, making sure the correct freight is delivered to the correct address.

Interline freight

Interline freight is freight picked up from or delivered to another carrier. Use the same care when dealing with interline freight as you would when dealing with any other consignor or consignee.

- Check for cargo shortage or damage before signing the connecting carrier's bill of lading or freight bill;
- Don't sign the bill of lading or freight bill if the connecting carrier refuses to acknowledge things such as shortages or damages;
- If equipment interchange is involved (leaving your trailer and/or hooking up a trailer belonging to another company), inspect the trailer and its contents before signing for possession; and
- Always check with your company for instructions.

▌ Summary

In this chapter, you have learned about bills of lading, freight bills, and the terms associated with these documents. You have also learned the basics of freight pickup and delivery.

23

CARGO DOCUMENTATION QUIZ

Directions: *Read each statement carefully and mark the response that best answers the question.*

1. The shipper is also called the _____.
   A. Consignor
   B. Consignee
   C. Receiver
   D. Bill of lading

2. The receiver is also called the _____.
   A. Consignor
   B. Consignee
   C. Shipper
   D. Bill of lading

3. A written transport contract between a shipper and carrier which identifies the freight, who it is consigned to, place of delivery, and terms of agreement is called the _____.
   A. Consignor
   B. Consignee
   C. Freight broker
   D. Bill of lading

4. Payment for goods is usually arranged between the shipper and receiver.
   A. True
   B. False

5. A bill of lading must be legibly written in ink, indelible pencil, or must be typed.
   A. True
   B. False

6. The name of the shipper is not required to be included on a freight bill.
   A. True
   B. False

7. When signing a bill of lading, you are acting as your company's agent, accepting the contract terms.
   A. True
   B. False

8. When picking up freight, you should never sign the bill of lading, as this should be done by a company supervisor.
   A. True
   B. False

9. A split shipment is one in which more than one container is picked up at a shipper.
   A. True
   B. False

10. _____ is freight picked up from or delivered to another carrier.
    A. Consignor
    B. Consignee
    C. Interline freight
    D. Split freight

CDL AIR BRAKE PRE-TEST

Read each question carefully and select the most correct answer.

1. The air loss rate for a straight truck or bus with the engine off and the brakes applied should not be more than:

   A. 1 psi in 60 seconds
   B. 1 psi in one minute
   C. 2 psi in 45 seconds
   D. 3 psi in one minute

2. Which of the following statements about brakes is true?

   A. The heavier the vehicle, the more work the brakes must do to stop the vehicle.
   B. Brakes have more stopping power when they get very hot
   C. Brake drums cool very quickly
   D. All of the above are true

3. The purpose of engine retarders is to:

   A. Provide emergency brakes
   B. Help slow the vehicle while driving and reduce brake wear
   C. Apply extra braking power to the non-drive axles
   D. Help prevent skids and slides

4. If your vehicle has an alcohol evaporator, it is there to:

   A. Get rid of alcohol that condenses in the air tanks
   B. Let the driver skip the daily tank draining
   C. Increase tank pressure the way superchargers boost engines
   D. Reduce the risk of ice in the air brake valves in cold weather

5. The air supply pressure gauge shows the driver how much pressure:

   A. Has been used in this trip
   B. Is available in the air tanks
   C. Is being sent to the brake chambers
   D. None of the above

OBJECTIVES

Upon completion of this chapter, you should have a basic understanding of:

- What a hazardous material is
- The CDL hazmat endorsement
- Hazard classes and divisions
- Why hazmat shipping papers must be filled out properly and easily accessed
- Loading and unloading hazmat
- What needs to be done when transporting hazmat

24 Hazardous materials

- WHAT IS A HAZARDOUS MATERIAL?
- THE CDL AND HAZMAT ENDORSEMENT
- HAZARD CLASSES AND DIVISIONS
- SHIPPING PAPERS
- SHIPPING PAPER ACCESSIBILITY
- LOADING AND UNLOADING
- ON THE ROAD
- SUMMARY

Transporting hazardous materials (hazmat) safely and securely today is more important than ever. Hazmat drivers need to receive special training associated with what they do on the job. If you are hired by a carrier to transport hazmat, additional training will be provided to you. This chapter will provide you with some basic background on requirements pertaining to the hazmat transportation process.

What is a hazardous material?

A hazardous material is defined in the Hazardous Materials Regulations (HMR) as a substance or material capable of posing an unreasonable risk to health, safety, and property when transported in commerce. The term includes hazardous substances, hazardous wastes, marine pollutants, elevated temperature materials, materials designated as hazardous in the Hazardous Materials Table, and materials that meet the defining criteria for hazard classes and divisions.

The CDL and hazmat endorsement

A hazardous materials endorsement is required on a driver's commercial driver's license (CDL) in order to haul placarded amounts of hazardous materials. An endorsement is also required for any quantity of a material listed as a select agent or toxin in 42 CFR Part 73.

In order to have a hazmat endorsement added to your CDL, you will need to pass a knowledge test. You will also need to complete a security threat assessment that includes a fingerprint-based criminal history records check and intelligence-based background check.

Hazard classes and divisions

Hazardous materials are classified by a hazard class or division number.

A hazard class is the category of hazard assigned to a hazardous material in the HMR. A material may meet the defining criteria for more than one hazard class, but is assigned to only one hazard class.

A division is a subdivision of a hazard class.

There are nine hazard classes, with some of the classes broken down into divisions.

- Class 1 — Explosives
- Class 2
  - Division 2.1 — Flammable gas
  - Division 2.2 — Non-flammable gas
  - Division 2.3 — Poison gas
- Class 3 — Flammable and combustible liquid

- Class 4
  - Division 4.1 — Flammable solid
  - Division 4.2 — Spontaneously combustible
  - Division 4.3 — Dangerous when wet
- Class 5
  - Division 5.1 — Oxidizer
  - Division 5.2 — Organic peroxide
- Class 6
  - Division 6.1 — Poisonous material
  - Division 6.2 — Infectious substance
- Class 7 — Radioactive
- Class 8 — Corrosive material
- Class 9 — Miscellaneous hazardous material

Shipping papers

No one wants to be involved in an accident, let alone one involving hazardous materials. However, accidents do happen. Accidents involving hazardous materials can potentially threaten lives, property, and the environment. That's why shipping papers have such an important role in the hazmat transportation process.

A hazmat shipping paper provides key information about the hazardous material being transported. Emergency responders use that information at the scene of an accident to determine what steps must be taken to keep damages to the lowest level possible. It is up to you, the driver, to make certain that information is correct and the shipping papers are easily accessible.

The HMR requires that a shipping paper have the basic description for each hazardous material being transported. For domestic transportation, the basic description must include, in this order:

- The UN or NA identification number;
- The proper shipping name;
- The hazard class or division number;
- The subsidiary hazard class or division number entered in parentheses; and
- The packing group (PG), if any.

The total quantity of the hazmat must be entered before and/or after the basic description. It must also include the appropriate unit of measure, which may be abbreviated. The number and type of packages must also be indicated.

Shipping paper accessibility

Shipping papers must be readily accessible to authorities in the event of an accident or inspection. You must:

- Clearly distinguish the hazmat shipping paper from other papers by tabbing it or having it appear first.
- Keep the shipping paper within immediate reach while at the vehicle controls and restrained by the lap belt, and visible to anyone entering the driver's compartment or in a holder mounted to the inside of the driver's door.
- Keep the shipping paper in a driver's side door pouch or on the driver's seat when you are not at the vehicle controls.

Loading and unloading

There are certain procedures that must be followed when loading and unloading hazardous materials from your vehicle. These procedures, as set out in the regulations, are intended to protect you and others around your vehicle during the loading and unloading process.

Set parking brake

During the loading and unloading of any hazmat, the vehicle's parking brake must be set and all precautions taken to prevent movement of the vehicle.

Tools

Any tools used in loading or unloading hazmat must be used with care not to damage closures on packages or containers, or to harm packages of Class 1 material and other hazmat in any way.

No smoking

Smoking on or near any vehicle while loading or unloading any Class 1, Class 3, Class 4 (flammable solid), Class 5 (oxidizer), or Division 2.1 is forbidden. Care should be taken to keep all fire sources (matches and smoking materials in particular) away from any vehicle hauling these materials.

24

Securing packages

Packages containing any hazmat not permanently attached to a vehicle must be secured against any movement, including shifting or movement between packages during normal transportation. Packages having valves or other fittings must be loaded to minimize the likelihood of damage during transportation.

Placards

The HMR requires most vehicles hauling hazmat to be placarded. The shipper is responsible for providing the appropriate placards. You, the driver, are responsible for putting them correctly on your vehicle and maintaining them during transportation.

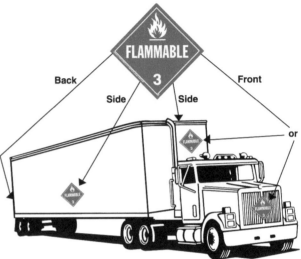

▌ On the road

There are certain procedures that must be followed when transporting hazardous materials. Like the loading and unloading procedures, they are covered in the regulations with the intention of protecting you and others around your vehicle.

Fueling

The engine of a placarded vehicle must be shut-off and someone must be in control of the fueling process at the point where the fuel tank is filled.

Smoking

No smoking or carrying lighted smoking materials is allowed on or within 25 feet of a placarded vehicle containing any Class 1, Class 5 (oxidizer) or flammable materials classified as Divisions 2.1, 4.1, 4.2, Class 3, or any empty tank vehicle that has been used to transport Class 3 or Division 2.1 materials.

Routing

Hazardous materials drivers must abide by designated hazardous materials routes that are posted around many cities and residential areas. Even if the route is not specified or pre-determined, placarded vehicles should avoid heavily populated areas, tunnels, narrow streets or alleys except when:

- There are no practicable alternatives;
- It is necessary to reach your destination, or facilities for food, rest, fuel, or repairs; or
- Emergency conditions require a deviation.

Tire checks

The tires of placarded vehicles must be checked at the beginning of each trip and each time the vehicle is parked. If any defect is found, the tire should be repaired or replaced immediately.

Parking

Placarded vehicles should not be parked on or within five feet of the traveled portion of any roadway. However, except for certain explosives, the vehicle may be stopped for brief periods when operational necessity requires parking and it would be impractical to stop elsewhere. Standard warning devices are to be set out, as required, when stopped along a roadway.

▌ Summary

In this chapter, you have learned about the CDL hazmat endorsement, hazard classes and divisions, shipping papers and accessibility, and procedures for loading and unloading hazardous materials. These are some of the basic requirements when it comes to transporting hazardous materials. Keep in mind that if you do transport hazardous materials for an employer, you will receive additional training.

24

Directions: *Read each statement carefully and mark the response that best answers the question.*

1. A driver transporting a placardable amount of hazardous materials needs a hazmat endorsement.
   A. True
   B. False

2. There are ____ hazard classes.
   A. 9
   B. 7
   C. 11
   D. 5

3. What items make up the basic description for a hazardous material on a shipping paper?
   A. The UN or NA identification number; the proper shipping name; the hazard class or division number; the subsidiary hazard class or division number; and the packing group (PG), if any
   B. The proper shipping name; the vehicle DOT number; the UN or NA identification letter; and the proper group (PG) number, if any
   C. The proper shipping name; the vehicle DOT number; the date; and the packing group (PG), if any
   D. The proper chemical name; the hazard class or division number; the UN or NA identification number; and the product group, if any

4. The total quantity of the hazmat must be entered:
   A. Before the basic description
   B. After the basic description
   C. Before and/or after the basic description
   D. None of the above

5. The driver should take the shipping papers with him/her when not at the vehicle controls.
   A. True
   B. False

6. Shipping papers must be readily accessible to authorities in the event of an inspection or accident.
   A. True
   B. False

7. It is the shipper's fault if the wrong placards are on the vehicle.
   A. True
   B. False

8. The engine of a placarded vehicle must be shut off when fueling.
   A. True
   B. False

9. Tires must be checked at the beginning of each trip and each time the vehicle is parked.
   A. True
   B. False

10. Placarded vehicles should not be parked within _____ feet of the traveled portion of any roadway.
    A. 2
    B. 4
    C. 5
    D. 10

Read each question carefully and select the most correct answer.

1. Which brake system applies and releases the brakes when the driver uses the brake pedal?

    A. The emergency brake system
    B. The service brake system
    C. The parking brake system
    D. None of the above

2. When using the parking brakes or emergency brakes, what type of pressure is being used?

    A. Fluid pressure
    B. Spring pressure
    C. Air pressure
    D. All of the above

3. Three different systems are found on modern air brake systems; service brakes, parking brakes, and the:

    A. Emergency brakes
    B. Foot brakes
    C. S-cam brakes
    D. Drum brakes

4. Air loss in a single vehicle (not a combination unit) should not be more than _____ with the engine off and the brakes applied.

    A. 1 psi in 30 seconds
    B. 1 psi in one minute
    C. 2 psi in 45 seconds
    D. 3 psi in one minute

5. The vehicle must have a warning device which comes on when the air pressure in the service air tanks falls below:

    A. 40 psi
    B. 50 psi
    C. 60 psi
    D. 80 psi

Hours of service

OBJECTIVES

Upon completion of this chapter, you should have a general understanding of the:

- 11-hour driving rule
- 14-hour duty limit
- Mandatory break provision
- 60-hour/7-day and 70-hour/8-day limit
- Driver's record of duty status /electronic logging device (ELD)
- Exceptions to the hours-of-service regulations (including short-haul, sleeper berth, and adverse weather conditions)

25 Hours of service

- WHO IS REGULATED?
- 11 HOURS DRIVING RULE
- 14 CONSECUTIVE HOURS DUTY RULE
- MANDATORY BREAK PROVISION
- ON-DUTY TIME
- 60-HOUR/7-DAY AND 70-HOUR/8-DAY LIMITS
- RECORD OF DUTY STATUS/ELECTRONIC LOGGING DEVICE
- EXCEPTIONS
- SUMMARY

INTRODUCTION

The hours-of-service regulations, located in Part 395 of the Federal Motor Carrier Safety Regulations (FMCSRs) limit the number of hours you can drive, as well as the number of hours you can be on duty. The hours-of-service regulations also require that you maintain a record of your duty status.

The specific requirements for drivers of property-carrying commercial motor vehicles (CMVs) are covered in this chapter.

■ Who is regulated?

If you operate any of the vehicles described below, you must comply with the hours-of-service requirements for drivers of property-carrying commercial motor vehicles (CMVs) as covered in this chapter:

- A vehicle with a gross vehicle weight rating, gross combination weight rating, gross vehicle weight, or gross combination weight (whichever is greater) of 10,001 pounds or more; or
- Any size vehicle transporting a placardable amount of hazardous materials.

Both you, the driver, and your motor carrier are responsible for compliance with these regulations.

There are also hours-of-service requirements for drivers of certain types of passenger-carrying vehicles. Refer to Part 395 for details.

■ 11 hours driving rule

All time spent behind the wheel of a CMV is considered driving time. After 11 hours of driving time, you must have at least 10 consecutive hours off duty before you can drive again.

The Federal Motor Carrier Safety Administration (FMCSA) takes this rule very seriously. Driving three or more hours beyond the driving time limit is considered an egregious violation. Committing this type of violation can result in fines and penalties for both you and your motor carrier.

Many states also have hours-of-service requirements that apply to intrastate operations within that specific state. State requirements may match federal requirements in whole or in part.

■ 14 consecutive hours duty rule

Your 11 hours of driving time must fall within a period of 14 consecutive hours of duty time.

Under the 14 consecutive hours duty rule, you cannot drive beyond the 14th consecutive hour after coming on duty. Once you have reached this limit you cannot drive again until you have 10 consecutive hours off duty. You may continue to work after the 14th hour, but you must not drive.

The 14 hours are consecutive from the time you start your tour of duty. Lunch breaks or other off-duty time do not extend this 14-consecutive-hour period.

Once you have reached the end of this 14-hour period, you cannot drive again until you have been off duty for at least 10 consecutive hours. You may continue to work after the 14th hour, but you must not drive.

> *For example, if you begin your work day at 6:00 a.m. you may not drive a commercial motor vehicle after 8:00 p.m. You must have at least 10 consecutive hours off duty before you may then drive again.*

Mandatory break provision

Under the mandatory break provision, you may not drive if more than 8 hours have passed since the end of your last off-duty or sleeper-berth period of at least 30 minutes.

This required break must be at least 30-minutes and can be taken at any time during your first 8 hours on duty. You may not perform any on-duty tasks during this break. Also, the break counts towards your 14-hour limit and does not extend your work day.

> *Meal breaks, resting in the seat of your parked vehicle, or a sleeper-berth period of 30 minutes or more all qualify as a break.*

Exceptions to the break provision

Division 1.1, 1.2, or 1.3 explosives — If you are required to be in attendance on a vehicle containing Division 1.1, 1.2, or 1.3 explosives, you may use 30 minutes or more of attendance time to meet the break requirement. In order to be considered a break, you may not be performing any other on-duty tasks while in attendance on the vehicle, must record the attendance time as on-duty time on your log, and include a remark or note indicating that this is your mandatory break.

Short-haul driver — If you are a "short-haul driver" who uses the 100 air-mile radius exception or the 150 air-mile radius (non-CDL short-haul) exception, you are not required to comply with the mandatory break provision.

Other exceptions — FMCSA grants exceptions to the mandatory break provision for certain types of operations. Check with your motor carrier for details.

On-duty time

Next we will be covering the 60-hour/7-day and 70-hour 8-day rule. To comply with this rule, you must understand the definition of on-duty time.

On-duty time is defined as all time from the time you begin work or are required to be ready for work until you are relieved from work and all responsibility for doing work. This includes time spent:

- Waiting to be dispatched;
- Inspecting, servicing, or conditioning a CMV;
- Driving (at the controls of your CMV);

- All time (other than driving time) in or on your CMV except:
  - ♦ Time spent resting on a parked vehicle (except when attending to a CMV containing Division 1.1, 1.2, or 1.3 (explosive) material),
  - ♦ Time spent resting in a sleeper berth, or
  - ♦ Up to 2 hours riding in the passenger seat of a property-carrying CMV moving on a highway immediately before or after a sleeper-berth period of at least 8 consecutive hours;
- Loading or unloading your vehicle;
- Repairing, obtaining assistance, or attending a disabled vehicle;
- Performing any other work for a motor carrier;
- Complying with drug or alcohol testing requirements; and
- Performing work for pay for any other employer (motor carrier or non-motor carrier).

60-hour/7-day and 70-hour/8-day limits

If you work for a company that does not operate CMVs every day of the week you and your motor carrier must comply with the 60-hour/7 day rule. Under this rule you may not drive after having been on duty for 60 or more hours in 7 consecutive days.

If you work for a company that operates CMVs every day of the week the company may use either the 60-hour/7-day or 70-hour/8-day rule. Under the 70-hour/8 day rule, you may not drive after having been on duty for 70 hours in any 8 consecutive days.

For example, if you work under the 70-hour/8-day schedule, at the end of the day, you would add the hours worked during the last 7 days (today plus the preceding 6 days). If the total is 70 or more, you would have no driving hours available for the next day.

Once you have reached the 60- or 70-hour limit you may not drive a CMV until you have hours available. You may do non-driving work after reaching either limit, but all of this time must be added to your total on-duty hours.

The 7 or 8 consecutive days is not a work week. It is any 7- or 8-consecutive day period. You don't start over counting hours. The oldest day's hours drop out of consideration as each new day's hours are added. A monthly summary sheet is one way to keep track of the 60 or 70 hour limit.

34-hour restart

The regulations include a restart provision. This optional provision allows you to restart your 60-or 70-hour clock at zero.

In order to use the restart, you must have at least 34 consecutive hours off duty. This restart can be done at any time. You do not have to wait until you have reached the end of your 60- or 70-hours to exercise this option.

There are two other provisions that are included in the 34-hour restart regulation that are not currently being enforced:

1. The 34 consecutive hour off-duty period must include two periods of time between 1:00 a.m. and 5:00 a.m.

2. You may only use the restart once within a period of 168 hours (7 days).

Congressional legislation, passed and signed into law December 16, 2014, suspended enforcement of these two provisions.

25

Record of duty status/electronic logging device

In order to monitor your compliance with the hours-of-service limits, you must keep track of your hours of service. This is done by using a record of duty status (daily log) or an electronic logging device that meets the requirements in Part 395 of the FMCSRs.

Record of duty status (daily log)

The regulations require you to record your duty status (in duplicate) for each 24-hour period.

You must use a form that includes a vertical or horizontal graph grid and the following information:

- Date;
- Total miles driven today;
- Truck or tractor and trailer number;
- Carrier's name;
- 24-hour period starting time (selected by the driver's home terminal);
- Driver's signature/certification;
- Main office address;
- Remarks section;
- Co-driver's name (if applicable);
- Total hours in each duty status (at end of grid); and
- Shipping document number(s), or shipper name and commodity.

Completing your record of duty status

You must complete the record of duty status in your own handwriting. Certain items, such as carrier name and main office address may be preprinted.

There are four categories to use when recording your time:

- Off duty;
- Sleeper berth;
- Driving; and
- On duty (not driving).

The total in all four categories must add up to 24 hours.

The record must be legible and kept current to the time shown for the last change of duty status.

The location (city, town, village and state) of all changes of duty status must be recorded in the remarks section.

If the change of duty status occurs at a location other than a city, town, or village the location can be recorded as the:

Though not required by the regulations, many motor carriers have a policy that requires the driver to indicate the reason for a short stop (tire check, cargo check, fueling). Make sure you know your motor carrier's policy on this issue.

- Highway number and nearest milepost followed by the name of the nearest city, town, village and state;
- Highway number and name of the service plaza followed by the name of the nearest city, town, village and state; or
- Highway numbers of the two nearest intersecting roadways followed by the name of the nearest city, town, village and state.

Short stops of less than 15 minutes can be shown by simply drawing a line from the appropriate time marker into the remarks section and noting the location and length of time stopped.

25

You must have in your possession a copy of each record for the last 7 consecutive days as well as the original record for the current day. They must be available for inspection while you are on duty.

The regulations require that you submit the original record of duty status and supporting documents to your motor carrier within 13 days of completion. Many motor carriers require their drivers to submit this information on a more frequent basis. Be sure to follow your motor carrier's policy.

A motor carrier must keep records of duty status, along with all supporting documents for a period of 6 months from the date of receipt.

Electronic logging devices (ELDs)

An electronic logging device (ELD) is an option that may be used to record your hours of service instead of paper logs. The ELD must contain all the same items required on the paper log.

When asked by an officer, you must be able to produce an electronic record of duty status (electronic log) for the current day and the previous 7 days. The information on the ELD must be current up to your last change of duty status.

In the event of an ELD's failure, you must be prepared to reconstruct the current day's log and any logs from the previous 7 days that the device is unable to display. Also, you should be prepared to maintain a handwritten paper log until the unit is repaired or replaced. This means you should have a logbook in your vehicle in the event you would need to maintain handwritten logs.

The ELD should be with you in the cab as well as instructions on how to store and retrieve data from the device, along with a list of any codes the ELD uses and their meanings.

If the device you use is not an approved ELD such as a laptop, smart phone, or tablet that is not automatically collecting data from the vehicle to determine when you are driving, then you must be able to print your logs on paper if requested by an officer.

As of December 18, 2017, you will be required to use an ELD that is registered and certified by the Federal Motor Carrier Safety Administration (FMCSA).

A motor carrier that installs and requires a driver to use an automatic on-board recording device (AOBRD) prior to December 18, 2017, may continue to use an AOBRD until December 16, 2019.

The device must be connected ("integrally synchronized") to the engine of the vehicle so that driving time can be automatically recorded. Also, the device must automatically capture date and time, vehicle position, and vehicle operational parameters.

There are exceptions to the ELD requirement for short-haul drivers, drivers involved in driveaway-towaway operations, and vehicles manufactured before model year 2000. Paper documentation will continue to be required for these operations.

Supporting documents

Currently, you are required to submit supporting documents along with your original record of duty status to your motor carrier within 13 days of completion.

As of December 18, 2017, the regulations become more specific as to the documents you must provide and how they are retained by your motor carrier.

Your motor carrier must retain supporting documents generated or received in the normal course of business in the following categories to verify on-duty not driving time:

- Bill of lading, itinerary, schedule, or equivalent document that indicates the origin and destination of each trip;
- Dispatch record, trip record, or equivalent document;
- Expense receipt related to any on-duty not driving time;
- Electronic mobile communication record, reflecting communications transmitted through a fleet management system; and
- Payroll record, settlement sheet, or equivalent document that indicates payment to a driver.

Your motor carrier is required to retain a maximum of eight supporting documents for your 24-hour period. If there are more than eight supporting documents for your 24-hour period, your motor carrier must retain the supporting documents containing the earliest and the latest time indications among the eight supporting documents retained.

Exceptions

The hours-of-service regulations include several exceptions. In general, the exceptions apply to certain types of industries, operations, and/or driving conditions. In this text we will address the hours-of-service exceptions that are most commonly used by professional drivers.

100 air-mile radius

You are not required to complete a record of duty status if the following criteria are met:

- You operate within a 100 air-mile radius of your normal work reporting location;
- You return to your normal work reporting location and are released from work within 12 consecutive hours;
- At least 10 consecutive hours off duty separate each 12 hours on duty;
- You do not drive more than 11 hours following 10 hours off duty; and
- Your motor carrier maintains your time records for 6 months showing the:
  - ◆ Time you report for duty each day,
  - ◆ Time you are released from duty each day,
  - ◆ Total number of hours you are on duty each day, and
  - ◆ Total time on duty for the preceding 7 days (if you are used for the first time or intermittently).

If you use this exception, you are still required to comply with the 11-hour driving rule, the 10 consecutive hour off-duty requirement, and the 60-hour/7day or 70-hour/8-day limit.

You are not required to comply with the mandatory break provision.

25

Short-haul provision (non-CDL)

Under this provision, you may extend your workday twice in any period of 7 consecutive days and are not required to maintain a record of duty status if the following criteria are met:

- You are not required to hold a commercial driver's license (CDL) to operate your vehicle; and
- You remain within a 150 air-mile radius of your normal work reporting location and return to and are released from your normal work reporting location at the end of each day.

Under this provision, you must:

- Comply with the 11-hour driving rule;
- Have at least 10 consecutive hours off duty separating each on-duty period; and
- Comply with the 60-hour/7-day limit or 70-hour/8-day limit (you may use the 34-hour restart provision if applicable).

If you use this exception, you are not required to comply with the mandatory break provision.

Under this provision, you must not drive:

- After 14 consecutive hours of duty time during 5 days of any period of 7 consecutive days; and
- After 16 consecutive hours of duty time during 2 days of any period of 7 consecutive days.

You are not required to keep a record of duty status, but your motor carrier is required to keep a time record showing the:

- Time you report for duty each day;
- Time you are released from duty each day;
- Total number of hours you are on duty each day; and
- Total time you are on duty for the past 7 days if you are used for the first time or intermittently.

If you use this exception, you are not eligible to use the 100 air-mile radius exception, sleeper-berth exception, or short-haul (16 hour) exception.

Short haul (16 hour) exception

There is an exception to the 14-hour duty limit that you can use on a periodic basis if you regularly return to your normal work reporting location.

Under this exception, you are allowed to accumulate 11 hours of driving time within 16 consecutive hours of duty once every 7 days, provided you:

- Return to your work reporting location on that day, and are released from duty at that work reporting location for the previous 5 on-duty days;
- Are released from duty within 16 hours after coming on duty (no additional on-duty time after 16 hours); and
- Have not used this exception within the previous 6 consecutive days (unless you have complied with the 34-hour restart provision and have started a new 7- or 8-day consecutive period).

Sleeper berth

Once you reach either your 11-hour driving limit or 14-hour duty limit, you must be off duty for at least 10 consecutive hours before you can resume driving.

This 10-hour off duty requirement can be met by resting in a sleeper berth. There are several ways you can use the sleeper berth to meet this off-duty requirement.

- The 10 hours of off-duty time can be accumulated by resting in the sleeper berth for one 10-hour period.

- The 10 hours of off-duty time can be accumulated by combining sleeper-berth time with off-duty time. These periods must be consecutive and not broken with any driving or on-duty activities.

- In a team driving situation, the 10 hours can be accumulated by resting in the sleeper berth for at least 8 hours and spending 2 additional hours in the passenger seat of your truck as it is moving. These 2 hours in the passenger seat must be immediately before or after the 8 hours in the sleeper berth and must be consecutive. No driving or on-duty activities may be performed during this time period.

- The equivalent of 10 hours can be accumulated by taking two rest periods:

  - One of the rest periods must be at least 8 consecutive hours (but less than 10 consecutive hours) and must be spent in the sleeper berth;

  - The other, separate rest period must be at least 2 consecutive hours (but less than 10 consecutive hours) and must be spent either in the sleeper berth, off duty, or a combination of the two.

When using the split-sleeper-berth option, you do not have the full 11 hours of driving time available after each sleeper-berth period. Compliance must be calculated from the end of the first two periods.

Calculation of the 14-hour duty limit includes all time except any sleeper-berth period of at least 8 (but less than 10) consecutive hours. Following the second sleeper-berth period, the hours available under the 14-hour duty rule must be recalculated from the end of the first of the two rest periods.

For example, you drive for 6 hours then spend 8 hours in the sleeper berth. After the 8 hours in the sleeper berth, you do not have the full 11 hours of driving time available. You must subtract the 6 hours of driving time prior to the sleeper-berth period from the 11 hours of driving time that is allowed to determine how many hours of driving time are available (11-6=5). You may drive for another 5 hours before you must take at least 2 hours in the sleeper berth, off duty, or a combination of the two.

This pattern continues until you have at least 10 consecutive hours off duty.

For example, using the same scenario as above, count the hours starting from the end of the first sleeper-berth period and subtract from 14. After the 8-hour sleeper-berth period, you drive for 5 hours and took 2 hours off duty for a total of 7 hours. Subtract the total number of hours (7) from the 14 allowed to determine the number of duty hours available under the 14-hour duty limit (14-7=7).

25

When using this option, you may not return to driving under the normal limits until you take:

- At least 10 consecutive hours off duty;
- At least 10 consecutive hours in the sleeper berth; or
- A combination of at least 10 consecutive hours of off duty and sleeper berth time.

Adverse driving conditions

The adverse driving conditions exception allows you to drive for an additional two hours under certain circumstances.

If you encounter weather, highway, or traffic conditions that prevent you from safely completing your run within the 11-hour driving time limit, you may drive for an additional 2 hours within your 14-hour duty window to complete the run. *However,* you must not have known or been able to foresee the situation at the time you began your run.

Another issue to consider when using the split sleeper-berth option is the mandatory break provision. You cannot drive if more than 8 hours have passed since the end of your last off-duty or sleeper-berth period of at least 30 minutes. You will need to make sure you take this into account when planning your sleeper-berth splits.

Adverse driving conditions do not include loading or unloading delays or conditions that were apparent before the run was dispatched. Examples of conditions that were apparent before a run was dispatched include a predicted winter blizzard or rush hour traffic in a metropolitan area.

▌ Summary

The purpose of the hours-of-service regulations is to keep tired drivers off the road. As we all know, a tired driver is an unsafe driver.

The FMCSA and law enforcement in general take these regulations seriously. Drivers and motor carriers are fined hundreds of thousands of dollars each year for violating these requirements.

Operating within legal limits and maintaining good records will help you operate legally, reducing the chance of a fatigue-related accident and keep you from receiving citations and fines.

25

HOURS OF SERVICE QUIZ

Directions: *Read each statement carefully and mark the response that best answers the question.*

1. After 11 hours of driving, you must have at least _____ consecutive hours off duty before you are allowed to drive again.
   A. 8
   B. 9
   C. 10
   D. 11

2. After 14 consecutive hours of duty time, you may not drive again until you have at least 10 consecutive hours off duty.
   A. True
   B. False

3. You may use lunch breaks to extend your 14 consecutive hours of duty time.
   A. True
   B. False

4. In order to restart your 60- or 70-hour clock, you must:
   A. Have at least 34-consecutive hours off duty
   B. Include two periods between 2:00 a.m. and 5:00 a.m. in your off-duty time
   C. Only use the restart once in the last 14 days
   D. All of the above

5. The regulations require you to record your duty status (in duplicate) for each 24-hour period.
   A. True
   B. False

6. There are three categories that must be recorded on your record of duty status: behind the wheel, sleeping, and working.
   A. True
   B. False

7. Weather conditions must be recorded at each change of duty status.
   A. True
   B. False

8. You must have in your possession a copy of each record of duty status for the last 7 consecutive days as well as the original record for the current day.
   A. True
   B. False

9. In adverse driving conditions, you may ignore the driving time requirements.
   A. True
   B. False

10. By using the sleeper-berth option, you can accumulate the equivalent of at least 10 consecutive hours off duty by taking four sleeper-berth periods.
    A. True
    B. False

CDL AIR BRAKE PRE-TEST

Read each question carefully and select the most correct answer.

1. Air brake equipped vehicles must have:
   A. At least three air tanks
   B. A hydraulic braking system, in case the air system fails
   C. An air pressure gauge, to show the pressure available for braking
   D. An air application gauge, to show air used by the brake chambers for braking

2. How do you check the free play in manual slack adjusters?
   A. Stop on level ground and apply the emergency brakes
   B. Park on level ground, chock wheels, release the parking brakes and pull slack adjusters
   C. Park on level ground and drain off air pressure before making adjustments
   D. Apply the service brakes by hand at the brake chambers and watch the slack adjusters move

3. The most common type of foundation brake found on heavy commercial vehicles is:
   A. Disc
   B. Wedge and drum
   C. S-cam drum
   D. None of the above

4. The air compressor governor controls:
   A. The rpms of the air compressor
   B. Whether the compressor is in good condition
   C. Air pressure applied to the brakes
   D. When the compressor will pump air into the storage tanks

5. The brake pedal:
   A. Is the main control in the system
   B. Can be a foot rest during normal driving
   C. Controls the air pressure applied to operate the brakes
   D. Exerts force on the slack adjusters by rods and connectors

OBJECTIVES

Upon completion of this chapter, you should have a basic understanding of:

- What to expect when crossing the border

- What to expect when operating in Canada

- The general differences between the U.S. and Canada when it comes to compliance issues including hours of service, daily vehicle inspections, and vehicle sizes and weights

26 International driving

- OPERATING IN CANADA
- CROSSING THE CANADIAN BORDER
- BORDER CROSSING PROGRAMS
- RETURNING TO THE UNITED STATES FROM CANADA
- MOTOR CARRIER SAFETY AND LICENSING
- VEHICLE SIZES AND WEIGHTS
- METRIC MEASUREMENTS AND CONVERSIONS
- SUMMARY

Every day, many professional drivers cross the U.S. borders without incident. For the new professional driver however, the thought of delivering goods into another country might seem like a daunting task.

Being aware of and knowledgeable about some of the processes and procedures can help make your border crossing experience smooth and relatively easy.

Operating in Canada

Travel into Canada is relatively common for the professional driver. Because U.S. drivers are allowed to operate into Canada without restriction, entry into and operation throughout Canada requires adequate preparation and paperwork.

Personal credentials/identification

To enter the country, Canada requires proof of identification and citizenship. This means carrying a current passport, passport card, your commercial operator's license, an "enhanced" driver's license, or a Free and Secure Trade (FAST) card.

If you are a permanent resident of the U.S. but not a citizen, then you will be required to present proof of your immigration status and show your visa.

Prior convictions

Certain types of convictions that are considered misdemeanors in the United States may be considered serious criminal (felony) offenses in Canada. If a professional driver has a felony conviction in the U.S., the driver may not be admitted into Canada. Through Canada's rehabilitation program, this denial of admittance may not be permanent. If you have been convicted of a crime that is considered to be a felony in Canada, you may be eligible for entry into Canada after five years from the end of your sentence.

If you have a felony conviction and need to enter Canada for a short time on a very limited basis, a special permit may be issued by the Citizenship and Immigration Canada consulate offices in the United States, but this is not guaranteed.

Declaring personal items

Certain personal items carried over the border into Canada must be "declared" to the Canada Border Services Agency (CBSA). Personal items that you must declare include:

- Tobacco;
- All animals, plants, and their products;

Know and follow the rules and regulations of the country you are traveling in, as enforcement does not consider ignorance of these requirements as a valid reason for noncompliance.

- Explosives, fireworks, ammunition;

- Firearms and weapons (certain weapons are prohibited and may be confiscated at the border);

- Prescription drugs with a clearly identifying label (if possible, you should also carry a letter from your doctor indicating your prescription).

Prohibited items

In Canada, professional drivers are prohibited from having alcohol in the cab of their vehicle under any circumstances. Other generally prohibited items include weapons, such as mace and handguns, as well as illegal drugs.

Vehicle credentials/safety compliance

Before leaving for Canada, you need to ensure that your vehicle registration, applicable safety certificates, fuel tax registration, permits, and operating authority are all in order. Carriers will usually provide the necessary credentials to their drivers, but it is your responsibility to make sure that you have everything you need and that it is current.

You will also want to make sure that your vehicle and load meet the vehicle size and weight limits for where you will be traveling in Canada. More information on sizes and weights will be discussed a little later in this chapter.

Border station hours

While many border crossing locations are in operation 24 hours a day, 7 days a week, some border crossings in rural areas may have limited operating hours. Be sure to check with your intended border crossing office to ensure the office will be open when you arrive.

▌Crossing the Canadian border

Crossing the border into Canada requires patience and a general understanding of the paperwork and procedures required by the CBSA. If you have done your homework in these areas, your border crossing should be relatively painless.

Border station entry

When you approach most border stations, you will find that there are certain lanes specified for the various vehicles entering the station. Use the designated commercial lanes, regardless of how long they are, at the border crossing station. Watch for signs that will direct you to the proper areas. It is important to remember crossing into Canada is a well-established systematic process. If you follow the signs and the directions of the officials at the border, your problems should be minimal.

Questioning

Upon arrival at the border, be prepared to answer a series of questions pertaining to your truck, your freight, your purpose for entering Canada, and your background or citizenship.

Officers will ask you questions to make sure you are not involved in any illegal activity and that you have met all documentation requirements for you, your vehicle, and your load. Some possible questions you may be asked include:

- How long will you be visiting Canada?
- Where will you be staying while in Canada?
- What will you be doing in Canada during your stay?
- What is your date of intended return to the United States?
- Do you have items to declare?
- Do you have any weapons in your possession?
- What are you hauling?
- Are you traveling alone?

Answer all questions directly and honestly. Be sure to listen closely and follow all further instructions from the CBSA officers.

Customs inspections

CBSA may inspect your cargo for illegal drugs/weapons and plants/animals that are not permitted into Canada. They may also search the cab of your truck for these items and may also search for illegal aliens or undeclared passengers. Last, they may inspect your cargo to insure that what you are carrying matches the paperwork you have provided.

Paperwork

The type of cargo you are hauling can determine what types of paperwork you will be required to submit at the border. Some shipments that are going to Canada are released or cleared by the CBSA at the border, and some shipments are released or cleared at warehouses or other inland locations. The manner in which cargo is released can also change the type of paperwork needed to transport a shipment into and out of Canada.

Some common forms/paperwork required to be submitted or shown at the Canadian border may include the following:

- *Form 7525–V, Shipper's Export Declaration.* Form 7525–V is actually a form required by U.S. Customs and Border Protection (CBP). This form notifies the CBP that you are exporting goods into Canada.
- *Form A8B, United States–Canada Transit Manifest.* This form is used to report shipments traveling through, but not delivering within, the United States and Canada.
- *B232, North American Free Trade Agreement (NAFTA)–Certificate of Origin.* Form B232 is used by importers to report goods qualifying under the NAFTA.
- *Bill of Lading.* The bill of lading describes the property you are carrying, as well as its origin and destination.

26

▌ Border crossing programs

There are several different types of border crossing programs in which you or your carrier may be involved. These border crossing programs were created to expedite shipments and drivers across the Canadian border while ensuring the shipments are legal and secure. Some of these programs are listed below.

PARS

The pre-arrival review system (PARS) is a program that allows shipments to be released directly into Canada without additional inspection at the border. The exporter/shipper will provide advance cargo documentation to CBSA, who will then look over the cargo documentation for accuracy and validity. When the driver arrives at the border, the driver's paperwork is matched to the information previously sent by the exporter or shipper. If everything matches, CBSA will then usually release the cargo without further inspection.

CSA

Customs Self Assessment (CSA) is a program under which carriers and drivers can take advantage of streamlined clearance options for eligible goods. Carriers must apply for the CSA program and meet certain conditions before becoming a CSA participant.

FAST

U.S. CBP and Canada's CBSA have aligned to create the Free and Secure Trade Program (FAST). This program establishes a harmonized clearance process for low-risk shipments and helps expedite shipments across the border. Dedicated FAST lanes at border crossings allow drivers and carriers with FAST clearance to cross the border much more quickly. Carriers and/or drivers must pre-apply for FAST through the U.S. CBP or the Canada's CBSA.

U.S. ACE/Canada eManifest

U.S. Customs and Border Protection's Automated Commercial Environment (ACE) provides a single, centralized online access point to connect U.S. Customs and Border Protection (CBP) and the trade community. The ACE online portal provides access to other government agencies with trade and border enforcement responsibilities.

ACE or another electronic data interchange (EDI) is required of motor carriers for submission of electronic manifest information for land entry into the U.S.

eManifest is Canada's equivalent to ACE and it can be used for land entry into Canada.

▌ Returning to the United States from Canada

Upon returning to the United States after your trip to Canada, you will be required to show identification, such as your CDL, and proof of citizenship. You should already have these items available, as you needed them to enter Canada.

If you are returning with freight, you will also be required to show proper credentials and paperwork for the freight, similar to what you needed when you entered Canada with a load.

■ Motor carrier safety and licensing

As referenced earlier, while operating in Canada, you need to be aware of some differences in the safety regulations as they apply to the professional driver. As in the United States, you need to be in compliance when operating in Canada.

Canada's hours of service

Canada's hours-of-service requirements are different from those in the United States. Canada's regulations compared to U.S. regulations can be summarized as follows:

Time, Cycle, Etc	Canadian HOS regulations	U.S. HOS regulations
Daily Driving Time	13 hours per day or workshift after 8 hours off	11 hours after 10 hours off duty
Daily on-duty time	No driving after 14 on-duty hours per day or workshift after 8 hours off	No driving after the 14th consecutive hour after coming on-duty
Daily off-duty time	8 hours before driving, 10 hours per day 24 consecutive hours within past 14 days	10 consecutive hours off duty; 30 minute break required before the end of the 8th consecutive hour of duty time
Length of workday	No driving after 16 consecutive hours	No driving after 14 consecutive hours
Duty Cycle	70 hours/7 days (Cycle 1) 120 hours/14 days (Cycle 2)	60 hours/7 days 70 hours/8 days
Cycle Reset	36 hours for Cycle 1; 72 hours for Cycle 2 (upon reaching 70th hour in Cycle 2, driver must take 24 consecutive hours off duty)	34-hour restart

Canada also requires additional items to be recorded in the daily log, such as:

- Starting/ending odometer reading and total distance traveled (minus any personal use);
- Drivers cycle identified;
- Starting/ending odometer reading for any personal use (up to 75 kilometers, approximately 47 miles travel per day); and
- Home terminal and address.

Vehicle trip inspections

Canada requires a documented pre-trip inspection of vehicles while the U.S. requires a documented post-trip inspection when vehicle defects or deficiencies are discovered.

The U.S. and Canada have a reciprocal agreement in place for trip inspection reporting. Part of the reciprocal

Though U.S. regulation only requires that a DVIR be completed when no defects or deficiencies are discovered, Canada requires that the last day's DVIR be carried on the vehicle (defect or no defect). This means that you need to have a completed DVIR on your vehicle even if you did not find any defects or deficiencies on your vehicle.

26

agreement is that a U.S.-based driver must carry his/her previous days' post-trip inspection when traveling in Canada. Be sure you have proof of a post-trip inspection before entering Canada, including when no defects or deficiencies are discovered on your vehicle.

Operating authority/Canadian safety credentials

Operating authority in the United States is granted by the Federal Motor Carrier Safety Administration (FMCSA). In Canada however, a federal operating authority does not exist. Instead, Canada-based carriers must obtain a safety operating authority called a safety fitness certificate. In most Canadian jurisdictions, the requirements for a carrier to obtain a safety fitness certificate only apply to Canada-based carriers. However, two provinces, Ontario and Quebec, both require U.S.-based carriers to obtain registration within the provinces.

In Ontario, it is called the Commercial Vehicle Operator Registration and in Quebec it is called the Registration Identification Number. Both registrations allow Ontario and Quebec to track the safety performance of U.S. carriers operating in the provinces. While operating in these provinces, you may have to produce credentials showing that your carrier is registered under these programs.

IFTA/IRP credentials

Because the International Fuel Tax Agreement (IFTA) and the International Registration Plan (IRP) apply to the lower 48 states and 10 Canadian provinces, you must have proper IFTA and IRP credentials when operating in Canada. For IFTA, you will have a copy of the IFTA license in your cab and IFTA decals on both sides of your cab.

For IRP, you will have a cab card listing vehicle weights and the states and provinces in which your vehicle can travel. The carrier will likely provide you with all necessary documentation and permits.

Canadian enforcement officers are authorized to ask to see your IFTA and IRP credentials at any time.

▊ Vehicle sizes and weights

The vehicle size and weight requirements in Canada are different, but similar to, the requirements in the United States.

In Canada, the vehicle size and weight requirements are established by each jurisdiction. For example, the size and weight requirements in British Columbia may not be the same as the requirements in Ontario. In order to create uniformity among the Canadian jurisdictions, all jurisdictions agreed to a "Memorandum of Understanding" (MOU) on vehicle size and weights.

The MOU establishes the following size and weight limitations:

- Height 4.15 m (13 ft. 6 in.)
- Width 2.60 m (8 ft. 6 in.)
- Length -
    - 1. Straight truck 12.5 m (41 ft.)
    - 2. Semitrailer 16.2 m (53 ft.)
    - 3. Truck-trailer 23.0 m (75 ft. 6 in.)

- Weight -
  - 1. Straight truck 24,250 kg (53,462 lb.)
  - 2. Tractor-semitrailer 46,500 kg (102,515 lb.)
  - 3. Truck-full trailer 53,500 kg (117,947 lb.)

Even though the MOU is in place, a Canadian jurisdiction may adopt less restrictive size and weight limits for roads within their jurisdiction. Refer to the individual jurisdictions' size and weight regulations for more information.

Metric measurements and conversions

Canada uses the metric system which is unlike the United States, where the English system is used. Common conversions of the English and metric systems include the following:

- 1 meter = 3.28 feet
- 1 kilometer = 0.621 miles
- 1 kilogram = 2.2046 pounds
- 1 foot = 0.3048 meters
- 1 mile = 1.6093 kilometers
- 1 pound = 0.454 kilograms

To convert a metric measurement to an English measurement, simply multiply by the English conversion equivalent. For example:

- To convert 80 kilometers to miles: 80 x 0.621 = 49.7 miles
- To convert 20 meters to feet: 20 x 3.28 = 65.6 feet

Canada uses degrees Celsius to represent temperature. To convert Celsius temperatures to Fahrenheit, multiply the degrees Celsius by 1.8 and add 32. For example, to determine the Fahrenheit temperature equivalent to 25° C, multiply (25°C x 1.8) + 32 = 77°F

Summary

In this chapter, you learned about the basic requirements you must be able to meet in order to cross the U.S./Canada border. Planning ahead, being patient, and acting professional go a long way when it comes to making a smooth transition across the border.

26

INTERNATIONAL DRIVING QUIZ

Directions: *Read each statement carefully and mark the response that best answers the question.*

1. To enter Canada, you need proof of identification and citizenship.
   A. True
   B. False

2. If you have a felony conviction on your record, you may not cross the border into Canada.
   A. True
   B. False

3. Canadians use the _____ system to measure everything including speed and fuel.
   A. Modified imperial
   B. U.S.
   C. Metric
   D. World trade

4. When crossing the border into Canada you must declare certain personal items including:
   A. Prescription drugs
   B. Animals
   C. Tobacco
   D. All of the above

5. The Free and Secure Trade (FAST) supports moving _____ across the border quickly.
   A. Race cars only
   B. Low-risk shipments
   C. All items manufactured in Europe
   D. Any items that originate in South America

6. When going through Canadian customs, you should be cordial and helpful with inspectors.
   A. True
   B. False

7. Regarding commercial drivers in Canada, which of the following is a correct statement?
   A. Maximum time on duty is 20 hours including driving time
   B. You are limited to 13 hours of daily driving time
   C. 6 hours off duty is required before a driver can drive again
   D. In any seven day period, drivers may be on duty for only 60 hours

8. Because it is a foreign country, you do not need IRP or IFTA credentials when operating in Canada.
   A. True
   B. False

9. Because you are a U.S. citizen, you do not need identification or proof of citizenship when coming back into the U.S. from Canada.
   A. True
   B. False

10. Canada requires a documented pre-trip inspection report.
    A. True
    B. False

CDL AIR BRAKE PRE-TEST

Read each question carefully and select the most correct answer.

1. What will determine how effectively the spring emergency brakes or the parking brakes work?

   A. The condition of the service brakes
   B. This can only be tested by highly trained brake service people
   C. The adjustment of the service brakes
   D. Braking power will increase when the service brakes are hot

2. When a failure occurs in the service brake system, the system you need to stop the vehicle is the:

   A. Parking brake system
   B. Emergency brake system
   C. Drum brake system
   D. Hand brake system

3. If your vehicle is equipped with an alcohol evaporator, every day during the winter weather you should:

   A. Check and fill the alcohol level
   B. Change the alcohol with a new bottle
   C. Oil the system with 5 wt. oil
   D. Drain out the alcohol which has accumulated

4. What turns on the electrical stop light switch in an air brake system?

   A. Spring pressure
   B. Hydraulic pressure
   C. Air pressure
   D. The driver, by hand

5. Which of the following is O.K. to find in the air brake system?

   A. Oil
   B. Air
   C. Water
   D. All of the above

Trip planning

OBJECTIVES

Upon completion of this chapter, you should have a general understanding of the five basic steps involved when planning a trip:

- Having up to date paperwork
- Selecting a route
- Estimating time
- Estimating fuel use and fuel stops
- Estimating trip expenses

27 Trip planning

- THE FIVE BASIC STEPS OF TRIP PLANNING
- PAPERWORK
- ROUTE SELECTION
- VEHICLE AND CARGO RESTRICTIONS
- ESTIMATING TIME
- ESTIMATING FUEL USAGE
- ESTIMATING TRIP EXPENSES
- SUMMARY

INTRODUCTION

The idea behind trip planning is to design the most effective, efficient, safe, and legal route between two points.

A well thought out trip plan can mean a savings of time and money for you and your motor carrier. A good plan can also mean a safe trip for you and the load you are hauling. If you have a solid plan before hitting the road, you are better able to relax and devote all of your time to paying attention to the road.

The five basic steps of trip planning

The following are the five basic steps of trip planning.

1. Make sure paperwork is up to date. Have proper freight documentation, current hours-of-service records, and proper permits and licenses.

2. Select the route. Remember, many variables are involved including cargo restrictions, traffic conditions, and weather.

3. Estimate time and plan for stops. Plan to meet the scheduled deadline, but consider driver and vehicle factors as well as weather and road conditions.

4. Estimate fuel use and fuel stops.

5. Estimate trip expenses. Understand the length and nature of the trip, what conditions to expect on the road, and plan for the unexpected.

Paperwork

After driving, paperwork is probably the largest task a driver deals with on a daily basis. Making sure you have all necessary paperwork and that the paperwork is accurate before your trip is essential to planning an efficient and profitable trip.

Generally, the paperwork you should carry with you falls under three categories — driver, cargo, and vehicle.

Driver

As the driver of a commercial motor vehicle (CMV), the Federal Motor Carrier Safety Regulations (FMCSRs) require you to carry certain documents to verify that you are a qualified driver.

Operator's license — You are required to have a valid operator's (driver's) license to operate a motor vehicle. You must carry this license when operating a motor vehicle.

The class of license you must hold is based on the type of vehicle you are operating.

The commercial driver's license (CDL) classes are federally mandated. (See Sec. 383.91 of the FMCSRs for details.) The CDL classes are as follows:

- Class A — Any combination of vehicles with a gross combination weight rating (GCWR) of 26,001 pounds or more provided the gross vehicle weight rating (GVWR) of the vehicle(s) being towed is in excess of 10,000 pounds.

- Class B — Any single vehicle with a GVWR of 26,001 pounds or more, or any such vehicle towing a vehicle not in excess of 10,000 pounds GVWR.

- Class C — Any single vehicle, or combination of vehicles that meets neither the definition of Class A nor that of Class B, but is designed to transport 16 or more passengers (including the driver) or is used in the transportation of a placardable amount of hazardous materials.

Non-CDL classes of license vary from state to state. Consult state laws and regulations for details.

Medical exam certificate — The driver qualification regulations in Part 391 of the FMCSRs place a great deal of emphasis on physical qualifications. This includes a requirement that you pass a physical exam and receive a valid physical exam certificate.

If you operate CMVs, and you do not possess a CDL you must carry a copy of this certificate at all times.

If you possess a CDL, you are not required to carry a copy of the medical exam certificate. A valid copy of the certificate must be on file at all times with your state licensing agency. See Chapter 1 for details.

Form MCSA-5876 (Revised: 12/06/2015)   OMB No. 2126-0006   Expiration Date: 8/31/2018

Public Burden Statement
A Federal agency may not conduct or sponsor, and a person is not required to respond to, nor shall a person be subject to a penalty for failure to comply with a collection of information subject to the requirements of the Paperwork Reduction Act unless that collection of information displays a current valid OMB Control Number. The OMB Control Number for this information collection is 2126-0006. Public reporting for this collection of information is estimated to be approximately 1 minute per response, including the time for reviewing instructions, gathering the data needed, and completing and reviewing the collection of information. All responses to this collection of information are mandatory. Send comments regarding this burden estimate or any other aspect of this collection of information, including suggestions for reducing this burden to: Information Collection Clearance Officer, Federal Motor Carrier Safety Administration, MC-RRA, 1200 New Jersey Avenue, SE, Washington, D.C. 20590.

U.S. Department of Transportation
Federal Motor Carrier
Safety Administration

Medical Examiner's Certificate
(for Commercial Driver Medical Certification)

I certify that I have examined **Last Name:** _____   **First Name:** _____   in accordance with *(please check only one)*:

○ the Federal Motor Carrier Safety Regulations (49 CFR 391.41-391.49) and, with knowledge of the driving duties, I find this person is qualified, and, if applicable, only when *(check all that apply)* **OR**

○ the Federal Motor Carrier Safety Regulations (49 CFR 391.41-391.49) with any applicable State variances (which will only be valid for intrastate operations), and, with knowledge of the driving duties, I find this person is qualified, and, if applicable, only when *(check all that apply)*:

☐ Wearing corrective lenses   ☐ Accompanied by a _____ waiver/exemption   ☐ Driving within an exempt intracity zone (49 CFR 391.62) *(Federal)*
☐ Wearing hearing aid   ☐ Accompanied by a Skill Performance Evaluation (SPE) Certificate   ☐ Qualified by operation of 49 CFR 391.64 *(Federal)*
                                                                    ☐ Grandfathered from State requirements *(State)*

Medical Examiner's Certificate Expiration Date
_____

The information I have provided regarding this physical examination is true and complete. A complete Medical Examination Report Form, MCSA-5875, with any attachments embodies my findings completely and correctly, and is on file in my office.

Medical Examiner's Signature _____   **Medical Examiner's Telephone Number** _____   **Date Certificate Signed** _____

Medical Examiner's Name *(please print or type)* _____   ○ MD   ○ Physician Assistant   ○ Advanced Practice Nurse
                                                                    ○ DO   ○ Chiropractor   ○ Other Practitioner *(specify)* _____

Medical Examiner's State License, Certificate, or Registration Number _____   **Issuing State** _____   **National Registry Number** _____

Driver's Signature _____   **Driver's License Number** _____   **Issuing State/Province** _____

Driver's Address   **CLP/CDL Applicant/Holder**
Street Address: _____   City: _____   State/Province: _____   Zip Code: _____   ○ Yes ○ No

ORIGINAL - DRIVER

Record of duty status — Each motor carrier must require every driver to record his/her duty status for each 24-hour period.

You must complete the record of duty status in your own handwriting (in duplicate) or by using an electronic logging device (ELD). The record must be legible and kept current to the time shown for the last change of duty status.

You must submit the original record of duty status to your motor carrier within 13 days of completion.

You must have in your possession a copy of each record for the last 7 consecutive days as well as the original record for the current day. They must be available for inspection while you are on duty.

The use of electronic logging devices (ELDs) by motor carriers and drivers to record the driver's hours of service is growing at a fast pace. For more information on the hours-of-service regulations, including the use of ELDs, see Chapter 25.

Many carriers require drivers to submit their original records of duty status prior to the regulatory requirement of 13 days.

Cargo

Paperwork regarding the freight you are hauling should be in proper order before you begin your trip. This ensures the safe and accurate delivery of goods to the appropriate party.

Bill of lading — The bill of lading is the document used in transactions between a shipper and carrier. There are three distinct and important functions served by the bill of lading:

1. It is a receipt issued by the carrier to a shipper for goods received for transportation.

2. It is a contract naming the parties involved, the rate/charge for transportation, and the agreement regarding the carrier's liability in the event of damage or loss of goods.

3. It serves as documentary evidence of title to the goods.

Unless specifically instructed otherwise, the carrier's duty is to deliver the shipment to the consignee named on the bill of lading. Possession of an original bill of lading, properly endorsed, indicates title to the goods.

This is an important document so make sure it's right from the beginning. If something looks incorrect, or incomplete, question it. If you are not getting answers, stop what you are doing and call your dispatcher.

Bills of lading must be legibly written.

The following information must be included on the bill of lading:

- Names of consignor and consignee;
- Origin and destination points;
- Number of packages;
- Description of freight; and
- Weight, volume, or measure of freight (if applicable to the rating of the freight).

In-depth information on the bill of lading requirements is covered in Chapter 23.

27

Vehicle

Paperwork regarding vehicle operations is completed throughout a trip. Accuracy is important, as the paperwork listed below is required by regulation and/or law.

Driver vehicle inspection report (DVIR) — At the end of your day's work on the vehicle you operated, you need to review the condition of your vehicle.

If during this post-trip inspection of your vehicle, you discover any defects or deficiencies which could affect the safe operation of your vehicle or cause a mechanical breakdown, you must complete a written report, commonly referred to as a driver vehicle inspection report (DVIR).

Though the regulations do not mandate that you carry this document on your vehicle, some motor carriers require that the DVIR stay with the vehicle as part of its vehicle maintenance policy.

Though a driver is not required by the FMCSRs to complete a DVIR when no defects or deficiencies are discovered during a post-trip inspection, many motor carriers do require a driver to complete a DVIR at the end of each day's work on a vehicle. This best practice and safety management control aids the motor carrier in minimizing the risk of operating unsafe vehicles and aids in protecting the motor carrier's Vehicle Maintenance BASIC score under the FMCSA's CSA program.

See Chapter 4 for additional information addressing DVIRs.

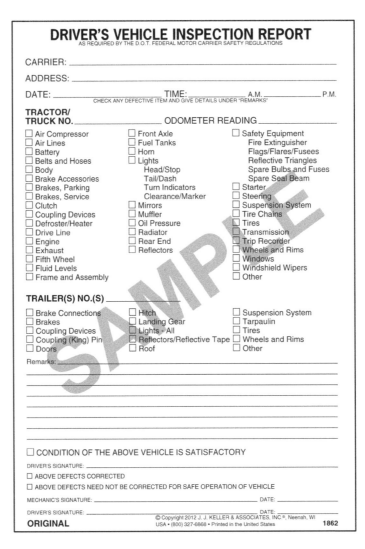

Trip report — A trip report or individual vehicle mileage report (IVMR) is used to record trip information including (but not limited to):

- Date of trip (starting and ending);
- Trip origin and destination;
- Route of travel and/or beginning and ending odometer reading of the trip;
- Total trip miles;
- Unit number or vehicle identification number.

The trip report must be accurate as this information is used by the carrier to file International Fuel Tax Agreement (IFTA) quarterly fuel tax returns and International Registration Plan (IRP) annual vehicle registration renewals. In the event the carrier is audited, the auditor will examine trip reports and fuel receipts for accuracy.

You should also complete a trip cost report. It tracks expenses incurred during the course of a trip. A trip cost report includes detailed information on:

- Fuel purchases;
- Brokerage fees;
- Permit fees;
- Tolls; and
- Scale fees.

Route selection

Many factors go into the selection of an appropriate route. Though, when reading a map, the shortest route (mileage-wise) may appear to be the best, this isn't always the case. Terrain, weather, traffic, road construction, and vehicle and cargo restrictions all play a part in selecting an appropriate route.

Reading maps

Being able to read and understand a road map is the first step in selecting an efficient route.

The road map is a necessary tool, helping you determine routes and locate specific destinations. Essential map reading skills you need to be proficient in include:

- Locating the starting point, intermediate stops, and the destination;
- Laying the route out on a map;
- Estimating point-to-point mileage using the map scale; and
- Reading map symbols.

Maps have many characteristics you need to understand in order to successfully plan a trip.

The majority of maps are set on a box or grid pattern with letters along the top and bottom and numbers along the sides of the map. A box or key within the map lists destinations (cities, towns, streets) and where to find them within the grid system.

All maps include a scale. The scale lists how many inches represent a given number of miles.

27

Map scales are good for figuring a rough mileage estimate. Mileage charts give a better idea of true distance.

Symbols are also included on all maps. Symbols represent everything from the size of a community to where to find a rest area. Symbols vary from map to map and all maps include a legend explaining the symbols used.

There are two types of maps most drivers rely on, highway maps and city maps.

Highway maps — Highway maps show an entire state or region. They sometimes include major cities in some detail. Features vary depending on the map, but all include major routes, road types, toll roads and freeways, population centers, and railroad crossings. Highway maps are best used to locate major highways and routes for long distance travel.

City maps — City maps provide the greatest detail. Major street names are readable and secondary streets can often be located on these types of maps.

Global positioning systems (GPS)

The use of an electronic navigation system, also referred to as a global positioning system (GPS) can make trip planning easier for the professional driver, if the driver uses the correct device and uses the device correctly.

Not all devices are the same. The device you may use in your personal vehicle is not the one you should be using in your CMV. You need to use a device that is designed specifically for truck drivers.

So what's the difference? In addition to general route information, a GPS designed for truck drivers includes information on low overpasses/bridges, route restrictions, and upcoming scales.

Using a GPS — Before beginning your trip, you will need to type in all relevant information about your vehicle so the GPS can provide you with the appropriate route, including:

Do not engage in distracted driving. Avoid typing and entering addresses or information into the GPS when behind the wheel.

- Your vehicle's length, width, and height;
- Your axle weights; and
- Hazardous materials you are transporting (if applicable).

Once you are on the road, follow the route recommended by the GPS, but always be alert to and obey all traffic signs and advisories (such as low bridge overpasses, weight limitations, detour signs). Also, do not be totally dependent on the directions provided, use common sense. Though the GPS provides a great deal of information, sometimes conditions change and the GPS may not include the most current information.

If your GPS does not provide automatic updates of the maps, be sure update your maps often so you have the most current information.

Online resources

Keep in mind that maps do not include information on delays caused by road construction or poor weather conditions. This information is available via the internet from several sources including the Federal Highway Administration (FHWA): http://www.fhwa.dot.gov/trafficinfo/.

Vehicle and cargo restrictions

Even the best planned trip can run into some unplanned delays and/or problems. Issues such as restricted routes and weight limits on roads and/or bridges must be dealt with while on the road.

Legal weight limits — Your vehicle must stay within legal limits. Federal requirements outlined in 49 CFR 658.17 are as follows:

- The maximum gross vehicle weight (GVW) is 80,000 pounds except where a lower GVW is dictated by the bridge formula.

- The maximum gross weight on any one axle, including any one axle of a group of axles, or a vehicle, is 20,000 pounds.

- The maximum gross weight on tandem axles is 34,000 pounds.

- Vehicles are not allowed on Interstate highways if the gross weight on two or more consecutive axles exceeds the limitations prescribed in the Bridge Gross Weight Formula, described below.

$$W = 500\left[\frac{LN}{N-1} + 12N + 36\right]$$

- W = the maximum weight in pounds that can be carried on a group of two or more axles to the nearest 500 pounds.

- L = the distance in feet between the outer axles of any two or more consecutive axles.

- N = the number of axles being considered.

This formula limits the weight on groups of axles in order to reduce the risk of damage to highway bridges. Allowable weight depends on the number of axles a vehicle has and the distance between those axles. However, the single- or tandem-axle weight limits supersede the Bridge Formula limits for all axles not more than 96 inches apart.

Truck routes — Communities often designate certain roads as truck routes, in many cases, prohibiting trucks from operating outside of these routes

Each state has its own weight limitations. Be aware of the regulations for the states you travel through. Also keep in mind that weight limits may be posted on individual roads or bridges. Vehicles exceeding the posted weights are prohibited.

Estimating time

Estimating time is crucial to your success as a professional driver. Most deliveries and pickups have scheduled times. If you miss those times, you may have to wait hours or even days to get loaded or unloaded.

Estimating the time a trip will take is necessary for planning stops, complying with hours-of-service regulations, estimating arrival time, and of course meeting schedules.

A general guideline that is used by many drivers is to allow two hours for every 100 miles traveled. This amount of time is a reasonable amount to cover driving time, meals, fuel stops, and rest stops.

27

If you drive mainly in the western states, you may be able to average better than this figure; however, it's important to understand that this is an average. If you drive 75 mph sometimes and 55 mph other times you may be averaging only 60 mph, so don't plan your entire trip at 75 mph just because that's what the posted speed limit is in the state you are running.

Many motor carriers set their vehicles' governors at between 60 mph and 65 mph (many at 62 mph). If you drive for a carrier that does this, make sure you take this into account when planning your trip.

This holds true conversely if you are running mainly in the northeast. Even though most posted speeds in that area are 55 mph, you may only average 45 or 50 due to increased traffic and congestion.

Keep in mind weather, traffic, and other conditions which could affect trip time. Remember, no driver is able to drive the maximum speed limit at all times.

Also take into consideration the hours-of-service regulations. Under these regulations, located in Part 395 of the FMCSRs, the driver of a property-carrying commercial motor vehicle may not drive:

- More than 11 hours following 10 consecutive hours off duty; or
- Beyond the 14th consecutive hour after coming on duty, following 10 consecutive hours off duty; or

See Chapter 25 for complete details on the hours-of-service regulations.

- After being on duty more than 60 or 70 hours in any 7 or 8 consecutive days.

Estimating fuel usage

Fuel usage estimates are needed to plan fuel stops.

The first step in estimating fuel usage is to determine the range of the vehicle. To find the range of a vehicle, multiply the tank capacity (in gallons) by the miles per gallon the vehicle delivers.

Tank capacity (gallons) x Miles per gallon (mpg) = Range

Average fuel usage is based on several factors including:

- Highway driving;
- City (town) driving;
- Slowdowns; and
- Idling time.

There are also factors/conditions that may not occur on a daily basis that you should keep in mind when estimating fuel use including:

- Idling for an extended period of time;
- Driving at higher speeds;
- Driving in the mountains; and
- Headwinds.

▌ Estimating trip expenses

Estimating the amount of money a trip will take means planning for food, fuel, tolls, and overnight stops. When estimating expenses, consider the:

- Distance to be traveled;
- Time the trip will take; and
- Possibility that emergency funds may be needed.

Items topping the expense list include meals, layovers, tolls, rest stops, and fuel stops. In an emergency, you may need funds for towing, a service call, or an unexpected layover.

▌ Summary

A well thought out trip plan can save your company time and money. Proper planning can save you from having to worry about certain details while on the road, allowing you to concentrate on driving safely.

27

TRIP PLANNING QUIZ

Directions: *Read each statement carefully and mark the response that best answers the question.*

1. When on the road, you do not need to carry your CDL.
   A. True
   B. False

2. Paperwork regarding the freight you are hauling should be in proper order before you begin your trip.
   A. True
   B. False

3. The information you record on a trip report must be accurate as it is used by auditors to verify payment of taxes.
   A. True
   B. False

4. What do you need to consider when selecting a route?
   A. Vehicle and cargo restrictions
   B. Local traffic conditions
   C. Weather conditions
   D. All of the above

5. Maps include information on delays caused by road construction or poor weather conditions.
   A. True
   B. False

6. All maps include a scale that can help you figure out a rough mileage estimate.
   A. True
   B. False

7. How many hours should you allow for each 100 miles traveled when estimating trip time?
   A. 1 hour
   B. 1.5 hours
   C. 2 hours
   D. 3 hours

8. When estimating a vehicle's fuel usage you need to determine the range of the vehicle.
   A. True
   B. False

9. When estimating trip expenses, you should consider:
   A. Distance traveled
   B. Time the trip will take
   C. Emergency funds
   D. All of the above

10. A well thought out trip plan can mean a savings of time and money for you and your company.
    A. True
    B. False

CDL AIR BRAKE PRE-TEST

Read each question carefully and select the most correct answer.

1. Air brakes use _____ to make the brakes work.

   A. Water
   B. Oil
   C. Processed air
   D. Compressed air

2. If your truck or bus has dual parking control valves, you can use pressure from a separate tank to:

   A. Release the spring brake to move in an emergency
   B. Apply more brake pressure for stopping if the main tank is getting low
   C. Stay parked without using up service air pressure
   D. Balance the service brake system while you drive

3. In air-brake equipped vehicles, you use the parking brakes _____.

   A. When slowing down
   B. As little as possible
   C. Whenever you park the vehicle
   D. Only during pre-trip and post-trip inspections

4. When driving, spring brakes (the parking and emergency brakes) are usually held back by:

   A. Air pressure
   B. Spring pressure
   C. Centrifugal force
   D. Bolts or clamps

5. Vehicles with an antilock braking system (ABS) have _____ to tell you something is not working.

   A. Green lights
   B. A red button
   C. Yellow malfunction lamps
   D. All of the above

Accident procedures

OBJECTIVES

Upon completion of this chapter, you should
have a basic understanding of:

- Accident procedures
- Accident preventability guidelines
- Vehicle fire procedures

28 Accident procedures

- DEFINITIONS
- ACCIDENT REGISTER
- SECURING THE SCENE
- AT THE SCENE
- HAZARDOUS MATERIALS
- VEHICLE FIRES
- SUMMARY

INTRODUCTION

No matter how safely you operate your commercial motor vehicle, there is always the possibility that you could be involved in an accident.

As a professional driver, it is important that you have a clear understanding of your responsibilities at the scene in the event of an accident, as well as your role afterward.

▌ Definitions

An **accident** is defined in Sec. 390.5 of the Federal Motor Carrier Safety Regulations (FMCSRs) as an occurrence involving a commercial motor vehicle (CMV) operating on a highway in interstate or intrastate commerce which results in:

- A fatality;
- Injury to a person who, as a result of the injury, immediately receives medical treatment away from the scene of the accident; or
- Disabling damage to one or more of the vehicles, requiring the vehicle(s) to be towed from the scene.

A **fatality** means any injury which results in the death of a person at the time of the accident or within 30 days of the accident.

Disabling damage includes vehicles that could have been driven, but would have been further damaged if driven. Excluded from the definition of disabling damage is:

- Damage which can be temporarily fixed at the scene without special tools or parts;

Sometimes the term "crash" is used instead of "accident." Both terms have the same meaning.

- Tire disablement without other damage (even if no spare is available);
- Headlamp or taillight damage; and
- Damage to turn signals, horn, or windshield wipers which makes them inoperative.

The term "accident" does not include incidents involving getting in or out of a parked vehicle, or which involve only the loading or unloading of a vehicle's cargo.

▌ Accident register

Section 390.15(b) of the FMCSRs, states that a motor carrier must keep an accident register. This register must include (at a minimum) the following information for each accident:

- Date of accident;
- Location (city/town and state) in which the accident occurred;

- Driver name;

- Number of injuries;

- Number of fatalities; and

- Whether hazardous materials, other than fuel spilled from the fuel tanks of the motor vehicles involved in the accident, were released.

The accident register must also include copies of all accident reports required by state or other governmental entities or insurers.

The motor carrier must retain all of this information for three years after the date of the accident.

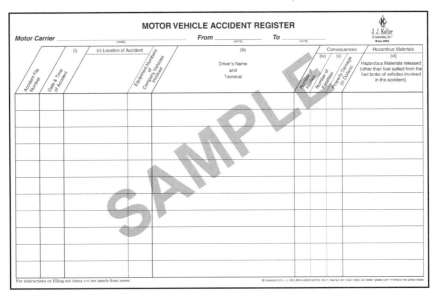

Securing the scene

No matter how safely you drive your vehicle, there's always a chance of being involved in an accident. When the unexpected happens, it is important that you know what to do and what to expect.

When an accident occurs, you must deal with immediate problems and gather and report accident information in a timely manner. The following steps can help you accomplish these tasks.

Stop immediately

Failure to stop (or leaving the scene), when involved in an accident is a serious offense; so serious that it is listed as a disqualifying offense in Sec. 383.51 and Sec. 391.15 of the FMCSRs.

As a commercial driver's license (CDL) holder, if you are convicted of this offense, you are disqualified from operating a CMV for one year.

See Sec. 383.51 of the FMCSRs for disqualification details.

In addition to being a disqualifying offense, failure to stop (or leaving the scene) is against the law and can result in fines and/or jail time.

When involved in an accident, remain calm and pull your vehicle as far off the road as possible.

If the accident involves an unoccupied vehicle, try to find the owner. If the owner can't be found, leave your name, the company's name, address, and phone number in a visible location, such as under a windshield wiper blade, and contact law enforcement. Also write down the make, model, year, license number, and description of the unoccupied vehicle to supply to your company.

Prevent additional accidents

Turn on your vehicle's four-way flashers and then set out emergency warning devices. The devices (in most cases reflective triangles) must be set out within 10 minutes of stopping.

Emergency warning device placement is spelled out in Part 392 of the FMCSRs and is described below:

Two-lane road — The devices should be placed as follows:

When placing the emergency warning devices, hold them in front of you to increase you visibility to traffic. Also consider wearing a high visibility vest.

- The first device should be placed on the traffic side of the vehicle four paces (about 10 feet) from the front or rear, depending on traffic direction.

- The second device should be placed 40 paces (about 100 feet) behind the vehicle.

- A third device should be placed 40 paces (about 100 feet) ahead of the vehicle on the shoulder or in the lane the vehicle is in.

One-way or divided highway — The devices should be placed 10, 100, and 200 feet from the rear of the vehicle, toward approaching traffic.

Within 500 feet of a hill, curve, or obstruction — A device should be placed 100 to 500 feet from the vehicle in the direction of the obstruction. The other two should be placed according to the rules for two-lane or divided highways.

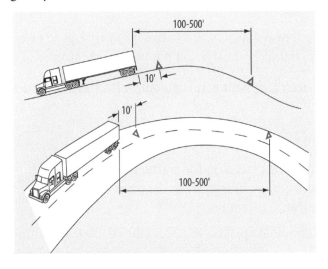

Three bidirectional emergency reflective triangles, six fusees, or three liquid burning flares are acceptable warning devices with which a vehicle must be equipped. The triangles must meet the specifications of 49 CFR 571.125. Fuses and liquid-burning flares must meet Underwriters Laboratories standards. Flame-producing devices are prohibited on vehicles carrying explosives, a flammable gas, a flammable liquid, or a motor vehicle using compressed gas as a motor fuel.

When placing emergency warning devices, be alert for other drivers who may not see you on the road.

Notify law enforcement

Call law enforcement officials. Provide as many details as possible, including the location of the accident, the number of vehicles involved, and the number of people involved.

Never leave the scene of an accident to notify law enforcement unless there is no means of communicating at the accident site.

Check for injuries

If anyone is hurt, you should call for medical assistance. Do not move an injured person unless there's a risk of fire or additional injury.

At a minimum, you should call for help, ask if the other party wants someone contacted, and keep him/her warm. Doing too much can be just as dangerous as doing nothing at all. Never attempt to do something you are not trained in.

Document the accident

Detail is important. The more detail you can provide can assist with insurance and legal issues. When documenting the accident, you should include:

- Time and location of accident;
- Description of damage to vehicles and property;

- Name and address of all individuals involved;
- Name and address of insurance companies of all individuals involved;
- Type, make, model, and license numbers of all vehicles involved; and
- Names and departments of any investigating officers.

Many motor carriers provide accident reporting kits in their trucks. These kits can be used to answer questions in a time when you may not be thinking straight. Also, a disposable camera may be a great resource to record how the event happened. Drawing a simple diagram of the situation is also a good idea.

Photographs — A disposable camera may be the most useful item you can have at the scene. Taking pictures will help determine how an accident occurred and how much damage was involved. But you need to know what to photograph, and what not to photograph.

- Take wide shots from the fog stripe at the edge of the road toward the point of impact, showing the final location of the vehicles.
- Take wide shots from the centerline and all sides of the vehicles, including the damage.
- Take close-up shots of damage and any skid marks or road debris.
- Never take pictures of individuals who have been injured or killed.

Contact your motor carrier

Notify your motor carrier of the accident as soon as possible. Know whom to call in the event of an accident. These names and phone numbers should always be available, possibly posted in a single place in each cab. Follow all company rules, be cooperative, and answer all questions posed by the company representative (safety director, dispatcher).

Post-accident testing —If certain conditions are met, your carrier will instruct you to go for a post-accident drug and alcohol test. The following table notes when a test is required under Sec. 382.303 of the FMCSRs.

Type of accident involved	Citation issued to the CMV driver	Test must be performed by the employer
Human fatality	YES	YES
	NO	YES
Bodily injury with immediate medical treatment away from the scene	YES	YES
	NO	NO
Disabling damage to any motor vehicle requiring tow away	YES	YES
	NO	NO

You are prohibited from consuming alcohol for eight hours after an accident, or until you submit to a post-accident alcohol test, whichever occurs first.

Damaged vehicle — The company representative will also direct you on how to handle a disabled or damaged commercial motor vehicle (towing, repair). If the vehicle is not disabled, the carrier may grant permission to drive the vehicle from the scene (providing it is given a thorough pre-trip inspection to ensure safety) to a garage.

Preliminary report

A preliminary accident report is often used as part of a motor carrier's investigation into an accident.

Depending on motor carrier policy, this type of report is completed by the driver or a representative of the motor carrier.

At the scene

Be polite and respectful at the accident scene. Note that anything said at the accident scene could be used against you and/or your motor carrier at a later date. You should not:

- Discuss specific details of the accident with others at the scene;
- Volunteer unnecessary information;
- Admit fault; and/or
- Try to settle anything at the scene — that's the job of law enforcement, insurance representatives, and the motor carrier.

To avoid problems after the accident you should:

- Honestly answer questions asked by the law enforcement officials investigating the accident;
- Be factual; and
- Never speculate or guess as to what may have caused the accident or who is at fault.

Hazardous materials

When an accident or incident involves a hazardous material, there may be additional risks to safety, health, and the environment. Because of this, there are additional regulatory requirements that must be followed.

If you haul hazardous materials, your employer must provide training to you on proper procedures for responding to leaks, spills, and other emergencies.

If you are involved in an incident or accident, you must immediately report this to your company. Regulatory requirements and company policy will dictate how you handle the situation. At the very least, keep bystanders away from the area.

If a hazardous material response team is called to the scene, follow their instructions.

Also, certain reports must be made by your company (See Sec. 171.15 and Sec. 171.16 of the Hazardous Materials Regulations for details.)

▌ Vehicle fires

A vehicle fire can be a dangerous and frightening experience. Common sense, good driving habits, and good housekeeping can prevent many vehicle fires but, unfortunately, not all fires can be prevented. You need to be prepared to face this potentially dangerous situation.

Prevention

All fires need fuel, air, and heat to ignite and spread. Fire prevention revolves around keeping those elements from coming together. Most vehicle fires occur in one of the following three areas:

- Cab/engine;
- Tires/brakes; and
- Cargo.

Cab/engine — Good housekeeping is important. The cab should be clean and free of debris at all times.

The engine compartment should be checked regularly. The engine should always be clean. If oils or fluids are spilled on the engine they should be wiped up immediately. After work is finished on the engine, all rags should be removed from the area and all fluid caps should be put back where they belong.

Regular checks should be made of the following items:

- Wiring and electrical system;
- Fuses;
- Battery; and
- Exhaust system.

When refueling, the engine should be turned off and all smoking materials should be extinguished. Turn off your cell phone. The fuel tank should be checked for signs of leakage. Also, make sure you have metal to metal contact while fueling.

Tires/brakes — Overheated tires are another way vehicle fires ignite. An underinflated tire can overheat, increasing the risk of a tire fire. A soft or flat tire should be changed as soon as possible.

If a hot tire is changed, it shouldn't be placed in the spare tire rack until it cools.

Brakes should also be checked regularly, as worn brakes can overheat, causing a fire.

All brakes (including the parking brake) should be fully released before a vehicle is moved.

Also, never ride the brakes. Riding the brakes can cause a fire in the brake linings that could spread to the tires.

Cargo — Periodically check your mirrors, looking for smoke. Smoking materials should never be used around a vehicle hauling hazardous materials or in the cargo area as freight is being loaded or unloaded.

Know what commodities you are hauling. This information is important so you and/or emergency crews can respond properly.

Putting out fires

The first consideration when a fire occurs is your safety and the safety of others. If possible, move the vehicle to a location away from other people, vehicles, and buildings. Getting the fire under control is the next step, but don't take unnecessary risks. If a fire is too large or dangerous to handle, leave it to the professionals.

Cab/engine fires — The following are basic steps to follow when dealing with a cab/engine fire.

- Turn off the vehicle's engine. If you can do it safely, also look for fuel leaks.
- Disconnect the battery cables from the terminals (if it can be safely done) if the fire is electrical.
- Don't open the hood more than necessary when fighting an engine fire. Remember, air is one of the ingredients that will help fuel a fire.
- Never use water on a petroleum-based fire. The use of water will cause a petroleum-based fire to spread.
- Follow the directions on the fire extinguisher. To avoid smoke and fumes, the extinguisher should be used with the wind behind the extinguisher.
- Never assume a fire is completely out. Fires often smolder, spark, and can reignite.

Tire fires — Tire fires are hard to extinguish and are dangerous. This is due to the fact that tires are made of highly flammable material. A tire fire can generate an intense amount of heat. There are several things that should be kept in mind when fighting a tire fire.

- Remove the hot tire (if it can be done safely) from the vehicle.
- Use water to fight a tire fire. Water helps cool a tire as well as extinguish flames. Fire extinguishers are good at suppressing flames, but will not be able to put out a tire fire.

Cargo fires — In many cases cargo fires are discovered by the sight or smell of smoke around cargo doors. There are several things to keep in mind when fighting a cargo fire.

- Do not open the doors if smoke is detected until the vehicle is in a safe place and help has arrived.
- Disconnect the tractor from the trailer (if possible) and move the tractor to a safe place away from the fire.
- Always know what type of cargo is in the trailer. This will help firefighters determine the safest way to extinguish the flames.

Extinguishers

Section 393.95 of the FMCSRs requires one or two (depending on the rating) properly filled and readily accessible fire extinguishers on all CMVs. The extinguisher(s) must be securely mounted on the vehicle and must be designed and maintained to visually show whether the extinguisher is fully charged.

If a vehicle is hauling hazardous materials, it must be equipped with one fire extinguisher having an Underwriters' Laboratories rating of 10 B:C or more.

If a vehicle is not hauling hazardous materials, it must be equipped with either one fire extinguisher having an Underwriters' Laboratories rating of 5 B:C or more or two fire extinguishers, each with an Underwriters' Laboratories rating of 4 B:C or more.

General classes of fires

The National Fire Protection Association (NFPA) has classified four general types of fires, based on the combustible materials involved and the kind of extinguisher needed to put them out. The four fire classifications are A, B, C, and D. Each classification has a special symbol and color identification.

Class A — This type of fire is the most common. The combustible materials are wood, cloth, paper, rubber, and plastics. The common extinguisher agent is water, but dry chemicals are also effective. Carbon dioxide extinguishers and those using sodium or potassium bicarbonate chemicals are not to be used on this type of fire.

Class B — Flammable liquids, gases, and greases create Class B fires. The extinguishers to use are foam, carbon dioxide, and dry chemical.

Class C — Class C fires are electrical fires and a nonconducting agent must be used. Carbon dioxide and dry chemical extinguishers are to be used. Never use foam or water-type extinguishers on these fires.

Class D — Combustible metals, such as magnesium, titanium, zirconium, and sodium fires are Class D fires. These fires require specialized techniques to extinguish them. None of the common extinguishers should be used since they can increase the intensity of the fire by adding an additional chemical reaction.

There are only two dry chemical extinguishers that can be used on Class A, B, and C fires, and those are multi-purpose ABC extinguishers, either stored pressure or cartridge operated.

Multi-purpose extinguishers (ABC) will handle all A, B, and C fires.

All fire extinguishers are labeled with either ABC, or A, or B, or C.

It is important to know what type of fire is in progress.

If you use a fire extinguisher, be sure to use one only on fires for which that fire extinguisher is designed. Using the wrong agent on a fire may increase the intensity of the fire. Check the label on the fire extinguisher. It should list the fire class(es) it is meant to put out.

▌ Summary

Even the best driver may be involved in an accident at some point in his/her career. When the unexpected happens, you need to safely and legally deal with the situation in a short period of time.

In this chapter, you learned about accidents; the definition of an accident, regulatory requirements, the procedures you should follow when an accident occurs, including documentation and reporting responsibilities. You also learned about preventing and fighting vehicle fires.

ACCIDENT PROCEDURES QUIZ

Directions: *Read each statement carefully and mark the response that best answers the question.*

1. You should document an accident by getting names, license numbers, and insurance company information from all drivers involved.
   A. True
   B. False

2. It is not a good idea to take photos of the accident scene.
   A. True
   B. False

3. Disabling damage includes damage to the vehicle's turn signals or horn.
   A. True
   B. False

4. _____ must be included in an accident register.
   A. Name and phone number of the driver's emergency contact
   B. Total cost of all vehicle damage
   C. Date of accident and driver name
   D. All of the above

5. Which is not true of Class A fires:
   A. They involve flammable materials
   B. The combustible materials are wood, cloth, paper, rubber and plastics
   C. They are the most common type of fire
   D. All of the above

6. After an accident, make sure that you either apologize or defend yourself, depending on the circumstances.
   A. True
   B. False

7. If you are involved in an accident, your company must record this in an accident register.
   A. True
   B. False

8. Required warning devices for two-lane roads include:
   A. One device on the traffic side of the vehicle 4 paces (approximately 10 feet or 3 meters) from the front or rear, depending on traffic direction
   B. One device 40 paces (approximately 100 feet or 30 meters) behind
   C. One device 40 paces (approximately 100 feet or 30 meters) ahead of the vehicle on the shoulder or in the lane the vehicle is in
   D. All of the above

CDL AIR BRAKE PRE-TEST

Read each question carefully and select the most correct answer.

1. The antilock braking system (ABS) only activates:

   A. In cold temperatures
   B. When wheels are about to lock up
   C. In warm temperatures
   D. When all other braking systems fail

2. You must make a quick emergency stop. You should brake so you:

   A. Can steer hard while braking hard
   B. Use the full power of the brakes and lock them
   C. Can stay in a straight line and maintain steering control
   D. Burn up the hand brake first

3. Tractor and straight truck spring brakes come on fully when the air pressure drops to a range of:

   A. 10 to 15 mph
   B. 10 to 15 psi
   C. 20 to 45 psi
   D. None of the above

4. Which of the following answers is most correct about using brakes on a long and/or steep downgrade?

   A. Use the braking effects of the engine and when the vehicle speed reaches the "safe" speed, apply brakes firmly until vehicle speed is reduced to approximately 5 mph below "safe" speed
   B. Use stab braking
   C. Use only the trailer brakes to maintain "safe" speed
   D. Apply brakes when the vehicle speed reaches 5 mph over "safe" speed and then release when speed of vehicle is back at the "safe" speed

5. To use the stab braking technique during emergency braking, you:

   A. Pump the brake pedal rapidly and lightly
   B. Brake hard with the pedal until the wheels lock, then get off the brakes until the wheels begin to roll again
   C. Brake hard with the pedal until the wheels lock, then get off the brakes for as long as the wheels were locked
   D. Brake hard with the pedal and hand valve until you stop

Security of cargo, truck, and driver

OBJECTIVES

Upon completion of this chapter, you should have a basic understanding of:

- Cargo theft prevention
- Ensuring your security while on the road
- The importance of safety protocols

- CARGO THEFT
- PERSONAL SECURITY
- IN-TRANSIT SECURITY TIPS
- SUMMARY

INTRODUCTION

This chapter discusses safety and security procedures that should be followed to help you avoid becoming a crime victim while on the road.

■ Cargo theft

Each year, thousands of drivers are injured and millions of dollars are lost in thefts and robberies. There are some simple safety and security procedures that you can follow to help you avoid becoming a crime victim while on the road.

Communicating in advance

Communication between the carrier and shipper is the first step in ensuring the safety of you and your vehicle.

All involved should be aware of who is picking up a given load. This includes the carrier and shipper knowing the:

- Name of the driver picking up the load;
- Carrier assigned vehicle number; and
- Carrier assigned trailer number (if applicable).

The shipper

When you arrive at the shipper, be prepared to show photo identification. The shipper may also ask you for the name of the receiver and the destination of the materials before releasing the shipment.

When it comes to loading the vehicle, you should:

- Supervise the process (if you are not loading the vehicle);
- Only accept scheduled cargo and never accept an unauthorized or unscheduled box, carton, or package;
- Always consider requests to load unauthorized or unscheduled freight as highly suspicious and contact your carrier if you are asked to load unauthorized or unscheduled freight;
- Load the most valuable cargo in the nose of the trailer and as far away from the doors as possible;
- Make sure all cargo being loaded is free of visual damage;
- Thoroughly review and verify all load-related documents; and
- Report and resolve any discrepancies on load-related documents before signing the paperwork or sealing the trailer.

Once the vehicle is loaded, secure the trailer doors with a heavy-duty padlock and/or trailer seal.

Trailer seals

Trailer seals are often used to deter theft and maintain cargo security. Typically, trailer seals fall into two categories, indicative seals and barrier seals.

Indicative seals — Indicative seals are manufactured for one time use and are typically made of plastic, wire, or thin strips of sheet metal marked with a serial number or an identifier. The seal is slipped through a hasp or around locking bars or handles.

They can be broken by hand or with the aid of simple tools, and are not strong enough to prevent intrusion. Plastic strip seals and metal strip seals are examples of indicative seals.

Barrier seals — Barrier seals are designed to prevent intrusion and are typically made out of metal or metal cable. They often require bolt cutters or cable cutters for removal.

Examples of barrier seals include high security cables, locking bars, and padlocks.

When sealing the trailer, make sure you record the seal number(s) on the bill of lading or other designated shipping document.

On the road

Many cargo thefts and hijackings occur within a few miles of a load's origin. Because of this, you should:

- Be on alert when leaving a shipper;
- Keep all doors locked and windows rolled up until on the road; and
- Pay extra attention when near prime vehicle hijack areas including signal-regulated highways, on ramps, and off ramps.

If you suspect that you are being followed, immediately contact law enforcement and your motor carrier.

At the receiver

When arriving at the receiver, you may be asked for identification as well as the bill of lading or shipping papers. When unloading the trailer, you and the receiver should:

- Match the bill of lading or other load-related numbers and paperwork;
- Inspect the seal(s) and match the number(s) with corresponding documentation;
- Break the seal(s);

- Unload the shipment; and
- Sign the bill of lading or other load-related paperwork.

Supervise the unloading process and report any discrepancies to your motor carrier as soon as possible.

Personal security

29

Safeguarding the cargo being transported is important, but it is equally important that drivers protect themselves from physical attacks and the loss of personal items.

Steps that you can take to ensure your safety include:

- Being conscious of vehicles that may be following;
- Being suspicious of anyone who asks about the load or its destination;
- Never sharing information about the load, pick-up and delivery schedules, or routing;
- Never leaving items of value in plain sight in your vehicle;
- Locking the vehicle when stopped;
- Always being aware of your surroundings;
- Safeguarding your wallet, credit card(s), and receipts;
- Never pulling large amounts of cash out of your wallet;
- Being alert at all times when using an ATM; and
- Inspecting the vehicle and its seals/locks at the end of each stop/rest period.

In-transit security tips

The security protocols that most employers have set up were created for a reason, your safety. They cannot be ignored or viewed as an inconvenience. To do so will put you and your vehicle at risk.

The following are just a few security best practices that you as a driver may be called upon to abide by:

Communications

Many motor carriers require drivers to maintain regular communication either through a phone or some sort of satellite communication system. While checking in, you should make sure the phone conversation is as private as possible and is not for everyone to hear. This includes the use of a cell phone, office phone, or pay phone. You just never know who is listening when you are checking in with the office, family, or friends.

Resting and parking

Stop at only reputable truck stops or high-traffic rest areas. Park in well-lighted areas where other trucks are present. When possible, the trailer should be backed against a wall, fence, or other closed trailer, for added security to the load.

When at truck stops, restaurants, or motels, the load should be parked so that you have a clear view of the vehicle. Trailer seals, pin locks, and other vehicle security devices should be used. Avoid stopping in dark or deserted areas while waiting to make deliveries. Always remember to lock your vehicle and keep the keys with you at all times.

Strangers asking you to stop

Anyone asking you to stop should be viewed as suspicious. A frequent ploy used by hijackers is to create a scenario that forces or compels a driver to stop. If someone tries to hijack or break into your truck, always assume the criminal is armed and dangerous. Do not try to be a hero. Call the police immediately for help.

Routes

A well-thought-out trip plan can be a security tool of its own. The best trip plan will involve driving directly to the destination without stopping, if possible, or with the least amount of stops or breaks needed. Never take a load home or to any unsecured or unauthorized parking area. Also, never ask for directions on the CB. You just don't know who you are talking to and they may be directing you right into trouble.

▌ Summary

Security, in general, is common sense. You need to watch what you say and look for anything that looks out of the ordinary or suspicious. Always keep a look out for anyone watching or listening to you or who is overly eager to learn more about your load or route.

29

SECURITY OF CARGO, TRUCK, AND DRIVER QUIZ

Directions: Read each statement carefully and mark the response that best answers the question.

1. When on the road, you should never share information with others about your:
   A. Load
   B. Pick-up/delivery schedules
   C. Routing
   D. All of the above

2. It is acceptable to take a load home or to any unsecured or unauthorized parking area.
   A. True
   B. False

3. You should always lock your vehicle when stopped.
   A. True
   B. False

4. Always inspect your vehicle and its seals/locks at the end of each rest stop.
   A. True
   B. False

5. When stopping, you should:
   A. Park in a high-traffic location
   B. Park as far away from the lights as possible
   C. Roll down your windows for better air circulation
   D. All of the above

6. It is okay to talk about your load if:
   A. The person is another driver
   B. The person at the counter of the truck stop is friendly
   C. The person seems interested
   D. It is never appropriate to discuss load-related information while on the road

7. Many highjackings occur within a few miles of the point of origin (the shipper).
   A. True
   B. False

8. Anyone who has been following you for a long distance:
   A. Just happens to be going the same direction
   B. Should be viewed as suspicious
   C. Should be ignored
   D. All of the above

9. Anyone asking you to stop (when on the road) should be viewed as:
   A. Concerned
   B. Nosey
   C. Suspicious
   D. Friendly

10. When stopped at a truckstop, rest area, or restaurant you should:
    A. Safeguard your wallet, credit card(s), and receipts
    B. Never pull large amounts of cash out of your wallet
    C. Be alert at all times when using an ATM
    D. All of the above

Read each question carefully and select the most correct answer.

1. When you are driving through construction zones, you should:
   A. Speed up and hurry through them so you aren't in them any longer than necessary
   B. Stop before entering them, get in low gear and proceed through
   C. Watch for uneven surfaces
   D. Reduce your speed only if construction workers are near the roadway

2. If you break down on a level, straight, four-lane, divided highway, where should you place the reflective warning triangles?
   A. One 10 feet from the rear of the vehicle, one approximately 100 feet from the rear of the vehicle and another one about 100 feet to the front of the vehicle
   B. One 10 feet from the rear of the vehicle, one approximately 100 feet from the rear of the vehicle, and one about 200 feet from the rear of the vehicle
   C. One 100 feet from the rear of the vehicle, one approximately 200 feet from the rear of the vehicle, and one about 300 feet from the rear of the vehicle
   D. One 50 feet from the rear of the vehicle, one about 100 feet from the rear of the vehicle, and one about 200 feet from the front of the vehicle

3. According to the Commercial Driver's manual, why should you limit the use of your vehicle's horn?
   A. If your vehicle has air brakes, the air horn may not work while you are applying your brakes
   B. It may startle other drivers
   C. You should keep both hands on the steering wheel at all times
   D. The Driver's Manual does not say that a driver should limit the use of the horn

4. Which of the following should you do when dealing with a tailgater?
   A. Increase your following distance
   B. Avoid quick changes
   C. Avoid tricks such as flashing your brake lights
   D. All of the above

5. The proper way to load a vehicle is:
   A. Keep the load balanced in the cargo area
   B. Place the load at the front of the trailer to give your drive wheels better traction
   C. Place the load at the rear of the trailer so your rear tires have better traction
   D. It makes no difference where the cargo is placed as long as you are not over the allowable gross weight

Personal health and safety 30

OBJECTIVES

Upon completion of this chapter, you should have a basic understanding of:

- Healthy diet and exercise habits

- Stress management

- Driver fatigue

- The prohibitions and regulations addressing the use and abuse of alcohol and drugs

- Safe workplace practices

30 Personal health and safety

- PERSONAL HEALTH AND DRIVING
- WEIGHT, DIET, AND EXERCISE
- STRESS
- FATIGUE
- ALCOHOL USE AND DRUG ABUSE
- SAFETY EQUIPMENT AND PRACTICES
- SUMMARY

INTRODUCTION

A healthy driver is a safe and alert driver. Achieving a healthy and safe lifestyle can be challenging when done on the road, but it can be done. This chapter will focus on several of the factors that contribute to driver health and wellness.

Personal health and driving

Life on the road can lead to a lot of bad habits including:

- Minimal exercise;
- Unhealthy eating habits;
- Over consumption of caffeine; and
- Smoking.

It is important to incorporate good habits including eating well, getting plenty of rest, and having an exercise routine. Remember, a healthy driver is an alert, safe driver.

Weight, diet, and exercise

Weight, diet, and exercise all work together when it comes to your health.

Being overweight can contribute to several health problems including unhealthy cholesterol levels, high blood pressure, diabetes, back pain, and joint stress. It can also cause you to feel fatigued. A healthy diet and physical activity can help control your weight, and in turn, prevent certain health problems.

Diet

Whether at home or on the road, it is important to maintain a healthy diet. A healthy diet includes eating a variety of foods on a daily basis that are rich in nutrients and low in calories. This includes vegetables and fruits, whole grains, low-fat dairy, and lean protein.

Vegetables and fruits — Vegetables and fruits are full of nutrients that help in promoting good health. Select vegetables and fruits of various colors and varieties. Choose red, orange, and dark green vegetables such as tomatoes, sweet potatoes, and broccoli with meals.

Also select a variety of fruits and vegetables as snacks such as apples, pears, berries, and carrots.

Whole grains — When selecting bread, rice, or pasta, try to select whole grains. Whole grains provide more nutrients than refined grains.

Examples of whole grains include oatmeal, brown rice, and whole wheat pasta. At least half of the grains consumed on a daily basis should be whole grains.

Low-fat dairy — Milk, cheese, and yogurt are included in the dairy group. Select fat-free (skim) or low-fat (one percent) milk, cheese, and yogurt.

Lean protein — Meat, poultry, seafood, eggs, nuts, and seeds are considered part of the protein group. Select lean cuts of meat or low-fat meat and poultry.

Limit fat, oil, added sugar, salt — Limiting fats, oils, and added sugars is also important when it comes to a healthy diet as these foods provide calories, but little in nutritional value. Too much sodium (salt) can increase blood pressure.

Drink water — Water is a key ingredient to health and wellness. You need water to process the nutrients you eat, cleanse your body of toxins and impurities, and replenish you after exercise or physical exertion, especially in extreme heat.

Normally, you should drink at least eight-8-ounce glasses of water every. If you are working in extreme heat, you will need to drink at least 8 ounces of cool water every 15 to 20 minutes.

Eating healthy on the road

Being on the road can present additional challenges when it comes to healthy eating. Your options can be limited when it comes to the menu at a truck stop or fast food outlet. Planning ahead and packing healthy foods before starting a trip is one way to combat this problem.

There are lots of healthy choices that can be purchased from the grocery store before leaving on a trip. They can be carried in a small cooler on the vehicle. These choices include fresh fruit, cut up vegetables, and string cheese. Ready to eat cereals and unsalted nuts are other healthy foods that can be taken on the road.

Making healthy food choices can be a challenge when stopping at a restaurant or truck stop. Being an informed diner is half the battle when it comes to being a healthy diner.

Many restaurant and fast food chains are starting to post calories on their menus. Also, many post nutritional information on their websites. If possible, this information should be checked out before ordering. If this isn't a possible, look for key words such as grilled, whole grain, and low fat to help in making informed mealtime decisions.

For breakfast, skip the sweet rolls and pancakes. Items such as oatmeal, whole grain cereals, and fresh fruit are healthier selections.

When it comes to lunch and dinner, look for terms such as grilled, steamed, or broiled when selecting meat, whole grain when selecting breads, buns, and pasta, and low fat when choosing dairy products.

When at a salad bar, select vegetables and fruit and use salad dressing sparingly. Avoid prepared salads such as potato or pasta salads as they often contain dressings or sauces that are high in fat.

Beverages are another issue to consider. Sodas and sweetened coffees are full of sugars and calories. Low-fat milk, unsweetened tea, and fruit and vegetable juices without added sugars are better choices.

Exercise

Regular physical activity is important to overall health and fitness. Being physically active can help with:

- Losing weight or maintaining a healthy weight (when combined with proper diet);
- Well-being;
- Sleep; and
- Strengthening muscles and bones.

Beneficial physical activity includes:

Consult with a medical professional before starting any diet or exercise program. A medical professional can make recommendations based on your health and lifestyle.

30

- Aerobic activities including brisk walking jogging, bicycling, and swimming;
- Resistance, strength building, and weight-bearing activities including lifting weights and push-ups; and
- Balance and stretching activities including gentle stretching, dancing, and martial arts.

So how much physical activity is necessary? The the U.S. Department of Agriculture (USDA) recommends that adults do at least two and a half hours of moderate physical activity each week.

Moderate physical activities include brisk walking, bicycling, and golf (when walking and carrying clubs). It is also recommended that strengthening activities such as push-ups, sit-ups, and lifting weights be done at least twice each week.

Exercise on the road

Being on the road can present challenges when it comes to getting in some physical activity on a regular basis. Having a "game plan" can help in getting in some form of physical activity.

The "game plan" may include making time during a stop to take a 30 minute walk or planning to stop at a facility that includes exercise equipment.

Some drivers carry exercise equipment such as hand weights or a bicycle or do simple stretching exercises in their vehicle.

▋ Stress

Stress is a physical or mental response to the pressures of an event or factors of living in general. Though we tend to speak of it in a negative context, stress can be positive or negative.

Biologically, when stress occurs, your body releases hormones which accelerate your breathing and heart rate, increase your blood sugar levels and blood pressure, and improve blood clotting. Your body gets into a survival mode, readying itself for a physical emergency.

As stress continues, your body temporarily adjusts to the stress. If stress is removed during this adjustment period, your body returns to normal. However, if stress goes on for prolonged periods of time, your body fails to adjust and wears out. This can weaken your defenses and lead to disease.

Medically, stress can cause you to suffer high blood pressure, pain, breathing trouble, digestive disorders, insomnia, and fatigue.

Psychologically, you may suffer frustration, irritability, anger, impatience, worry, and/or a lack of self-confidence. To compound matters, your job can be affected too. Stress can lead to accidents, a loss of priorities, rushing, and anger or inappropriate behavior.

Use one or more of the following stress-reduction techniques to help you deal with stress:

- Take breaks;
- Exercise;
- Maintain a balanced diet;
- Get proper rest;
- Practice deep breathing or yoga;
- Manage your time/set priorities and do the most important things first;
- Laugh and cry to release tension; and
- Share your stress with others/talk to a friend.

Fatigue

Fatigue is a generic term used to describe anything from being sleepy to exhausted. Two major causes of fatigue are sleep loss and changes to the body's circadian rhythm (internal clock).

Sleep loss — Sleep, like food and water, is necessary for human survival. Depriving your body of sleep is like starving yourself or not eating.

In general, most adults need 7 to 8 hours of uninterrupted sleep to feel well-rested. Sleep loss of as little as 2 hours can affect alertness and performance. This can include reduced judgment, slowed reaction time, lack of coordination, and poor attitude/mood.

Circadian rhythm — Put simply, circadian rhythm is your body's internal or biological clock. For most people, their clock runs on a 24-hour basis with some highpoints and low points in that 24-hour span of time.

Time cues, such as sunlight and darkness and your work/rest schedule keep your body clock set to a certain schedule.

Most everyone's clock is set for two low points. One is between 2:00 a.m. and 6:00 a.m. The other is between 1:00 p.m. and 5:00 p.m. The more dangerous of the two is between 2:00 a.m. and 6:00 a.m. as most people are programmed to sleep when it is dark and fighting fatigue is difficult.

Signs of fatigue

There are several signs that can tell you that you are about to fall asleep including:

- Lack of alertness;
- Drowsiness;
- Yawning;

- Trouble focusing eyes/trying to keep them open;
- Head drooping;
- Reduced reaction time;
- Erratic shifting, intermittent braking, following vehicles too closely;
- Lane deviations; and
- Bad driving decisions.

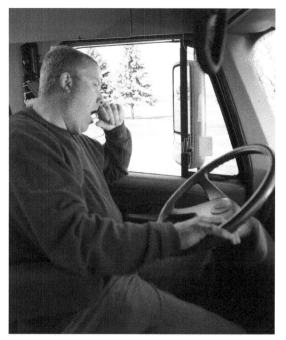

30

Fighting fatigue

There are several things that can be done to fight fatigue including getting a solid 8 hours of sleep, trying to establish a regular sleep and waking schedule, and avoiding driving during "down" times.

Sleep apnea

Sleep disorders can also contribute to fatigue. One of the more common sleep disorders is sleep apnea.

Sleep apnea is a breathing disorder characterized by brief pauses of breathing during sleep. When this happens, the person who is sleeping gasps for air, wakes up enough to get back into a normal breathing pattern, then falls back to sleep. Often, this happens in such a short period of time that the person sleeping doesn't realize what just occurred.

The process can repeat itself up to 600 times a night. Though a person with sleep apnea doesn't fully wake up during these breathing episodes, his/her sleep pattern is disrupted enough that the sleep period isn't refreshing, causing daytime sleepiness and poor concentration.

Early detection and treatment for sleep apnea is important because sleep apnea may be linked with serious medical conditions including irregular heartbeat, high blood pressure, heart attack, and stroke.

Alcohol use and drug abuse

Driving, drugs, and drinking are a deadly mix. Alcohol and/or drug use can decrease your skill and thinking abilities. It can reduce coordination, slow your reaction rate, and dull mental processes.

You should never use alcohol or drugs to help you stay awake or remain alert. Part of being a professional driver is knowing when it is safe to drive.

It is your responsibility to comply with the applicable alcohol and drug regulations as well as you company's policy on this subject.

Prohibitions

The Federal Motor Carrier Safety Regulations (FMCSRs) address the use of alcohol by commercial drivers. Prohibited behaviors, as listed in Sec. 392.5 of the FMCSRs include:

- Alcohol consumption 4 hours prior to coming on duty, or while having physical control of, or operating a commercial motor vehicle;

- Alcohol use, being under the influence of alcohol, or having any measurable amount of alcohol concentration or detected presence of alcohol, while on duty, operating, or in physical control of a commercial motor vehicle; or

- Being on duty or operating a commercial motor vehicle with alcohol in possession, with the exception of transporting a manifest shipment of alcoholic beverages.

The FMCSRs also address the use of drugs by commercial drivers. Section 392.4 of the FMCSRs states that drivers may not be on duty and possess, be under the influence of, or use any of the following drugs or substances:

- Any 21 CFR 1308.11 *Schedule I* substance;

- An amphetamine or any formulation thereof (including, but not limited, to "pep pills," and "bennies");

- A narcotic drug or any derivative thereof; or

- Any other substance, to a degree which renders the driver incapable of safely operating a motor vehicle.

Alcohol and drug testing

The alcohol and drug regulations, located in Parts 40 and 382, apply to every person who operates a commercial motor vehicle (CMV) in interstate or intrastate commerce in the United States, and is subject to the commercial driver's license (CDL) requirements of Part 383 and his or her motor carrier. It also applies to drivers who operate CMVs in the United States and are subject to the Licencia Federal de Conductor (Mexico) or the CDL requirements of the Canadian National Safety Code and their motor carriers.

Safety-sensitive function means all time from the time a driver begins to work or is required to be in readiness to work until the time he or she is relieved from work and all responsibilities for performing work. Driving, loading and unloading a CMV, and inspecting or servicing equipment are all included in the definition of a safety-sensitive function. See Sec. 382.107 for the complete definition.

Alcohol misuse and drug use — Alcohol misuse and drug use that could affect the performance of a safety-sensitive function is prohibited.

Alcohol prohibitions include:

- Use while performing a safety-sensitive function;

- Use during the 4 hours before performing a safety-sensitive function;

- Reporting for duty or remaining on duty to perform a safety-sensitive function with an alcohol concentration of 0.04 or greater;

- Use during the 8 hours following an accident, or until the driver undergoes a post-accident test; and

- Refusal to take a required test.

A driver found to have an alcohol concentration of 0.02 or greater but less than 0.04 may not perform, nor be permitted to perform, safety-sensitive functions for at least 24 hours.

Drug prohibitions include:

- Use of any drug or substance as defined in 21 CFR 1308.11 Schedule I;

- Use of any non-Schedule I drug or substance, except under the direction of a licensed medical practitioner who is familiar with the driver's medical history and has advised the driver that the drug will not adversely affect the driver's ability to safely operate a commercial motor vehicle);

- Testing positive for drugs;

- Having an adulterated or substituted test specimen; and

- Refusal to take a required test.

A motor carrier may require a driver to inform the motor carrier of any drugs the driver is using to treat a medical condition.

Types of tests — There are six types of tests required under the Part 382 regulations:

- **Pre-employment (drug)** — A pre-employment drug test is given before a driver performs any safety-sensitive functions for an employer. The employer must receive a negative result before allowing the driver to drive or perform other safety-sensitive functions. See Sec. 382.301 for specific details.

- **Post-accident (alcohol and drug)** — If a driver is involved in an accident while driving a commercial motor vehicle, he/she may be required to undergo post-accident testing if certain criteria are met. See Sec. 382.303 for specific details.

- **Random (alcohol and drug)** — Unannounced random testing is required of a certain percentage of drivers each year. The tests must be reasonably spaced throughout the year and each driver must have an equal chance of being tested each time a selection is made. See Sec. 382.305 for specific details.

- **Reasonable suspicion** — If an employer has reason to believe that a driver's appearance or behavior may indicate drug or alcohol use, the driver may be sent for a reasonable suspicion test. Reasonable suspicion testing must be based on the observations of a trained supervisor. See Sec. 382.307 for specific details.

- **Return-to-duty** — Return-to-duty testing is required before a driver returns to duty after testing positive for drugs, failing an alcohol test, or refusing to take a drug or alcohol test. In addition to this test, there are referral, evaluation, and treatment requirements that must be met. See Sec. 382.309 and Part 40, Subpart O for specific details

- **Follow-up** — Follow-up testing is required after the driver returns to duty. The regulations require a minimum of six tests in the first year after returning to a safety-sensitive function. Follow-up testing can go on for a total of five years. See Sec. 382.311 and Part 40, Subpart O for specific details.

Test results and return to duty — A driver who fails an alcohol and/or drug test or refuses to take an alcohol and/or drug test must complete the return-to-duty process before he/she is again able to perform any safety-sensitive functions, including driving a CMV. This process includes evaluation by a substance abuse professional (SAP), completing the treatment prescribed by the SAP and passing a return-to-duty test. The driver is then subject to a minimum of six follow-up tests in the next 12 months and could be subject to follow-up testing for up to a total of five years. See Part 40, Subpart O for complete details.

30

Driver disqualification

Under Sec. 383.51 of the FMCSRs, certain offenses committed in *any* kind of vehicle (work or personal) will be held against a CDL driver. This means that any CDL driver who is convicted of being under the influence of alcohol or drugs (in any kind of vehicle) as prescribed by state law will be disqualified from operating a vehicle requiring a CDL for a period of one year for a first offense. If the offense occurred in a vehicle hauling hazardous materials, the penalty is stiffer with a three-year disqualification. Any subsequent offenses in any kind of vehicle will lead to a lifetime disqualification.

■ Safety equipment and practices

Safety on the job includes more than a general knowledge of the regulations. It includes common sense and following your motor carrier's policies and procedures related to safe workplace practices.

Accidents often occur when you face a new job or a change at work. When something in your workplace changes, think about your safety. If you are not sure about how to proceed, ask questions. Also, if you discover a hazard, report it.

Vehicle entry and exit

Believe it or not, there are proper ways of climbing up, getting into and out of cabs and seats, and getting down from motor vehicles:

- Always use handrails, face the ladder or steps, and maintain three points of contact (two feet and one hand, or one foot and two hands) at all times;

- Always use anti-slip surfaces for climbing or stepping; and

- Never jump from or to ladders, steps, or walkways.

Personal protective equipment (PPE)

It is important that appropriate personal protective equipment (PPE) be used to prevent injury when loading or unloading your vehicle or working at a warehouse, dock, or other facility.

Occupational Safety and Health Administration (OSHA) regulations require that all PPE fit correctly, be in good shape, and be appropriate for the job. OSHA regulated PPE that may be used includes:

- Hand protection (gloves);
- Foot protection (steel-toed work shoes);
- Eye protection (goggles); and
- Head protection (hard hat).

Proper lifting

Injury to the back must be taken seriously, as it can cause a lifetime of pain and discomfort. There are five steps to a proper lifting technique:

Step 1: Size up the load before trying to lift it. If it's too heavy get some help.

- Stretch before you lift, and stretch out frequently during sessions of repeated lifting;
- Test the weight by lifting one of the corners;
- Anything over 50 pounds is considered a heavy lift;
- Request help if you need it; and
- Use mechanical aids such as hoists, carts, or dollies as needed.

Step 2: Bend your knees. Let your legs do the work.

- Place your feet apart and close to the object;
- Center yourself over the load, bend your knees, and get a good handhold;
- Lift straight up, smoothly; and
- Never bend at the waist, or lift with a rounded back.

Step 3: Never twist or turn your body once you have made the lift.

- Keep the load steady and close to your body; and
- Never carry a load above your head or at your side.

Step 4: Make sure you can carry the load to its destination before attempting the lift.

- Make sure your path is clear of all obstacles; and
- Break up a long carry by stopping halfway to reposition your grasp.

Step 5: Set the load down properly.

- Bend your knees;
- Keep your back upright;
- Let your legs do the work;
- Take your time;
- Keep your head up;
- Tighten the abdominal muscles; and
- Pivot your feet before you move another direction, do not twist.

Also, always push, don't pull an object. Pushing puts less strain on the back.

Summary

A successful, professional driver needs to take health and safety seriously, whether on the road or at the terminal. Health and safety must be a way of life for the commercial driver in order to succeed. It is all a matter of choices, from healthy lifestyles to the conscious effort to follow safety policies and procedures.

PERSONAL HEALTH AND SAFETY QUIZ

Directions: Read each statement carefully and mark the response that best answers the question.

1. A healthy driver is an alert, safe driver.
   A. True
   B. False

2. A healthy diet includes eating a variety of foods on a daily basis that are rich in nutrients and low in calories.
   A. True
   B. False

3. Ways to deal with stress include:
   A. Taking breaks and relaxing
   B. Maintaining proper rest and diet
   C. Managing your time, setting priorities
   D. All of the above

4. A good way to fight fatigue is by:
   A. Getting three hours of sleep each night
   B. Driving during your "down times"
   C. Establishing a regular sleep and waking schedule
   D. All of the above

5. The regulations allow you to transport a small amount of alcohol on your vehicle for use when off duty.
   A. True
   B. False

6. A driver must be removed from all safety-sensitive functions if he/she tests positive for drugs.
   A. True
   B. False

7. When entering or exiting a vehicle, you should:
   A. Jump
   B. Wear a hardhat
   C. Maintain three points of contact at all times
   D. All of the above

8. Proper lifting technique includes:
   A. Sizing up the load
   B. Bending your knees, letting your legs do the work
   C. Lifting straight and smoothly
   D. All of the above

9. Always push, don't pull an object, as pushing puts less strain on the back
   A. True
   B. False

10. Never twist or turn your body once you have made the lift.
    A. True
    B. False

Read each question carefully and select the most correct answer.

1. If you aren't sure that you have safe space to pass under an object, you should:
   A. Assume all clearances are of sufficient height
   B. Height clearance is not a concern as long as you stay on state or federal roadways
   C. Take another route
   D. All of the above

2. Controlled braking is:
   A. Applying brakes hard enough for the wheels to lock up
   B. Pressing the brakes hard enough to lock-up the wheels, then releasing and then reapplying again
   C. Applying firm brake pressure, but not to the point of lock-up
   D. Only used if the vehicle does not have anti-lock brakes

3. You are driving on a straight and level roadway at 60 mph and suddenly a tire blows out on your vehicle. What should you do first?
   A. Immediately begin light, controlled braking
   B. Immediately begin stab braking
   C. Grip steering wheel firmly with both hands and stay off the brakes until the vehicle has slowed down
   D. Immediately begin emergency braking

4. Which of the following is true?
   A. Tires with tread separation or cuts should not be used on a vehicle
   B. Tires which are mismatched sizes should be used on a vehicle
   C. $\frac{1}{32}$ inch tread depth is allowed on drive tires
   D. $\frac{1}{32}$ inch tread depth is permissible for steering tires

5. Why do hazardous materials regulations exist?
   A. To provide for safe drivers and equipment
   B. To communicate a risk
   C. To contain the product
   D. All of the above

Public and employer relations 31

OBJECTIVES

Upon completion of this chapter, you should have a basic understanding of:

- The image of the trucking industry
- Appropriate contact with the public
- Good customer relations
- Job requirements
- How to apply for a job

31 Public and employer relations

- TRUCKING INDUSTRY IMAGE
- CONTACT WITH THE PUBLIC
- CUSTOMER RELATIONS
- WHAT DO EMPLOYERS LOOK FOR?
- COMPANY POLICY
- WHISTLEBLOWER PROTECTION
- OPPORTUNITIES FOR ADVANCEMENT
- APPLYING FOR A JOB
- SUMMARY

INTRODUCTION

As a professional driver, your workplace is the nation's highways and the facilities you travel to when making deliveries. A successful driver maintains his/her professionalism at all times. This chapter will address the skills, techniques, and regulatory requirements you need to master in order to be a true professional and land a job within the trucking industry.

▌ Trucking industry image

As with any group or industry, it only takes the bad actions of a few individuals to give the whole group a poor public image. This is especially true for the trucking industry. Drivers who are rude and aggressive, including those who speed, tailgate, and cut off other drivers are responsible for leaving fellow motorists with a bad impression of the professional driver and the trucking industry.

There are many consequences for an industry that has a poor public image. Public and media outcry can have a strong effect on the entire industry. In some cases this can spur new or changed laws and regulations that can be costly to the trucking industry. How does this affect you? Legislation that is unfavorable to the industry (increased use taxes, road restrictions) can lead to less profit, which can mean fewer jobs.

Remember, it is often said that when something bad happens to someone, that individual tells ten others of his/her experience.

▌ Contact with the public

You are face of your company. Everything from your conduct to your attitude and appearance play a part in how your company is viewed by the public.

The rules of the road

Projecting a professional image on the road includes following all laws and regulations as well as practicing good driving habits, including:

- Following posted speed limits;
- Maintaining a safe distance between vehicles;
- Making sure there is a clear path when changing lanes;
- Signaling at the appropriate time when planning to turn;
- Making sure there is adequate space to safely pass;
- Being courteous when using high-beam headlights — don't blind other drivers;
- Never using the vehicle's size to intimidate others; and
- Being aware of other drivers, vehicles, and the flow of traffic

Laws and regulations are intended to protect everyone. Follow all laws and regulations.

Appearance

Often, the first impression is a lasting one. Vehicle and personal appearance are important factors when it comes to first impressions.

Vehicle — Your vehicle is a rolling advertisement for your company. Because a first impression is a lasting one, how you drive and how your vehicle is cared for plays a role in how your company is viewed by your current customers, potential customers, and the general public.

Your vehicle should be clean and well maintained. A dirty or poorly maintained vehicle sends the message that your company doesn't care.

Include vehicle neatness and condition in your regular vehicle inspection process.

Driver — When it comes to your personal appearance, neatness counts. As previously stated, you are a representative of your company.

Your clothes should be neat, clean, and appropriate for the workplace. Your hair should be neat and if you have a beard or moustache, keep it trimmed.

▎Customer relations

In today's business world, the majority of contact between a business and its customers is done via phone or computer. In many cases, the professional driver is the only representative of the company the customer deals with face-to-face.

Because of this, how you conduct yourself plays a huge part in how your company is viewed by both current and potential customers.

Punctuality

Be on time. The customer is probably setting his/her work schedule around when the shipment will arrive. If you are going to be late, you or your company's dispatcher should make a short phone call to the customer letting him/her know you will be late. This can save a lot of time and problems for both your company and your customer.

Courtesy

Always be polite and friendly when dealing with customer personnel.

Frustrations should never be taken out on the customer. You should never argue with the customer.

A customer's impression can lose or gain business for your company. You should make every effort to be courteous at all times.

Knowledge

Know and follow company rules in handling cargo and documentation.

Know your company's procedure for dealing with freight problems. A prompt solution is good customer service.

Also be aware of what types of services your company offers. A customer may ask if your company can handle a certain type of shipment, deliver to a specific area, or carry a specific product.

Respect

Respect the customer's property. Make all deliveries as you would like deliveries made to your home. All cargo must be handled carefully. No one wants to see their order mishandled.

Respect the requests of the customer. Make every effort to follow the customer's rules and be aware of special delivery or pick-up instructions.

Always use extra caution when driving on the customer's property. Watch for low telephone and power lines as well as porches, overhangs, steps, and loading docks that stick out from buildings. Follow posted directions, don't speed, and watch for pedestrians.

Angry customer

When a customer is angry, how you handle the situation can make or break your company's relationship with the customer.

Never take a customer's anger personally. Instead, focus on fixing the problem that caused the customer's anger. Always be courteous and remain calm.

The following steps should be followed when dealing with this type of situation:

- Apologize for the situation, even if it isn't your fault. You don't have to take blame for the situation, but should apologize for the situation.
- Express concern that things didn't go as planned, but never be patronizing. An angry customer wants to know that you and your company care.
- Even if your company isn't at fault, accept responsibility and assure the customer that the company will do its best to make things right.
- Determine what steps the company can take to make things right. This may require contact with the your supervisor for advice and/or directions as to what can or cannot be done.
- Try to come to some sort of solution with the customer before leaving. If you need to return to your company to work with your supervisor or others at the company to correct the problem, assure the customer that you will contact the customer as soon as possible. Make sure that you follow up on this promise.
- If you are able to offer solutions to the problem before leaving, let the customer choose the course of action that is most convenient.

Also, follow up with the customer to make sure the course of action agreed to worked out as planned.

Following up shows that you and your company care about the customer and want to continue a positive business relationship.

31

▍ What do employers look for?

As previously mentioned, as a professional driver, you are the face of your company. Because of this, employers are looking for just the right professional to fit their company's image when hiring. They are looking for someone who is qualified based on federal regulations and company policy.

The regulations

Parts 383 and 391 of the Federal Motor Carrier Safety Regulations (FMCSRs) address driver qualification as well as disqualification.

You must be qualified according to the standards in Sec. 391.11 of the FMCSRs. This includes passing a physical exam, possessing a valid commercial driver's license (CDL), and passing a road test.

Your motor carrier is required to maintain a driver qualification file. The items that must be in the file, as listed in Sec. 391.51 of the FMCSRs includes an employment application, your motor vehicle record, and road test documentation.

As the holder of a CDL certain type of offenses, committed in any type of vehicle (work or personal), can disqualify you from operating a commercial motor vehicle (CMV) for anywhere from 60 days to life depending on the offense. Disqualifying offenses include a conviction for a drug or alcohol related offense, leaving the scene of an accident, speeding, and reckless driving.

See Chapter 1 of this text for a full discussion of the driver qualification and disqualification regulations.

General job qualifications

The following are some of the things a prospective employer is looking for when hiring a driver:

- A general knowledge of the various types of vehicles used by the trucking industry as well as vehicle systems and components;
- An understanding of the language of the industry;
- General knowledge about required paperwork (record of duty status, inspection reports, etc.);
- The ability to safely drive assigned vehicles; and
- A basic understanding of cargo handling techniques and procedures.

A prospective employer is also looking for an individual who has a good, positive attitude. This means being interested in the job, mature, responsible, enthusiastic, and safe.

▍ Company policy

Motor carriers have their own policies and procedures. Some of the policies may vary from what you have learned in this driver training program, but do keep in mind that you should always operate safely and legally. It is illegal for an employer to require you to violate federal, state, or local laws/regulations.

A typical company policy covers:

- Hours of work;
- Compensation (pay and benefits);
- Safety rules;
- Vehicle inspection and maintenance requirements;
- Rules for trips; and
- Public/customer relations.

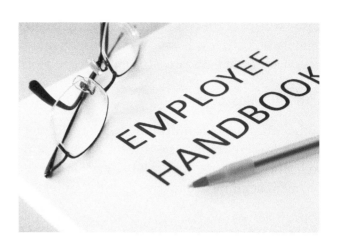

■ Whistleblower protection

Whistleblower protection laws are in place to protect you from retaliation if you report CMV safety violations to the Federal Motor Carrier Safety Administrtaion (FMCSA). You're also protected if you testify before FMCSA or if you refuse to operate an unsafe vehicle, drive in conditions that may cause serious bodily injury, or violate a CMV safety law.

These Department of Labor, Occupational Safety and Health Administration (OSHA) regulations (29 CFR Part 1978) prohibit your employer from discharging, disciplining, or discriminating against you regarding pay, terms, or privileges for taking any one of the following actions:

- Filing a complaint related to the violation of a CMV safety or security regulation;
- Having testified in or testifying in the future in a proceeding related to a violation of a CMV safety or security regulation;
- Refusing to operate a CMV because:
  - ◆ You would have violated a federal safety, health, or security regulation, or
  - ◆ You had a reasonable apprehension that you, or someone else, would have been seriously injured or impaired had you operated an unsafe vehicle;
- Accurately reporting your hours on duty (refuse to inaccurately report);
- Cooperating with a federal safety or security investigation; or
- Providing information to an enforcement agency relating to an accident or incident resulting in injury or death to an individual or property damage in connection with CMV transportation.

To qualify for the protection, you must have sought from your employer, and were unable to obtain, correction of the hazardous safety or security condition.

Filing a Complaint

Complaints should be filed with the OSHA office in the area where you live or work. You can find information online at www.osha.gov.

A complaint should be filed within 180 days of when the alleged violation occurred. However, there are situations where the time limit will be waived.

There are no special forms to use to file the compliant. The complaint may be filed orally or in writing.

31

Upon receipt of the complaint OSHA will begin its investigation. Within 60 days of filing the complaint, OSHA will issue written findings as to whether there is reasonable cause to believe the employer retaliated against the employee in violation of the whistleblower protection regulations.

OSHA findings

If the investigation confirms a violation, the employer will receive a preliminary order. The order will include, where appropriate, a requirement that the employer end the violation, reinstate the employee to his/her former position, and/or pay for compensatory damages. The order may also require payment of punitive damages up to $250,000.

If the investigation finds that a violation did not occur, OSHA will notify the parties of the finding.

Coercion

A motor carrier, shipper, receiver, broker, or freight forwarder cannot coerce you to operate a CMV in violation of the Federal Motor Carrier Safety Regulations (FMCSRs), Hazardous Materials Regulations (HMRs), or commercial regulations.

Coerce means threatening to or withholding business, employment, or work opportunities, or threatening job action against you to get you to violate the FMCSRs, HMRs, or commercial regulations.

If you believe you were coerced to violate the regulations described above, you may file a written complaint with the Federal Motor Carrier Safety Administration (FMCSA).

The complaint must be filed with the National Consumer Complaint Database at http://nccdb.fmcsa.dot.gov or the FMCSA Division Administrator for the state in which you are employed within 90 days of the event.

Upon the filing of the complaint of coercion, the appropriate FMCSA Division Administrator will determine whether the complaint meets the coercion complaint requirements. If the complaint meets the requirements, it will be investigated, and you will be notified of the results of the investigation in a timely manner.

Opportunities for advancement

Experience plays a part in the hiring process. As with most professions, the higher paying, more lucrative driving jobs go to drivers with a certain level of experience and skill as well as a safe driving record.

Know that completing your driving education is a solid first step in achieving whatever driving goal you may have. Many experienced drivers will tell you that their first job was hauling local freight or working in a motor carrier's yard jockeying trailers, spotting trailers, and/or loading and unloading freight.

When working in this type of situation, put your best foot forward, show enthusiasm, and above all do a good job. This will help you in advancing your career.

▮ Applying for a job

The application process for a tractor-trailer driver involves a certain amount of paperwork, tests, and an interview process.

Much of the paperwork you will be required to fill out is mandated by the FMCSRs.

Application for employment

Section 391.21 of the FMCSRs requires a motor carrier to obtain certain, specific information from you including (but not limited to):

- Your name, address, date of birth, and Social Security number;
- The issuing state, number, and expiration date of your CDL;
- Information on your experience operating motor vehicles;
- A list of all motor vehicle accidents in the past 3 years;
- A list of all violations of motor vehicle laws in the past 3 years; and
- A list of all employers in the past 10 years.

Investigations and inquiries

Section 391.23 of the FMCSRs requires a motor carrier to obtain information about your work and driving history. You will be required to fill out paperwork giving your permission to the motor carrier to conduct these investigations.

The motor carrier is also required to check your drug and alcohol testing history for the past 3 years. You will be required to fill out paperwork giving your permission for the motor carrier to obtain this information from your past employers (driving jobs only).

Testing

You will also be required to complete a certain battery of tests before you can operate a commercial motor vehicle for a prospective employer.

Road test — Section 391.31 of the FMCSRs requires that you complete a road test before operating a commercial motor vehicle for a motor carrier.

In order to pass the road test, you will need to successfully complete several tasks including:

A motor carrier may accept another motor carrier's road test if it was conducted in the last 3 years. Also, your valid CDL may be accepted if you do not have a double/triple or tanker endorsement. Keep in mind that a motor carrier may still require a road test even though you could meet the exception.

- A pre-trip inspection;
- Coupling and uncoupling a combination;
- Placing a vehicle in operation and driving in traffic; and
- Braking and parking.

Upon successful completion of the road test, you will be given a certificate and a copy will be placed in your qualification file.

31

Written exam — Though a written exam hasn't been required for several years, some carriers still require this test as a way of evaluating a driver's understanding of the FMCSRs.

Physical exam — Section 391.41 of the FMCSRs requires you to pass a physical exam before you can operate a commercial motor vehicle. As a CDL holder, you must present a valid copy of this certificate to your state licensing agency to be added to your driving record. Your carrier must have evidence of a valid medical exam in your qualification file by maintaining a current copy of your driving record.

In addition to turning in the medical card, you must self-certify with your state of license. See Chapter 1 for additional details.

Pre-employment drug test — Section 382.301 of the FMCSRs requires you to pass a pre-employment drug test before driving a commercial motor vehicle. Though a pre-employment alcohol test isn't required by the FMCSRs, some companies do require this as company policy.

Job interview

The job interview is an important part of the application process. Be prepared for the interview:

- Learn all you can about the company. Ask current and past employees and/or visit the company's website.

- Be prepared to ask intelligent questions.

- Make sure you have the necessary paperwork and information with you, including information to fill out the paperwork mentioned earlier in this chapter.

- Dress neatly.

- Be well rested.

- Get to the interview site a little early.

- When asked, present your qualifications honestly.

- Be positive and responsive to questions asked.

- Keep the conversation focused on the job and why you are the best candidate.

The interviewer should volunteer information about the company, work conditions, and company policies. If they don't, you should ask. Don't wait until you are on the job to find this out.

Keep in mind that most people are nervous in job interviews. Be yourself. Try to relax and enjoy the experience. Make sure you end the interview on a positive note. Thank the interviewer for his/her time and interest and make sure you express your interest in the job and company. Before leaving, ask what will happen next, including what procedure the company will follow in making a decision.

▌Summary

In this chapter, you have learned what it takes to become a trucking professional. This includes professional image, good customer service, and the skills required to land a job within the trucking industry.

31

PUBLIC AND EMPLOYER RELATIONS QUIZ

Directions: *Read each statement carefully and mark the response that best answers the question.*

1. A successful driver maintains his/her professionalism at all times.
   A. True
   B. False

2. Good driving habits include:
   A. Giving little or no warning when planning to turn
   B. Using the vehicle's size to intimidate other drivers
   C. Following posted speed limits and maintaining a safe distance between vehicles
   D. All of the above

3. You should look at your vehicle as a rolling advertisement for both the trucking industry and your employer.
   A. True
   B. False

4. Good customer service includes being:
   A. On time
   B. Polite and friendly with the customer
   C. Knowledgeable of your company's services
   D. All of the above

5. When searching for a new driver, a motor carrier is looking for someone who is qualified based on federal regulations and company policies.
   A. True
   B. False

6. Whistleblower protection laws are in place to protect you from retaliation if you report CMV safety violations to FMCSA.
   A. True
   B. False

7. The FMCSRs require a motor carrier to obtain information about your work and driving history.
   A. True
   B. False

8. The FMCSRs do not require a physical exam prior to operating a commercial motor vehicle.
   A. True
   B. False

9. In preparing for a job interview, you should:
   A. Learn all you can about the company
   B. Dress neatly
   C. Make sure you have necessary paperwork with you
   D. All of the above

10. Always try to end a job interview on a positive note.
    A. True
    B. False

GENERAL KNOWLEDGE CDL PRE-TEST

Read each question carefully and select the most correct answer.

1. Which of the following statements about backing a commercial motor vehicle is NOT true?

   A. Since you can't see behind you, you should back quickly until you bump the dock
   B. Use mirrors on both sides of your vehicle
   C. You should always back toward the driver's side when possible
   D. Both A and C

2. Alcohol use impairs:

   A. Muscle coordination
   B. Reaction time
   C. Depth perception
   D. All of the above

3. Which of the following is true concerning cold weather driving?

   A. Exhaust system leaks are not of concern during cold weather
   B. If the temperature is below 32 degrees Fahrenheit, the engine cannot overheat
   C. Using bleach on tires will provide increased traction
   D. You should use windshield washer fluid which contains an anti-freeze

4. _____ are signs put on the outside of a vehicle which identify the hazard class of the cargo.

   A. Labels
   B. Shipping papers
   C. Placards
   D. All of the above

5. Controlled braking is used when:

   A. The goal is to keep the vehicle in a straight line while braking
   B. You must stop as quickly as possible
   C. Is only used with hydraulic brakes
   D. Is only used when the vehicle is equipped with anti-lock brakes

Basic business practices

OBJECTIVES

Upon completion of this chapter, you should have a basic understanding of:

- Cost determination and control
- Fuel management
- Growing revenue

32 Basic business practices

- COST DETERMINATION AND CONTROL
- FUEL MANAGEMENT
- GROWING REVENUE
- SUMMARY

INTRODUCTION

In this chapter we will touch on just a few of the many business concepts and ideas that you should be aware of when it comes to operating a profitable trucking business.

Cost determination and control

Cost is the greatest single issue that you will deal with as a trucking professional. Excessive costs, or lack of an effective cost control program, can cause any truck driver to become unprofitable.

There are two main categories of costs that you should be familiar with as a business person, rolling (or variable) costs and fixed costs.

It is important to understand these concepts as they apply to both company drivers and owner-operators.

Rolling costs

Rolling costs, also referred to as variable costs, are difficult to predict because they are always changing. These types of costs typically get budgeted as an estimate or assumption. When you look at what type of freight you want to haul, and where you want to run, rolling costs can become a substantial factor in your decision.

Rolling costs included such things as:

- Your pay;
- Fuel;
- Tires;
- Road tax;
- Tolls;
- Vehicle depreciation;
- Loading and unloading fees;
- Fines; and
- Accidents and claims.

As you can see from this list, there are many rolling costs that can use up a substantial portion of your revenue. How you control these costs will have a direct impact on how successful you are as a truck driver and professional business person.

Fixed costs

Fixed costs are those costs that can be placed into a budget and don't change over time. They are known costs that do not change based on how many miles you drive, or how long you sit at home. This is important to remember as these costs will continue, whether you spend the majority of your time on the road or take time off.

Fixed costs include:

- Vehicle payments;
- Finance charges;
- Liability insurance;
- Health insurance;
- Vehicle insurance;
- Cargo insurance;
- Facility rent or mortgage (if you have one);
- Property taxes;
- Professional services (legal, accounting, etc); and
- Professional dues and subscriptions.

Fixed costs are the easiest to budget for because they are always there and don't change. Your fixed costs become a base for what you need to create in revenue each month to succeed.

Fuel management

Fuel costs will be one of the biggest expenses you will deal with as a truck driver. Even if you don't own your own truck, it's important to understand how fuel and fuel mileage strategies can affect your bottom line.

Driving habits and performance

Your driving habits can be one of the largest factors when it comes to fuel mileage, as driving technique can influence fuel mileage by as much as a mile per gallon.

The following are some of driving techniques that can improve fuel mileage:

- Progressive shifting;
- Low rpm driving;
- Operating at a slower speed; and
- Idle reduction.

Many companies currently have fuel bonus programs in place for their company drivers. This incentive could create thousands of dollars in extra revenue for you, as a company driver, just by doing some of the things that you have been taught in this course about proper driving technique. As an owner/operator, your fuel bonus program is the realization that you have saved thousands of dollars in fuel costs every month just by exercising good driving practices.

Growing revenue

Whether you get paid by the mile, the trip, or the hour, revenue is controlled by you, the driver. How much you make is directly determined by how much you want to do and what you want to pay others to do for you.

You may think that as a company driver or even as an owner/operator you have little control over what you get paid. That is incorrect. While you may not be able to adjust your rate per mile whenever you want to, you can control how many miles you run, how you run those miles, and how you schedule your time off.

As we talked about earlier, your creation of revenue should initially be driven by your costs; how much do you need to make to break even. In addition to that, you should have an amount in mind as to what you want and/or need to realize an acceptable standard of living for yourself and your family. Keeping this in mind, you can now determine how much revenue is necessary to accomplish these benchmarks, and operate accordingly.

As an owner/operator, how you run your truck affects your bottom line. Remember those fixed costs? Well, they don't change as you drive more or less each month. If you want to realize a larger net revenue (what's in your pocket at the end of the month) this month, then try running more miles than you did the previous month. The fixed costs won't increase but your gross revenue will. This in turn, creates more money to you.

How do you do this? Run smart, not hard. Decide ahead of time where it makes the most sense to run, based on freight availability, and schedule accordingly. The end result could be a greater realization of income without sacrificing home time.

▌ Summary

In this chapter, you have learned just a few of the business concepts involved with being a company driver and/or owner/operator. Although there are many other business concepts and practices, far too many to mention in this manual, the ideas of costs and revenue are the most important for you to know.

Everything you do in the future as a professional in the transportation industry will be associated to either a cost or revenue. If you look at your truck driving career not as a job, but as a business, you can be extremely successful. A successful driver is one who learns how to be a professional truck driver, and learns how to be a professional business person as well.

32

BASIC BUSINESS PRACTICES QUIZ

Directions: *Read each statement carefully and mark the response that best answers the question.*

1. There are many types of costs associated with trucking but you only need to worry about variable costs.

   A. True
   B. False

2. Fuel cost is considered to be a fixed cost.

   A. True
   B. False

3. Which of the following is not a rolling cost?

   A. Tires
   B. Road Tax
   C. Vehicle payment
   D. Scale fees

4. Fuel is one of the biggest expenses that an owner/operator deals with every day.

   A. True
   B. False

5. Methods of improving your fuel mileage include _____.

   A. Driving fast
   B. Revving the engine to get the oil to flow better
   C. Coasting
   D. Progressive shifting

GENERAL KNOWLEDGE CDL PRE-TEST

Read each question carefully and select the most correct answer.

1. Shifting gears properly is important because:
   A. Doing so helps you maintain control of the vehicle
   B. It helps to keep the oil flowing through the crankcase
   C. It keeps the radiator cool
   D. It keeps the engine at the proper operating temperature

2. The braking effect of the engine is greatest when:
   A. It is above the governed RPMs and the transmission is in the high gears
   B. It is near the governed RPMs and the transmission is in the lower gears
   C. It is above the governed RPMs and the transmission is in the lower gears
   D. It is near the governed RPMs and the transmission is in the high gears

3. Water will extinguish which of the following fires?
   A. Electrical
   B. Diesel fuel
   C. Gasoline
   D. Tire

4. Convex (curved) mirrors will:
   A. Make objects appear to be larger than they really are
   B. Make objects appear to be closer than they really are
   C. Make objects appear closer and larger than they really are
   D. Show a wider area than flat mirrors

5. The Driver's Manual says you should use your horn:
   A. To make the deer standing alongside the road to move further away
   B. When a car gets in the way
   C. If it may help you to avoid a collision
   D. When you begin to change lanes

CHAPTER 32

OBJECTIVES

Upon completion of this chapter, you should have a basic understanding of:

- What CSA is and how it affects your professional driving career
- The four major components of the CSA system
- CSA-related data

- WHAT IS CSA?
- DATA COLLECTION
- SAFETY MEASUREMENT SYSTEM (SMS)
- BEHAVIOR ANALYSIS AND SAFETY IMPROVEMENT CATEGORIES (BASICS)
- ASSIGNING VALUE
- SAFETY EVALUATION
- INTERVENTIONS
- YOUR ROLE IN CSA
- CSA-RELATED DATA
- SUMMARY

INTRODUCTION

When it comes to topics of importance in the motor carrier industry, Compliance, Safety, Accountability (CSA) is at the top of the list. So what is CSA and how does it affect you and your future as a professional driver? This chapter will help you answer this and many more questions about this issue.

▎ What is CSA?

CSA is a compliance and enforcement program implemented by the Federal Motor Carrier Safety Administration (FMCSA) that focuses on both motor carriers and drivers. CSA applies to:

- Any interstate motor carrier that operates commercial motor vehicles (CMVs) and has a US DOT number;

- Any interstate or intrastate motor carrier that operates vehicles transporting hazardous materials; and

- All drivers who drive CMVs in interstate commerce.

A CMV is defined in Section 390.5 of the Federal Motor Carrier Safety Regulations (FMCSRs) as:

- Having a gross vehicle weight rating or gross combination weight rating, or gross vehicle weight or gross combination weight of 10,001 pounds or more, whichever is greater; or

- Designed or used to transport more than 8 passengers (including the driver) for compensation; or

- Designed or used to transport more than 15 passengers (including the driver), and is not used to transport passengers for compensation; or

- Transporting hazardous materials in a type or quantity requiring placarding.

The goal of CSA is to improve large truck and bus safety by reducing crashes, injuries, and fatalities on the nation's highways. It addresses enforcement in a way that allows for contact with a larger number of motor carriers and drivers earlier in the safety evaluation process. This allows FMCSA to address problems before they become serious.

In the past, FMCSA's enforcement system focused on motor carriers and didn't include drivers. Under CSA, FMCSA's focus includes both motor carriers and drivers. FMCSA believes that by tracking both motor carriers and drivers, the agency has a more complete picture of compliance.

The CSA system consists of four major components:

- Data collection;

- Safety measurement;

- Safety evaluation; and

- Interventions.

▌Data collection

The first component in the CSA system is data collection. FMCSA uses three data sources to gather information about motor carrier and driver compliance:

- Roadside inspections;
- Crash reports; and
- Investigations.

The roadside inspection is where the majority of data about motor carriers and drivers is gathered. The roadside inspection is an examination of both the driver and his/her CMV by law enforcement. This examination determines if the driver and his/her vehicle are in compliance with the FMCSRs and Hazardous Materials Regulations.

Data collection takes place during all roadside inspections. Violations found during the roadside inspection are entered into the system. When no violations are found, that is also entered into the system.

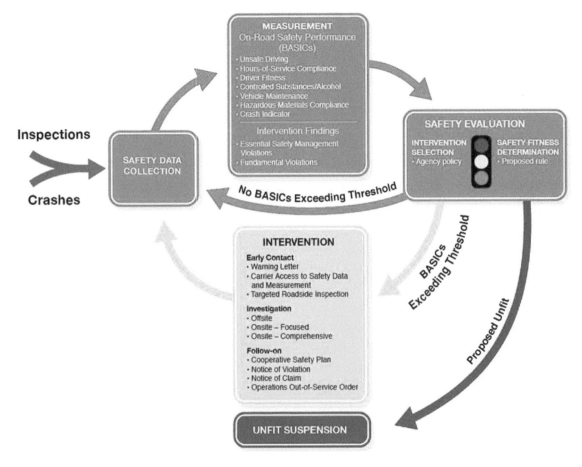

▌Safety measurement system (SMS)

The second component of the CSA system is the Safety Measurement System (SMS). The SMS quantifies the on-road safety performance and compliance history of motor carriers and drivers to:

- Identify candidates for interventions;
- Determine the specific safety problems exhibited by a driver or motor carrier; and
- Monitor whether safety problems are getting worse.

Every month, the SMS measures roadside violation and crash data performance and calculates a score in the seven Behavior Analysis and Safety Improvement Categories (BASICs).

Motor carriers are measured on the previous 24 months and drivers are measured on the previous 36 months.

Behavior Analysis and Safety Improvement Categories (BASICs)

The Behavior Analysis and Safety Improvement Categories (BASICs) are seven categories of safety behaviors measured in the SMS. The BASICs are behaviors that can lead to crashes. The seven BASICs are:

- Unsafe driving;
- Hours-of-service compliance;
- Driver fitness;
- Controlled substances and alcohol;
- Vehicle maintenance;
- Hazardous materials (HM) compliance; and
- Crash indicator.

Unsafe driving

Unsafe driving addresses the operation of CMVs by drivers in a dangerous or careless manner. Examples of violations that fall under this BASIC include:

- Speeding;
- Reckless driving; and
- Improper lane change.

Hours-of-service compliance

Hours-of-service compliance covers the operation of CMVs by drivers who are ill, fatigued, or in non-compliance with the hours-of-service regulations. Examples of violations that fall under this BASIC include:

- Operating a CMV while ill or fatigued;
- Hours-of-service violations; and
- Logbook violations.

One of the most cited offenses during a roadside inspection is the log book violation. It is important that you understand and follow the hours-of-service regulations. See Chapter 25 for additional information on the hours-of-service regulations.

33

Driver fitness

Driver fitness addresses operation of CMVs by drivers who are unfit due to a lack of training, experience, or medical qualifications. Examples of violations that fall under this BASIC include:

- Failure to have a valid and/or appropriate license;
- Failure to have proper endorsements;
- Failure to have a valid medical certificate/card; and
- Failure to train hazmat employees.

Controlled substances and alcohol

Controlled substances and alcohol covers operation of CMVs by drivers who are impaired due to alcohol, illegal drugs, and misuse of prescription or over-the-counter medications. Examples of violations that fall under this BASIC include:

- Use or possession of drugs; and
- Possession, use, or under the influence of alcohol within four hours prior to duty.

Vehicle maintenance

Vehicle maintenance addresses failure to properly maintain a CMV and prevent shifting loads. Examples of violations that fall under this BASIC include:

- Defective brakes, lights, and other mechanical components;
- Failure to make required repairs;
- Failure to inspect the vehicle or prepare inspection reports; and
- Improper load securement.

The condition of your vehicle is an extremely important issue, as the roadside inspection is where most data will be gathered. Chapter 4 addresses vehicle inspections and Chapters 20 and 21 address preventive maintenance and diagnosing and reporting vehicle malfunctions.

Hazardous material (HM) compliance

Hazardous materials (HM) compliance addresses the unsafe handling of hazardous materials on a CMV. Examples of violations include:

- Leaking containers;
- Improper placarding;
- Failure to have proper hazmat documentation; and
- Hazmat routing violations.

Crash indicator

Crash indicator covers histories or patterns of high crash involvement, including frequency and severity. It is based on law enforcement crash reports.

Assigning value

Each safety-related event is assigned to one of the seven BASICs. It then receives a number value between one and ten. This number value is based on the violation's relation to causing a crash.

Violations not often related to causing crashes receive a low value and violations that have a high relation to causing crashes receive higher values.

Examples of low value violations include:

- A general form and manner violation on your record of duty status;
- A defective/inoperative windshield wiper on your vehicle; and
- Not carrying spare fuses on your vehicle (when required).

Remember, under this system, both the driver and motor carrier are scored. Data stays with the motor carrier for 24 months and with the driver for 36 months.

Examples of high value violations include:

- A false record of duty status;
- No or improper load securement; and
- Violating an out-of-service order.

As well as receiving a number value between one and ten, safety-related events are also time weighted. This means that recent events count more than events that occurred a year earlier.

Safety evaluation

The safety evaluation is the third component in the CSA system. This is where FMCSA determines what, if any actions will be taken against the motor carrier or driver.

After a score is determined, the carrier and driver are then placed in a peer group of carriers and drivers. Percentiles of 0 to 100 are then determined by comparing the BASIC scores to the scores of others in the peer group. A score of 100 indicates the worst performance. In other words, the lower the score the better.

If one or more of the BASIC percentiles exceed a threshold, the carrier or driver becomes a candidate for an intervention.

Interventions

Interventions are the fourth component in the CSA system. Interventions are actions FMCSA can take against a motor carrier and driver based on safety measurement scores and enforcement history.

Motor carrier interventions

Motor carrier interventions can be triggered by one or more deficient BASICs, a high crash rate, a complaint, or a fatal crash.

Intervention selection is influenced by safety performance, hazardous material or passenger carrier status, and intervention history.

Interventions range from mild to severe. Interventions include:

- Warning letter;
- Targeted roadside inspection;
- Off-site investigation;
- Focused on-site investigation;
- Comprehensive on-site investigation;
- Cooperative safety plan;
- Notice of violation;
- Notice of claim/settlement agreement; and
- Operations out-of-service order (unfit suspension).

33

Driver interventions

Generally, driver interventions are triggered by an on-site investigation of the motor carrier for whom the driver is working. During an on-site investigation, the investigating officer reviews the safety performance of the drivers who work for the company. This review determines whether any drivers will be subject to intervention.

Your role in CSA

As you can see, your actions (or inactions) can play a huge part in the scoring of both you and your motor carrier under CSA. So, how do you ensure positive scores?

Since the majority of data will be gathered during roadside inspections, it is important to have roadside inspections with no violations. How do you do this?

Take care of your vehicle:

- Conduct thorough pre-trip and post-trip vehicle inspections;
- Get problems with your vehicle repaired as soon as possible; and
- Make sure your vehicle is on a regular maintenance schedule.

Remember that appropriate conduct and courtesy can help when it comes to ensuring a positive outcome during a roadside inspection.

Also, make sure all of your paperwork is current and up to date including your:

- Records of duty status;
- Commercial driver's license; and
- Medical certificate/card.

Remember, positive scores will reflect well on you as a professional driver.

CSA-related data

As part of the CSA initiative, FMCSA has been working to make accurate and timely information about motor carriers and drivers available to the industry.

As a new driver who will be applying for work with motor carriers in the near future, it is important that you are aware of and understand one of these initiatives, FMCSA's Pre-Employment Screening Program (PSP).

PSP allows motor carriers to electronically access driver inspection and crash records as part of the hiring process.

Your records will be reviewed by prospective employers as part of the hiring process.

Drivers must give their written consent before records may be released to a motor carrier and records will be protected in accordance with federal privacy laws.

Drivers may also access this data to verify its accuracy and correct any discrepancies. The information provided includes the most recent five years of crash data and three years of roadside inspection data from FMCSA's Motor Carrier Management Information System (MCMIS).

MCMIS is comprised of driver data including:

- Inspection and compliance review results;
- Enforcement data;
- State-reported crashes; and
- Motor carrier census data.

FMCSA states that by accessing this data, motor carriers will be able to better assess the potential safety risks of prospective driver-employees.

▌ Summary

Safe driving practices, maintaining a safe vehicle, and accurate paperwork all have a role in your success as a professional driver. Maintaining positive scores in the CSA Safety Measurement System and making sure prospective employers are able to receive and review positive records under the PSP will go a long way in forwarding your career as a professional driver.

33

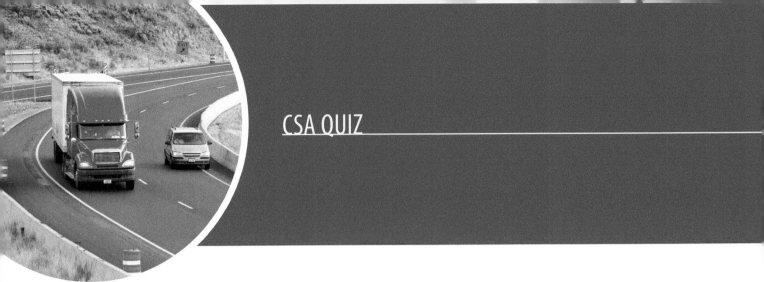

Directions: Read each statement carefully and mark the response that best answers the question.

1. CSA is a program designed to improve truck and bus safety.
   A. True
   B. False

2. CSA applies to:
   A. Any interstate motor carrier that operates CMVs and has a US DOT number
   B. Any interstate or intrastate motor carrier that operates vehicles transporting hazardous materials
   C. Drivers who drive CMVs in interstate commerce
   D. All of the above

3. The majority of CSA data is collected during roadside inspections.
   A. True
   B. False

4. In the CSA Safety Measurement System (SMS), motor carriers are measured on the previous 12 months of data.
   A. True
   B. False

5. The BASICs are seven categories of safety behaviors measured in the SMS.
   A. True
   B. False

6. The unsafe driving BASIC addresses CMV incidents resulting from the unsafe handling of hazardous materials.
   A. True
   B. False

7. Speeding is an example of a violation that falls under the driver fitness BASIC.
   A. True
   B. False

8. A false record of duty status is an example of a low value violation in the SMS.
   A. True
   B. False

9. Interventions are actions that can be taken against a motor carrier and driver based on safety measurement scores and enforcement history.
   A. True
   B. False

10. To ensure a positive score under CSA, you should:
    A. Take care of your vehicle
    B. Make sure your records of duty status are up to date
    C. Always carry a current and valid license and medical certificate
    D. All of the above

GENERAL KNOWLEDGE CDL PRE-TEST

Read each question carefully and select the most correct answer.

1. What is hydroplaning?

   A. An emergency situation created when an aircraft must make an emergency landing on a highway
   B. Excessive heat built up in the radiator
   C. Something that only occurs at high vehicle speeds
   D. When water or slush collects on the road, and your vehicle's tires lose contact with the road

2. If you are being tailgated you should:

   A. Motion for the tailgater to pass you when it is safe
   B. Increase your following distance
   C. Turn your 4-way flashers on
   D. Slam on the brakes

3. Which of the following conditions may produce a skid?

   A. Driving too fast for conditions
   B. Overbraking
   C. Oversteering
   D. All of the above

4. When fighting a fire, which is most correct?

   A. Get as close to the fire as possible
   B. Aim the fire extinguisher at the base of the fire
   C. Aim the fire extinguisher at the top of the fire
   D. All of the above

5. If a state or federal inspector determines that your vehicle is unsafe, it will be put out of service:

   A. For 24 hours
   B. For 48 hours
   C. Until you can contact your carrier and make arrangements for repair
   D. Until it is fixed

WHAT'S THE SYMPTOM	WHERE'S THE PROBLEM	WHAT COULD BE WRONG	WHAT SHOULD YOU DO
Ammeter shows continuous maximum charge	Electrical	Short circuit in wiring. Regulator malfunction.	Disconnect battery, check regulator, find short
Ammeter shows discharge while motor is running	Electrical	Loose wiring connection. Alternator malfunction. Bad battery.	Tighten connections, check battery, check alternator, check belts
High engine temperature	Cooling	Low water level. Broken fan belt. Defective fan clutch. Defective thermostat.	Add water, replace fan belt, check fan clutch, check/replace thermostat
Coolant, oil, or fuel dripping	Cooling, Lubricating, or Fuel system	Bad connections and/or hoses. Loose filters. Bad fuel pump or water pump.	Identify source of leak and repair
Excessive exhaust smoke	Exhaust or turbo system	Air filter dirty. Poor grade fuel. Fuel pump malfunction. Return fuel line blocked.	Change filter, check fuel pump, treat fuel, check return line
Excessive black smoke	Engine, fuel system	Restricted air supply. Malfunctioning injector(s). Overloading engine.	Change fuel filters, check/replace injectors, use better shifting technique
White exhaust smoke	Engine, fuel system	Engine is cold. Worn injector. Water in fuel. Fuel is beginning to gel.	Treat fuel, warm up engine, check/replace injectors
Blue exhaust smoke	Engine, fuel system	Worn valves. Malfunctioning turbo. Excessive oil overfill.	Check oil level, have turbo checked, have valves and rings (compression) checked

WHAT'S THE SYMPTOM	WHERE'S THE PROBLEM	WHAT COULD BE WRONG	WHAT SHOULD YOU DO
Low oil pressure <20 psi	Lubricating system	Cracked engine seals or rings. Oil temperature very high. Worn oil pump. Dirty filters. Worn bearings. Oil leak.	Change oil and filters, have engine components checked, check oil pump
Mettalic click in time with wheels revolving	Suspension, wheels, tires	Loose wheel. Loose lug nuts. Object in tire.	Check and tighten lug nuts, tighten axle nut, check wheel bearings, check tire for object/damage
Dull thud in time with wheel rotation	Wheels or tires	Flat tire. Loose lugs or wheel. Rock between duels.	Change tire, tighten lugs, remove rock
Dull thud or loud rap in time with engine	Engine	Burned out connecting rods or main bearing. Piston slap.	Shut off motor immediately. Contact mechanic for instructions.
Air escaping or hissing noise	Tires, air system, braking system	Damaged tire. Open air petcock. Air lines or fittings leaking. Brake application valve sticking. Ice in brake valves or lines. Air bag going bad.	Change/check tires, check all air lines and connections, apply brakes several times to dislodge ice, apply heat to brake canisters and/or lines carefully, check and/or replace air bag
Snap or click when starting from dead stop	Drive train, fifth wheel	Loose u-joints. Excessive wear in differential. Worn or broken fifth wheel lock. Loose or broken mounting bolts.	Tighten bolts, adjust fifth wheel, check differential and u-joints
Clunking or grinding noise under floor	Drive train	Clutch going bad or out of adjustment. Bad throw-out bearing. Bent or damaged drive shaft. Broken teeth in transmission.	Have all listed parts checked by mechanic
Whine - harsh high pitch	Drive train at engine	Worn accessory drive. Loose belts	Check drive gears, tighten belts
Whine - short high pitch	Engine	Ball bearing in housing. Generator or alternator malfunction. Water pump malfunction.	Shut off engine. Check listed parts

WHAT'S THE SYMPTOM	WHERE'S THE PROBLEM	WHAT COULD BE WRONG	WHAT SHOULD YOU DO
Clicking sound in engine with loss of power, sluggishness, or overheating	Engine	Broken valve spring. Worn timing gear.	Shut off engine. Contact mechanic
Sudden loss of power	Brake, drive train, engine, or fuel system	Brakes dragging. Clutch slipping. Engine severely overheated. Blocked fuel filter. Fuel pedal linkage failure.	Adjust brakes, adjust clutch, determine cause of overheating and fix, change fuel filters, check fuel linkage
Engine surges	Fuel or engine system	Air or water in fuel system. Throttle linkage loose. Fuel level low.	Check fuel for air and/or water, check throttle linkage, refill fuel
Brakes grab	Braking system	Grease on brake lining. Brakes adjusted improperly. Ice in brakes.	Cleans brake drums of grease, check and readjust brakes, thaw (warm) brake system
Brakes don't hold	Braking system	Brakes out of adjustment. Grease on linings. Water or ice on linings. Air tanks full of oil or water. Broken air line or fitting.	Readjust brakes, check linings for grease, warm brake system to remove ice, drain air tanks, repair and/or replace air lines and/or fittings
Constant pull to right or left on steering	Tires, suspension, braking, or steering system	Soft tire. Broken spring. Front brake dragging or our of adjustment. Axles out of alignment.	Check tires, check springs, readjust brakes, align all axles
Tractor does not want to come back straight after lane change or turn	Steering or fifth wheel	Dry fifth wheel.	Grease fifth wheel
Excessive vibration in engine	Engine system	Broken valve. Blown cylinder head gasket. Unbalanced or damaged fan. Engine mount loose. Clutch out of balance. Bad injectors. Air in fuel.	Check all listed parts and systems for damage or wear.
Gradual loss of power	Fuel or engine system	Fuel filter dirty or clogged. Air filter dirty or clogged. Faulty valve. Jelling fuel. Freezing fuel filter. Injectors going bad.	Check fuel system, replace bad or blocked fuel and/or air filters, treat fuel for jelling, check and replace injectors

A

A Train — Combination of vehicles composed of a tractor and a semi-trailer towing a full trailer: 1) connected with an A dolly; or 2) without a convertor dolly.

Accelerator pedal — Located on the floor under the steering wheel. Operated by driver's right foot. Driver depresses accelerator pedal to increase engine speed.

Agent — A person authorized to transact business for and in the name of another. A driver becomes an agent of the trucking company when signing for freight.

Aggregated shipments — Several shipments from different shippers to one consignee that are consolidated and treated as a single consignment.

Agitator body — Truck body designed and equipped to mix concrete in transit.

Agreed valuation — Freight value mutually agreed upon by shipper and carrier as a basis for transportation charges. It also may represent an agreed maximum amount that can be recovered in case of loss or damage.

Air application pressure gauge — Indicates how much air pressure is being applied by the brakes during brake operation.

Air brakes — Brakes that utilize compressed air to activate brakes.

Air cleaner — Air or filter device for cleaning air entering engine. There may be two, one on each side of the tractor.

Air compressor — Device to build up and maintain required air pressure in the brake system reservoir.

Air dryer — A device for cleaning and removing moisture from air systems.

Air filter restriction gauge — Provides indication of filter's obstruction by dirt and other contaminants which would restrict the flow of air to the engine.

Air intake manifold — Distributes air to the various cylinders of the engine. It attaches to the cylinder heads at the intake ports.

Air lines — Used to carry compressed air from one part of the air brake system to another and from tractor to the trailer. One line is called the emergency or supply line and is always charged with compressed air. The other line is called the service or control line. When the air brake treadle valve is depressed, air flows from the supply reservoir through the service line and causes the brakes to apply.

Air operated (fifth wheel) release — Located under the fifth wheel plate, but operated by a release lever in the cab, this device locks and unlocks the sliding fifth wheel's locking mechanism.

Air pressure gauge — Indicates the amount of air pressure in the air tanks.

Air reservoirs — Storage tanks for compressed air, used in tractor and trailer air systems.

Air slider — A cab-controlled sliding fifth wheel that can be unlocked by air to be moved backward or forward. See sliding fifth wheel.

Air suspension — Located between the axle and the frame of a truck, the suspension system uses air bags to cushion vibration and road shocks and dampen the ride. See air tag.

Air tag — A tag axle that has two bellows-like air bags that, when filled, force the tractor's rear axle harder against the ground for a smoother ride and for weight distribution between the two axles of the tractor.

Ammeter — An instrument that measures the amount of battery being charged or discharged.

Anti-lock brake system (ABS) — While the driver holds the brake pedal firmly down during a hard stop, the computer operated system senses wheel speeds and rapidly applies and releases the brakes to each wheel, thus avoiding wheel lock-up, providing steering control during the stop.

Articulated — Having parts connected by joints. A tractor-trailer is an articulated vehicle.

Authority — Operating rights granted to for-hire, common, and contract carriers by the FMCSA.

Authorized carrier — Person/company granted common or contract carrier operating rights by the FMCSA.

Automobile transporter — Company authorized to transport motor vehicles on special vehicles or by driving them.

Automobile transporter body — Truck or trailer body with ramps for loading and low-road clearance, designed for the transportation of vehicles, also known as a car carrier.

Auxiliary transmission — Second transmission connected with the main transmission to provide a wider range of speeds and gear ratios.

Average speed calculation — Average speed (miles per hour) may be calculated by dividing the distance driven (in miles) by time (the number of hours it took to drive that distance).

Axle — The housing or beam that connects opposite wheels. There are two types of axles: 1) live axles, which transmit power from the drive shaft to the wheels; and 2) dead axles, which do not transmit power and are used only to help carry the load or to steer.

Axle group — Any number of consecutive axles on a vehicle through which weight is: 1) intended to be equally distributed for transmission to a public highway; and 2) transmitted to a public highway.

Axle load — Weight existing on a motor vehicle's axle; an axle weight limit on a highway refers to the maximum weight allowed on the truck's heaviest axle.

Axle ratings — Rear axles on a truck generally carry three ratings: 1) carrying capacity rated at the ground; 2) total weight the axle is capable of carrying/pulling in service, gross combined weight; 3) the maximum horsepower limit the axle is capable of carrying in normal service.

Axle ratio — Ratio of axle to drive line; the number of turns of the drive line in relation to one full turn of the drive wheels. The higher the numerical ratio, the slower the road speed. See gear ratio.

Axle spread — The distance between the extreme axle centers of an axle group.

Axle temperature gauges — Indicate temperature of lubricant in drive axles.

Axle weight — The gross weight of a rig that rests on any truck axle; axle weights are used as part of the bridge formula when setting bridge weight limits.

B

B Train — A combination of vehicles composed of a tractor and a semi-trailer towing another semi-trailer attached to a fifth wheel mounted on the rear of the first semi-trailer.

Backhaul — 1) Return transportation movement, usually at less revenue than the original move (headhaul); 2) movement in the direction of lighter traffic flow when traffic is generally heavier in the opposite direction; or 3) to move a shipment back over part of a route already traveled.

Baffle — A perforated divider or wall inside the tank of a liquid cargo tanker truck that moderates the movement or surging of liquids carried in a less-than-full tank.

BASIC(s) — See Behavior Analysis and Safety Improvement Categories.

Battery — An electrochemical device for storing and supplying electrical energy.

Bead — The inner edge of the outer wall of a rubber tire, fitting on the rim. The "foundation" of a tire. It is made of high tensile steel wires and wrapped and reinforced by the plies.

Behavior Analysis and Safety Improvement Categories (BASICs) — Seven categories of safety behaviors measured in the Compliance, Safety, Accountability (CSA) Safety Measurement System (SMS). The BASICs represent behaviors that can lead to crashes: unsafe driving, fatigued driving, driver fitness, controlled substances/alcohol, vehicle maintenance, cargo-related, and crash indicator.

Belly dump — Trailer that unloads by opening an air-operated gate in its bed; bulk materials like sand, grain, coal or other dry products are usually belly-dumped.

Berm — The shoulder of the road.

Bill of lading (B/L) — The written transportation contract between shipper and carrier. It identifies the freight, who it is consigned to, the place of delivery, and gives the terms of the agreement.

The straight bill of lading provides that goods be delivered to the consignee indicated. The consignee does not have to surrender his copy to receive the goods.

Bill of sale — Formal document issued by a seller to a buyer as evidence of transfer of title to an item of personal property.

Binders — 1) Load stabilizing equipment such as chain, wire/manila/synthetic fiber rope, steel strapping or nylon webbing used to secure a load; or 2) slang term for brakes.

Bingo card — Slang term for authority cab card; designed with open squares on the back where driver places vehicle's authority identification stamps (or PSC#) as received from various states. Card is to be carried in the cab of the power unit to which it has been assigned. See cab card.

Black ice — A very dangerous, nearly invisible patch of ice on a clear road formed when temperatures drop very rapidly when the road surface is wet.

Blanket permit — A master type permit issued to a carrier by a state or province and which does not have any particular vehicle identification indicated. The permit may be photocopied, with a copy placed in the carrier's vehicles as the required permit for those vehicles in that state.

Blanket waybill — A waybill covering two or more consignments of freight.

Bleed the air tanks — To drain the accumulated water out of the air tanks of a tractor to prevent the condensed water from reducing air tank capacity and thus cutting braking efficiency.

Bleed the fuel lines — To remove trapped air from the fuel lines.

Blocking or bracing — Pieces of wood or other material used to prevent movement of goods in rail, vessel, or truck shipments in order to prevent breakage.

Blood Alcohol Content (BAC) — A measurement or calculation of the amount of alcohol in the bloodstream. The blood alcohol content is considered an indirect indicator of the level of someone's intoxication.

Blower — A device that forces additional air into the engine to increase its efficiency and horsepower.

Bobtail — Slang term for a tractor driven without its trailer, can also refer to a straight truck or a truck with a short rear overhang.

Bogie — 1) An assembly of two or more axles; or 2) removable set of rear axles and wheels used to support a van container.

Bogie truck — Low skeleton platform mounted on two centrally located load-carrying wheels and fitted with two or four smaller diameter stabilizing wheels; also known as a restless dolly.

Boomers — Slang term for the binder devices used to tighten chains around cargo on flatbed trailers.

Booster axles — An axle generally having an air or hydraulic cylinder suspension system that can be actuated independently to assume a portion of the load that would otherwise be carried by adjacent axles.

Bottom dump — Trailer that unloads through bottom gates; same as belly dump.

Brake chamber — Air chamber mounted near each wheel and connected to the brake itself by a push rod and slack adjuster (cam brake) or a push rod (wedge brake).

Brake drum — Metal, drum-shaped compartment that revolves with the wheel and provides a friction surface for the brake lining.

Brake horsepower — The actual horsepower of an engine, measured by a brake attached to the drive shaft and recorded on a dynamometer.

Brake lining — Material designed to create friction when pressed against the brake drum. It is fastened to the brake shoe and contacts the drum during the braking process.

Brake shoe — The nonrotating unit of the brake (to which the brake shoe is attached) that contacts the rotating unit to supply braking force.

Break down the unit — Slang term for the process of uncoupling a tractor from a trailer.

Breakaway protection — Process which applies brakes on the trailer(s) in case of a broken air hose or some other emergency.

Breakaway valve — Valve positioned between the tractor and trailer; automatically cuts off air going to trailers if pressure drops below 60 pounds, causing trailer brakes to activate.

Bridge — The distance between one axle and another, or between two sets of axles. Used in some states to ascertain the permissible gross weight for the vehicle. Also called spread. See spread tandem.

Bridge formula — Formula used to determine maximum gross weight that can be carried on any given arrangement of consecutive axles.

Broker — A broker arranges, for compensation, the truck transportation of cargo belonging to others, utilizing authorized for-hire carriers to provide the actual truck transportation. A broker does not assume responsibility for the cargo and usually does not take possession of the cargo.

Brokerage license — Granted by the Federal Motor Carrier Safety Administration to allow licensee to arrange for transportation in interstate commerce.

Bulkhead — Found on each end of a tanker, it is used to seal the tank. Also a wall or metal divider used inside a tanker to divide it into smaller compartments.

Bulk cargo container — Shipping container employed in handling/hauling dry fluid materials.

Bulk freight — Dry or liquid freight not in packages/containers and transported in bulk, e.g., potatoes, grain, citrus, ore, etc.

Buttonhook turn — A right turn procedure for tractor-trailers that lets the trailer's rear wheels clear the inside corner of the turn. The rig proceeds through the intersection until the rear tires will clear the corner and then the driver sharply turns right and holds the turn (creating the "hook" of the turn) until the tractor can be turned left to straighten itself in the turn lane.

C

C Train — A combination of vehicles composed of a tractor and a semi-trailer towing a full trailer connected with a C dolly.

C Dolly — A converter dolly with two parallel arms which connect to two hitches located on a towing unit so as to prevent any rotation in a horizontal plane through the hitch points.

Cab — Driver compartment of a truck or tractor-trailer.

Cab card — Registration document issued by base jurisdiction for a vehicle in an apportioned/prorated fleet which identifies vehicle, base plate, registered weight by jurisdiction (if IRP); also shows jurisdictions where vehicle is registered.

Cab-over-engine (COE) — Truck tractor unit with engine located under the cab; face of the vehicle is flat.

Camber — Inward or outward tilt of wheels on vertical axis of truck or other motor vehicle; proper camber affects tire wear.

Camshaft — Long, straight shaft covered with elliptical knobs called cams; as the camshaft turns, cams push the push rods and open the cylinder valves.

Carbon monoxide (CO) — A colorless, odorless, highly poisonous gas, produced by the incomplete combustion of fuel. It is usually expelled by the exhaust system.

Carburetor — Device in an engine to mix air with gasoline spray; mixture is then distributed to cylinders by intake manifold so it can be ignited by a spark.

Cargo — Freight transported in a vehicle.

Cargo manifest — Document listing all consignments on a truck, vessel or aircraft and giving quantity, identifying marks, consignor/consignee of each item.

Cargo-related BASIC — One of seven categories of safety behaviors measured in the CSA Safety Measurement System. Commercial motor vehicle incident resulting from shifting loads, spilled or dropped cargo, and unsafe handling of hazardous materials are included in this BASIC. Violations include improper load securement and hazardous material handling.

Carrier — Individual, partnership or corporation engaged in the business of transporting goods or passengers.

Casing — The tire structure, excepting tread and sidewall rubber.

Caster — Forward (or rearward) inclination of kingpin or support arm of wheel; amount of tilt in axle beam.

Center of gravity — The point within the length and width of a vehicle around which its weight is evenly distributed or balanced.

Cetane number — Rating applied to ignition properties of diesel fuel; the higher the number, the better the ignition quality. See octane number.

Chain binders — A device used to remove slack from chains used to tie down loads. See boomers.

Check valve — Device to automatically isolate one part of the air brake system from another. A one-way check valve provides free air flow in one direction only. A two-way check valve permits actuation of the brake system by either of two brake application valves.

Chocks — Block or stop barriers placed behind/in front of wheels to keep vehicle from rolling.

Circuit breaker — A device that automatically interrupts the flow of an electric current when the current becomes excessive.

Clutch — The part of the drive train that allows the driver to disconnect or connect the engine to the transmission.

C.O.D. — Collect on delivery. The payment for goods is made at the delivery point. The driver must collect payment before the cargo is unloaded.

Code of Federal Regulations (CFR) — U.S. Government Printing Office publications containing regulations various federal agencies have created/promulgated.

Coercion — A threat by a motor carrier, shipper, receiver, or transportation intermediary, or their respective agents, officers or representatives, to withhold business, employment or work opportunities from, or to take or permit any adverse employment action against, a driver in order to induce the driver to operate a commercial motor vehicle under conditions which the driver stated would require him/her to violate motor carrier safety, hazardous materials, or commercial regulations.

Combination ramp and arrester bed — An emergency escape ramp built off of steep road grades to slow and stop a rig in emergency situations. The ramp uses loose surface materials and/or an upward grade and ramp length to safely slow and stop the rig.

Combination vehicle — Truck/truck tractor coupled to one or more trailers, including semi-trailers. Also referred to as a "rig". See rig.

Combined gross vehicle weight — The total unladen weight of a combination of vehicles plus the weight of the load carried on that combination of vehicles.

Commercial carrier — Any motor carrier transporting persons or property for-hire on the public highways.

Commingling — Mixing types of goods from separate shipments and sending them as a combined shipment.

Commodities — 1) Articles, goods, or merchandise; or 2) goods shipped.

Common carrier — A for-hire carrier that holds itself out to serve the general public at reasonable rates and without discrimination. To operate, the carrier must secure a Certificate of Public Convenience and Necessity from the FMCSA.

Compliance, Safety, Accountability (CSA) — A Federal Motor Carrier Safety Administration initiative to improve large truck and bus safety and reduce commercial vehicle-related crashes, injuries, and fatalities.

Compression pin — Hardware used to join two 20-foot containers into a single 40-foot unit.

Compression ratio — Volume of air above the piston at bottom dead center compared with volume of air at top dead center.

Compression stroke — A phase of the four-stroke cycle when the air-fuel mix is compressed.

Compressor — See air compressor.

Compressor belt — Belt running between engine pulley and air compressor that uses power of engine to operate air compressor.

Connecting carrier — Carrier that interchanges trailers/freight with another carrier to complete shipments.

Connecting rod — Rod that connects the piston to the crankshaft.

Consign — To send goods to purchaser or agent to sell.

Consignee — Person who receives goods shipped from the owner.

Consignment — Goods shipped when an actual purchase has not been made, but when the consignee agrees to sell the goods

Consignor — The person or company (usually the owner) that ships goods to customers.

Consolidation — Practice of combining less-than-carload (LCL) or less-than-truckload (LTL) shipments to make carload/truckload movements.

Container (van body type) — A truck or trailer body provided with means for ready removal from and attachment to a vehicle.

Containerization — 1) Practice/technique of using box-like device to store, protect, and handle a number of packages as a unit in transit; or 2) shipping system based on large cargo-carrying containers (usually 20 or 40 feet in length) that can be interchanged between trucks, trains, and ships without rehandling contents.

Continuous seal — A term denoting that the seals on a truck remained intact during the movement of the truck from origin to destinations or, if broken in transit, that it was done by proper authority and without opportunity for loss to occur before new seals were applied.

Contraband — Illegal or prohibited traffic or freight.

Contract carrier — A for-hire carrier that does not serve the general public but serves shippers with whom the carrier has a continuing contract. A Permit from the FMCSA is required.

Controlled substances/alcohol BASIC — One of seven categories of safety behaviors measured in the CSA Safety Measurement System. The operation of commercial motor vehicles by drivers who are impaired due to alcohol, illegal drugs, and misuse of prescription or over-the-counter medications are included in this BASIC. A violation under this category could be issued for use or possession of controlled substances or alcohol.

Conventional tractor — Power unit with engine under the hood of the tractor, in front of driver compartment.

Converter gear or dolly — The coupling device composed of one or two axles and a fifth wheel by which a semi-trailer can be coupled to the rear of a tractor-trainer combination, forming a double-bottom rig, i.e. it converts a semi-trailer into a full trailer.

Convex mirror — A type of mirror having a convex shape in order to show a larger field of view than can be obtained from a flat mirror of the same size.

Coolant — The fluid that circulates around an engine to help it maintain a safe working temperature, usually it is a combination of antifreeze and water.

Coolant alarm — A warning light that indicates if the level of coolant in the engine's system is too low.

Coolant temperature gauge — Indicates the current temperature of the coolant in the engine.

Coolant temperature warning — A warning light that indicates if the coolant is overheating causing severe internal engine damage.

Coupling — Act of connecting truck (or tractor) and trailer.

Coupling device — Any mechanical means for connecting trailer or semitrailer to truck or truck-tractor, e.g., fifth wheel.

Crash indicator BASIC — One of seven categories of safety behaviors measured in the CSA Safety Measurement System. Histories or patterns of high crash involvement, including frequency and severity are included in this BASIC. It is based on information from state-reported crash reports.

Creeper gear — Lowest gear/combination of gears on a tractor used when extra power is needed.

CSA — See Compliance, Safety, Accountability.

Cubic capacity — The carrying capacity of a truck measured in cubic feet.

Cubic foot — A common measure of the capacity of a truck, 1,728 cubic inches.

Curb weight — The weight of an empty tractor-trailer minus driver and cargo but including fuel, oil, and all standard equipment.

▌D

DOT — See Department of Transportation.

Dead axle — An axle that does not transmit power. Used to steer and support the load.

Deadheading — Returning to home base without a load after delivery has been made.

Declared combined gross vehicle weight — The total unladen weight of any combination of vehicles plus the maximum load to be carried on that combination of vehicles for which registration fees have been paid.

Delivery — The act of transferring possession of a shipment. This could be from consignor to carrier, one carrier to another, or carrier to consignee.

Demountable body — Box of motor freight vehicle (chassis or trailer) constructed so it can be used interchangeably on railroad flatcars for piggyback hauling or on trucks for highway loads.

Department of Transportation (DOT) — A cabinet-level executive department of the United States government. The DOT consists of the Office of the Secretary and eleven individual Operating Administrations, including the Federal Motor Carrier Safety Administration (FMCSA).

Depth perception — The ability to judge distances.

Detention — Delay of a driver and freight vehicle or container beyond a stipulated time.

Diesel engine — An internal combustion engine that uses compression to raise air temperature to the igniting point, whereas fuel is ignited by a spark in a gasoline engine.

Differential — The part of the power train that permits one wheel to turn at a different rate of speed from the other, as occurs when going around a turn.

Differential lock, interaxle type — Used on twin-screw tractors, this valve can be set to lock both rear axles together so that they pull as one for off-the-road operation. Never used for over-the-road operation.

Direct current (D.C.) — Electrical current that always flows in one direction only and is the type used in automotive equipment.

Direct drive — Refers to a condition in which the transmission is in a gear having a 1:1 ratio, that is, when the engine crankshaft is turning at the same rate as the vehicle drive shaft. See overdrive and underdrive.

Disc brakes — Brakes that function by causing friction pads to press on either side of a disc rotating along with the wheel.

Dispatcher — Person in charge of dispatching trucks and drivers to and from destinations.

Dispatching — The scheduling and control of freight distribution.

Distance calculation — Distance traveled can be determined by multiplying driving speed (miles per hour) by time (the number of hours driven).

Diversion — A change made in the route of a shipment in transit. See reconsigment.

Divisible load — Any load consisting of a product, material or equipment which can be reduced to meet the specified regulatory limits for size and/or weight.

Dock — A platform where trucks load and unload.

Dock plate — Removable ramp used between dock and trailer/railcar so forklift can drive into unit, used for ease/safety in loading/unloading.

Dock receipt — A receipt given for a shipment received or delivered at a pier or dock.

Documentation — 1) The supplying of anything printed, written, etc., relied upon to record or prove something (documents); or 2) the documents that are supplied.

Dolly — 1) Auxiliary axle assembly equipped with fifth wheel used to convert semitrailer to full trailer; 2) small square or rectangular platform on rollers/wheels used to handle freight in warehouse; or 3) landing gear on a trailer (dolly wheels).

Double-axle — See tandem axle.

Double bottom — Combination of tractor, semi-trailer and full trailer, also called twin trailers or doubles.

Double-clutching — Shifting the gears of a nonsynchronized truck transmission without clashing them, by depressing and releasing the clutch pedal twice.

Double drop frame — A drop frame trailer with one drop behind the kingpin and one in front of the rear axles. See drop frame.

Driveaway operation — Transportation of new/used motor vehicles where units being transported are loaded with the front axles resting on the back of the power unit being driven and the wheels of the rear axles on roadway, one or more units can be transported in tandem; or power units can be driven on their own.

Drive axle — An axle that transmits power to the wheels. A drive axle is a powered axle that actively pulls the load.

Drive shaft — A heavy-duty tube that connects the transmission to the rear-end assembly of the tractor.

Drive train — A series of connected mechanical parts for transmitting motion.

Driver fitness BASIC — One of seven categories of safety behaviors measured in the CSA Safety Measurement System. The operation of commercial motor vehicles by drivers who are unfit to operate a commercial motor vehicle due to lack of training, experience, or medical qualifications are included in this BASIC. Violations include failure to have a valid and appropriate commercial driver's license and being medically unqualified to operate a commercial motor vehicle.

Driver's daily log — Daily record required to be kept by driver which shows driving, on-duty/not driving, sleeper berth, and off-duty time. See record of duty status.

Drop frame trailer — Open flatbed trailer sometimes equipped with van body (household goods movers) designed with minimum floor-to-highway distance except for raised section for rear wheel housings and raised forward section. This increases cargo capability without increasing the vertical clearance of the vehicle.

Dry tank — Part of brake system. Air passes from wet tank to dry tank. Dry tank is the air reservoir from which the air is drawn for operating the brake system.

Dual wheels — Wheel assembly with two wheels on each side of axle, generally found only on rear.

Dummy coupler — A fitting used to seal the opening in an air brake hose connection (glad hands) when the connection is not in use. Sometimes called a dust cap.

Dump body — Truck body which can be tilted to discharge load.

Dunnage — The material used to protect or support freight in trucks. The weight of dunnage is shown separately on the bill of lading since it is material used around cargo to prevent damage. Often, it is transported without charge.

Duty — A tax levied by a government on imports and exports.

DVIR — Driver vehicle inspection report.

Dynamometer — A device for measuring the work output of an engine. See brake horsepower.

E

Electronic logging device (ELD) — A device or technology that automatically records a driver's driving time and facilitates the accurate recording of the driver's hours of service.

Electronic logging device (ELD) record — A record of duty status, recorded on an ELD, that reflects the data elements that an ELD must capture.

Embargo — To resist or prohibit the acceptance and handling of freight. A formal notice that certain freight will not be accepted.

Emergency (air line) — See air lines.

Emergency brake release — Will override the spring brake control in the event air pressure is lost. You must hold it while pulling out on the spring brake control. For emergency use only.

Emergency engine stop — See Stop (Engine) and emergency stop.

Emergency movement — Movement by motor carrier in an instance which is not covered by ordinary circumstances, law, regulation or permit, which usually requires the acquisition of authority from a regulatory body.

Emission — Refers to gases and other materials vented to the atmosphere by the exhaust system.

Encroachment — The act of intruding or going beyond the proper limits, such as encroachment on another lane of traffic or off-tracking.

Engine brake — Sometimes called a Jake Brake or compression brake. Part of the truck's retarder system, activated by a switch on the dash or by taking your foot off of the accelerator pedal. The engine brake changes valve timing so instead of providing engine power, it acts as an air compressor, powered by the wheels, which slows the truck vs. total reliance on wheel brakes. See exhaust brake, hydraulic retarder and retarder systems.

Engine oil temperature gauge — Indicates the temperature of the engine oil.

Engine water jackets — Hollow chambers that surround the cylinder liners and other parts exposed to high temperatures in the engine. The coolant circulates within these chambers to cool the engine.

En-route inspection — See inspection.

Escape ramp — A ramp on a steep downgrade that can be used by a truck driver to stop a runaway truck when brakes have failed. The ramp often has a soft gravel surface and forms a steep upgrade to stop the truck. Sometimes called a runaway truck ramp.

Excess freight — Freight in excess of the quantity shown on the freight bill.

Exempt carrier — Motor carrier engaged in for-hire transportation of commodities exempt from federal economic regulation under 49 USC 13506 and 49 CFR 372.115.

Exhaust brake — Part of a truck retarder system. It closes a valve in the exhaust system which restricts the flow of exhaust gases, creating back pressure and slowing the engine. See engine brake, hydraulic retarder and retarder systems.

Exhaust manifold — That part of the exhaust system that carries the exhaust gases from the cylinders to the turbocharger.

Exhaust ports — Connecting passages from the inside to the outside of the cylinder heads.

Exhaust stack — Pipe connected to the muffler through which exhaust gases are released.

Exhaust stroke — The last phase of the four-stroke cycle when waste gases are pushed out of the exhaust valve.

Exhaust valves — Open to discharge the burned gases from the combustion chambers.

Export — To send goods to a foreign country.

Eye lead time — Term used to describe the distance that a driver is looking ahead on the road. A 12-second eye lead time means that the driver is looking ahead the distance he/she will travel in 12 seconds time.

F

Fatigued driving BASIC — One of seven categories of safety behaviors measured in the CSA Safety Measurement System. The operation of commercial motor vehicles by drivers who are ill, fatigued, or in non-compliance with the hours-of-service regulations are included in this BASIC. Violations include hours of service, logbook, and operating a commercial motor vehicle while ill or fatigued.

Federal Motor Carrier Safety Administration (FMCSA) — An administration within the U.S. Department of Transportation. FMCSA's primary mission is to reduce crashes, injuries, and fatalities involving large trucks and buses. FMCSA develops and enforces the Federal Motor Carrier Safety Regulations (FMCSRs).

Federal Motor Carrier Safety Regulations (FMCSRs) — Federal regulations that establish safe operating requirements for commercial vehicle drivers, carriers, vehicles, and vehicle equipment.

Federal Register — Government publication that prints rules/regulations of federal agencies on a daily basis.

Fifth wheel — The coupling device located on the tractor's rear frame that is used to join the front end of the trailer to the tractor. It is a flat, rounded plate with a V-shaped notch in the rear.

First aid — The immediate and temporary care given to the victim of an accident or sudden illness until the services of medical personnel can be obtained.

Flatbed — Trailer with level bed and no sides or top.

Flexi-van — Trailers with detachable container bodies that are loaded on specially constructed flat cars equipped with two turntables.

FMCSA — See Federal Motor Carrier Safety Administration.

FMCSRs — See Federal Motor Carrier Safety Regulations.

Fog lamps — Amber colored auxiliary lights for use during foggy and misty conditions.

Foot brake valve — Valve which the driver depresses with his foot, which controls the amount of air pressure delivered to or released from the brake chambers. Also called a treadle valve.

Forklift — A self-propelled vehicle for lifting, stacking, etc., heavy objects that may be loaded on pallets or skids; it consists typically of projecting prongs that are slid under the load then raised or lowered.

For-hire carriage — Motor carrier services in which charge is made to cover cost of transportation, generally provided by common or contract carrier.

For-hire carrier — A company that can be engaged to haul cargo by truck.

Foundation brake — A type of brake designed with the brake shoes on the inside of the braking drum to expand against the inner surface of the drum. A common braking mechanism for trucks.

Frame or chassis — A metal support for the body, power unit, and running gear; the backbone structure around which the vehicle is assembled. Contains the engine mounts, fuel tank supports, etc.

F.O.B. (Free on board) — Contractual terms between a buyer and a seller which define where title transfer takes place and the exchange point where responsibility for risk/expense transitions from seller to buyer.

Freight — Goods being transported from one place to another.

Freight bill — The carrier's invoice for payment of transport services rendered.

Freight charge — The rate established for transporting freight.

Freight claim — A charge made against a carrier for loss, damage, delay, or overcharge.

Freight forwarder — 1) Individual/company that accepts less than truckload (LTL) shipments and consolidates them into truckload lots on a for-hire basis; or 2) agent who helps expedite shipments by preparing necessary documents/making other arrangements for moving freight. Forwarders must obtain operating authority from the FMCSA.

Front haul — 1) The front portion of a trip, from start to destination; or 2) freight carried on the front portion of the trip. See back haul.

Fuel filter — Device for cleaning engine fuel.

Fuel gauge — Registers amount of fuel in fuel tank. One for each tank.

Fuel pump — Pump that moves a fuel from the fuel tank to the engine.

Fuel taxes — Excise taxes on gasoline and other fuels.

Full trailer — A trailer with both front and rear axles; used as the second trailer in a double-bottom rig or hooked behind a straight truck to form a truck-trailer combination. A semi-trailer can be converted into a full trailer by the use of converter dollies. See semi-trailer.

Furniture van body — Truck body designed for the transportation of household goods; usually a van of drop-frame construction.

Fuse — A wire or strip of easily melted metal, usually set in a plug, placed in a circuit as a safeguard; if the current becomes too strong, the metal melts, thus breaking the circuit.

Fusee — A colored burning flare used as a signal to warn other road users.

G

Gear box temperature gauge — Indicates temperature of lubricant in transmission.

Gear pump — Located at the rear of the fuel pump. Driven by the fuel pump main shaft. Consists of a single set of gears to pick up and deliver fuel throughout the fuel system. From gear pump, fuel flows through the filter screen and to the pressure regulator.

Glad hands — Connectors mounted on the front of a trailer for connecting air lines from the tractor.

Gooseneck — Part of a lowbed trailer that reaches up from the deck to attach to the fifth wheel.

Governor (air) — Device to automatically control the air pressure being maintained in the air reservoirs. Keeps air pressure between 90 and 120 psi. Prevents excessive air pressure from building up.

Governor (fuel) — Maintains sufficient fuel for idling with the throttle control in "Idle" position, and cuts off fuel above maximum rated rpm.

Grain body — Low side, open-top truck body designed to transport dry flowable commodities.

Gross combination weight (GCW) — The weight of the tractor, trailer, and cargo.

Gross combination weight rating (GCWR) — The value specified by the manufacturer as the loaded weight of a combination motor vehicle.

Gross ton — 2,240 pounds. More commonly called a long ton.

Gross vehicle weight (GVW) — The weight of an empty tractor or trailer.

Gross vehicle weight rating (GVWR) — The value specified by the manufacturer as the loaded weight of a single motor vehicle.

Gross weight — 1) The weight of an article together with the weight of its container and the material used in packing; 2) as applied to a truck, the weight of a truck together with weight of its entire contents. See gross vehicle weight and gross combination weight.

H

Half-cab — A tractor having only a half of a cab along the left side of the engine.

Hand valve — The valve that controls only the trailer brakes. See trailer brake.

Hazardous materials — Substance/material determined and designated by Secretary of Transportation to be capable of posing unreasonable risk to health, safety and property when transported in commerce.

Hazmat — Slang for hazardous materials.

Headache rack — Slang for a heavy bulkhead mounted behind the tractor cab to protect the driver from a shifting load.

Header bar — A hinged, rear cross piece on open-top trailer, that can be swung out of the way to load high objects.

Heavy hauler — A trucking company authorized to transport articles which require special equipment for loading/unloading/transporting because of size/shape/weight/other inherent characteristics.

Hopper body — Truck or trailer body capable of discharging its load through a bottom opening without tilting.

Hose tenders — Devices that keep air and electrical lines between the tractor and trailer suspended and out of the way. Also known as "pogo sticks."

Hours of service — The number of hours tractor-trailer drivers may drive and be on duty after meeting off-duty requirements, according to Part 395 of the Federal Motor Carrier Safety Regulations.

Household goods carrier — Motor carrier authorized to transport furniture, household goods and other properties involved in change of residence. Includes moving offices, stores, etc.

Hydraulic brakes — Brakes that depend on the transmission of hydraulic pressure from a master cylinder to the wheel cylinders.

Hydraulic retarder — A driveline retarder consisting of a spinning rotor enclosed in a stationary housing with vanes. Oil (transmission fluid or engine oil) is pumped into the retarder and movement of the oil by the rotor, and against the fixed vanes, uses up energy and creates a slowing action. Part of a truck's retarder system. See engine brake, exhaust brake, and retarder systems.

Hydrometer — An instrument used to determine the state of charge of a battery.

Hydroplaning — Action produced by water on the roadway, in which tires lose traction (contact with the road) and skim along the water's surface, thus causing dangerous loss of directional control.

I

In bond — Storage of goods in custody of government/bonded warehouse or carrier from whom goods can be taken only upon payment of taxes/duties to an appropriate government agency.

Independent trailer brake (trolley valve) — Located on the dash or steering column, this hand operated brake applies brakes only to the trailer.

Indivisible load — Any vehicle or load which cannot be dismantled, disassembled, or loaded to meet specific regulatory limits for size and/or weight.

Initial carrier — The transportation line that picks up a shipment from the shipper; in other words, the "first" carrier.

Initial point — The point at which a shipment originates.

Injector — A device found in a diesel engine that changes liquid fuel oil into a mist or spray and meters it to each cylinder.

Injector pump — A pump used to deliver fuel to the injectors under very high pressure.

Inner bridge — The distance between the extreme of any group of two or more consecutive axles, e.g., between the front and rear axles of a tractor, or between axles 2 and 5 of a tandem tractor and tandem trailer. The measurement, taken at the center of the wheel hubs, is used to determine the gross weight that can be carried on any consecutive set of axles.

Inspection (vehicle) — Checking over the vehicle parts and systems for problems and malfunctions and to see that everything is in order and in place. Pre-trip inspection is a thorough inspection done before the trip. En-route inspections are made periodically during the trip. Post-trip inspections are done after the trip, so that problems and malfunctions can be reported to maintenance personnel.

Intake manifold — That part of the fuel system that carries the air or air/fuel mixture to the cylinders.

Intake ports — Provide the connecting passages from the outside of the cylinder heads to the inside head openings (the valves).

Intake stroke — Phase of the four-stroke cycle when fuel and air enter the cylinder.

Intake valves — Valves used in an engine to admit air into the combustion chambers of the cylinders.

Interaxle differential lock — See differential lock.

Interaxle differential lock control — Used for slippery conditions, it is activated by the driver from the cab by a switch which locks or unlocks two differentials. When the differential lock is engaged, it maximizes the traction output of both axles. Do not engage if wheels are spinning.

Interchange point — A station at which freight in the course of transportation is delivered by one transportation line to another.

Interline — Transferring loaded trailer from one carrier to another to avoid loading/unloading. Daily rental/lease agreement usually used in this circumstance.

Internal combustion engine — Any engine that burns fuel within itself, as a source of power.

Intermodal transportation — Using more than one mode to deliver a shipment.

Interstate commerce —- Trade, traffic, or transportation in the United States — 1) Between a place in a state and a place outside of such state (including a place outside of the United States); 2) Between two places in a state through another state or a place outside of the United States; or 3) Between two places in a state as part of trade, traffic, or transportation originating or terminating outside the state or the United States.

Interstate operating authority — The right to transport regulated goods across state lines issued by the FMCSA and required by all for-hire interstate carriers of regulated commodities.

Interventions — Action FMCSA would take under Compliance, Safety, Accountability (CSA) to correct unsafe behavior and achieve safety compliance. An intervention is triggered by: (1) one or more BASICs above a pre-determined FMCSA threshold/score, (2) a high crash indicator, (3) a complaint, or (4) fatal crash.

Intrastate commerce — The transportation of persons or property between points within a state having origin, destination, and all travel within the same state. A shipment between two points within a state may be interstate if the shipment had a prior or subsequent move outside of the state and the shipper intended an interstate shipment at origin.

Intrastate operating authority — Permission granted by an individual state to conduct intrastate transportation within that state. Some states require authority registration for for-hire, private, and exempt carriers.

Invoice — An itemized list of goods shipped to a buyer stating quantities, prices, fees, shipping charges, etc., often with a request for payment.

J

Jackknife — 1) To place the trailer at a sharp angle to the tractor; or 2) a type of skid in which either the tractor or the trailer loses traction and slides sideways.

Jake Brake — Slang for the Jacobs engine brake. Used as an auxiliary braking device on a tractor. See engine brake.

K

Kingpin — The "peg" or "pin" permanently attached to a trailer which is inserted and locked into the pulling frame of a fifth wheel or the power unit, and serving as the attachment by which the trailer is pulled.

Kingpin weight — Weight of the trailer at the kingpin or the trailer weight applied to the fifth wheel.

L

Laden weight — Weight of vehicle and its load.

Lading — That which constitutes a load. The freight in a vehicle.

Landing gear — The support legs that hold up the front end of a semi-trailer when it is disconnected from a tractor. See dolly.

Layover time — The non-working time that a road driver spends away from his home terminal before being dispatched to some other destination.

Lift axle — Normally kept in the raised position unless heavier loads require it to be used. The axle can be raised or lowered, to meet the requirements for the load.

Line haul — The movement of freight between major cities or terminals. Line haul operations do not include pick-ups or deliveries. Line haul service is also commonly referred to as over-the-road (OTR) operations.

Live axle — Same as drive axle or powered axle.

Livestock body — Truck or trailer designed for the transportation of farm animals.

Lock ring — In two-piece wheel rims, the lock ring holds the side ring firmly on the rim base.

Log book — See record of duty status.

Log body — Truck or trailer body designed for the transportation of long items. See pole trailer.

Long ton — 2,240 pounds. Also called a gross ton.

Low bed — An open trailer with drop frame construction used primarily to haul heavy equipment. Also known as flat bed or low boy.

Low boy — See low bed.

Low-air warning device — Any mechanical means of warning a truck driver that his/her vehicle is not maintaining the proper amount of air pressure needed to operate the brakes, etc. Can be a buzzer, a flashing red light on the instrument panel, or a small red metal flag that drops into the driver's line of vision.

Lumber body — Platform truck or trailer body with rollers designed for the transportation of lumber.

M

Manifest — See bill of lading.

Mixed truckload — A truckload of different freight articles combined into a single shipment.

Mode — Frequently used to refer to the basic divisions of the transportation industry. The principal modes of transportation are truck, rail, air and water.

Motor carrier — A for -hire motor carrier or a private motor carrier. The term includes a motor carrier's agents, officers, and representatives as well as employees responsible for hiring, supervising, training, assigning, or dispatching of drivers and employees concerned with the installation, inspection, and maintenance of motor vehicle equipment and/or accessories.

Motor vehicle — Any vehicle, machine, tractor, trailer, or semi-trailer propelled or drawn by mechanical power and used upon the highways in the transportation of passengers or property, or any combination thereof determined by the Federal Motor Carrier Safety Administration, but does not include any vehicle, locomotive, or car operated exclusively on a rail or rails, or a trolley bus operated by electric power derived from a fixed overhead wire, furnishing local passenger transportation similar to street-railway service.

Muffler — Noise-absorbing chamber used to quiet the engine's noise.

N

Net ton — 2,000 pounds. Also called a short ton.

Net weight — 1) The weight of an article clear of packing and container; 2) as applied to a truckload, the weight of the entire contents of the truck; or 3) as applied to a rig, the weight of a tractor-trailer when empty or curbweight.

Non-divisible load — A unit load which cannot be broken down into smaller, more convenient units for transportation.

Nozzle — See injector.

O

Occupational Safety And Health Administration (OSHA) — The regulatory and enforcement agency within the Department of Labor (DOL) responsible for ensuring safe and healthy workplaces in the U.S.

Odometer — An instrument attached to a power vehicle to measure the distance traveled.

Off-road recovery — The use of the road shoulder as an escape way by a truck that is then able to safely return to the highway.

Off-tracking — A term used to refer to the path taken by the rear end of a vehicle when turning. The path of the rear wheels is shorter than the path of the front. The off-track is much shorter on a tractor-trailer. Drivers must compensate for off-tracking in turns and on curves.

Oil filter — Device for cleaning and purifying the engine lubricating oil.

Oil pressure gauge — Measures pressure of engine lubricating oil. Pressure varies with engine speed and oil viscosity. Sudden drop of pressure indicates a problem.

Oil seal — A device used to retain lubricant in the bearing area of the wheel. The sealing part of the seal is usually made of a resilient material such as synthetic rubber or leather, which is assembled into a wheel or the hub bore.

Open top (trailer) — A truck or trailer body with sides but without any permanent top, often used for heavy equipment that must be lowered into place by crane.

Out-of-service order — A declaration by an authorized enforcement officer of a Federal, State, Canadian, Mexican, or local jurisdiction that a driver, a commercial motor vehicle, or a motor carrier operation, is out of service pursuant to Sections 386.72, 392.5, 395.13, 396.9 or compatible laws, or the North American Uniform Out-of-Service Criteria.

Outer bridge — The distance from the center of the wheel hub of the steering axle to the center of the wheel hub of the last axle of the rig. The measurement is used to determine gross weight limits and meet the requirements of bridge law.

Outriggers — Devices used for increasing width of low boy trailer.

Overage — Freight in excess of the quantity or amount shown on the bill of lading or other shipping document.

Overdimensional (OD) — Term which denotes a vehicle that exceeds a state's maximum, allowable length, width, height, and/or weight.

Overdrive — Refers to a condition in which the vehicle's transmission is in a gear having a ratio greater than 1:1, that is, the engine crank shaft turns at a slower rate than the vehicle drive shaft.

Overdriving the headlights — Driving at a speed that will not permit you to stop your vehicle within the distance you can see ahead.

Overriding the governor (overspeeding) — When the weight of the vehicle drives the engine beyond governed speed. Happens on hills when vehicle is not in a low enough gear and is not supplemented as necessary by light, steady brake application. The governor does not control the engine speed when the vehicle is driving the engine.

Oversized vehicle — Any vehicle whose weight and/or dimensions exceeds state regulations.

Owner-operator — Driver who owns and operates his own truck; he may be a common carrier, contract carrier or exempt carrier; such contractor may lease vehicle and driver to another carrier.

P

Packing list — A detailed specification of packed goods.

Pallet — A portable platform for holding material for storage or transportation.

Pallet jacks — Powered or manual mechanical lifts for loading or unloading cargo shipped on pallets.

Palletized — Stacked on pallets.

Parking brake control valve — Controlled from the dashboard by either a switch or a push-pull control, this valve engages the springbrakes.Use theparking brake anytime the rig is parked and engage only after it is completely stopped.

Payload — The cargo or freight that a vehicle hauls.

Peddle run — Truck route with frequent delivery stops.

Piggyback — Transportation of a highway trailer on a railway flat car.

Pigtail — Slang for the electrical cable used to transmit power from the tractor to the trailer.

Pintle hook — Coupling device at rear of truck or trailer for the purpose of towing trailers.

Piston — A device that moves up and down in the engine cylinder and provides power to the crankshaft.

Placards — Diamond-shaped signs required by regulation to be displayed on all four sides of a motor vehicle when it is hauling hazardous materials.

Plane or west coast mirror — Flat-surfaced side mirrors positioned on both sides of a truck tractor so the driver can see both sides of the rig and its immediate environment from the cab.

Platform body — Truck or trailer body with a floor, but no sides or roof. Also called a stake truck.

Point of origin — The terminal at which a shipment is received by a transportation line from the shipper.

Pole trailer — Trailer composed of a single telescopic pole, a tandem rear-wheel unit, and a coupling device used to join the trailer to a tractor. Pole trailers are used to transport logs or similar items. When chained together it becomes a rigid unit and thereby serves as its own trailer body. Pole trailers are adjustable in length.

Post-trip inspection — See inspection (vehicle).

Power-lift tail gate — A power-operated tailgate capable of lifting load from street level to the level of the truck or trailer floor.

Power stroke — Phase of the four-stroke cycle when fuel is ignited and combustion take place.

Power train — The series of parts that transfer the power of the engine to the wheels. Same as drive train.

Powered axle — Commonly called a live axle. See drive axle.

Prepaid — A term denoting that transportation charges have been or are to be paid at shipping point.

Pre-trip inspection — See inspection (vehicle).

Preventive maintenance — A systematic checking and care of equipment to keep repairs to a minimum.

Private carrier — A company that carries/hauls its own property in its own vehicles.

Progressive shifting — A process of shifting high torque rise engines that involves shifting at lower rpms at slower speeds, and at progressively higher rpms as the speed of the vehicle increases.

Pro number — The abbreviation of the word progressive and is usually prefixed to an agent's record numbers on freight bills, which are used to identify the freight bill.

Proof of delivery — A motor carrier establishes proof of delivery from delivery receipt copy of freight bill signed by consignee at time of delivery. This is legal proof of delivery.

Property broker — A company that arranges for the truck transportation of cargo belonging to others utilizing for-hire carriers to provide the actual truck transportation. The broker does not assume responsibility for the cargo and usually does not take possession of the cargo. Brokers must obtain operating authority from the FMCSA.

PSI — Pounds per square inch. A measurement of pressure, for example, the amount of air pressure in a tire.

Pup — Slang term for short semi-trailer used in combination with dolly and another semi-trailer to create twin trailers.

Pusher axle — Dead axle (non-powered) mounted in front of powered axle, single or tandem, increases weight-carrying capacity of vehicle.

Pyrometer — An instrument that registers the temperature of the exhaust gases.

R

Radiator — A device of tubes and fins through which circulating water from the engine water jackets passes to give off excess heat and thus cool the engine.

Ragtop — Slang term for open-top trailer using a tarpaulin cover.

Rain cap — Protection device used on exhaust stacks to prevent rain entry when the engine is stopped.

Reaction time — The time that elapses between the point that a driver recognizes the need for action and the time that he takes the action.

Recap (tires) — 1) To recap a tire by bonding new tread rubber to the used tire; or 2) a tire that has been recapped.

Reciprocity — 1) An exchange of rights, in motor transportation may involve granting equal rights to vehicles of several states in which reciprocity agreements are in effect; or 2) to give preference in buying to vendors who are customers of a buying company.

Reconsigment — A change (made in transit) in the route, destination, or consignee as indicated in the original bill of lading.

Record of duty status (Driver's log) — Daily record required to be completed by driver which shows driving, on-duty/not driving, sleeper-berth, and off-duty time. See driver's daily log.

Reefer — Slang for refrigerated trailer.

Refrigerated trailer — An insulated van-type truck or trailer body equipped with a refrigeration unit. Used for carrying perishable goods. Also called a reefer.

Regular route common carrier — Motor carrier operating over definite routes between specified points with fixed termini on regular schedule.

Relay emergency valve — A combination valve in an air brake system, which controls brake application and which also provides for automatic trailer brake application should the trailer become disconnected from the towing vehicle.

Relay valve — Valve used to speed up the application and release of the rear wheel brakes.

Repower — When dispatch sends a replacement tractor and driver to recover a load in transit.

Reshipment — Goods sent to another destination under conditions which do not make the act subject to reconsignment rules and charges of the carrier. See reconsignment.

Restricted articles — Types of freight that cannot be handled at all or may only be handled under certain specific conditions.

Retarder systems — Retarders supplement diesel truck service brakes and assist in reducing brake shoe overheating and resulting brake fade on long, steep downgrades. See engine brake, exhaust brake and hydraulic retarder.

Revolutions per minute (RPM) — The number of turns or rotations the engine makes in a minute. Engine RPM is expressed in hundreds on the tachometer.

Rig — Slang for truck, tractor-semi-trailer, truck and full trailer, or other combination vehicle.

Rocky mountain double — A tractor pulling a 40 to 53 foot semi-trailer and a 26 to 29 foot full trailer. Overall lengths range from 80 to 100 feet.

Route — 1) The course or direction that a shipment moves; 2) to designate the course or direction a shipment shall move; or 3) the carrier or carriers over which a shipment moves.

Runaway truck ramp — See escape ramp.

S

Saddle tanks — Barrel type fuel tanks that hang from the sides of the tractor's frame.

Saddlemount combination — Is a combination of vehicles in which a truck or tractor tows one or more trucks or truck tractors, each connected by a saddle to the frame or fifth wheel of the vehicle in front of it. The saddle is a mechanism that connects the front axle of the towed vehicle to the frame or fifth wheel of the vehicle in front and functions like a fifth wheel kingpin connection.

Safety evaluation — FMCSA's process of determining how to address motor carriers with poor safety performance.

Safety measurement system (SMS) — Quantifies the safety performance of motor carriers and drivers under Compliance, Safety, Accountability (CSA) to identify candidates for interventions, to determine the specific safety problems exhibited by a motor carrier or driver, and to monitor whether safety problems are improving or worsening.

Security seals — Seals used by shippers to ensure a cargo container, and/or the truck's rear doors haven't been opened while in transit

Semi — Slang for either a tractor-trailer combination, or for a semi-trailer.

Semi-trailer — A trailer that has only rear axles. The front of a semi-trailer either rests on the tractor or is supported by its landing gear when coupled. See full trailer.

Service brake system — Under normal braking conditions the braking system uses air pressure controlled by the brake pedal on the floor to move the brake shoes against the brake drum to slow a vehicle or bring it to a stop.

Severity weighting — Places a value on each safety-related violation in Compliance, Safety, Accountability (CSA) that is determined by its association with crash causation.

Shipper — A person or agent that ships freight.

Shipper's load and count — Indicates that the contents of a truck were loaded and counted by the shipper and not checked or verified by the carrier.

Shipping papers — Papers used in connection with movement of freight.

Shock absorber — A device added to an axle that dampens axle momentum and tire bounce caused by rough road surface.

Short ton — 2,000 pounds. Also called a net ton.

Shortage — When quantity of freight received is actually less than that shown on the documents.

Sight side — The side of the tractor visible by driver, i.e., driver's side. Opposite of blind side.

Single axle — Term commonly used to refer to a power unit (tractor) having only one rear axle, thus, actually a two axle unit (one axle steering at the front and one at the rear), or a semi-trailer having one axle only.

Single drop frame — A drop frame trailer with one drop, immediately behind kingpin. See drop frame.

Skid — 1) A wooden platform or pallet on which heavy articles or packaged goods are placed to permit handling; or 2) failure of tires to grip the roadway because of loss of traction.

Slack adjuster — An adjustable device located on the brake chamber pushrod that is used to compensate for brake shoe wear.

Sleeper berth — Area in a tractor where a driver can sleep. Sleeper berths must meet standards set by the Federal Motor Carrier Safety Regulations.

Sleeper — Tractor cab equipped with bunk facilities so a driver may rest.

Sliding fifth wheel — Fifth wheel assembly capable of being moved forward/backward on tractor to give desired load distribution between tractor and trailer axles.

Sliding tandem — An adjusted bogie beneath the trailer that can be moved forward or backward to distribute the weight between tractor and trailer axles.

Space management — Maintaining a safe distance between your vehicle and other vehicles, people or objects above, below ,and around your truck.

Speedometer — An instrument that indicates the speed of a vehicle.

Splitter — Mechanism that divides a gear into two or more ratios such as direct, overdrive, or underdrive. Controlled by a switch on the gearshift.

Spotter — 1) Someone who assists another driver in a backing maneuver; 2) a worker in terminal yard who parks vehicles brought in by regular drivers; or 3) a supervisor who checks the activities of drivers on the road.

Spread tandem — A two-axle assembly in which the axles are separated by distances substantially greater than that in conventional assemblies.

Stabilizer — Device used to stabilize vehicle during turns. Also called a sway bar.

Stake body — Truck or trailer platform body with readily removable stakes which may be joined by chains, slats, or panels.

Starter motor — An electric or air powered motor used to set the crankshaft in motion in order to start the engine.

Steering axle — Axle through which directional control of vehicle is applied. It may be powered or non-powered and there may be more than one steering axle on the unit.

Stop (engine) and emergency stop — Some tractors are equipped with a starter button and an "engine stop" switch. The engine stop is used to shut off the engine. Some tractors are equipped with an "emergency engine stop" switch to be used only when the engine starts to "run away" (exceeding the safe upper RPM limits). Once the emergency stop has been used, the engine will not start again until a mechanic has made repairs.

Straight bill of lading — See bill of lading.

Straight truck — Power unit/cargo body mounted on the same chassis.

Supercharger — A type of blower, connected to the engine crankshaft, that forces air into the intake manifold at higher than atmospheric pressure to increase engine power and performance. See blower.

Supply lines (fuel) — The lines that carry a supply of fuel to each injector. Fuel enters the inlet connection and then the injectors.

Supporting document — A document, in any medium, generated or received by a motor carrier in the normal course of business that can be used, as produced or with additional identifying information, by the motor carrier and enforcement officials to verify the accuracy of a driver's record of duty status.

Suspension — The system of springs, etc., supporting a vehicle upon its undercarriage or axles.

Sway bar — See stabilizer.

Synchronized transmission — A transmission in which the gears are so constructed as to allow smooth shifting without the need to double-clutch.

T

Tachograph — A recording device in a tractor that automatically records the number of miles driven, the speed, the number of stops, and other pertinent statistics.

Tachometer — A device in the tractor, located on the instrument panel, that indicates the revolutions per minute of the engine's crankshaft.

Tag axle — The rearmost axle of a tandem-axle tractor if that axle serves only to support additional gross weight. A tag axle does not transmit power.

Tailgating — Following the vehicle ahead of you at an unsafe distance i.e., less than your total stopping distance.

Tandem axle — An assembly of two axles, either, none or both of which may be powered.

Tank trailer — Any trailer on which tanks are mounted to contain fluid commodities in bulk, tanks may contain baffles to stop liquid from surging while in motion, pumps for loading/unloading may be self-contained.

Temperature gauge — A device that indicates the temperature of such things as coolant, lubricating oil, and gear lube.

Terminal — A building for the handling and temporary storage of freight as it is transferred between trucks, i-e., from a city pickup to a line haul truck.

Terminal carrier — The line haul motor carrier making delivery of a shipment at its destination. Terminal carrier means the last or final carrier.

Throttle — Controls the engine speed.

Through bill of lading — See bill of lading.

Tie rod — Part of the tractor's steering system, it is the connecting rod between the steering arms.

Time weighted — Assigning a value to a violation based on when it occurred under Compliance, Safety, Accountability (CSA). The time weight of an event decreases with time, resulting in more recent events having a greater impact on an entity's BASIC than events from the more distant past.

Toll — A charge made for the use of a facility such as a bridge or turnpike.

Ton-mile — A unit of measure. The movement of a ton of freight one mile.

Tonnage — Number of tons.

Total stopping distance — The distance the vehicle travels between the time the driver recognizes the need to stop and the time the vehicle comes to a complete stop. Total stopping distance includes perception distance, reaction distance, brake lag distance, and braking distance.

Traction — Adhesive friction, as of tires on pavements.

Tractor — Power unit designed primarily for pulling other vehicles and not constructed to carry load other than part of weight of vehicle and load being drawn.

Tractor protection valve — Controls flow of compressed air from tractor to trailer; when closed, stops flow of air to trailer. When this happens, the trailer brakes will apply. Used to make sure that air is always available for tractor brakes.

Trailer — See full trailer; semi-trailer.

Trailer brake — A hand-operated remote control that applies trailer brakes only. Located on the steering column or dash. Must never be used for parking. Also called hand valve, trolley brake, trolley valve handle, trailer hand brake, and independent trailer brake.

Trailer-on-flatcar — Popular piggyback arrangement which features conventional highway trailers placed on rail flatcars.

Transfer pump — A pump used to move fuel from fuel tank to injectors.

Transmission — Selective gear box providing various combinations of gear ratios.

Treadle valve — See foot brake valve.

Tri-axle — An assembly of three rear axles, any or all of which may be powered.

Triple-bottom — Double-bottom unit, plus an additional trailer.

Triples — A combination consisting of a tractor, a semi-trailer and two full trailers, coupled together.

Truck — 1) Vehicle for hauling; or 2) weight-bearing, wheeled device used to move goods from place-to-place.

Truck tractor — Motor vehicle used for drawing other vehicles (trailers and semi-trailers), built so that the only load it carries is part of the weight of vehicle it draws.

Truckload — 1) Quantity of freight that will fill a truck; 2) quantity of freight weighing the maximum legal amount for a particular type of truck; or 3) when used in connection with freight rates, the quantity of freight necessary to qualify a shipment for a truckload rate, which is cheaper than a less-than-truckload rate..

Turbocharger — A type of blower, powered by engine exhaust gases, that forces air into the intake manifold at higher than atmospheric pressure to increase engine power and performance. See blower.

Turn around — A type of trip or "run" in which the driver returns to the origin point immediately after his vehicle is unloaded and reloaded.

Turnpike double — A tractor pulling two trailers between 35 and 48 feet in length. Total length is about 100 feet or more.

Twin screw — A truck or tractor with two rear axles, both driven by the engine. Same as tandem drive axles.

Two-speed axle — A drive axle capable of being shifted through two gear ranges in order to double the number of gears available from the transmission

U

Unclaimed freight — Freight which has not been called for by the consignee or owner, or freight that cannot be delivered.

Underdrive — Refers to a condition in which the vehicle's transmission is in a gear having a ratio less than 1:1, that is, the engine crankshaft turns at a faster rate than the vehicle's drive shaft. Opposite of overdrive. See direct drive.

Underpass and bridge clearance — The minimum vertical clearance from the surface of the roadway to an overhead structure.

Unladen vehicle weight — See curb weight.

Universal joint — A joint or coupling that permits a swing of limited angle in any direction; used to transmit rotary motion from one shaft to another not in line with it.

Unsafe driving BASIC — One of seven categories of safety behaviors measured in the CSA Safety Measurement System. The operation of a commercial motor vehicle in a dangerous or careless manner is included in this BASIC. Violations can include speeding, reckless driving, improper lane change, and inattention.

V

Valve — A device that opens and closes openings in a pipe, tube, or cylinder,.

Vehicle identification number (VIN) — The numbers and letters assigned to a vehicle for the purpose of titling and registration.

Vehicle maintenance BASIC — One of seven categories of safety behaviors measured in the CSA Safety Measurement System. Commercial motor vehicle failure due to improper or inadequate maintenance is included in this BASIC. A roadside inspection report might show violations associated with brakes, lights, and other mechanical defects, and failure to make required repairs.

Vehicle scale — Scale designed to determine weight of motor truck or other vehicle, loaded or unloaded.

Voltage regulator — A device that controls the voltage output of a generator.

Voltmeter — indicates output of alternator in volts.

W

Warehouse receipt — A receipt for goods placed in a warehouse (may be issued as a negotiable or non-negotiable document).

Water level warning light — Lights up when coolant level in radiator drops below required level. Similar lights will indicate low oil pressure or high coolant temperature, depending on the type of engine.

Water pump — Pump that circulates the coolant through the engine cooling system.

Water temperature gauge — Indicates temperature of engine coolant.

Waybill — A document prepared by a transportation line at the point of origin of a shipment, showing the point of origin, destination, route, consignor, consignee, description of shipment and amount charged for the transportation service. Forwarded with the shipment, or sometimes direct by mail, to the agent at the transfer point or waybill destination. The waybill is basically a description of goods and shipping instructions.

Weigh station — Permanent station equipped with scales at which motor vehicles transporting property on public highways are required to stop for checking of gross vehicle and/or axle weights. Many states also use portable scales to check compliance with the state's weight limits. Also often combined with port of entry facilities.

Western double — Standard A-train with two equal-length trailers, typically 24-31 feet long, and an overall length of 60-75 feet.

Wet tank — Part of the air brake system. Compressed air produced by the compressor goes to the wet tank, which collects any water and engine oil that the air has in it.

Wheelbase — Distance in inches from center of hub of front wheel of a vehicle to center of hub of back wheels or the center of the space between the tandems.

Wrecker — Truck designed for hoisting and towing disabled vehicles.

Y

Yard jockey — Slang for person who operates a yard tractor or yard mule, a special tractor used to move semi-trailer around the terminal yard.

Yard mule — Slang for tractor used to move semi-trailers around the terminal yard.

GLOSSARY

Symbols

11 hours driving rule   *301*

14 consecutive hours duty rule   *301*

34-hour restart   *303, 308, 308*

60-hour/7-day and 70-hour/8-day limits   *303*

100 air-mile radius   *307*

A

ABS light   *29*

Accelerator   *21, 64*

Accident procedures   *343–351*

Accident register   *343*

Accidents   *149, 193, 345*

Active warning devices   *202*

Actual valuation   *280*

Adaptive/intelligent cruise control   *148*

Address   *282*

Adjusting mirrors   *128*

    Left side convex   *128*

    Left side plane/west coast   *128*

    Right side convex   *128*

    Right side plane/west coast   *128*

Advance warning sign   *203*

Adverse driving conditions   *148, 310*

Aftercooler   *39*

Aggregate working load limit   *269*

Air application pressure gauge   *46*

Air bag suspension   *36*

Air blockage   *217*

Air brakes *45*

  Air application pressure gauge *46*

  Air pressure gauge *46*

  Air tanks *45*

  Brake chamber *47*

  Compressor *45*

  Drain cocks *46*

  Emergency relay valve *47*

  Glad hands *46*

  Governor *45*

  Independent trailer brake *46*

  Low-pressure warning signal *46*

  One-way check valve *46*

  Quick release valve *47*

  Relay valve *47*

  Safety valves *46*

  Tractor parking valve *46*

  Treadle valve *46*

Air brake system operation *47*

Air intake and exhaust system *39*

Air intake system *39*

Air lines *174*

Air pressure gauge *26, 46*

Alcohol and drug testing *, 11*

Alcohol misuse and drug use *11*

Alcohol use and drug abuse *371*

Alley dock backing *103*

All-wheel skids *228*

Alternator *41*

Ammeter *26, 41*

Antifreeze *173*

Antilock brakes *23*

Antilock brake systems *47*

Applying for a job *387*

Automatic transmission *95*

Autoshift transmission *95*

Auto transporters *241*

Auxiliary brakes *23*

Axles *37*

Axle temperature gauge   *28*

Axle weight   *270*

B

Backing   *101–105*

    Alley dock backing   *103*

    Backing maneuvers   *102*

    Blind side backing   *102*

    Parallel parking   *104*

    Rules for safe backing   *101*

    Sight side backing   *102*

    Steering principles   *101*

    Straight line backing   *102*

Backing maneuvers   *102*

Barrier seals   *358*

Basic documents   *281*

BASICs   *See Behavior Analysis and Safety Improvement Categories (BASICs)*

Basis of rates   *280*

Battery   *41*

Behavior Analysis and Safety Improvement Categories (BASICs)   *405*

    Controlled substances and alcohol   *406*

    Crash indicator   *406*

    Driver fitness   *405*

    Hazardous material (HM) compliance   *406*

    Hours-of-service compliance   *405*

    Unsafe driving   *405*

    Vehicle maintenance   *406*

Belted bias tires   *48*

Bias ply tires   *48*

Bill of lading   *279, 281, 331*

    Straight bill of lading   *279*

    Through bill of lading   *279*

Blind side backing   *102*

Blocked vision   *192*

Blocking   *270*

Blowouts   *218*

Border crossing programs   *320*

    Canada eManifest   *320*

    CSA   *320*

FAST   *320*

PARS   *320*

U.S. ACE   *320*

Border station entry   *318*

Bracing   *270*

Brake chamber   *47*

Brake controls   *23*

Brake fade   *217*

Brake failure   *217*

Brake lag distance   *145*

Brake lights   *165*

Brakes   *174, 248*

Brakes, Emergency   *45*

Brake system   *44*

   Disc brakes   *45*

   Drum brakes   *44*

   Emergency brakes   *45*

   Parking brakes   *45*

   Service brakes   *44*

Braking distance   *145*

Braking system defects   *60*

Braking technique   *183*

Breakdowns   *181*

B-trains   *237*

C

Cab-over-engine (COE)   *14*

Camber   *51*

Canada eManifest   *320*

Canada's hours of service   *321*

Canadian safety credentials   *322*

Cargo handling   *267–273*

Cargo problems   *63*

Cargo securement   *267*

Cargo theft   *357*

Carrier   *279*

Caster   *51*

CB radio   *137*

CDL   *See Commercial driver's license (CDL)*

CDL classes   *5*

CDL/Med card merger   *8*

Cell phone   *137*

Charging circuit   *41*

Children   *193*

Circadian rhythm   *370*

CLP   *See Commercial learner's permit (CLP)*

Clutch   *42, 89, 249*

Clutch brake   *22*

Clutch pedal   *22*

CMV   *See Commercial motor vehicle (CMV)*

COD   *280*

COE   *See Cab-over-engine (COE)*

Coercion   *386*

Cold weather starting   *176*

Combination vehicle   *15*

Combination Vehicle (Group A)   *5*

Commercial driver's license (CDL)   *5*

Commercial learner's permit (CLP)   *5*

Commercial motor vehicle (CMV)   *14*

Communicating intent   *135*

Communicating presence   *136*

Communication from others   *138*

Company policy   *384*

Completing your record of duty status   *305*

Conducting an inspection   *59*

Confused drivers   *193*

Connecting carrier   *279*

Consignee   *279*

Consignor   *279*

Contact with the public   *381*

Controlled braking   *215*

Controlled substances and alcohol   *406*

Conventional tractor   *14*

Convex   *127*

Coolant level   *173*

Coolant level alarm   *28*

Coolant temperature gauge   *27*

Coolant temperature warning light   *28*

Cooling system   *41*

Coupling device capacity   *270*

Coupling devices   *175*

Coupling system   *52*

　　Fifth wheel   *52*

　　Kingpin   *53*

　　Landing gear   *53*

Coupling system defects   *62*

Coupling tractor-trailers   *111*

Coupling twin trailers   *117*

Cranking circuit   *42*

Crash indicator   *406*

Crossbuck signs   *203*

Crossing the Canadian border   *318*

Crossing traffic   *157*

Cruise control   *21, 148*

　　Adaptive/intelligent cruise control   *148*

CSA-related data   *408*

Curves   *83, 147*

Customer relations   *382*

Customs inspections   *319*

Customs Self Assessment   *320*

D

Daily log   *304*

Deck plates   *174*

Defrosting   *173*

Delivery receipt   *280*

Demurrage   *281*

Destination   *282*

Detention   *281*

Diet   *367*

Differential   *44*

Differential warning   *29*

Directing traffic   *136*

Disabled vehicles   *193*

Disc brakes   *45*

Disc wheels   *48*

Disengaged   *22*

Distance scanning   *125*

Do not stop on tracks sign   *204*

Double-drop low bed with two axles   *238*

Doubles   *235*

    B-trains   *237*

    Rocky Mountain doubles   *237*

    Turnpike doubles   *236*

    Western doubles   *236*

Downgrade procedures   *218*

Downgrades   *182*

Downshift   *217*

Downshifting   *90, 91*

DQ file   *See Driver qualification file (DQ File)*

Drag link   *51*

Drain cocks   *46*

Drive axle   *14*

Driver disqualification   *, 202, 9*

Driver fitness   *405*

Driver qualification file (DQ File)   *8*

Driver qualifications   *6*

Drive shaft and universal joints   *43*

Drive train   *42*

Driving at night   *166*

Driving hazards   *178*

    Reduced traction   *178*

    Reduced visibility   *178*

Driving too fast for conditions   *225*

Drug abuse   *371*

Drug testing   *372*

Drum brakes   *44*

Dry bulk tankers   *239*

Duals   *15*

Dunnage   *270, 281*

Duties   *280*

DVIR requirements   *260*

    Driver vehicle inspection report   *332*

E

Eating healthy on the road   *368*

Eaton® Fuller® Nine Speed   *92*

Eaton® Fuller® Super Ten   *93*

Eaton® Fuller® Thirteen Speed   *94*

ELD   *See Electronic logging device (ELD)*

Electrical system   *41*

Electric retarders   *24*

Electronic logging device (ELD)   *304, 306*

Emergency equipment   *, 62*

Emergency maneuvers   *213–219*

Emergency relay valve   *47*

Emergency stopping   *215*

Endorsements   *6*

Engaged   *22*

Engine   *37, 250*

    Engine shutdown   *78*

    Engine warm-up   *77*

    Not starting   *177*

    Starting the engine   *77*

Engine brakes   *24*

Engine controls   *21*

Engine control switch   *21*

Engine shutdown   *78*

Engine warm-up   *77*

En-route inspection   *68*

Entering traffic   *157*

Escape ramps   *184*

Escape route   *218*

Estimating fuel usage   *336*

Estimating time   *335*

Estimating trip expenses   *337*

Evasive steering   *213*

Excessive idling   *78*

Exempt sign   *204*

Exercise   *367, 369*

Exhaust brakes   *24*

Exhaust pyrometer gauge   *28*

Exhaust system   *39, 175*

Exhaust system defects   *62*

Exposed wiring   *174*

Extinguishers   *350*

F

Familiarity with route   *164*

FAST   *320*

Fatigue   *163, 370*

    Fighting fatigue   *371*

    Signs of fatigue   *370*

    Sleep apnea   *371*

Federal Motor Carrier Safety Administration (FMCSA)   *4*

Fifth wheel   *, 15*

    Fixed-mount   *52*

    Sliding/adjustable   *52*

Filing a Complaint   *385*

Fixed costs   *395*

Fixed-mount   *52*

Flashing light signal   *203*

Fluid leaks   *60*

FMCSA   *See Federal Motor Carrier Safety Administration (FMCSA)*

Folding gooseneck low bed   *238*

Foot brake control valve   *23*

Force of motion   *225*

Forklift   *272*

Frame   *35, 61*

Free play   *22*

Freight broker   *279*

Freight delivery   *285*

Freight (expense) bill   *284*

Freight forwarder   *279*

Freight pickup   *284*

Front tractor axle   *37*

Front wheel skids   *227, 229*

Fuel economy   *149*

Fuel filters   *38*

Fuel gauge   *26*

Fueling   *294*

Fuel management   *396*

Fuel system   *38*

Fuel system heaters   *39*

Fuel tank   *38, 174*

Full trailer   *15*

G

Gas vs. diesel   *37*

GCW   *See Gross combination weight (GCW)*

GCWR   *See Gross combination weight rating (GCWR)*

Gear box   *51*

Generator   *41*

Glad hands   *46*

Glare   *163*

Global positioning systems (GPS)   *334*

Glow plugs   *177*

Good shifting skills   *91*

GPS   *See Global positioning systems (GPS)*

Grades   *147*

Gross combination weight (GCW)   *270*

Gross combination weight rating (GCWR)   *270*

Gross vehicle weight (GVW)   *270*

Gross vehicle weight rating (GVWR)   *270*

Growing revenue   *396*

GVW   *See Gross vehicle weight (GVW)*

GVWR   *See Gross vehicle weight rating (GVWR)*

H

Hand holds   *174*

Hazard classes and divisions   *291*

Hazardous material (HM) compliance   *406*

Hazardous materials   *291–295*

Hazard recognition   *191*

Hazmat endorsement   *291*

Heating   *173*

Heavy Straight Vehicle (Group B)   *5*

Helper service   *280*

High center-of-gravity vehicles   *239*

Hitting/hunting a gear   *91*

Horn   *137*

Hours of service

    11 hours driving rule   *301*

    14 consecutive hours duty rule   *301*

    34-hour restart   *303*

    60-hour/7-day and 70-hour/8-day limits   *303*

    100 air-mile radius   *307*

    Canada   *321*

    Completing your record of duty status   *305*

    Electronic logging devices   *306*

    Exceptions   *307*

    Mandatory break provision   *302*

    On-duty time   *302*

    Record of duty status   *304*

    Short haul (16 hour) exception   *308*

    Short-haul provision   *308*

    Sleeper berth   *309*

Hours-of-service compliance   *405*

Hub piloted   *48*

Hydraulic retarders   *24*

Hydraulic sliding axle trailer   *238*

Hydraulic tail low bed   *238*

I

Ice   *146*

IFTA   *322*

Ignition circuit   *42*

Impaired drivers   *164*

Inattentive drivers   *193*

Independent trailer brake   *46*

Indicative seals   *358*

Inside delivery   *280*

Interaxle differential lock   *24*

Interline freight   *285*

Intermodal equipment   *70*

Intersections   *192*

Interstate commerce   *3*

Interventions   *407*

In-transit security   *359*

Intrastate commerce   *3*

IRP   *322*

J

Jackknifing   *179*
>   *Tractor jackknife*   *227*
>   *Trailer jackknife*   *226*

Job interview   *388*

K

Kingpin   *53*

L

Landing gear   *53*

Leaf spring suspension   *36*

Left side convex   *128*

Left side plane/west coast   *128*

Left turns   *82, 157*

Legal weight limits   *270, 335*

Lighting and accessory circuits   *42*

Lights   *165, 174*

Liquid tankers   *239*

Livestock trailers   *240*

Loading tools   *272*

Load locking bars   *270*

Loss of air pressure   *217*

Low bed with jeep dolly   *238*

Low-clearance vehicles   *239*

Low ground clearance sign   *205*

Low pressure warning alarm/light   *28*

Low-pressure warning signal   *46*

Lubrication system   *39*
>   *Maintaining the lubrication system*   *40*

Lug tread   *49*

Lumper   *280*

M

Maintenance costs   *149*

Major offenses   *9*

Malfunctions   *259–261*
>   *Detection of problems*   *260*
>   *Driver responsibility*   *259*

Mechanic responsibility   259

Troubleshooting   260

Warning signs   260

Managing space   155

Above   156

Ahead   155

Behind   155

Below   156

To the sides   156

Mandatory break provision   302

Manifest   279

Maximum rate   280

Medical exam certificate   330

Merging vehicle   214

Metric measurements and conversions   323

Minimum rate   280

Mirrors   126, 165, 174

Adjusting mirrors   128

Convex   127

Plane/west coast   126

Mountain driving   182

Braking technique   183

Downgrades   182

Escape ramps   184

How brakes can fail   183

Upgrades   182

Multiple articulation vehicles   235

Multiple trailers   71

N

Night driving   163–167

Night driving procedures   165

Number sign   205

O

Obtaining your commercial driver's license   4

Odometer   25

Off-ramps   192

Off-road recovery   215

Off-tracking   81

Oil filter system   *40*

Oil level alarm   *28*

Oil pressure gauge   *27*

Oil pressure warning light   *28*

Oil temperature gauge   *28*

Oncoming vehicle   *214*

On-duty time   *302*

On-ramps   *192*

On-the-road (en-route) inspection   *, 59*

Operating in Canada   *317*

Operator's license   *329*

Order notify shipment   *280*

Originating (pickup) carrier   *279*

Other road users   *164*

Out-of-service violations   *10*

Overacceleration   *179, 225*

Overbraking   *179, 225*

Overinflation   *50*

Overloading   *271*

Oversize vehicles   *238*

    Double-drop low bed with two axles   238

    Folding gooseneck low bed   238

    Hydraulic sliding axle trailer   238

    Hydraulic tail low bed   238

    Low bed with jeep dolly   238

    Removable gooseneck low bed   238

Oversteering   *179, 225*

P

Packing slip   *280*

Pallet jacks   *272*

Parallel parking   *104*

Parallel track sign   *205*

Parked vehicles   *193*

Parking   *295*

Parking brake control valve   *23*

Parking brakes   *45*

PARS   *320*

Passive warning devices   *203*

Pavement drop-offs   *191*

Pavement markings   *205*

Penalties   *149*

Perception distance   *145*

Personal health   *367*

Personal protective equipment   *374*

Personal security   *359*

PHMSA   *See Pipeline and Hazardous Materials Safety Administration (PHMSA)*

Physical qualification and examination   *7*

Pipeline and Hazardous Materials Safety Administration (PHMSA)   *4*

Pitman arm   *51*

Placards   *294*

Plane/west coast   *126*

Pole trailers   *241*

Poor vehicle maintenance   *253*

Poor visibility   *164*

Post accident test   *12*

Post-trip inspection   *, 59, 69*

Power steering   *52*

Pre-employment test   *12*

Preheaters   *177*

Prepaid   *280*

Pre-trip inspection   *, 59, 63*

    Seven-step pre-trip inspection   63

Primary vehicle controls   *21*

Proper lifting   *374*

Proper tire care   *49*

Proper tire inflation   *49*

Putting a tractor-trailer in motion   *79*

Putting the vehicle in motion   *78*

Pyrometer   *39*

Pyrometer warning light   *29*

Q

Quick release valve   *47*

R

Radial tires   *48*

Railroad crossings   *201–207*

Railroad-highway grade crossing violations   *11*

Rain *146*

Random testing *12*

Reaction distance *145*

Reading maps *333*

Rear tractor axles *37*

Reasonable suspicion testing *13*

Receiver *279*

Record of duty status *, 304, 304*

Reduced traction *178*

Reduced visibility *178*

Reefers *See Refrigerator units*

Reflectors *174*

Refrigerated trailers *240*

Refrigerator Units *71*

Regulated industry *3*

Relay valve *47*

Released valuation *280*

Removable gooseneck low bed *238*

Residential delivery *281*

Restrictions *6*

Retarders *23*

Return-to-duty/follow-up testing *13*

Rib tread *49*

Right side convex *128*

Right side plane/west coast *128*

Right turns *81, 157*

Road conditions *146*

Road construction *191*

Road debris *192*

Road hazards *191*

Road shape *147*

    Curves *147*

    Grades *147*

Roadside inspections *252*

Roadway factors *164*

    Familiarity with route *164*

    Impaired drivers *164*

    Other road users *164*

    Poor visibility *164*

Rockwell Ten Speed   *94*

Rocky Mountain doubles   *237*

Rolling costs   *395*

Route selection   *333*

Routine servicing   *247*

Routing   *294*

Rules for safe backing   *101*

S

Safe loading responsibilities   *272*

Safety evaluation   *407*

Safety measurement system (SMS)   *404*

Scanning to the sides   *126*

Scheduled preventive maintenance   *247*

Secondary vehicle controls   *24*

Securement devices   *269*

Seeing to the rear   *128*

Semiautomatic transmission   *95*

Semitrailer   *15*

Serious traffic violations   *10*

Service brakes   *44*

Shifting   *89*

Shifting controls   *89*

    Accelerator   89

    Clutch   89

    Shift lever   89

Shifting gears   *90*

    Downshifting   91

    Good shifting skills   91

    Hitting/hunting a gear   91

    Upshifting   90

Shifting patterns   *92*

    Eaton® Fuller® Nine Speed   92

    Eaton® Fuller® Super Ten   93

    Eaton® Fuller® Thirteen Speed   94

    Rockwell Ten Speed   94

Shift lever   *89*

Shipper   *279*

Shipping paper accessibility   *293*

Shipping papers   *292*

Shock absorbers   *37*

Short haul (16 hour) exception   *308*

Short-haul provision   *308*

Sight side backing   *102*

Signals   *203*

Signs   *203*

Skidding   *179*

Skid dynamics   *225*

Skid recovery   *229*

Skids   *225*

    All-wheel skids   *228*

    Front wheel skids   *227, 229*

Sleep apnea   *371*

Sleeper berth   *309*

Sleep loss   *370*

Sliding/adjustable   *52*

Slippery surfaces   *179*

Slowing down   *136*

Small Vehicle (Group C)   *6*

Smoking   *294*

SMS   *See Safety measurement system (SMS)*

Snow   *146*

Spacing of duals   *50*

Special cargo vehicles   *241*

Special rigs   *, 235–241, 70*

    Doubles   *235*

    Triples   *237*

Speed   *148*

Speed limit   *149*

Speedometer   *25*

Split shipments   *285*

Spoke wheels   *48*

Stab braking   *215*

Standard bell   *204*

Standard gates   *204*

Starter button   *21*

Starting the engine   *77*

Steering arm   *51*

Steering a tractor-trailer   *79*

Steering axle   *14*

Steering principles   *101*

Steering shaft   *51*

Steering system   *50*

    Drag link   *51*

    Gear box   *51*

    Pitman arm   *51*

    Steering arm   *51*

    Steering shaft   *51*

    Steering wheel   *51*

    Tie rod   *51*

Steering system defects   *61*

Steering wheel   *21, 51*

Steps   *174*

Stopped vehicle   *214*

Stopping a tractor-trailer   *79*

Stopping distance   *145*

Stop sign   *205*

Storage and delay charges   *281*

Straight bill of lading   *279*

Straight line backing   *79, 102*

Stress   *369*

Stuck on the tracks   *206*

Stuck vehicle   *180*

Stud piloted   *48*

Supporting documents   *307*

Suspension system   *36*

Suspension system defects   *61*

Systematic maintenance   *250*

▌T

Tachometer   *26*

Tailgate delivery   *280*

Tandem axle   *14*

Tankers   *71*

Tariffs   *280*

Tarps   *270*

Terminal carrier   *279*

Testing the tractor-trailer hook-up *78*

Texting *138*

Through bill of lading *279*

Tiedowns *269*

Tie rod *51*

Tire care *49, 50*

Tire chain installation *175*

Tire chains *174*

Tire checks *294*

Tire defects *60*

Tire inflation *49*

Tire load *270*

Tire maintenance *49*

Tires *48, 173, 249*

    Belted bias tires *48*

    Bias ply tires *48*

    Mixing radial and bias ply tires *49*

    Radial tires *48*

    Tire maintenance *49*

    Tire tubes *49*

    Tread design *49*

    Tubeless tires *49*

Tire tubes *49*

Toe-in *52*

Toe-out *52*

Top-heavy loads *271*

Total stopping distance *145*

Towing *181*

Tracks out of service sign *205*

Traction *225*

Tractor *14*

Tractor jackknife *227*

Tractor parking valve *46*

Tractor-trailer skids *226*

Traffic flow *148*

Trailer *15*

Trailer air supply valve *23*

Trailer brake hand-control valve *23*

Trailer jackknife *226*

Trailer seals   *358*

> *Barrier seals*   *358*

> *Indicative seals*   *358*

Transmission   *43*

Transmission controls   *22*

Tread design   *49*

> *Lug tread*   *49*

> *Rib tread*   *49*

Treadle valve   *46*

Triples   *237*

Trip planning   *329–337*

Trip report   *333*

Trucking industry image   *381*

Truck routes   *335*

Tubeless tires   *49*

Turbocharger   *39*

Turning   *81*

Turning space   *157*

Turnpike doubles   *236*

Turn signals   *135, 165*

Two-wheel dolly   *273*

Types of inspections   *59*

> *On-the-road (en-route) inspection*   *59*

> *Post-trip inspection*   *59*

> *Pre-trip inspection*   *59*

U

Uncoupling tractor-trailers   *115*

Uncoupling twin trailers   *118*

Underinflation   *50*

Unloading tools   *272*

Unsafe driving   *405*

Unscheduled maintenance   *247*

Upgrades   *182*

Upshifting   *89, 90*

U.S. ACE   *320*

Use of mirrors   *126*

User hazards   *192*

Using your horn   *137*

▌ V

Value of cargo   *280*

Vehicle entry and exit   *374*

Vehicle factors   *164*

  Brake lights   *165*

  Lights   *165*

  Mirrors   *165*

  Turn signals   *165*

  Windshield   *165*

Vehicle fires   *349*

Vehicle inspections   *59–71*

Vehicle instruments   *25*

Vehicle maintenance   *406*

Vehicle sizes and weights   *322*

Visibility   *148*

Vision   *163*

Voltage regulator   *41*

Voltmeter   *26, 41*

▌ W

Warehousing receipt   *280*

Warning devices   *28, 136, 202*

Weight   *367*

Weight and distance   *280*

Weight balance   *271*

Weight distribution   *270*

Welcome to the trucking industry   *3*

Western doubles   *236*

Wet brakes   *180*

Wheel alignment   *51*

  Camber   *51*

  Caster   *51*

  Toe-in   *52*

  Toe-out   *52*

Wheel and rim defects   *60*

Wheel load   *225*

Wheels   *48*

  Disc wheels   *48*

  Hub piloted   *48*

Spoke wheels   *48*

Stud piloted   *48*

Whistleblower protection   *385*

Windows   *174*

Windshield   *165*

Windshield washers   *173*

Windshield wipers   *173*

Work zones   *191*

Y

Yield sign   *204*

INDEX

NOTES

NOTES

NOTES

NOTES

NOTES

NOTES

NOTES

NOTES